Energy Tax and Regulatory Policy in Europe

CESifo Seminar Series

Edited by Clemens Fuest

See http://mitpress.mit.edu for a complete list of titles in this series.

Energy Tax and Regulatory Policy in Europe
Reform Priorities

Edited by
Ian Parry, Karen Pittel, and Herman R. J. Vollebergh

CESifo Seminar Series

The MIT Press
Cambridge, Massachusetts
London, England

This book was set in Palatino by Sharon D. Ray, St. Pete Beach, FL. Printed and bound in the United States of America.

Library of Congress Cataloging-in-Publication Data

Names: Parry, Ian W. H. (Ian William Holmes), 1965- editor. | Pittel, Karen, 1969- editor. | Vollebergh, Herman R. J., editor.
Title: Energy tax and regulatory policy in Europe : reform priorities / edited by Ian Parry, Karen Pittel, and Herman Vollebergh.
Description: Cambridge, MA : MIT Press, [2017] | Series: CESifo seminar series | Includes bibliographical references and index.
Identifiers: LCCN 2016054314 | ISBN 9780262036399 (hardcover : alk. paper)
Subjects: LCSH: Energy policy—Europe. | Energy tax—Europe.
Classification: LCC HD9502.E852 E56 2017 | DDC 336.2/7833379094—dc23
LC record available at https://lccn.loc.gov/2016054314

10   9   8   7   6   5   4   3   2   1

Contents

Series Foreword

This book is part of the CESifo Seminar Series. The series aims to cover topical policy issues in economics from a largely European perspective. The books in this series are the products of the papers and intensive debates that took place during the seminars hosted by CESifo, an international research network of renowned economists organized jointly by the Center for Economic Studies at Ludwig-Maximilians-Universität, Munich, and the Ifo Institute for Economic Research. All publications in this series have been carefully selected and refereed by members of the CESifo research network.

Glossary of Technical Terms and Abbreviations

Agency for the Cooperation of Energy Regulators (ACER). EU Agency created to further the completion of the internal energy market.

Aggregator. Holds a portfolio of electric power contracts with a range of individual consumers and/or producers and trades this contracted power on the wholesale market.

Area licensing scheme. A scheme charging motorists for driving in a restricted zone with high congestion. The charge applies both to trips that enter the zone as well as trips within the zone.

Asymmetric information. Where one party has more or better information than another.

Auto oil program of the European Union. Assesses future trends in emissions and air quality and policies to reduce emissions.

Automatic frequency control. A system for adjusting the power of multiple generation plants or consumption devices in response to changes in the load as measured by system frequency.

Automatic indexation. A benefit payment that increases in tandem with increases in the level of consumer prices (in response to higher energy prices).

Back-loading. The postponement (until 2019–2020) of 900 million tons of auctioned emissions allowances to reduce the buildup of surplus emissions allowances in the EU ETS.

Balancing. In the context of electricity markets, increases or reductions in energy from reserves to balance the differences between supply and demand in the system.

Balancing reserves. Sources of extra power in the form of either generation or demand reduction, to deal with demand and supply imbalances.

Basic research. Research (conducted mostly by universities, other nonprofits, and laboratories) to gain improved knowledge or understanding of the subject under study without specific applications in mind (though it can be directed to areas or technologies of potential interest).

Behavioral failures. When people fail to behave as predicted by rational economic theory.

Biofuel. Fuels that contain energy from recent production of carbon in living organisms such as plants and algae. Biodiesel is the most common biofuel in Europe and is produced, for example, from animal fats, vegetable oils, soy, and algae. Biodiesel can be used in any diesel engine when mixed with regular diesel.

Border tax adjustments (BTAs) or border carbon adjustments (BCAs). These measures impose charges on the embodied carbon content of certain imported products.

Bunker fuels. Any type of fuel oil used aboard ships.

Carbon capture and storage (CCS). An (as yet unproven) technology for extracting CO_2 emissions from smokestacks and transporting them via pipelines to underground geological storage sites.

Carbon dioxide (CO_2). The predominant greenhouse gas.

Carbon leakage. Refers to a possible increase in carbon emissions in other regions in response to an emissions reduction in one country or region. Leakage could result from the relocation of economic activity; for example, the migration of energy-intensive firms away from countries whose energy prices are increased by climate policy. Alternatively, it could result from increased demand for fossil fuels in other countries as world fuel prices fall in response to reduced fuel demand in countries taking mitigating action.

Carbon tax. A tax imposed on CO_2 emissions released largely through the combustion of carbon-based fossil fuels.

Clean Development Mechanism (CDM). Under this program, emission reduction projects in developing countries can earn certified emission reduction credits that can be purchased by industrialized countries as one method of meeting their emissions obligations.

Climate and Energy Package. This package is a legally binding set of three key targets for the European Union as a whole and specifies (1) a minimum 20 percent reduction of overall EU GHGs (CO_2, CH_4, N_2O, F-gases) relative to 1990 levels; (2) a 20 percent share of renewable energy in final energy consumption; and (3) a 20 percent reduction in primary energy use by 2020.

Climate and Energy 2030 Framework. This framework (also pledged at COP 21 in Paris as an INDC) sets three key targets for the year 2030:

(1) at least 40 percent cuts in GHGs (from 1990 levels); (2) at least 27 percent share for renewable energy; and (3) at least 27 percent improvement in energy efficiency. The framework was adopted by EU leaders in October 2014. It builds on the 2020 Climate and Energy Package.

Command and control regulation. Direct regulation of an industry or activity by legislation that states what is permitted and what is illegal.

Compressed natural gas (CNG). Natural gas stored at high pressure that can be used in modified internal combustion engine vehicles. It is environmentally cleaner than traditional fuels, but the cost and placement of fuel storage tanks is the main barrier to its wider use.

Consumption basket. Amount spent by a particular income group on different consumer products.

Cordon toll. A scheme charging motorists for driving in a restricted zone with high congestion. The charge applies only when entering the zone, while trips within the zone are free.

Corrective tax. A charge levied on a source of environmental harm and that is set at a level to reflect, or correct for, environmental damage.

Council of European Energy Regulators (CEER). Forum for the cooperation of the independent energy regulators of Europe.

Credit trading. Allows firms covered by an ETS with high pollution abatement costs to do less mitigation by purchasing allowances from relatively clean firms with low abatement costs. Similarly, in regulatory systems credit trading allows firms with high compliance costs to fall short of an emissions (or other) standard by purchasing credits from other firms that exceed the standard.

Cross-border externality. When the actions of firms or households in one country impose costs on firms or households in neighboring countries.

Crowding out. In the energy R&D context, refers to reduction in R&D in other sectors of the economy in response to higher short-term prices for scientists and other research inputs, following an increase in energy-related R&D.

Day-ahead market. Market for forward trade of electricity to be delivered the following day.

Deadweight loss, economic, or welfare cost. Measure of the economic cost of a particular policy (gross of any environmental or other benefits). Primarily reflects changes in production costs and changes in household benefits from consumption.

Demand management. In the content of electricity markets, refers to the modification of consumer demand, usually to encourage less energy use during peak hours or to move energy use to off-peak times such as nighttime and weekends.

Demonstration. Seeks to prove the viability of new technologies (from R&D) at the commercial scale (prior to deployment).

Diminishing returns. The decrease in the incremental output of a production process as the amount of a single factor of production is incrementally increased, while the amounts of all other factors of production stay constant.

Director-General (DG) Energy. A department in the European Commission.

Distance charges. Taxes that vary directly in proportion to how much a vehicle is driven, for example, on busy roads at peak period.

Distribution network. A system of low-voltage electricity lines in a given area, typically transporting electricity from the transmission network to consumers.

Distribution system operator (DSO). Responsible for operating, maintaining, and developing the distribution network.

Distributional incidence or burden. Refers to whose economic welfare is reduced by a policy, and by how much. It is quite different from formal or legal incidence—fuel suppliers, for example, may be responsible for remitting tax payments to a revenue administration, but they may bear little economic incidence if they can charge higher prices.

Divestment. The opposite of investment; that is, reducing capacity by closure or mothballing.

Dynamic efficiency. In the context of ETSs, refers to the equalization of (discounted) incremental emissions abatement costs in different years to minimize mitigation costs over time.

Economies of density. Decline in unit costs (e.g., of providing transit service) due to taking advantage of access to high population densities.

Economies of scale. Refers to lower costs per unit of operation that might be obtained with greater scale, for example, lower costs per passenger for transit systems when transit vehicles have higher passenger occupancy rates.

Effort sharing decision. EU Member States have agreed on binding GHG targets for the period 2013–2020 and these targets concern emissions from most sectors not included in the EU ETS, such as transport (except aviation and international maritime shipping), buildings, agriculture, and waste. Relevant policies are implemented both at the EU and MS level.

Emissions Trading System or Scheme (ETS). A market-based policy to reduce emissions (sometimes referred to as cap-and-trade). Covered sources are required to hold allowances for each ton of their emissions or (in an upstream program) embodied emissions content in fuels. The total quantity of allowances is fixed and market trading of allowances establishes a market price for emissions. Auctioning the allowances provides a valuable source of government revenue.

Energy Efficiency Directive. This 2012 directive establishes a set of binding measures to help the European Union reach its 20 percent energy efficiency target by 2020. Under the Directive, all EU countries are required to use energy more efficiently at all stages of the energy chain from its production to its final consumption. EU countries were required to transpose the Directive's provisions into their national laws by June 5, 2014.

Energy efficiency gap or energy paradox. The observation that consumers fail to adopt energy-efficient technologies that appear to more than pay for their up-front investment costs in terms of the expected savings in energy costs over the life of the technology.

Energy-intensive and trade-exposed (EITI) firms. Firms (e.g., cement, aluminum, and chemicals producers) exposed to international trade whose production costs would increase disproportionately in response to higher energy prices.

Energy Star labelling. In the United States, a government-backed symbol certifying that various products or equipment meet a certain level of energy efficiency.

Energy Tax Directive (ETD). Sets minimum tax rates for fuels outside the EU ETS—including motor fuels, heating fuels, and electricity—that Member States typically need to incorporate into their national tax systems.

Energy Union. Proposal by the EU Commission for closer coordination of energy policies in Europe.

EU GHG monitoring system. As parties to the UNFCCC and its Kyoto Protocol, the European Union and its member countries are required to report to the UN annually on their GHG inventories and regularly on their climate change policies and measures and progress toward the targets ("biennial reports" and "national communications").

Euronorm. European emission standards define the acceptable limits for exhaust emissions of new vehicles sold in EU Member States. The emission standards are defined in a series of EU directives staging the progressive introduction of increasingly stringent standards.

European Economic Area (EEA). Provides for the free movement of people, goods, services, and capital within the internal market of the 28 EU Member States as well as Iceland, Liechtenstein, and Norway.

European Emissions Allowance (EUA). Climate credits used in the EU ETS.

European Energy Strategy. This strategy has its legal foundation in the Lisbon treaty in which the general goals of EU energy policy are stated in Article 194 (EU 2010). The aim is to (a) ensure the functioning of the energy market; (b) ensure security of energy supply in the Union; (c) promote energy efficiency and energy saving and the development of new and renewable forms of energy; and (d) foster the interconnection of energy networks.

European Network for Transmission System Operators of Electricity (ENTSO-E). Association of all European TSOs.

European Research Executive Agency. Funding body created by the European Commission to maximize the efficiency and impact of EU research and innovation programs.

External cost or externality. A cost imposed by the actions of individuals or firms on other individuals or firms (possibly in the future, as in the case of climate change) that the former do not take into account.

Feebate. This policy would impose a fee on firms with emission rates (e.g., CO_2 per kWh) above a "pivot point" level and provide a corresponding subsidy for firms with emission rates below the pivot point. Alternatively, the feebate might be applied to energy consumption rates (e.g., gasoline per km) rather than emission rates. Feebates are the pricing analog of an emissions (or energy) standard, but they circumvent the need for credit trading (across firms and across time periods) to contain policy costs.

Feed-in premiums (FIP). As applied to the power sector, these provide an output subsidy per kilowatt hour of electricity produced from renewables.

Feed-in tariffs (FIT). These provide renewable energy producers with long-term contracts that guarantee access to the grid at a fixed price (normally decreasing over time). Payments are usually higher for more expensive technologies like photovoltaic or offshore wind energy.

Flexible fuel vehicles. These can run on traditional motor fuels or a blend of these fuels and biofuels. Since biofuels contain less energy per liter compared with traditional fuels, fuel economy tends to deteriorate when vehicles use the blended fuel.

Flue gas desulfurization. A set of technologies used to remove SO_2 from exhaust flue gases of fossil-fuel power plants.

Free rider problem. In the climate context, the reluctance of an individual country to incur mitigation costs when the climate benefits accrue largely to other countries.

Gate closure. The last time at which bids and offers are accepted for a trading electricity contracts in a specific time period.

Grandfathering of allowances. Giving away free allowances in a trading system to pre-existing sources of emissions.

Greenhouse gas (GHG). A gas in the atmosphere that is transparent to incoming solar radiation but traps and absorbs heat radiated from the earth.

High speed rail (HSR). A type of rail transport operating faster than traditional rail traffic, using an integrated system of specialized rolling stock and dedicated tracks.

Imperfect appropriation. Where one firm that develops a new technology is unable to fully capture the spillover benefits of the technology to other firms.

Independently nationally determined contributions (INDCs). These are the emissions mitigation pledges countries made for the 2015 Paris Conference of Parties (COP 21).

Induced innovation hypothesis. In the context of energy technologies, the idea that higher energy prices should lead to more rapid increase in energy efficiency and investment in low-emission technologies.

Input-output analysis. A method for computing (in the present context) how higher energy prices will be passed forward into higher prices for consumer products.

Intellectual property (IP) rights. Refers to intellectual advancements for which a monopoly is assigned to designated owners by law (e.g., through patents and copyrights).

Intermediate inputs. Products (e.g., energy, raw materials, or semi-finished goods) that are used in the production process to produce other goods or services rather than for final consumption.

Intermittent generation capacity. Production capacity that is not continuously available due to some factor outside direct control, such as weather-dependent wind and solar power.

International Civil Aviation Organization (ICAO). A specialized agency of the United Nations whose objectives include providing safe, secure, sustainable, and efficient global civil aviation while minimizing aviation's adverse environmental effects.

Intraday market. Market for trade of electricity contracts during the day of delivery.

Knowledge spillovers. Where information about new technologies, products, or production techniques at one firm potentially benefit other firms.

Kyoto Protocol. An international agreement linked to the United Nations Framework Convention on Climate Change, committing advanced countries to emission reduction targets. The Protocol was adopted in 1997 and entered into force in 2005, but expired in 2012.

Learning-by-doing. When a firm improves productivity or lowers production costs through continued learning about using equipment or technologies more efficiently.

Learning curve. The relationship between learning about a technology or product (usually measured by production costs) and experience or use of the product or technology.

Linear reduction factor. Refers to the fixed annual percent decrease of the emissions cap in the EU ETS.

Linking. In the context of an ETS, refers to the joining of trading systems establishing a common price on emissions across all the covered regions.

Liquefied natural gas (LNG). Natural gas converted to liquid form for ease of storage or transport by ships or trucks (e.g., over long distances where pipelines do not exist) where it is re-gasified and distributed as pipeline natural gas.

Liquidity constraint. Limit on the amount an individual can borrow against future income to pay for an investment.

Lisbon Treaty. International agreement, signed in 2007, that amends the two previous treaties that form the constitutional basis of the European Union.

Loop flow. Power flow along an unintended path in the electricity transmission network that loops away from the most direct path.

Low emission zones. These ban or impose charges on high emission vehicles entering a restricted zone with poor air quality.

Lump-sum compensation. A payment made that is not contingent on an individual's circumstances and therefore does not affect their behavior (as opposed, for example, to a tax cut that increases incentives for work effort).

Marginal congestion cost. Cost that one vehicle imposes on other road users through contributing to congestion, slowing average travel speeds, and raising travel times for other vehicle occupants.

Marginal tax rate. The tax rate paid on an extra unit of income.

Market-based policies. These establish a price on emissions, either directly through taxes, or indirectly through use of permits that can be traded in markets.

Market coupling. Simultaneous clearing of multiple electricity markets, based on all bids and offers in these markets.

Market failure. A situation where the private sector by itself would not make production and consumption decisions that would be efficient from society's perspective; for example, excessive generation of emissions due to the failure to price them for environmental damages.

Market stability reserve. Designed to balance out the allowances in the EU ETS from one year to another. If one year sees the total of emission allowances crossing a set threshold, a percentage of allowances will be automatically withdrawn from the market and placed in the reserve. In other years, when the quantity of allowances is low, they will be returned from the reserve to the market.

Means-tested benefits. Benefits paid only to households whose income falls below some low-income threshold.

Methane. GHG produced largely from agricultural sources and oil and gas field operations. Methane has a shorter atmospheric lifespan than CO_2; however, it is a far more powerful GHG. A ton of methane is equivalent to about 300 tons of CO_2 in global warming equivalents over a century.

Modal split. Share of trips or travelers using a particular type of transportation (e.g., roads, bus, or rail).

Myopic consumers. In an energy context, refers to consumers who undervalue the future energy savings from improvements in energy efficiency.

NACE classification. The industry standard classification system used in the European Union (for the French term "nomenclature statistique des activités économiques dans la Communauté européenne").

National Allocation Plans (NAPs). EU Member States submit these as part of the process for determining the allocation of allowances for installations covered by the EU ETS.

National Renewable Energy Action Plans. National action plans on renewable energy that all Member States of the European Union were obliged to notify the European Commission of in 2010. The plans provide detailed road maps of how the Member States expect to reach the legally binding 2020 target for the share of renewable energy in total energy consumption.

New Entrants Reserve (NER300). Funds demonstration projects for CCS and renewables with proceeds from the sale of 300 million emissions allowances to new firms in the EU ETS. Its successor program, NER400, will be endowed with revenues from 400 million allowances.

Nitrogen oxides (NO$_x$). Pollutants caused by the combustion of fuel, primarily coal, that reacts in the atmosphere to form fine particulates with potentially harmful effects on human health.

Non-tradable outputs. Sectors that are largely insulated from adverse impacts on competitiveness from higher energy prices.

Oligopoly. An industry with a limited number of producers that are able to set prices above levels that would occur in a more competitive market.

Output-based rebate. In the context of a carbon tax, this is a payment per unit of output to compensate firms whose production costs rise significantly in response to higher energy prices.

Particulates. Pollutants that are either emitted directly from fuel combustion, or formed indirectly from chemical reactions in the atmosphere involving other pollutants (e.g., SO$_2$ or NO$_x$). Fine particulates are small enough to penetrate the lungs and bloodstream and increase the prevalence of strokes, and various heart and lung diseases.

Pass-through. When a (carbon) tax is reflected in higher prices for energy consumers (as opposed to lower prices for producers).

Passed-backward. When a (carbon) tax lowers prices for (energy) suppliers.

Peak-load or peak-period pricing. A form of congestion pricing where people pay an additional fee (e.g., for road use) during peak periods of high demand.

Performance standards. Used to set a uniform emissions control target for firms, such as pounds of SO$_2$ per unit of energy, but do not dictate how the target is met.

Pollution Abatement Costs and Expenditures (PACE) survey. A comprehensive source of pollution abatement costs and expenditures related to environmental protection for the manufacturing sector of the United States. The PACE survey collects facility-level data on pollution abatement capital expenditures and operating costs associated with compliance to local, state, and federal regulations and voluntary or market-driven pollution abatement activities.

Power exchange. A market where electricity is traded, including for intraday, day-ahead, and longer terms.

Price collar. Establishes a price ceiling and a price floor for emissions prices in an ETS.

Private good. A good for which consumption of it by one individual or firm reduces the amount available to other individuals or firms.

Progressive policy. A policy that imposes a larger burden as a proportion of income (or some other measure of household well-being) on higher income groups and a smaller burden on lower income groups.

Public good. A good (e.g., new knowledge) where use of it by one individual or firm does not reduce the amount available for other individuals or firms.

R&D or RD&D. The former refers to research and development and the latter to R&D plus demonstration.

R&D tax credit. These credits allow businesses to apply for a euro-for-euro reduction of tax liability for qualified expenditures on research activities.

Ramping. Changing the output of a power generating plant, including start and stop.

Rebound effect. The increase in fuel use (or emissions) resulting from increased use of energy-consuming products following an improvement in energy efficiency, which lowers their operating costs.

Regressive policy. A policy that imposes a larger burden as a proportion of income (or some other measure of household well-being) on lower income groups and a smaller burden on higher income groups.

Renewable energy. Energy sources such as hydro, wind, solar, and biofuels.

Renewable Energy Directive 2009/28/EC. Sets binding, specific, national targets for each EU Member State for renewable energy ranging from 10 percent in Malta to 49 percent in Sweden.

Renewable portfolio standard (RPS). Defines minimum required shares for renewables in power generation, and creates a market allowing generators to fall short of the requirement by purchasing credits from generators going beyond the requirement.

Rent-seeking. Efforts by lobby groups to secure government favors like subsidies or exemptions from regulations.

Reserve price auction. A minimum price that must be paid for emissions allowances sold in periodic auctions of allowances.

Shale (or unconventional) gas. Natural gas that is found trapped within shale formations (i.e., fine-grained, organic-rich, sedimentary rock).

Smart grid. An electricity grid which includes a variety of operational and energy measures including smart meters, smart appliances, renewable energy resources, and energy efficiency resources.

Social cost of carbon (SCC). Refers to the net present value of damages (e.g., to agriculture or human health) due to the change in future global climate resulting from an additional ton of CO_2 emissions in a given year. It is expressed in monetary units and usually reflects worldwide damages (rather than damages to a particular country).

Social discount rate. In the climate context, this refers to the rate at which damages in the future from climate change caused by current emissions are discounted back to the present.

Social rate of return to R&D. The gain on an R&D investment, expressed as a percent of the initial investment cost, and where the gain includes both the private benefits to the firm conducting the research as well as the spillover benefits of the research to other firms that might copy a new technology or use the new knowledge in their own research programs.

Stock pollutant. Refers to a pollutant with a long residence time in the environment. For example, the average atmospheric lifespan of CO_2 emissions is around 100 years.

Strategic Energy Technologies Information System (SETIS). Identifies energy technology and research objectives to help the European Union achieve its environmental goals, as laid out in the Strategic Energy Technologies Plan.

Sulfur dioxide (SO_2). A pollutant caused by the combustion of fuel, primarily coal, that reacts in the atmosphere to form fine particulates with potentially harmful effects on human health.

Supply adequacy. Long-term balance between demand and supply in electricity systems, including network capacity.

Supply security. Short-term balance between demand and supply within limits dictated by available network capacity.

Swedish NO_x tax. A charge implemented in 1992 on nitrogen oxide emissions with the revenues redistributed among covered sources in proportion to their energy production.

System code. Regulations covering technical aspects relating to the operation and use of electricity networks.

Tax competition. The risk of one country setting excessively low tax rates to attract a mobile tax base from other countries.

Tax sheltering. A legal way of reducing taxable income, for example, by receiving compensation in the form of untaxed fringe benefits rather than wages or spending on goods that are tax deductible.

Technology prizes. These can provide financial rewards for specific (high-priority) technological advances.

Technology-based standards. These specify the method, and sometimes the actual equipment, that firms must use to comply with a particular regulation.

Time consistency. A time-consistent policy is one that will be sustained as circumstances change over time (a time-inconsistent policy is not sustained over time).

Ton. Taken here to mean a metric tonne (1,000 kilograms). This is the standard unit for measuring CO_2 emissions (rather than a short ton, which is 2,000 pounds or 907 kilograms).

Transmission network. A system of high-voltage electricity lines, typically connecting generators to distribution network.

Transmission system operator (TSO). Responsible for operating, maintaining and developing the transmission network, including ensuring balance between demand and supply to avoid system failure.

Twenty-twenty-twenty (20-20-20) targets. Adopted in 2009, consisting of a 20 percent reduction in EU GHGs relative to 1990 levels by 2020, a 20 percent share of renewables in EU energy production by 2020, and 20 percent energy savings by 2020 relative to a baseline projection for that year.

Two-speed system. In the context of the EU ETD, this would allow low-income members to meet lower energy tax floors than higher income states.

UK carbon tax floor. A domestic tax that varies inversely with the emissions price in the European Union to prevent the overall UK price (the tax plus the emissions price) falling below a floor level.

Unanimity. Requires approval of all EU Member States (rather than a qualified majority) for a new measure at the EU level. Unanimity usually applies to tax measures (e.g., an EU-wide carbon tax).

Unitary patent. Ensures uniform protection for an invention in 25 EU Member States to reduce patenting costs for innovators.

U.S. Acid Rain Program. Trading program introduced in 1990 by the U.S. Environmental Protection Agency to reduce SO_2 emissions from power plants.

Vignettes. Truck charges or passes based on period of time (rather than distance travelled); applied in Austria, Bulgaria, the Czech Republic, Hungary, Moldova, Romania, Slovakia, Slovenia, and Switzerland.

Waxman-Markey bill. A 2010 bill, introduced in the U.S. by Congressmen Waxman and Markey, with an ETS as its centerpiece. The bill passed the House but the Senate version was never put to a vote.

Willingness to pay. The amount individuals are willing to sacrifice in terms of income to reduce something undesirable, such as a health risk.

Introduction and Summary for Policymakers

Ian Parry, Karen Pittel, and Herman Vollebergh

The European Union faces many critical challenges in energy policy. Most obvious is how to reach the deep greenhouse gas (GHG) reductions (up to 90 percent by 2050) promised by the EU Commission and its Member States, for instance at the UN Conference of the Parties (COP 21) in Paris, December 2015. This challenge should be considered against the background of already implemented and related policies, such as the European Trading System (ETS), energy taxes, renewables incentives, and air quality standards, as well as important international developments in energy markets such as the rise of shale gas in the United States and the recent, unexpected drop in oil prices. Indeed, dealing simultaneously with environmental (climate and air quality) impacts of different economic activities (e.g., power generation) and with broader adverse side effects (e.g., interconnection problems in electricity grids and congestion in the case of road vehicles) is the major challenge for the years ahead.

Setting ambitious targets is one thing, but finding appropriate instruments, particularly in the face of interacting market failures, is something different. European policymakers are grappling with an unprecedented range of issues in this regard, including:

- Reforming the ETS, the centerpiece of climate mitigation efforts at the EU level;
- Reforming the regulatory structure for electricity markets to accommodate growth in renewable generation and integration of power grids;
- Rationalizing the consistency of EU-level objectives, and the policies underpinning them, for emissions, energy efficiency, and renewables;

- Introducing tax floors under the Energy Tax Directive for non-ETS fuels to more effectively promote climate and energy objectives;
- Understanding the prospects, and appropriate policy regimes, for emerging energy sources, most obviously unconventional gas;
- Improving the effectiveness of clean technology development and deployment policies to ameliorate trade-offs between environmental and economic concerns;
- Restructuring the taxation for vehicles, their fuels, and use to more effectively address not only global warming and air pollution, but also broader side effects like road congestion;
- Overcoming obstacles, most obviously the burdens on vulnerable households and firms, to the most efficient reforms, for example, carbon and energy pricing.

There are numerous inter-connections between these issues; for example, there is less need for aggressive renewable policies if carbon pricing is progressively reducing emissions and power grids are not ready for rapid penetration of intermittent generation. However, energy policy has always been mainly a Member State responsibility and only recently have opinions changed, not least because of the close connection between climate and energy policy (Helm 2015). Indeed, proper coordination of EU energy policy in the face of deep reductions in climate change emissions, adding to the Member States' own policies, is likely to be helpful in finding better, more coherent, and more efficient policies—that is, policies coordinating what is needed at the EU level while leaving room for differences in Member States' preferences on their energy and environmental policy mix.

Policymakers therefore need an overarching view of the main issues in energy policy and its interaction with environmental policies, and how changes to one component of energy or environmental policy may affect appropriate policies elsewhere in the energy system. This volume has two main goals: (1) to provide concise and readable introductions to the issues that are at the table in several of the main areas where energy and climate policy meet; and (2) to come up with practical suggestions to find effective and efficient solutions, taking stock where appropriate of relevant interactions. These papers, written by individuals with widely diverse expertise, were presented for discussion at a workshop involving a mix of participants from academia, government, the European Commission, and other international organizations, held at CESIfo in Munich in November 2014. The rest of this introduction first presents a very brief introduction to the history of energy and climate regulation in the European Union and its Member States. Next, to set the stage, we provide a short overview of key energy and environmental statistics as well as EU policies. Subsequently, we discuss the challenges the different chapters in this book address and the broader policy lessons that can be drawn from them.

Energy and Climate Policy in the European Union: A Brief Introduction

Until 2007, no explicit legal basis existed for European energy policy (apart from the regulation covered by the Euratom treaty on nuclear technology and security) and energy policy was mainly justified on the grounds of environmental policy and by the strive for a common European market. Since 2007, EU energy policy has had its legal foundation in the Lisbon Treaty, in which the general goals of energy policy are stated in Article 194 (EU 2010):

To (a) ensure the functioning of the energy market; (b) ensure security of energy supply in the Union; (c) promote energy efficiency and energy saving and the development of new and renewable forms of energy; and (d) promote the interconnection of energy networks.

While it is stated that these goals should be aimed for in "a spirit of solidarity," Member States also retain their individual rights to translate these aims into policy measures. Consequently, European energy policy comprises a mix of regulation on the EU level and of country-specific measures reflecting national circumstances.

Of all the above goals, those related to climate policy have featured most prominently in public discussion. As fossil fuel combustion accounts for about 80 percent of EU GHGs (EEA 2015c), mitigation efforts are inextricably tied to energy policy. Climate policy in the European Union is based on three pillars: reducing GHGs, increasing the share of renewables in energy consumption, and increasing energy efficiency. While the first pillar is not featured directly in Article 194, it can be seen as a key motivation behind the renewability, efficiency, and energy-saving goals. Consequently, GHG regulation is often treated as part of energy policy—the most prominent example being the EU ETS. The close interrelation of energy and climate policy is also reflected by the fact that climate change mitigation is one of the three long-term goals (along with energy security and competitive energy provision to foster growth and employment) of the European Energy Strategy.

From 2007 to 2015, European energy policy covered a variety of different goals, measures, and initiatives in the fields of energy and electricity markets, energy technologies, energy efficiency, energy security (technological as well as political), renewable energy, and transport. The goals to be attained in 2020 include the 20-20-20 targets of the Climate and Energy Package (EC 2015a), specifying a minimum 20 percent reduction of overall EU GHGs (CO_2, CH_4, N_2O, and F-gases) relative to 1990 levels, a 20 percent share of renewable energy in final energy consumption, and a 20 percent reduction in primary energy use by 2020.

The 20 percent GHG mitigation target puts forth a 21 percent goal for the EU ETS sector (relative to 1990), while remaining emissions for the non-ETS sectors are supposed to fall by 10 percent (compared with 2005 levels). Country-specific goals for non-ETS sectors have been set in the so-called Effort Sharing Decision, depending on the Member States' relative wealth, ranging from -20 percent (Denmark, Luxembourg, and Ireland) to +20 percent (Bulgaria). Member States agreed on binding targets for most non-ETS sectors, including transport (except aviation and international maritime shipping), buildings, agriculture, and waste. The 20 percent renewable goal has been translated into national targets (EC 2015a), ranging from 10 percent (Malta) to 49 percent (Sweden), and domestic, legally binding policies have been put in place to implement these targets. The 2012 Energy Efficiency Directive (EC 2012) establishes a set of binding measures to help the European Union reach its 20 percent energy efficiency target by 2020. Although no explicit fines can be imposed, the EC can impose binding policies on Member States in case of severe incompliance. The legislation for land use, land-use change, and forestry (EU Decision 529/2013) is based on the existing accounting rules under the second commitment period of the Kyoto Protocol.

In 2014, partially in preparation for COP 21, the 20-20-20 targets were supplemented by targets for 2030. The Climate and Energy Framework includes at least 40 percent cuts in GHGs from 1990 levels, at least a 27 percent share for renewable energy, and at least a 27 percent improvement in energy efficiency (EC 2015b). The GHG reduction goal was also submitted for COP 21 as the EU's Intended Nationally Determined Contribution (INDC).[1] Legislative proposals to implement the 2030 framework for both ETS and non-ETS sectors were submitted by the EC to the Council and European Parliament in 2015–2016 on the basis of the general political directions by the European Council, accounting for environmental integrity.

Due to the subsidiarity element in European energy policy, the measures adopted to implement the 20-20-20 targets on the Member State level are to some degree uncoordinated, leading to unintended side effects in other Member States and implications for the effectiveness of EU-wide instruments such as the EU ETS. The rapid increase of solar and wind power in Germany, with its spillover effects on neighboring countries and potential feedback effects on neighboring electricity prices as well as on the EU ETS price, is probably the most prominent example. In an effort to better coordinate the transformation of European energy supply, and to better address reliance on energy imports, the EC launched the Energy Union in 2015 (EC 2015e). Besides energy security and the decarbonization of the energy supply, the Energy Union strives for a fully integrated European energy market, a reduction of energy demand, and the fostering of research, innovation, and competitiveness. Measures to reach these goals will be taken in a step-by-step process until 2017.

Energy and Emissions in the EU: Some Key Statistics and Policy Measures

Following this short introduction to the foundations of energy and climate policy in the European Union, some additional statistics with respect to the three fundamental targets—GHG emissions, energy use, and renewable energy, as well as a brief mention of fiscal and air pollution issues—will help to provide background for the following chapters.[2]

GHG Emissions
Regarding GHG mitigation, the European Union has seen an overall decrease of 21 percent from 1990 levels until 2013 with emissions from the energy sector declining almost proportionally by about 19 percent (figure 0.1). With respect to GHG intensity of the GDP, this implied a decrease of about 37 percent in total during this period and 35 percent with respect to energy related emissions. Since the introduction of the EU ETS, emissions from sectors covered by the ETS and emissions of non-ETS sectors have followed a similar downward trend (see figure 0.2).

At a national level, the GHG intensity of the GDP varies considerably, depending, for example, on a country's fuel mix and household budget shares for energy. In fact, in 2012 (figure 0.3), the emissions

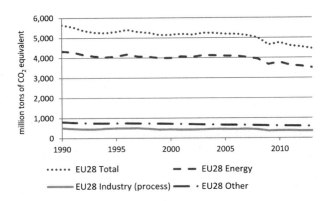

Figure 0.1
EU-28 emissions as reported to the UNFCCC and to the EU Greenhouse Gas Monitoring Mechanism

Source: EEA (2015d).

Note: Process emissions are releases from industrial processes (e.g., iron and steel, aluminum) involving chemical or physical reactions other than combustion and where the main purpose of the process is not energy production.

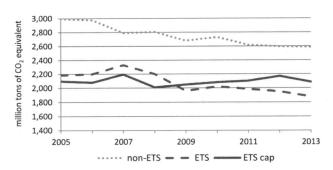

Figure 0.2
Total GHG emissions in non-ETS EU sectors, EU ETS sectors, and EU ETS cap (in Mt CO_2-equ.)

Sources: EEA (2014; 2015c), EC (2015d).

Note: GHG totals exclude emissions from Land Use, Land-Use Change and Forestry (LULUCF) and international bunker fuels.

intensity of the most intensive country (Bulgaria) was almost ten times as large as that of the least intensive country (Sweden).

About 45 percent of EU GHGs were covered by the EU ETS in 2012.[3] To reach the 40 percent reduction in total GHGs stipulated in the EU Climate and Energy Framework, the European Union plans to cut ETS emissions by 43 percent (compared to 2005). To this end, the yearly

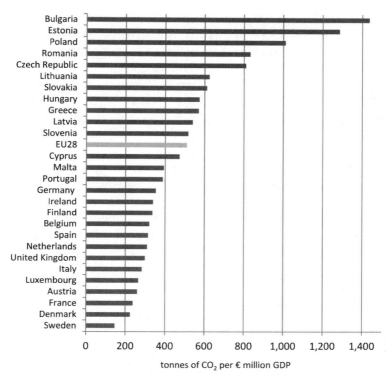

Figure 0.3
GHG intensity of GDP in EU-28 Member States, 2012 (in tCO$_2$/€ mGDP)
Source: Eurostat (2015).

decrease in emissions certificates will ramp up from 1.74 percent currently to 2.20 percent starting in 2020.

At the end of 2015, emission certificates in the EU ETS were trading at a price of about 8€/tCO$_2$. Coming from a record high of 32€/tCO$_2$ in the summer of 2008, prices followed a downward trend in the following years, reflecting a rising oversupply of certificates (see figure 0.2) caused, in part, by the economic recession, increased renewables deployment, and international credit use (Koch et al. 2014). To reduce this excess supply, the European Union committed to a reduction of certificates by 900 million tons over a period of three years starting in 2014. Initially, this supply reduction was planned to be temporary, with the retained certificates issued in 2019 and 2020, though the effects of this "backloading" on emissions prices were (as is to be expected in a system with allowance banking and borrowing) relatively modest (Brink et al. 2015).

For the next trading period beginning in 2021, it is now planned, however, to enhance the EU ETS by a mechanism ("market stability reserve") allowing the European Union to remove certificates from the market if demand is low to stabilize prices (and vice versa in the case of high demand). The already back-loaded certificates are planned to be placed into this reserve, making the initially temporary measure permanent.

To reach the 2030 goal of 40 percent GHG emission reduction, non-ETS sectors will need to cut emissions by 30 percent (compared to 2005).[4] As for the 2020 target, this goal needs to be translated into individual binding targets for Member States in an update of the Effort Sharing Decision.[5] For the 2020 goals, Member States have already set their own national energy efficiency targets and put instruments and programs into place that help achieve them. Under the Energy Efficiency Directive, all EU countries are required to use energy more efficiently at all stages of the energy chain, from its production to its final consumption. Contributions to the reduction in emissions come from road transport and buildings, aided by, for example, eco-design requirements for energy-related products and energy-labelling systems to inform consumers. In the transport sector, EU CO_2 emission standards for new cars and vans (Euronorm 6) will cut emissions. In addition, Member States can implement national measures such as the introduction (or increase) of a carbon (or fossil fuel) energy tax. The EU Energy Tax Directive sets minimum tax rates for motor fuels, heating fuels, and electricity.

Energy Demand

Overall gross inland energy consumption (GIC) in the EU-28 rose by 10 percent between 1995 and 2005, but fell back to 1990 levels (equivalent to about 1,666 million tons of oil) by 2013 (figure 0.4). In other words, the potential growth in energy demand from rising GDP between 1990 and 2013 was fully offset by improvements in energy efficiency. In its reference scenario 2013 (EC 2013a), the European Commission foresaw a continuation of this trend with energy efficiency almost doubling until 2050 compared to 2010 levels. This development is especially driven by high projected international energy prices, low growth rates of energy-intensive industries and the indirect effect of the EU ETS on energy use. Overall GIC in this scenario is projected to fall by about 8 percent until 2050. Future energy demand will especially be characterized by a trend toward electrification, due to a shift toward electricity in heating and cooling as well as in transport but also an

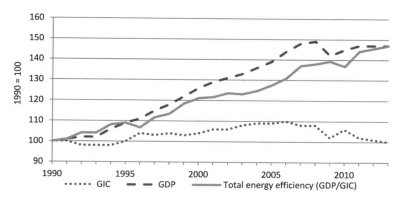

Figure 0.4
Trends in gross inland energy consumption (GIC), GDP, and energy efficiency in the EU-28 (1990 = 100; GDP at 2005 market prices)
Source: Eurostat (2015).

increasing use of electric appliances in the residential and the tertiary sector (EC 2013a).

Energy Mix and Renewables

During the 1990–2013 period, the energy mix changed noticeably, with the share of coal, gas, and petroleum products in energy consumption declining from 83 percent to 74 percent (figure 0.5). Overall coal and petroleum consumption declined by about 15 percent, but was partially substituted by less carbon-intensive gas (whose energy share rose from 18 to 23 percent). With the share of nuclear energy staying almost constant (at roughly 13 percent), the decrease in fossil fuels was mainly compensated by an increase of renewables, whose share rose from 4 to 12 percent. The EU reference scenario 2013 foresees a further increase in the share of renewables in GIC to about 25 percent in 2050 while the share of solid fuels is projected to further decrease to 7.6 percent (EC 2013a). Absolute levels of oil and gas consumption are both predicted to decrease as well. Yet in combination with the overall decrease in GIC, this implies only a slight decrease of the share of oil in energy demand and an almost constant share in the case of gas. The increasing electrification, however, goes hand in hand with an increasing share of intermittent energy generation from wind and solar.

Looking at the renewable shares of individual Member States, large differences exist. Renewable energy shares were less than 10 percent of energy consumption in nine countries in 2013, and above 25 percent in

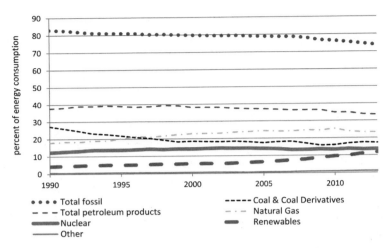

Figure 0.5
Trends in fuel shares in total gross inland consumption of energy (EU-28)
Source: Eurostat (2015).

seven countries (figure 0.6). These differences are also reflected by the differentiated, country-specific renewable targets mentioned above.

At the EU level, renewable energy shares have been growing steadily across the electricity, heating, and transport sectors, though large differences in these shares across sectors have persisted. For example, as shown in figure 0.7, the share of renewables in power generation increased from 15 percent in 2004 to 25 percent in 2013, while the renewables share in transportation increased from a very low base of 1 percent up to 5 percent (half of what is targeted for in 2020; see EC 2015g).

The strong increase of renewables in power generation reflects major policy interventions (feed-in-tariffs, renewable quotas, and/or market premiums) by Member States. Growth in renewable generation capacity was especially striking for solar energy (up from 0.2 GW to 89 GW—of which 38 GW were built in Germany alone) and wind energy (from 10 GW to 129 GW). Hydro power still has the largest absolute capacity in the EU-28 (149.5 GW), though the increase was much less pronounced (less than 1 percent per year). Figure 0.8 provides an overview of the renewable capacity mix in different Member States in 2000 and 2014 and also depicts the average growth rate of renewable capacity per year. With respect to absolute numbers, the largest country of the European Union, Germany, also has the largest installed capacity by far. Yet,

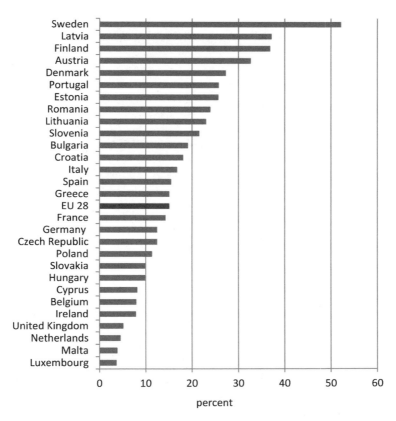

Figure 0.6
Share of renewable energy in gross final energy consumption in 2013
Source: Eurostat (2015).

although the share of renewable capacity also exceeds the country's population share considerably (25 percent of the European Union installed capacity versus 15 percent of EU population), its share of renewables in electricity generation in 2013 was only average for the European Union (25 percent), compared with 68 percent in Austria and 68 percent in Sweden (Eurostat 2015). The gap between installed capacity and power generation reflects the relatively low capacity to generation ratio for intermittent renewables like wind and solar. The impact of the rapid increase of intermittent generation on the functioning and optimal design of power markets is one of the key challenges that European energy policy will face in the decarbonization of its energy supply.

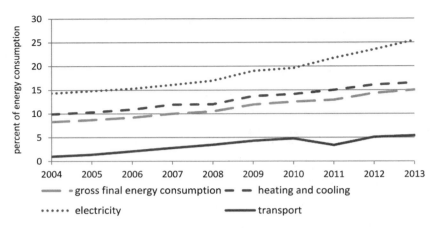

Figure 0.7
Share of renewable energy in electricity, heating/cooling, and transport (EU-28)
Source: Eurostat (2015).

Fiscal Perspective

From a fiscal perspective, carbon pricing via the ETS has had a relatively small impact on national and EU budgets during the first two trading phases (2005–2012), as most allowances were freely allocated ("grandfathered"). Although up to 10 percent of the certificates could have been sold during the second phase (2008–2012), only 4 percent were actually auctioned (EC 2015e). From 2013 onward, however, more and more certificates have been auctioned, including 100 percent of certificates used by power generators (exceptions are made for some new Member States) while the industry and heating sectors have begun with an auctioned share of 20 percent with the intent of increasing this to 100 percent by 2027 (except for sectors that are deemed to be exposed to carbon leakage). Revenues from these auctions will largely be distributed to the Member States.

According to the revised EU ETS Directive at least 50 percent of the auctioning revenues should be used by Member States for climate and energy-related purposes. 300 million allowances stemming from the so-called New Entrants Reserve are dedicated to funding the deployment of innovative renewable energy technologies as well as carbon capture and storage (NER300 Program; EC 2015f). How much Member States benefit financially from the auctioning revenues will of course depend crucially on the development of allowance prices. However, in 2013, total revenues amounted to 3.6bn€ (EC 2015c), or only about

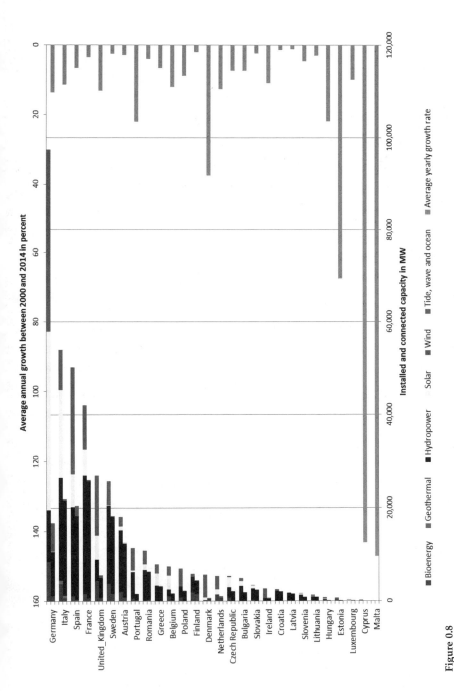

Figure 0.8
Left and lower axis: Installed and connected capacity of renewable energies in 2000 (lower bar) and 2014 (upper bar). Right and upper axis: Average growth rate per Member State.
Source: IRENA (2015).

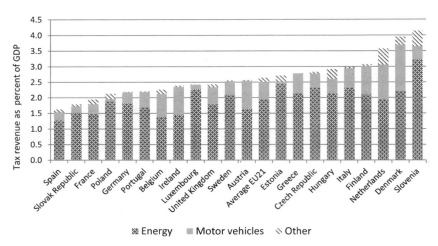

Figure 0.9
Green tax revenues as percent of GDP for EU-21 countries (2012)
Source: OECD (2015).

0.03 percent of GDP, which is very small relative to revenues from energy taxes.

On average, green taxes raised 2.6 percent of GDP across the selected 21 EU countries shown in figure 0.9, varying from about 1.5 percent of GDP in Spain to about 4 percent in Slovenia. The biggest component is energy taxes (e.g., taxes on motor fuels, heating oils, and electricity consumption), accounting, on average, for almost 2 percent of GDP, followed by motor vehicle taxes (0.6 percent) and other sources like taxes on waste or water (0.1 percent). The large diversity in revenue from green taxes reflects the difficulties within the European Union to harmonize excise taxation. Efforts for harmonization started back in 1985 in order to improve the internal market within the European Union. They were not very effective, though, due to the unanimity requirement that applies to all fiscal decisions. Instead, Member States agreed to minimum excise rates, e.g., under the Energy Tax Directive, on a wide range of fuels. Proposals to reform this ETD, however, have been notoriously difficult to implement in the last few years and are currently on hold.

Local Air Pollution

Finally, as regards local environmental damages from fossil fuel use, the main concern is fine particulates ($PM_{2.5}$), which are small enough to penetrate the lungs and bloodstream and increase the prevalence of

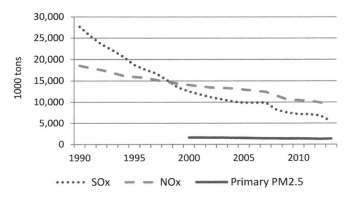

Figure 0.10
Emissions of major air pollutants in the European Union (in 1,000 tons)
Source: EEA (2015b).

various fatal illnesses from strokes and heart and lung diseases. These particulates can be emitted directly during fuel combustion but are also formed indirectly from chemical reactions in the atmosphere from SO_x and NO_x emissions.

Although these local air pollutants feature less prominently in the current political discussion than GHGs, considerable efforts have been undertaken to reduce them including a number of EU directives dating back to 1980 (EC 2013b). In fact SO_x emissions in particular, as well as NO_x emissions, have decreased dramatically over the last quarter century (figure 0.10).

Nonetheless, air pollution emissions (from fossil fuels and other sources) were still responsible for a large number—an estimated 475,000—of premature deaths in the European Union in 2012, mostly from exposure to direct and indirect sources of fine particulates. These mortality rates vary considerably across countries depending on use of coal and diesel fuel, in particular the deployment of technologies to control emissions from these fuels, the density of population exposed to emissions, and the existing health of the local population. As indicated in figure 0.11, annual mortality rates are highest in Bulgaria at 2,202 per 1,000,000 inhabitants and lowest in Ireland at 262, compared with an EU average of 943.

Currently, a new Clean Air Programme for Europe is under discussion, which aims to ensure that existing targets are met in the short term, and new air quality objectives are agreed upon for the period up to 2030 (see EC 2013b). The package also includes a revised National

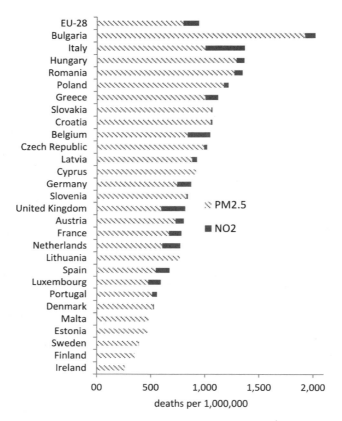

Figure 0.11
Premature deaths from $PM_{2.5}$ and NO_2 in EU-28 (per 100,000 inhabitants) in 2012
Sources: EEA (2015a); Eurostat (2015).

Emission Ceilings Directive with stricter national emission ceilings for the six main pollutants, as well as a proposal for a new Directive to reduce pollution from medium-sized combustion installations, such as energy plants for street blocks or large buildings, and small industry installations. Interactions with continued efforts to mitigate climate change through reduced fossil fuel combustion will certainly be of help to further reduce these emissions as well.

Main Messages for Policymakers

What are the main challenges for the European Union to make progress toward the goal of deep climate change emission reduction and its consequence for the wide range of related policies to date? The chapters in this book discuss several of the most important issues mentioned in the introduction. We now summarize some of the messages for policymakers from the rest of the book.

Emissions Trading System (Chapter 1)

The EU Emissions Trading System (ETS) is the world's largest carbon market, has been a catalyst for pricing schemes in other countries, and is the EU's flagship climate policy. As discussed by Cameron Hepburn and Alexander Teytelboym, however, there are some basic (but legally and politically challenging) design issues that will need to be resolved at some point as the European Union makes progress on its pledge to cut GHGs by 40 percent below 1990 levels by 2030.

One critical issue is the need for a more robust and predictable emissions price to encourage emissions-saving investments and improve cost effectiveness of the system over time. The prospective "market stability reserve" may help, but does not create the needed explicit price signal—this might instead be established through including a reserve price on allowance auctions. Another issue is that the trading system covers less than half of EU GHGs—in principle, the system could be expanded to other major emissions sources by incorporating upstream suppliers of transportation fuels (both domestic and international) and heating fuels.

Currently, allowance auction revenues are at a small fraction of their potential. Transitioning more rapidly to full allowance auctions would provide national governments with a significant revenue source which might help to alleviate other tax burdens or reduce budget deficits (trade-sensitive sectors would still need some transitory relief, though there are better ways of doing this than the current approach of granting them free allowances).

Price Floors in the EU ETS (Chapter 2)

This chapter, by Ottmar Edenhofer, Christina Roolfs, Beatriz Gaitana, Paul Nahmmachera, and Christian Flachsland, continues the discussion of the EU ETS and is slightly more technical than the other chapters, but provides an important quantitative analysis of the most critical design issues with the EU ETS. These are the insufficient incentives for mitigation provided by the current emissions price and the inability of national level policies to affect EU-wide emissions, given that they are fixed by the cap. The chapter evaluates current policies, especially in light of the subsidiarity principle in EU energy policy given the prevailing differences between Member States with respect to income as well as CO_2 emissions.

The authors show that a minimum price for emission allowances would result in considerable additional emission reduction. A transfer system that redistributes EU ETS revenues between richer and poorer Member States would furthermore increase the efficiency of emission mitigation by reducing incentives to strategically distort the carbon price. While a theoretically optimal transfer system might not be politically feasible, other transfer systems taking into account solidarity between Member States can also improve economic efficiency.

Electricity Markets (Chapter 3)

Rapid growth in renewable power generation in Europe has led to greater price and quantity volatility in electricity markets and a greater mismatch between the location of power generation and available transmission capacity. As a result, regional price differentials tend to be more pronounced, causing significant inefficiency in allocation of power generation across different markets. Nils-Henrik von der Fehr discusses a variety of regulatory and market reforms to improve the operation and integration of power grids.

For example, new network capacity is needed to better integrate remote regions where renewable capacity is expanding (such as Germany, Italy, and Spain) with urban areas or locations where previous generation capacity is being retired. Transmission networks, and the operation of those networks, needs to be better coordinated across borders, and ultimately, perhaps, at the EU level. On the supply side, the intermittency of renewables can be accommodated in part through greater coupling of day-ahead and intraday markets across different power exchanges. Regulatory and other obstacles to new demand-side technologies (e.g., smart meters and remote control of appliances to optimize electrical usage) enabling consumers to better deal with price volatility also need to be addressed.

Energy Tax Directive (Chapter 4)

Recent attempts to reform the EU's Energy Tax Directive, which sets tax floors for fuels outside the ETS, have stalled. However, the issue will likely resurface at some point with pressure for harmonization of carbon prices across ETS and non-ETS fuels as the European Union moves forward with its climate mitigation pledges.

Ian Parry and Herman Vollebergh discuss a variety of possible reforms to the ETD. Recent proposals (increasing tax floors for diesel and natural gas but not gasoline) make sense on economic grounds, though the environmental, fiscal, and economic benefits would be limited. Instead, there are much larger gains from extending tax floors to also cover fuels in the ETS, particularly coal (with the ETS cap tightened to maintain allowance prices). Policymakers might also consider the possibility of a two-speed system granting lower-income Member States (who are most concerned about higher energy prices) lower tax minima, as this need not sacrifice a great deal in terms of climate benefits.

Coherence of Climate, Renewables, and Energy Efficiency Policies (Chapter 5)

Besides its emissions mitigation pledge, the European Union has additional targets for the share of renewable generation and energy efficiency. As discussed by Andreas Löschel and Oliver Schenker, the rationale for these supplementary targets and policies to implement them hinge critically on whether there are additional impediments hindering investments in renewable and energy-saving technologies.

The first priority is to establish a robust emissions price, applied across all emissions sources, to provide across-the-board incentives for the advancement of clean technologies. Beyond that, evidence suggests there is a strong case for supplementary policies to promote research and development (R&D) into renewables and other clean technologies, though the case for heavy policy intervention to promote deployment of renewable and energy-efficient technologies is more nuanced. This suggests some need for rebalancing current policies, which emphasize deployment over research.

The choice between, and design of, specific deployment instruments is also important. For example, policies providing a fixed subsidy per kilowatt hour of renewable power generation would permit the needed supply responses to changes in market conditions while guaranteed prices per kilowatt hour (the more common approach in practice) would not. Policies also need to be carefully tailored according to the severity of market impediments to different technologies, and progressively phased out as new technologies mature.

Clean Technology Development (Chapter 6)

Spending on clean technology R&D in the European Union seems small in comparison with other sectors (e.g., power sector companies spend less than 1 percent of turnover on innovation compared with 10-15 percent for information technology and pharmaceuticals) and is 30 percent below levels in the early 1980s. Antoine Dechezleprêtre and David Popp recommend a doubling of direct support for R&D at the EU level, phased in gradually over ten years, to allow for training of new scientists (and avoid crowding-out of other R&D).

They also recommend that R&D be funded at the EU level, using 10 percent of the future revenues from ETS allowance auctions to provide a stable, long-term funding commitment. The research funding should be directed at potential breakthrough technologies that are currently further from the market (and have received less support) than wind and solar, but that are potentially critical for a low-carbon transition, such as carbon capture and storage, energy storage, smart grids, energy efficiency, and infrastructure for electric vehicles.

Shale Gas (Chapter 7)

While there has been a dramatic boom in shale gas development in the United States, some European countries (e.g., the United Kingdom and Poland) are just now taking the first steps to develop reserves, while others (e.g., France and the Netherlands) have blocked development. As discussed by Alan Krupnick and Zhongmin Wang, a number of factors were all favorable to shale gas development in the United States, such as geology, the ability to buy private mineral rights, high gas prices, a large number of small-scale producers, ample water resources, and pipeline infrastructure. Conditions are generally less favorable in European countries (e.g., the geology and business climate are different, mineral rights are state-owned, and there is greater public opposition to development), though changing market conditions and concerns about energy dependence could favor some development in the future.

Potential environmental risks from shale gas development are wide-ranging, including water stress, contamination of surface and groundwater, local air pollution, seismic activity (from pumping wastes into deep disposal wells), GHGs (especially from methane venting and leakage), and habitat disruption. However, the severity of the risks is highly site-specific and there is little quantitative evidence on their magnitude.

Enforceable regulatory frameworks (e.g., requirements for well casing, distances from wells to streams and buildings, restrictions on venting, etc.) should be a prerequisite for shale gas development. And policy frameworks are best developed at the Member State, or local, rather than EU, level (perhaps with the exception of methane regulations). Liability also has a key role, given that regulators may know a lot less about environmental risks, and the costs of mitigating them, than producers.

Transportation Policies (Chapter 8)

A key theme of the chapter on transportation policies by Stef Proost and Bruno de Borger is the fundamental imbalance in the way current policies treat the major external costs of motor vehicles. In particular, tax incentives to purchase fuel-efficient vehicles, high fuel taxes, and fuel economy regulations combine to provide strong incentives for reducing carbon emissions and petroleum use, while very little is done to alleviate urban traffic congestion, the largest externality. The latter is best managed through charging motorists for distance traveled on busy roads at peak periods, and the electronic metering technologies needed to do this are now available.

There are some promising signs toward reducing traffic congestion; for example, the usefulness of pollution, congestion, accident, road damage, and other external cost assessments for guiding the efficient structure and rates of transportation taxes is widely accepted among EU policymakers. And several countries have taken the first steps in implementing distance-based charges for trucks. But governments are only at the start of the process, as charges need to vary with place and time of driving, in line with external costs, and, most importantly, they need to cover cars.

Proost and de Borger provide a variety of other recommendations for policy reform. These include scaling back targets for the penetration of alternative fuel vehicles and ridership on public transit; removing tax incentives for diesel fuel; sticking to fuel taxes to reduce carbon emissions from vehicles; varying parking charges with location and time of day; and complementing congestion pricing with peak period pricing of transit.

Overcoming Obstacles to Policy Reform (Chapter 9)

A key obstacle to the reform of carbon and energy pricing is the potential impacts on low-income households and energy-intensive, trade-exposed industries. As discussed by Stephen Smith, these considerations should not block policy reform—holding down energy prices below levels warranted by supply and environmental costs is an inefficient way to help low-income households (most of the benefits leak away to higher income groups) and prevents the efficient long-term allocation of scarce resources across energy-intensive and other sectors. Instead, ideally, reforms should move ahead, but be phased in gradually to allow households and firms time to adjust. Reforms should also be accompanied by targeted measures to help vulnerable groups, though these need to be carefully designed, not least because they divert revenues from the general budget that could be used for other productive purposes (e.g., alleviating tax burdens on labor and capital).

For low-income households, some compensation might come from broader tax cuts and automatic indexing of social benefits, but other measures (e.g., strengthened social safety nets, improvements in the energy efficiency of homes) are also needed. Vulnerable firms and workers might receive assistance to ease the adjustments (e.g., through temporary exemptions, other reliefs, worker retraining). In principle, charges on the embodied carbon of imported products might also help to level the playing field and encourage other countries to price carbon; however, there are practical challenges to their implementation and they may run counter to free trade obligations. The best way to address competitiveness concerns would be to promote international coordination over carbon pricing.

This short overview of the manifold dimensions of energy policy and regulation in the European Union provides a broad sense of the complex challenges lying ahead in the transformation and decarbonization of European energy supply, but also offers some practical steps forward. The chapters of the book are self-contained and can be read individually. Yet the chapters also show that the different fields of energy policy are inextricably interwoven and that policymakers need a broad sense of the issues and the policy interactions in setting priorities for reform. We hope that this book helps to inform and stimulate the policy dialogue, as there is much at stake for the environment and the economy.

Notes

1. For the EU pledge, see http://www4.unfccc.int/submissions/INDC/Published%20Documents/Latvia/1/ LV-03-06-EU%20INDC.pdf and for an overview of all INDCs, see http://infographics.pbl.nl/indc/.

2. EU air quality policies also interact with climate change policy, but we only touch briefly upon those interactions in the current volume.

3. The EU ETS covers essentially point sources from industrial installations, a large part of which fall under the power generation sector. Other covered sectors include cement

production, iron and steel, coking plants and oil refining, as well as paper, glass, ceramics production, and (since 2012) emissions from aviation (within EU airspace).

4. Contributions from international credits are not foreseen.

5. http://ec.europa.eu/clima/policies/effort/index_en.htm.

References

Brink, C., H. R. J. Vollebergh, and E. van der Werf. 2016. "Carbon Pricing in the EU: Evaluation of Different EU ETS." *Energy Policy* 97: 603–17.

EC (European Commission). 2012. "Directive 2012/27/EU of the European Parliament and of the Council of 25 October 2012 on Energy Efficiency." *Official Journal of the European Union* 315/1. http://eur-lex.europa.eu/legalcontent/EN/TXT/?qid=1399375464230&ur i=CELEX:32012L0027.

EC. 2013a. *EU Energy, Transport and GHG Emissions, Trends to 2050, Reference Scenario 2013.* Luxembourg: Publications Office of the European Union. https://ec.europa.eu/energy/sites/ener/files/documents/trends_to_2050_update_2013.pdf.

EC. 2013b. "Clean Air Policy Package." http://ec.europa.eu/environment/air/clean_air_policy.htm and http://ec.europa.eu/environment/air/legis.htm.

EC. 2015a. "2020 Climate & Energy Package." *European Commission: Climate Action.* http://ec.europa.eu/clima/policies/strategies/2020/index_en.htm.

EC. 2015b. "2030 Climate & Energy Framework." *European Commission: Climate Action.* http://ec.europa.eu/clima/policies/strategies/2030/index_en.htm.

EC. 2015c. "Emissions Trading System (EU ETS): Auctioning." *European Commission: Climate Action.* http://ec.europa.eu/clima/policies/ets/cap/auctioning/index_en.htm.

EC. 2015d. "Emissions Trading System (EU ETS): Emissions Cap and Allowances." *European Commission: Climate Action.* http://ec.europa.eu/clima/policies/ets/cap/index_en.htm.

EC. 2015e. "Priority: Energy Union and Climate." *European Commission: Priorities.* http://ec.europa.eu/priorities/energy-union/docs/energyunion_en.pdf.

EC. 2015f. *EU ETS Handbook.* https://ec.europa.eu/clima/policies/ets/ets-summer-university/system/files/ged/EU-ETS-Handbook.pdf.

EC. 2015g. "Renewable Energy Directive." *European Commission: Energy.* https://ec.europa.eu/energy/en/topics/renewable-energy/renewable-energy-directive.

EEA (European Environment Agency). 2014. "Total Greenhouse Gas (GHG) Emission Trends and Projections." *European Environment Agency: Indicators.* http://www.eea.europa.eu/data-and-maps/indicators/greenhouse-gas-emission-trends-5/assessment-1.

EEA. 2015a. *Air Quality in Europe—2015 Report.* Luxembourg: Publications Office of the European Union. http://www.eea.europa.eu/publications/air-quality-in-europe-2015.

EEA. 2015b. "Emissions of the Main Air Pollutants." *European Environment Agency: Data Visualisations.* http://www.eea.europa.eu/data-and-maps/daviz/emission-trends-for-the-main-2.

EEA. 2015c. "EU Emissions Trading System (ETS) Viewer." *European Environment Agency: Interactive Data Viewers.* http://www.eea.europa.eu/data-and-maps/data/data-view ers/emissions-trading-viewer.

EEA. 2015d. "National Emissions Reported to the UNFCCC and to the EU Greenhouse Gas Monitoring Mechanism." *European Environment Agency: Datasets.* http://www.eea .europa.eu/data-and-maps/data/national-emissions-reported-to-the-unfccc-and-to-the-eu-greenhouse-gas-monitoring-mechanism-3.

EU (European Union). 2010. "Consolidated Versions of the Treaty on European Union and the Treaty on the Functioning of the European Union (2010/C 83/01)." *Official Journal of the European Union* 53: 1-361. http://eur-lex.europa.eu/legal-content/EN/ TXT/PDF/?uri=OJ:C:2010:083:FULL&from=EN.

Eurostat. 2015. "Database." *Eurostat: Your Key to European Statistics.* http://ec.europa.eu/ eurostat/data/database.

Helm, Dieter. 2015. *Carbon Crunch: How We're Getting Climate Change Wrong—And How to Fix It.* London, UK: Yale University Press.

IRENA (International Renewable Energy Agency). 2015. "Renewable Electricity Capacity and Generation Statistics 2000–2014." *IRENA: Data and Statistics.* http://resourceirena .irena.org/gateway/dashboard/.

Koch, Nicolas, S. Fuss, G. Grosjean, and O. Edenhofer. 2014. "Causes of the EU ETS Price Drop: Recession, CDM, Renewable Policies or a Bit of Everything? New Evidence." *Energy Policy* 73: 676-85.

OECD (Organisation for Economic Co-operation and Development). 2015. "The OECD Database on Policy Instruments for the Environment." Organisation for Economic Co-operation and Development. http://www2.oecd.org/ecoinst/queries.

1   Reforming the EU ETS: Where Are We Now?

Cameron Hepburn[1] and Alexander Teytelboym

Key Points for Policymakers

- The EU ETS has suffered from inadequate coverage, excessive free allocation of permits, and carbon prices that are too low.
- Current reforms aimed to address these problems include the market stability reserve (MSR), increased incentives for greater coverage by allowing Member States to keep their own auction revenues, and an increase in the upper limit on auctioning to 40 percent.
- Superior solutions—unfortunately unlikely to be implemented due to European politics—include a reserve price on auctions and a ceiling EUA price; upstream coverage of road transport, household, and heating; and a move to full auctioning with border adjustments to address competitiveness concerns.

1. Introduction

Classic economic theory suggests that pricing carbon dioxide (CO_2) should be the most efficient way to reduce CO_2 emissions as this promotes—with one single instrument—the full range of opportunities for mitigating emissions across the economy (Baumol and Oates 1988). The two main mechanisms used to supply an explicit price on CO_2 emissions are direct taxation (Pigou 1920) or an emission-trading scheme (ETS) (Montgomery 1972). An ETS, also referred to as a "cap-and-trade scheme," caps the total quantity of emissions and allows participants to trade emission permits, thereby encouraging (within a period) emission reduction to take place at the lowest aggregate cost. In an (unrealistic) world without uncertainty and other constraints, taxation and ETS could both achieve an efficient outcome. But in a (realistic) world with scientific and political uncertainty and long-term investments, the choice between taxes and an ETS depends on a host of factors (Weitzman 1974; Hepburn 2006). Broadly speaking, the conclusion of the economics literature is that although economic considerations tend to favor the use of taxation for a problem such as climate change, political considerations around the world have, thus far, appeared to favor the adoption of an ETS (World Bank 2014).

At the European level, after much discussion of carbon taxation in the 1990s, the European Commission's (EC) original 1992 proposal for a carbon tax was eventually scrapped in 1997 (Convery 2009). New taxes are unpopular in any country, and harmonizing or ceding taxation powers from Member States to Europe simply did not attract the necessary political support. The Lisbon Treaty continues to require unanimity in the European Council for any EU-wide taxation decisions, making any EU carbon tax especially challenging from a political perspective.[2] Individual European Member States, such as Denmark, France, and Sweden, did introduce (and have retained) carbon taxation regimes at national level in the 1990s, and these now sit (somewhat uncomfortably) alongside the European ETS. In more recent times, Ireland has implemented a carbon tax, and the United Kingdom a "carbon price floor," which operates as a tax that varies inversely with the price level in the EU ETS. Outside the European Union, countries that have introduced a carbon tax without also having a nationwide cap-and-trade scheme include Mexico and Japan. South Africa is considering introducing a carbon tax, although it has been subject to delays. British Columbia has a very well-designed revenue-neutral carbon tax that was introduced quickly without either a great debate in the public press or time for industry lobbying to oppose it (Jaccard 2012).

The signature of the Kyoto Protocol in 1997 instead stimulated the EC to consider options for introducing an ETS. This shift in direction was partly influenced by the intellectual and practical success of the U.S. SO_2 cap-and-trade scheme (Stavins 1998).[3] The EU ETS went live with a "learning phase" of emissions trading from 2005–2007, had a second phase from 2008–2012, and is currently in the third phase, running from 2013–2020. Since its birth, the EU ETS has been the largest such scheme in the world. It covers around 11,000 polluting installations (as well as aviation within the European Economic Area [EEA]) in 31 countries (three of which are outside the European Union), which are responsible for 45 percent of the EU's total greenhouse gas emissions. The key sectors that have not been covered by the EU ETS as of mid-2015 are road transport, heating fuels, and bunker fuels.

Since the creation of the EU ETS, other ETSs for greenhouse gases have proliferated around the world. At the national level, legislated cap-and-trade schemes exist in Switzerland, New Zealand, and Kazakhstan. There are subnational schemes in the United States (the Regional Greenhouse Gas Initiative that covers the northeastern United States, and a separate scheme in California), Canada (Alberta and Quebec), and Japan and China (seven regional or city-level schemes). South Korea rolled out an ETS in 2015. Several other countries, including Ukraine, Turkey, Brazil, Chile, and Thailand, are planning to introduce either an ETS or a carbon tax (World Bank 2014). The point is that many jurisdictions are watching and learning from European experiences with the EU ETS, both positive and negative, so the reforms to the EU ETS not only have important implications within the European Union, but also guide other policy decisions around the world.

We proceed as follows. In section 2, we briefly review the objectives of cap-and-trade schemes and the history of the EU ETS. In sections 3 and 4, we look at the current issues facing the EU ETS and analyze the proposed solutions, focussing in particular on three key issues—low and dynamically inefficient prices, inadequate coverage of emissions, and excessive free allocation of allowances. In section 5, we make an economic and political case for a better solution. Finally, we state our conclusions.[4]

2.   Three Key Objectives of ETS Design

An ETS is designed to reduce regulated emissions to an agreed level, ideally reflecting a calculation of appropriate environmental benefits and economic costs of reducing emissions. There are several important economic considerations that ideally would be taken into account into ETS design. Broadly speaking, most of these considerations relate to either temporal, spatial, or fiscal issues (Fankhauser and Hepburn 2010a; 2010b). Temporal issues include the length of commitment periods, and issues such as banking and borrowing of allowances into the future to achieve dynamic efficiency. Spatial issues involve coverage of sectors by the ETS within a particular country and, for a global externality such as climate change, linking to other ETSs. Fiscal issues relate to the potential auctioning of emissions allowances and use of revenues. We consider three issues—dynamic efficiency, coverage and competitiveness, and fiscal recycling—in more detail below.[5]

2.1 Dynamic Efficiency

A cap-and-trade scheme is dynamically efficient if it achieves a given cumulative amount of emissions reductions while minimizing the costs *over time*. For a long-run challenge such as the reduction of carbon dioxide emissions, this requires more than the lowest-cost reduction of emissions within a given year. Rather, it also requires that the system as a whole provides firms with appropriate incentives to reduce emissions optimally over time—to equate (discounted) incremental abatement costs at different points in time—through efficient timing of, for instance, long-term investments into mitigation technologies, low-carbon research and development (R&D), and retirement and replacement of high-carbon capital stock with low-carbon equivalents.

There are at least four key policy choices that pertain to delivering dynamic efficiency. First, the regulator must decide on the appropriate time horizon for the cap-and-trade scheme. A cap-and-trade scheme for a long-lived, stock pollutant such as CO_2 would ideally have a very long time horizon (Fankhauser and Hepburn 2010a), perhaps of several decades. In practice, most cap-and-trade schemes are legislated for a short, fixed time period with a possibility of rolling over emissions allowances to future periods. However, short-term abatement targets may be socially inefficient if they leave uncertainty over medium- and longer-term emissions prices, thereby reducing firms' incentives to invest in expensive mitigation technology (e.g., renewable plants) with long-range emissions reductions (Vogt-Schilb, Hallegatte, and de Gouvello 2014).

Second, in the absence of tight price collars, banking (saving permits for future use) and borrowing (using allowances from future allocations today) rules are important. Without the ability to bank and to borrow to some (normally limited) degree, participants do not have the flexibility to reduce emissions in the year when it is cheapest to do so, thus increasing overall social costs.

Third, the credibility of future caps is critical, so that investors have a clear signal on which they can base their investment decisions and thus avoid the lock-in of carbon intensive infrastructure (Aghion et al. 2014). An ETS design that is responsive to changing market conditions in a predictable (if not formulaic) way helps to avoid the need for politicians to intervene to correct problems in the market (Fankhauser and Hepburn 2010a).

Finally, on a related note, price instability is itself a problem that can create uncertainty. In artificial markets such as an ETS without price stability mechanisms, the supply curve of permits in a given period is often steeply sloped (if not vertical), leading to greater price volatility (Fankhauser and Hepburn 2010a). Prices are more stable when the market participants have timely information about the market fundamentals, which allows them to form reasonable expectations. Temporarily incorrect prices distort firms' expectations, affect their short-run investment decisions, and potentially increase long-run mitigation costs. Mechanisms to increase the responsiveness of supply, or at least minimize price volatility, are advisable. Examples of such mechanisms are auction reserve prices (i.e., setting a minimum price for the periodic auction of the allowances), allowance reserves (where a limited number of additional allowances can be issued once a quantity safety valve is triggered), or more direct price ceilings and floors.

2.2   Wide Coverage

One ton of carbon dioxide does the same damage no matter where it is emitted on the planet. Therefore, to achieve emissions reductions at the lowest cost, ideally, every (polluting) sector in every country should be covered by a single (or linked) cap-and-trade scheme. If all sectors in all countries faced the same carbon price, emissions would be reduced wherever it was cheapest. In practice, there are two large distortions to this ideal.

First, it is impossible or at least highly infeasible to cover all emissions from all sectors within a given jurisdiction. Non-CO_2 emissions, such as methane, which is prevalent in the agricultural sector, are harder and more expensive to monitor. Emissions from mobile sources (e.g., cars) are very difficult to monitor directly, and emissions from extremely small sources may also not be worth the costs associated with measuring, monitoring, verifying, and accounting. Rather, carbon pricing in these sectors can be more easily achieved by integrating carbon charges in road fuel excises (which are long established in most countries), or by incorporating such sectors into an upstream ETS as we discuss below. Other sectors may have enough political power to prevent themselves from coming under the ETS, or at least may be able to ensure that their oligopoly profits are protected by an adequate free allocation of pollution permits (Hepburn, Quah, and Ritz 2013). As such, in any jurisdiction there will be "covered" or "ETS" sectors and "uncovered" or "non-ETS" sectors. While the price faced by the ETS sectors is the same, a variety of different taxes and regulations tend to be put in place to address emissions from the "non-ETS" sectors, and these will impose a large range of different carbon prices. Fankhauser, Hepburn, and Park (2010) argue that "price intervention may not always have the desired effect" and can "undermine the carbon price in the rest of the trading regime, likely increasing costs without reducing emissions" when the ETS overlaps with other taxes and regulations.

Second, even when an explicit carbon price does exist in a given country, that carbon price will not necessarily be the same as carbon prices elsewhere in the world, for a whole variety of reasons. The consequence is that firms with emissions-heavy production processes have a (normally mild) incentive to locate their manufacturing outside a cap-and-trade scheme and sell their products back into the domestic (capped) market. For some sectors, such as the domestic power sector, it may be difficult or impossible to move outside the European Union and consumers or intermediary firms cannot switch easily to imports. Firms in these sectors typically pass a high proportion of the costs on to consumers (Sijm, Neuhoff, and Chen 2006; Bruyn et al. 2010; Jouvet and Solier 2013; Fabra and Reguant 2014), so there is relatively little justification for free allowances to such firms. In other sectors, such as cement, steel, and aluminium, if the cost of emissions in countries without an ETS is lower, and if this has a significant impact on final consumer prices, then domestic consumers may prefer to buy cheaper goods produced in countries without a carbon price. The carbon leakage rates for very vulnerable sectors are estimated to be between 50 percent and 150 percent for carbon prices between €5 and €50 (Vivid Economics 2014, 78).[6] To address this, the EU ETS provides firms with freely allocated permits provided that they continue to operate in the European Union.[7] These free allowances as well as compensation schemes create additional distortions (see section 5.3). Border carbon adjustments, which impose costs on the carbon content of imported goods, are an alternative way to prevent loss of international competitiveness and leakage (Helm, Hepburn, and Ruta 2012), but these have not yet been properly trialled. The relative merits of free allowances and border carbon adjustments are generally difficult to assess with the available data (Monjon and Quirion 2011; Keen and Kotsogiannis 2014).

2.3   Sensible Fiscal Properties

There are sound economic arguments that suggest the starting point should be no free allocation of permits to firms (Hepburn et al. 2006) unless good reasons to the contrary can be demonstrated. For instance, free allocation leads to inefficient rent-seeking and creates political lock-in. Instead, allowances to emit may be sold via an auction, which helps to ensure that those who value them hold the allowances at the start of trading.[8] Thus, auctions deliver efficiency and raise revenue for the government. This revenue may be used to reduce distortions elsewhere in the economy, e.g., to reduce taxes on labor and capital (Parry and Bento 2000) or subsidize innovation and deployment of green technologies (Dechezleprêtre and Popp, this volume). Therefore, productive use of auction revenues can increase the overall efficiency of the economy. We will return to consider the use of auction revenues later in the paper—politically, this is a key challenge of cap-and-trade design.

3.   A Brief History of the EU ETS

The EU ETS was created in 2003 by the EU Directive 2003/87/EC and established in 2005 following several small-scale experimental carbon trading schemes across the European Union (Convery 2009). The EU ETS covers three greenhouse gases: carbon dioxide, nitrous oxide (from the production of acids), and perfluorocarbons (from aluminium production). One EU Allowance (EUA) allows the holder to emit one ton of carbon dioxide equivalent (tCO_2e). EUAs can be traded on exchanges or bought through brokers. Exchanges offer spot and derivative (e.g., futures) trading.

3.1   Phase I: 2005–2007

During Phase I, over 95 percent of the EUAs were given away for free, leading to considerable allocative inefficiencies. Prices (in nominal terms) started out at around €7 and stayed between €20 and €30 for a year, before crashing to €15 after the first verified emissions report came out in April 2006 and pointed to a significant over-allocation of emissions allowances. The decision to allow banking of Phase I allowances for use in Phase II was left at the discretion of Member States.[9] Due to the over-allocation of allowances and the inability to bank Phase I allowances for Phase II, the price of Phase I EUAs eventually

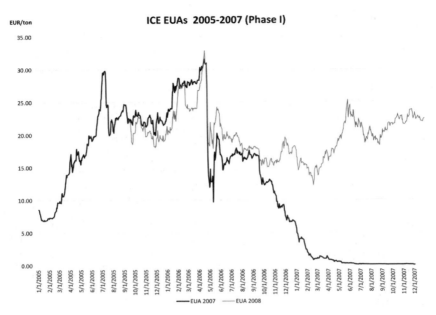

Figure 1.1
Evolution of EUA spot prices in Phase I
Source: Sendeco.

collapsed to near zero (see figure 1.1) as firms tried to sell off all Phase I allowances they accumulated in previous years (Ellerman and Buchner 2007; Hintermann 2010; Anderson and Di Maria 2011).

3.2 Phase II: 2008–2012

Various design flaws in Phase I were addressed in Phase II, which coincided with the first Kyoto Protocol commitment period. First, the revised EC directive mandated EU Member States to allow EU ETS participants to bank their Phase II allowances for Phase III. Second, the EU ETS was broadened to cover more sectors, including glass and petrochemicals. Third, the EC revised and simplified its guidelines for the publication of National Allocation Plans (NAPs), which Member States submit as part of the process for determining the allocation of allowances for installations covered by the EU ETS. The EC then used the NAPs to determine the number of allowances allocated to each Member State: most states did not receive as many allowances as they asked for. Fourth, Clean Development Mechanism (CDM), Certified Emission Reduction (CER), and Joint Implementation (JI) Emission

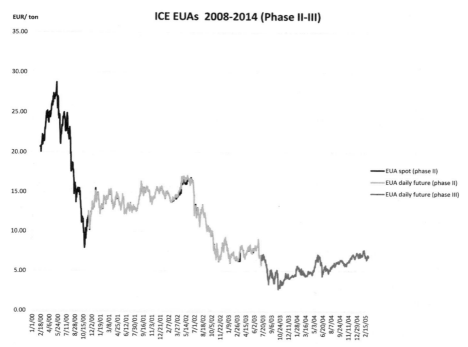

Figure 1.2
Evolution of EUA spot and futures prices in Phases II and III
Source: Bloomberg.

Reduction Unit (ERU) credits created under the flexibility mechanisms of the Kyoto Protocol became tradable alongside EUAs at a one-to-one exchange rate.[10] Fifth, in 2012, within-EEA aviation emissions were included in the EU ETS. Finally, the directive increased the ability of Member States to auction off allowances. Member States were permitted to auction off at most 10 percent of their allowances, though only the United Kingdom and Germany came close to that cap. It is likely that the governments chose to forego these auction revenues because of successful lobbying by emission-intensive industries.

The economic crisis that began in late 2008 has been associated with a fall in the price of EUAs. Since reaching a peak of €35 in July 2008, EUA prices fell to around €15 between early 2009 and early 2011, before declining to around €5-€7 (Creti, Jouvet, and Mignon 2012). The number of surplus EUAs grew to 2.1 billion by the end of 2012. Figure 1.2 illustrates the evolution of the EUA spot and future prices over Phases II and III. The futures show the price of a contract for the delivery of an EUA (of any eligible vintage) in December of the relevant year.

3.3 Phase III: 2013–2020

Phase III is the longest EU ETS phase so far. In Phase III, there are several major changes compared to Phase II and the EU ETS decision-making process shifts significantly from Member States to Brussels. First, there is an EU-wide cap on emission allowances, which is reduced by 1.74 percent annually. Second, the limit on the proportion of EUAs that can be auctioned by Member States rose to 40 percent in 2013 and around half of allowances will be auctioned off between 2013 and 2020. Some exempt manufacturing sectors and aviation will continue to receive 30 percent and 85 percent of their allowances for free, respectively. Third, even more sectors and greenhouse gases are covered (see figure 1.3). Phase III also saw the first step back for the EU ETS. The emission reduction requirements of the aviation sector for 2012 were retrospectively suspended[11] in 2013 and only within-EEA aviation is covered by the EU ETS between 2013–2016, pending a negotiation with the International Civil Aviation Authority (which in October 2016 signed a global deal to begin compulsory offsetting of aviation emissions from 2027).

4. Current Challenges for the EU ETS

4.1 Low EUA Prices

The EC has recognized that the persistent low EUA price (figure 1.2) is promoting only limited abatement efforts in the near term and beginning to undermine the ability of the EU ETS to deliver an appropriate long-term price signal to polluting firms. The low price has reduced firms' incentives to invest into clean technologies. In the power sector, producers have reacted in this (and lower international coal prices) in the short term by switching from natural gas back to coal.[12] The December 2020 EUA future price of under €8 (see figure 1.2) at the end of March 2015 appears to be substantially below the socially optimal price, that, one that would incentivize firms to undertake the necessary long-term investment into clean infrastructure in a manner that balances costs and benefits. The price is also too low relative to the implicit price used internally by many companies when making their investment decisions. For instance, several multinational oil companies use internal screening prices of $40/€35 or more,[13] even though they operate in jurisdictions that are, on the whole, subject to even more lax carbon regulation than Europe.

Low EUA prices are at least partially caused by low levels of current demand for EUAs, driven by a combination of reduced energy demand caused by the economic crisis, support for renewables on the national level, support for energy efficiency, and the use of CDM/JI credits. However, it may be that such current demand-side factors account for only 10 percent of the observed price variation (Edenhofer, Normark, and Tardieu 2014), with expectations about future conditions—in particular, expectations of low future prices—playing a more important role in price formation. Notwithstanding the large current surpluses in EUAs, for instance, the carbon price remains positive, indicating that the market implicitly expects the emission cap to be binding at least at some point in the future.

4.2 Limited Coverage (and Overlapping Policies)

Currently, only half of the EU's emissions are covered by the EU ETS (see figure 1.3). This compares to 60 percent coverage in the South Korean ETS (and the repealed Australian Carbon Pricing Mechanism) and 85 percent in the California and Quebec cap-and-trade schemes (World Bank 2014). Carbon-intensive sectors outside the EU ETS include road transport, agriculture (which produces methane), and the natural gas used for heating homes and buildings.

While this is for understandable reasons—covering the downstream emissions in these sectors by including every motorist in the EU ETS would not be sensible—it is nevertheless problematic because it leads to ad hoc and inconsistent national responses instead. Some EU countries have carbon taxes on top of their EU ETS participation, partly in order to stimulate emission reductions in these sectors; firms that participate in the EU ETS are generally exempt of legislation (the UK carbon price floor is a notable exception). Tax rates vary dramatically from $28/tCO_2$ in Ireland to $168/tCO_2$ in Sweden (World Bank 2014). In addition to direct carbon pricing policies, all EU countries implement emissions standards (e.g., euro 6 for cars or building regulations, see De Borger and Proost in this volume), which carry a high *implicit* carbon price, although other market failures are also arguably addressed by such policies. Moreover, there are country-specific energy policies and targets: the United Kingdom, for example, has introduced an obligation for electricity providers to supply renewable power while Germany provides generous feed-in tariffs.[14] Given these other policies, even the inclusion of sectors such as power in the EU ETS does not necessarily imply that marginal abatement costs are equalized across

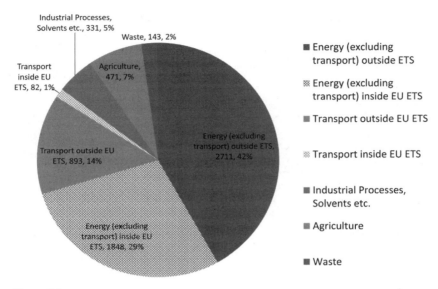

Figure 1.3
Sectoral breakdown of emissions covered by the EU ETS in 2012
Sources: EEA (2016a; 2016b).

sectors. Indeed, national emissions reduction policies that overlap with sectors covered by the EU ETS would be expected to push down the EU ETS price unless such national policies were coordinated with an explicit reduction in the number of permits (Fankhauser, Hepburn, and Park 2010). After the collapse of the Australian cap-and-trade scheme, there are no near-term candidate cap-and-trade carbon markets that will link to the EU ETS (except for Switzerland), and a lack of global links creates further inefficiencies in the overall global response.

4.3   Excessive Free Allocation
Finally, decision-making at the level of the EC remains slow, involving a large number of veto players and regulatory capture through lobbying (Helm 2012). Theoretical and some empirical work suggests that the level of free allocation that has been historically provided by the EC to firms has been overly generous—profit-neutral allocations require only a minority of allowances to be freely allocated, even in trade-exposed sectors (Hepburn et al. 2013).[15] Under the EU ETS, allowances are allocated for free according to new and existing capacities independent of current production, using industry benchmarks. In California, an output-based system has been adopted (Meunier,

Ponssard, and Quirion 2012). The EU allocation system reduces free allocations around specific thresholds of *past* production levels, which incentivizes firms to strategically increase production to guarantee more free allocations in the future (Branger et al. 2014). While political deals obviously do need to be struck to get policies through, the level and specifics of free allocation clearly deserve additional focus in further reform efforts. It has been estimated that auctioning in a reformed EU ETS could raise as much as €64 billion (Flachsland 2014)—18 times more than the current revenue. For Germany and Poland, this would constitute as much as 3.9 percent and 8.9 percent of the central government budget spending, respectively.

5.   Current Approaches

In this section, we review how the EC and various EU Member States are dealing with the three problems described in the previous section.

5.1   Addressing Low Prices

Back-loading   In order to limit current supply, the EC decided to back-load the auctioning of 900m EUAs until 2019–2020. The EC will correspondingly reduce auction volumes by 400m in 2014, 300m in 2015, and 200m in 2016. As the aggregate cap remains unchanged, this decision was arguably more about political signalling than about sensible economic policy.

Unsurprisingly, the back-loading decision had no immediate effect on price of allowance futures. It is possible, of course, that in the absence of back-loading, the price would have fallen further. But the slight increase in the price of EUA (from just under €5 in April 2014 to just under €7 by April 2015) could also be explained by macroeconomic factors, including slowly increasing economic growth across the European Union.

Market Stability Reserve   The first major compromise proposal to address the low allowance price is the market stability reserve (MSR). It is not certain whether the MSR will commence in 2017 or 2021. It can be summarized as a quantity-based rule: if the total number of allowances in circulation[16] is

- less than 400m, then the MSR releases 100m allowances into circulation.
- between 400m and 833m, then the market functions without intervention.

- greater than 833m, then the MSR absorbs 12 percent of allowances in circulation each year.

The MSR is an ad hoc quantity-based solution to a problem of low prices. However, it does not deal with the issue of low prices directly. Instead, when the quantity of surplus permits falls below 400m or exceeds 833m, permits are released or removed from the market respectively. Nevertheless, this mechanism is designed to affect prices so that they are neither too high nor too low, effectively targeting some notion of price stability or dynamic efficiency.

Like the EU ETS itself, because the MSR affects carbon prices only indirectly, it does not constitute a "fiscal measure" and therefore does not require unanimity of the EU Member States to be adopted. The need to avoid the unanimity requirement is arguably why the EU's price stabilization mechanism has such an unusual design. While it is likely to bring about an improvement on back-loading, for instance, there are various problems with the MSR proposal. First, the mechanism is a complicated, indirect way of addressing the real objective—price stability—with the potential for the "law of unintended consequences" to apply. Several teams of academics are currently working on identifying these unintended consequences (including strategic behavior to shift the system across a threshold to trigger a subsequent intervention) ex ante, with the intention of avoiding them (their conclusions are summarized in a special issue of the *Journal of Environmental Economics and Management*). Second, it is not impossible that the MSR will actually increase price volatility because the total number of allowances in circulation is calculated with a two-year lag (Edenhofer et al. 2014). The uncertainty created by new data that arrives out of sync with current investment decisions could lead to pro-cyclical dynamics. Volatility could also increase if it is expected that the trigger levels could change over time (for example, because the power sector's demand for hedging forward sales of electricity falls). Third, the MSR creates unusual incentives at the thresholds. As emission reductions occur, the number of allowances in circulation increases. At the threshold, the MSR would function to remove EUAs from the market, which would push up EUA prices, incentivizing greater emission reductions.

Adjusting the Emissions Reduction Path The second proposal approved by the European Council, now to be implemented by the EC, is to increase the annual reduction in the number of allowances from 1.74 percent currently to 2.2 percent. This proposal will affect the futures price of allowances because it affects the aggregate emission cap.[17] The adjustment to the reduction path will apply at the start of Phase IV from 2021. Overall, this is a sensible move. However, it should be stressed that meddling with the emissions pathway too much could damage the credibility of the EC and exacerbate time-inconsistency problems. Firms may fear that if they invest in abatement technologies today, there is some risk that the EC could subsequently loosen the emissions cap (and increase reduce carbon prices in the future), damaging the value of their investments (Helm, Hepburn, and Mash 2003).

5.2 Expanding Coverage

Road transport is one of the sectors with the most rapidly growing worldwide emissions, but as the sources of emissions are mobile, no regional cap-and-trade scheme has included road transport yet. However, in 2015 the California cap-and-trade scheme will extend to all fuel *distributors* (including heating and transportation fuels).[18] The application of the ETS upstream (i.e., fuel producers, refineries, importers of refined fuels)[19] is sensible as it minimizes administrative costs. Regulated players, such as competitive refineries, will then pass the costs on to consumers (Creutzig et al. 2011; Flachsland et al. 2011). It is notable that the EC has already introduced regulations that address other externalities caused by road transport, including emission standards for air pollutants, and several EU countries have introduced additional taxes on road fuels (including its carbon content). Including road transport in the EU ETS will not in principle affect the EUA price provided that an appropriate corresponding number of additional allowances are issued (Creutzig et al. 2010).

Some countries would like to include road transport within the EU ETS. And Member States are currently entitled to "opt in" to additional sectors to the EU ETS. However, current auction revenue redistribution arrangements serve as an impediment that tempers enthusiasm for greater coverage. Ten percent of allowances are distributed to the least wealthy Member States. So while a country such as Sweden may wish to bring the transport sector into the EU ETS, some of its potential auction revenue would automatically be distributed to other Member States, including, for instance, Poland.

The good news is that this perversity is likely to be corrected with the forthcoming package of amendments from the EC. Once auction revenues from new sectors are no longer redistributed, countries wishing to include road transport will be free to do so. However, this is unlikely to be extended to road transport across the European Union as a whole, so a patchwork of national arrangements is likely to result. While suboptimal, this should be manageable, just as excise duties currently vary from Member State to Member State.[20] Given that EU countries already raise substantial revenues from fuel excise duties, it is unclear whether there will be a stampede by Member States to include road transport within the EU ETS.

While sectoral coverage could also be expanded to cover maritime transport emissions (bunker fuels), aviation remains the most contentious issue in this domain. Aviation was originally due to be completely included in the EU ETS, but after the political ruckus of 2013, the scope was limited to only flights within the EEA, which is to say flights that both take off and land at EEA airports. Breathing room was granted to ICAO to develop a global mechanism by 2016, at which point the EU ETS would be amended to line up with the ICAO mechanism. In October 2016, ICAO signed the Carbon Offsetting and Reduction Scheme for International Aviation (CORSIA). The goal is to stabilize net emissions from aviation at their 2020 level. The scheme does not commit ICAO members to any direct emission reductions, focussing instead on offsetting and continued efficiency improvements introduced in 2007. The scheme begins its two-year testing phase in 2021 and is voluntary until 2027 with exemptions for less developed countries and small-island states.

Despite the justifiable nature of the EU position on aviation, a reversion to full coverage may well trigger a re-run of an aggressive response from other nations, followed by a likely concession from the EU leaders as a result of political pressure focussed on the export of airplanes manufactured by Airbus (Vihma and van Asselt 2014). So, the current question is whether to preemptively adjust aviation coverage so that the EU ETS covers only outward-bound flights from EU Member States. However, those advocating a preemptive change are faced with the accusation that they are already stepping back from a negotiation before it has even begun. It seems that the easier option for Europe is to do nothing now, then accept the fight in 2016 (as the ICAO progress has been insufficient), with a subsequent EU concession.*

---

* At the time of writing, the European Union has not yet responded to the ICAO agreement with new legislation.

5.3   Reducing Free Allocation

Currently, sectors covered by the EU ETS that are deemed at risk of foreign competition can receive up to 100 percent of their allowances free. Recent evidence suggests that this sector-based compensation is grossly inefficient and does not equalize the marginal probabilities of firms' relocation (Martin et al. 2014). Free allowances divert funds from the government budget, potentially implying that other taxes must be higher. Free allowances are equivalent to a marginal subsidy, which undermines the impact of the ETS and distorts firms' incentives toward carbon-intensive production. Firms can also apply for compensation schemes that cover their indirect emissions cost even though these schemes constitute state aid.[21] Both of these forms of compensation may create "ratchet" problems, if firms have an incentive to strategically increase their emissions today in order to guarantee free allowances in the future (Weitzman 1980).

Nevertheless, because the EC is concerned about the loss of competitiveness of its energy-intensive industry, some proportion of free allocation could continue until 2030.[22] Indeed, free allocation has even been contemplated for the power sector (which is not exposed to imports) by the continued use of Article 10c of the ETS directive 2003/87/EC, in order to prolong the phasing-out of free allocation. This is thought to be justified on the basis that because the cap is in place, there are no negative environmental consequences from the free allocation of permits. However, free allocations reduce revenues available to correct other market failures (e.g., inadequate innovation in clean technology), and differential free allocation increases overall social costs because some sectors face higher effective carbon prices than others (Bruyn et al. 2010). And when social costs rise, the political motivation to continue to reduce emissions falls. Despite this, there is little by way of serious proposals to accelerate the proportion of allowances that are auctioned.

6.   Preferable Solutions

We recognize that European policy-making is subject to a raft of institutional and political constraints, in addition to rent-seeking and regulatory capture. Brexit is likely to put further strains on the political consensus around the EU ETS (Hepburn and Teytelboym 2017). In some sense, it is remarkable that anything at all is achieved. Nevertheless, our view is that the following three recommendations, which represent improvements in economic efficiency, are not so wildly outside the bounds of political feasibility, and should be considered in the medium term. Preferable solutions to the three key problems identified are as follows:

1. Set reserve prices in auctions to support EUA prices, rather than deploy a convoluted market stability reserve.
2. Increase sectoral coverage to road transport across the European Union and ensure a strong position is taken on aviation and bunker fuels.
3. Advance full auctioning of EUAs as soon as possible, with border carbon adjustments to address competitiveness concerns or, failing that, at least ensure that the payoffs to successful industry lobbyists are designed in a manner that reduces perverse ratchet effects.

6.1   Auction Price Floor and Ceiling to Address Low EUA Prices

In theory, the simplest solution to meet the objective of dynamic efficiency, and the current challenge of low prices, is a price collar, i.e., a minimum and a maximum price (Roberts and Spence 1976; Pizer 2002; Grüll and Taschini 2011). A minimum price is just as important as a maximum price for this sort of problem (Burtraw, Palmer, and Kahn 2010). Price collars help firms form more accurate expectations both about prices and about policy (commitment) of the EC. Therefore, the outcome will be more dynamically efficient (Burtraw et al. 2010).

However, the theoretically simple "hard" price collar has at least two potential disadvantages. On the one hand, if prices are so low that the authorities have to enter the market to repurchase allowances, there is a liability on the public balance sheet (Fankhauser and Hepburn 2010a). Moreover, if prices remain too low for a considerable amount of time, a surplus of allowances may build up. Ideally, when the number of allowances in circulation exceeds a certain threshold, further allowances will be cancelled permanently. If prices are so high that additional allowances need to be released, this would cause the EC to sacrifice its emission reduction target (Fankhauser and Hepburn 2010a).

In practice, therefore, it may be more sensible to establish a minimum price through setting an auction price floor (Hepburn et al. 2006; Murray, Newell, and Pizer 2009) or with an extra fee on acquittal of allowances (Wood and Jotzo 2011). This need not be complicated, and is considerably simpler than the currently proposed market stability reserve. The main political disadvantage appears to be that it involves fixing a minimum price, which might be interpreted legally as a tax and thus, as a "fiscal measure," would be subject to the unanimity rule of the European Union, requiring the agreement of all 28 Member

States. While there is at least some doubt about the legal position (Edenhofer et al. 2014), there is little doubt that politically at least one Member State would use the opportunity to launch a challenge. Edenhofer et al. (chapter 2 of this volume) delve deeper into the issue of price floors for the EU ETS. They show empirically that a carbon price floor, combined with appropriate transfers between Member States, can ensure that no Member State loses out and that some are made better off. This redistribution, which is consistent with the EU principles of solidarity and subsidiarity, is a possible step toward overcoming political and economic obstacles to a carbon price floor. Even though the proposed MSR attempts to achieve the same end, the absence of a lower- and upper-bound price—effectively the very vagueness that is economically problematic—is politically beneficial. This vagueness also has political appeal to those with the view that the "market" should determine prices, but it also comes with a real social cost in that firms are unable to determine where the bounds to future prices are supposed to lie, and cannot be sure that there will not be further intervention if prices again turn out to be "too low," or for that matter, "too high."

6.2 Wider Coverage

Sectoral Expansion The EC has considerable work to do to encourage Member States to harmonize national carbon reduction policies and include as many sectors as possible in the EU ETS. This is the only way to guarantee the equalization of marginal abatement costs across countries and to achieve emission reduction at the lowest cost. In particular, the EC should cover maritime emissions (Miola, Marra, and Ciuffo 2011), road transport (Santos et al. 2010), buildings and agriculture emissions (and therefore include methane into the EU ETS gases), and ensure that extra-EU aviation (Anger and Köhler 2010) is either covered by ICAO or another mechanism, if not the EU ETS.

Greater Linking Linking of cap-and-trade schemes around the world is the most efficient way to prevent leakage and achieve global emission reduction (Anger 2008; Fankhauser and Hepburn 2010b; Flachsland, Marschinski, and Edenhofer 2009). While we accept that there are considerable political difficulties in ensuring that the preconditions for linking are met, wherever possible the EC should look to link with as many sufficiently stringent and compatible cap-and-trade schemes as possible. These linkages are beginning to emerge around the world, the most notable being the cap-and-trade schemes of California and Quebec.

6.3 Greater Auctioning and Border Carbon Adjustments

The 2030 Framework for Climate and Energy, adopted in October 2014, has extended free allowance allocation until 2030. This happened despite previous plans to end free allowance allocation in 2027. Centralized (EU-level), small-scale, frequent auctions (perhaps with an auction price floor) would improve distortions associated with free allocations (static efficiency), create appropriate dynamic investment incentives (dynamic efficiency), have negligible impact on competitiveness, and greatly improve countries' fiscal positions (Hepburn et al. 2006).

Concerns about the international loss of competitiveness that have been behind the high levels of free allocation can be better addressed by border carbon adjustments (Kuik and Hofkes 2010; Helm et al. 2012), which should be seriously considered. While BCAs can in principle be designed so that they are WTO compatible, there is disagreement about which design features to implement, and how they would need to be implemented, for a BCA to be legal under WTO rules.

The revenue raised from BCAs would ideally be used to sensibly address other economic problems, including reducing other distorting taxes (Parry and Bento 2000; Jorgenson et al. 2013), or be applied to correct important market failures in clean energy innovation and deployment. The European Union currently recycles EUA auction revenue into low-carbon innovation programs, such as the NER300 (Dechezleprêtre and Popp, this volume), which funds carbon capture and storage as well as renewable technologies with proceeds from the sale of 300 million EUAs from the New Entrants' Reserve. Any subsidies for clean energy innovation should be ideally allocated through a competitive process, to the extent possible, along the lines of the notion of auctioning carbon contracts (Helm and Hepburn 2007) but for earlier stage activity.

Alternatively, and if BCAs are still considered politically unpalatable, a portion of the revenue raised could be used to provide lump-sum compensation to emissions-intensive, trade-exposed firms, provided they continue to operate in Europe. Free allocation of allowances is a pollution subsidy on the margin, which distorts their incentives to reduce emissions and creates deadweight loss. Lump-sum compensation avoids this, along the lines of the second fundamental theorem of welfare economics.[23] As we noted in sections 2.2, 4.3, and 5.3, the current free allocation and financial compensation measures are far even from the politically feasible third-best.

Finally, a way to clear out the list of sectors that receive free allocation would be to change the reference price for the evaluation of the need for support. Currently, €30 is used as the reference price, merely because this was the figure used in the EU's 2020 Climate and Energy Package of legislation, adopted in December 2008.[24] A price of around half this level would be more realistic and would reduce the absurd number of sectors receiving "compensation" in the form of free allowances.[25] And any such "compensation" should be progressively phased out as other countries introduce carbon pricing and the playing field is levelled.

7. Conclusion

The EU ETS is far from perfect. Indeed, it might be said, to adapt the famous quote from Churchill, to be "the worst form of carbon regulation in Europe, except for all others." But reform is on the agenda, and much of what is proposed represents a modest improvement on the status quo.

But much more could be done. This paper has focussed on three critical problems, and has proposed three more suitable solutions— auction reserve prices to address low EUA prices, the inclusion of more sectors at the EU level to reduce inefficiencies, and much greater auctioning with BCAs to address competitiveness concerns, or failing that, at least the use of lump-sum rather than output-based free allocation to reduce economic distortions (table 1.1).

Going beyond these measures, to address credibility of targets and time-consistency problems that hamper investment, and the continued need to "reform" the system after the conclusion of each phase, the EC might consider setting up an independent carbon authority (Helm et al. 2003; de Perthuis and Trotignon 2014). The arguments for delegating both setting an (annual or aggregate) emission reduction cap and managing the price collars are similar to arguments for delegating the setting of an interest rate to an independent central bank. The independent carbon authority would be likely to be more responsive than the EC (where the back-loading decision took 20 months),[26] more transparent, less prone to regulatory capture, and able to commit to long-term reduction targets that are necessary to prevent investment hold-up. The

Table 1.1
Summary of Problems and Solutions

#	Challenge	Current approach	Recommended solution
1	Low prices; dynamic inefficiency	Back-loading; market stability reserve; more rapid emission reductions	Auction reserve prices; price collars
2	Insufficient coverage	Excluding aviation from non-EU to EU Member States	Several additional sectors
3	Competitiveness concerns	National compensation schemes; free allowance allocation	Lump-sum compensation; BCAs; sectoral deals

independent carbon authority should have well-defined short- and long-term objectives (low price volatility, renewable capacity targets, and so on). Although long-term commitment can reduce flexibility in policy-making (Brunner, Flachsland, and Marschinski 2012), if the long-term commitments were to a set of rules or principles that provide for adjustments that are prescribed ex ante, several key problems with the EU ETS could be solved.

Notes

1. Hepburn thanks Dieter Helm, Ian Parry, Peter Vis, Herman Vollebergh, and Peter Zapfel for helpful comments with the usual caveat.

2. As there are now 28 EU Member States, the difficulties of reforming the EU Energy Tax Directive (applying to fuels outside the ETS) are considerable (Parry and Vollebergh, this volume).

3. Since 2003, the United States has also been using a trading scheme to control the emissions of nitrogen oxides (Burtraw and Szambelan 2009).

4. The paper builds on an excellent recent review that discusses many similar issues by Edenhofer, Normark, and Tardieu (2014) and a 2015 special issue of the *Journal of Environmental Economics and Management* edited by Hepburn.

5. Other issues concerning the design of an ETS, such as the optimal length of commitment periods and relationships between the ETS and the overall tax system, are beyond the scope of this paper.

6. Carbon leakage rate is calculated by dividing increase in foreign emissions by the reduction in domestic (regulated emissions). Hence, a carbon leakage rate of over 100 percent means that there is an overall increase in worldwide emissions. This can happen because a firm may relocate to a region not covered by the ETS and switch to a

more carbon-intensive mode of production. Irrespective of whether its production increases or falls, its emissions may rise relative to its original emission levels, pushing the carbon leakage rate to over 100 percent. Refining and aluminum (and cements, for high carbon prices) are sectors where carbon leakage is expected to exceed 100 percent (Vivid Economics 2014, 78).

7. Paragraph 10(a)15 of Directive 2009/29/EC states:

A sector or subsector shall be deemed to be exposed to a significant risk of carbon leakage if:

a) the sum of direct and indirect additional costs induced by the implementation of this Directive would lead to a substantial increase of production costs, calculated as a proportion of the gross value added, of at least 5%; and

b) the intensity of trade with third countries, defined as the ratio between the total value of exports to third countries plus the value of imports from third countries and the total market size for the Community (annual turnover plus total imports from third countries), is above 10%.

8. Unless there is a binding reserve price at the auction, the permit price should not be affected by the allocation of permits. However, free allocation of allowances can have significant adverse distributional effects on the covered sectors by allowing firms that value allowances more to reap windfall gains.

9. Banking has since been permitted from the second phase of the EU ETS onward. Borrowing, in contrast, remains more limited. A firm is allowed to use its allowances for year t (allowances are distributed in January) in order to cover its emissions in year $t - 1$ (as allowances must be surrendered by April of year t). Borrowing across phases is not permitted, except when facing non-compliance charges (Chevallier 2012).

10. Countries and companies subject to Annex B of the Kyoto Protocol could earn CERs and ERUs by financing emission reduction projects in developed (for CERs) and other Annex B (for ERUs) countries. The market for these permits is much smaller than for EUAs. Countries and firms have a limit on the fraction of their emissions that they can cover with CERs/ERUs. The limit varies substantially between countries and sectors, but does not typically exceed more than a fifth of all freely allocated EUAs. This partly explains why there are often substantial discrepancies in prices of EUAs and CERs/ERUs.

11. See EU Parliament Decision No. 377/2013/EU.

12. See *Financial Times* (2014).

13. See Carbon Disclosure Project (2013).

14. Parry and Vollebergh (this volume) discuss European energy taxes introduced through the EU Energy Tax directive.

15. Hepburn et al. (2013) estimate that even in the British cement sector (an energy-intensive oligopoly) the profit-neutral allocation of free permits is under 50 percent of total permits.

16. The "allowances in circulation" are essentially a measure of the current surplus of EUAs in the system. It is defined by the European Union as "the difference between all allowances issued plus international credits used since 2008 up to the end of each year, and verified emissions recorded since 2008 plus allowances in the reserve at the end of that same year."

17. The proposal (see COM (2014) 20/2) was part of a broader 2030 Climate and Energy Policy Framework (see COM (2014) 15 at http://eur-lex.europa.eu/legal-content/EN/TXT/?uri=CELEX:52014DC0015).

18. The cancelled Australian Carbon Pollution Reduction Scheme was intended to apply to large upstream suppliers of liquid transportation fuels (Mortimore 2010).

19. For biofuels production, only refineries should be included, as farms will face very high transaction costs.

20. Including natural gas supplied to residential buildings in the ETS is likely to be a very divisive political issue.

21. The EC published its guidelines on state aid for environmental protection and energy in June 2014 (2014/C 200/01). Previously the EC raised no objections to the Dutch compensation scheme (while recognizing that it constitutes state aid; see paragraph 15 in State aid SA.37084 (2013/N)) or to the British compensation scheme for the indirect costs associated with the carbon price floor.

22. See, for example, Cover Note EUCO 169/14, paragraph 2.4. And see http://www.ft.com/cms/s/0/b7de8ac2-7b98-11e3-a2da-00144feabdc0.html#axzz3LKQuEuV3.

23. Another solution is to use output-based allocation of allowances with sectoral distributions based on value added rather than based on historical emissions (Fischer and Fox 2007).

24. See Commission Staff Working Paper SWD (2012) 5, pages 22 and 25. See also Vivid Economics (2014).

25. Commission Decision 2014/746/EU defines around 150 sectors as exposed to carbon leakage.

26. Between April 19, 2012 and January 8, 2014.

References

Aghion, P., C. Hepburn, A. Teytelboym, and D. Zenghelis. 2014. "Path Dependence, Innovation, and the Economics of Climate Change" (Policy Paper and Contributing Paper to New Climate Economy, Centre for Climate Change Economics and Policy/Grantham Research Institute on Climate Change and the Environment, London School of Economics and Political Science, UK). http://www.lse.ac.uk/GranthamInstitute/wp-content/uploads/2014/11/Aghion_et_al_policy_paper_Nov20141.pdf.

Anderson, Barry, and Corrado Di Maria. 2011. "Abatement and Allocation in the Pilot Phase of the EU ETS." *Environmental and Resource Economics* 48 (1): 83-103.

Anger, Annela, and Jonathan Köhler. 2010. "Including Aviation Emissions in the EU ETS: Much Ado about Nothing? A Review." *Transport Policy* 17 (1): 38-46.

Anger, Niels. 2008. "Emissions Trading Beyond Europe: Linking Schemes in a Post-Kyoto World." *Energy Economics* 30 (4): 2028-49.

Baumol, William J., and Wallace E. Oates. 1988. *The Theory of Environmental Policy,* 2nd ed. Cambridge, UK: Cambridge University Press.

Branger, Frédéric, J. Ponssard, O. Sartor, and M. Sato. 2014. "EU ETS, Free Allocations and Activity Level Thresholds, the Devil Lies in the Details" (Working Paper 190, Centre for Climate Change Economics and Policy Working Paper; Working Paper 169, Grantham Research Institute on Climate Change and the Environment, London School of Economics and Political Science, UK). http://www.lse.ac.uk/GranthamInstitute/wp-content/uploads/2014/10/Working-Paper-169-Branger-et-al-20142.pdf.

Brunner, Steffen, C. Flachsland, and R. Marschinski. 2012. "Credible Commitment in Carbon Policy." *Climate Policy* 12 (2): 255-71.

Bruyn, Sander de, A. Markowska, F. de Jong, and M. Bles. 2010. "Does the Energy Intensive Industry Obtain Windfall Profits through the EU ETS? An Econometric Analysis for Products from the Refineries, Iron and Steel and Chemical Sectors" (CE Delft Report). http://www.ce.nl/publicatie/does_the_energy_intensive_industry_obtain_windfall_profits_through_the_eu_ets/1038.

Burtraw, Dallas, and Sarah Jo Szambelan. 2009. "U.S. Emissions Trading Markets for SO_2 and NO_x" (Discussion Paper 09-40, Resources for the Future, Washington, DC, US). http://rff.org/RFF/Documents/RFF-DP-09-40.pdf.

Burtraw, Dallas, K. Palmer, and D. Kahn. 2010. "A Symmetric Safety Valve." *Energy Policy* 38 (9): 4921-32.

Chevallier, Julien. 2012. "Banking and Borrowing in the EU ETS: A Review of Economic Modelling, Current Provisions and Prospects for Future Design." *Journal of Economic Surveys* 26 (1): 157-76.

Convery, Frank J. 2009. "Origins and Development of the EU ETS." *Environmental and Resource Economics* 43 (3): 391-412.

Creti, Anna, P. A. Jouvet, and V. Mignon. 2012. "Carbon Price Drivers: Phase I versus Phase II Equilibrium?" *Energy Economics* 34 (1): 327-34.

Creutzig, Felix, E. McGlynn, J. Minx, and O. Edenhofer. 2011. "Climate Policies for Road Transport Revisited (I): Evaluation of the Current Framework." *Energy Policy* 39 (5): 2396-406.

Creutzig, Felix, C. Flachsland, E. McGlynn, J. Minx, S. Brunner, and O. Edenhofer. 2010. "CITIES: Car Industry, Road Transport and an International Emission Trading Scheme—Policy Options" (Report, BMW Group). https://www.bmwgroup.com/content/dam/bmw-group-websites/bmwgroup_com/responsibility/downloads/en/2010/cities_de.pdf.

de Perthuis, Christian, and Raphael Trotignon. 2014. "Governance of CO2 Markets: Lessons from the EU ETS." *Energy Policy* 75: 100-06.

Edenhofer, Ottmar, B. Normark, and B. Tardieu. 2014. "Reform Options for the European Emissions Trading System (EU ETS)" (Policy Position Paper, Euro-CASE, Paris). http://www.euro-case.org/images/stories/pdf/position-paper/Euro-CASE-policy-paper-ETS-reform.pdf.

EEA. 2016a. EEA Greenhouse Gas—Data Viewer. http://www.eea.europa.eu/data-and-maps/data/data-viewers/greenhouse-gases-viewer.

EEA. 2016b. EU Emissions Trading System (ETS) Data Viewer. http://www.eea.europa.eu/data-and-maps/data/data-viewers/emissions-trading-viewer.

Ellerman, A. Denny, and Barbara K. Buchner. 2007. "The European Union Emissions Trading Scheme: Origins, Allocation, and Early Results." *Review of Environmental Economics and Policy* 1 (1): 66-87.

Fabra, Natalia, and Mar Reguant. 2014. "Pass-Through of Emissions Costs in Electricity Markets." *American Economic Review* 104 (9): 2872-99.

Fankhauser, Samuel, and Cameron Hepburn. 2010a. "Designing Carbon Markets. Part I: Carbon Markets in Time." *Energy Policy* 38 (8): 4363-70.

Fankhauser, Samuel, and Cameron Hepburn. 2010b. "Designing Carbon Markets, Part II: Carbon Markets in Space." *Energy Policy* 38 (8): 4381–87.

Fankhauser, Samuel, C. Hepburn, and J. Park. 2010. "Combining Multiple Policy Instruments: How Not to Do It." *Climate Change Economics* 1 (3): 209-25. doi:10.1142/S2010007810000169.

Fischer, Carolyn, and Alan K. Fox. 2007. "Output-Based Allocation of Emissions Permits for Mitigating Tax and Trade Interactions." *Land Economics* 83 (4): 575-99. http://www.jstor.org/stable/27647795.

Flachsland, Christian. 2014. "Public Finance and the EU ETS: A Brief History and Implications of Potential Reform." Presentation *Closing the Carbon Price Gap: Public Finance and Climate Policy.*

Flachsland, Christian, R. Marschinski, and O. Edenhofer. 2009. "To Link or Not to Link: Benefits and Disadvantages of Linking Cap-and-Trade Schemes." *Climate Policy* 9 (4): 358-72.

Flachsland, Christian, S. Brunner, O. Edenhofer, and F. Creutzig. 2011. "Climate Policies for Road Transport Revisited (II): Closing the Policy Gap with Cap-and-Trade." *Energy Policy* 39 (4): 2100-10.

Grüll, Georg, and Luca Taschini. 2011. "Cap-and-Trade Properties under Different Hybrid Scheme Designs." *Journal of Environmental Economics and Management* 61 (1): 107-18.

Helm, Dieter. 2012. *The Carbon Crunch: How We're Getting Climate Change Wrong—And How to Fix It.* New Haven, CT, US: Yale University Press.

Helm, Dieter, and Cameron Hepburn. 2007. "Carbon Contracts and Energy Policy." In *The New Energy Paradigm,* ed. Dieter Helm. Oxford, UK: Oxford University Press.

Helm, Dieter, C. Hepburn, and R. Mash. 2003. "Credible Carbon Policy." *Oxford Review of Economic Policy* 19 (3): 438-50.

Helm, Dieter, C. Hepburn, and G. Ruta. 2012. "Trade, Climate Change, and the Political Game Theory of Border Carbon Adjustments." *Oxford Review of Economic Policy* 28 (2): 368-94.

Hepburn, Cameron. 2006. "Regulation by Prices, Quantities, or Both: A Review of Instrument Choice." *Oxford Review of Economic Policy* 22 (2): 226-47.

Hepburn, Cameron, and A. Teytelboym. 2017. "Climate Policy After Brexit." *Oxford Review of Economic Policy,* forthcoming.

Hepburn, Cameron, J. K. H. Quah, and R. A. Ritz. 2013. "Emissions Trading with Profit-Neutral Permit Allocations." *Journal of Public Economics* 98: 85-99.

Hepburn, Cameron, K. Neuhoff, M. Grubb, F. Matthes, and M. Tse. 2006. "Auctioning of EU ETS Phase II Allowances: Why and How?" *Climate Policy* 6 (1): 137-60.

Hintermann, Beat. 2010. "Allowance Price Drivers in the First Phase of the EU ETS." *Journal of Environmental Economics and Management* 59 (1): 43-56.

Jaccard, Mark. 2012. "The Political Acceptability of Carbon Taxes: Lessons from British Columbia." In *Handbook of Research on Environmental Taxation*, eds. by J. E. Milne and Mikael Skou Andersen, 175-91. Cheltenham, UK, and Northampton, MA, US: Edward Elgar Publishing.

Jorgenson, Dale W., R. J. Goettle, M. S. Ho, and P. J. Wilcoxen. 2013. *Double Dividend: Environmental Taxes and Fiscal Reform in the United States*. Cambridge, MA, US: MIT Press.

Jouvet, Pierre André, and Boris Solier. 2013. "An Overview of CO_2 Cost Pass-through to Electricity Prices in Europe." *Energy Policy* 61: 1370-76. doi:10.1016/j.enpol.2013.05.090.

Keen, Michael, and Christos Kotsogiannis. 2014. "Coordinating Climate and Trade Policies: Pareto Efficiency and the Role of Border Tax Adjustments." *Journal of International Economics* 94 (1): 119-28.

Kuik, Onno, and Marjan Hofkes. 2010. "Border Adjustment for European Emissions Trading: Competitiveness and Carbon Leakage." *Energy Policy* 38 (4): 1741-48.

Martin, Ralf, M. Muûls, L. B. De Preux, and U. J. Wagner. 2014. "Industry Compensation under Relocation Risk: A Firm-Level Analysis of the EU Emissions Trading Scheme." *American Economic Review* 104 (8): 2482-508.

Meunier, Guy, P. Ponssard, and J. Quirion. 2012. "Carbon Leakage and Capacity-Based Allocations: Is the EU Right?" *Journal of Environmental Economics and Management* 68 (2): 262-79.

Miola, A., M. Marra, and B. Ciuffo. 2011. "Designing a Climate Change Policy for the International Maritime Transport Sector: Market-Based Measures and Technological Options for Global and Regional Policy Actions." *Energy Policy* 39 (9): 5490-98.

Monjon, Stéphanie, and Philippe Quirion. 2011. "Addressing Leakage in the EU ETS: Border Adjustment or Output-Based Allocation?" *Ecological Economics* 70 (11): 1957-71.

Montgomery, W. David. 1972. "Markets in Licenses and Efficient Pollution Control Programs." *Journal of Economic Theory* 8: 395-418.

Mortimore, Anna. 2010. "Managing Transport Emission Through Tradable Permits and Regulatory Emission Standards: A Comparative Analysis Evaluating Australia's Carbon Pollution Reduction Scheme." In *Critical Issues in Environmental Taxation*, Volume VII, eds. Claudia Dias Soares, Janet Milne, Hope Ashiabor, and Kurt Deketelaere, 236ff. Cheltenham, UK, and Northampton, MA, US: Edward Elgar Publishing.

Murray, Brian C., R. G. Newell, and W. A. Pizer. 2009. "Balancing Cost and Emissions Certainty: An Allowance Reserve for Cap-and-Trade." *Review of Environmental Economics and Policy* 3 (1): 84-103.

Parry, Ian W. H., and Antonio M. Bento. 2000. "Tax Deductions, Environmental Policy, and the 'Double Dividend' Hypothesis." *Journal of Environmental Economics and Management* 39 (1): 67-96. http://linkinghub.elsevier.com/retrieve/pii/S0095069699910938.

Pigou, Arthur C. 1920. *The Economics of Welfare*. London, UK: Macmillan Publishers Ltd.

Pizer, William A. 2002. "Combining Price and Quantity Controls to Mitigate Global Climate Change." *Journal of Public Economics* 85: 409-34.

Roberts, Marc J., and Michael Spence. 1976. "Effluent Charges and Licenses under Uncertainty." *Journal of Public Economics* 5 (3-4): 193-208.

Santos, Georgina, H. Behrendt, L. Maconi, T. Shirvani, and A. Teytelboym. 2010. "Part I: Externalities and Economic Policies in Road Transport." *Research in Transportation Economics* 28 (1): 2-45.

Sijm, Jos, K. Neuhoff, and Y. Chen. 2006. "CO_2 Cost Pass-Through and Windfall Profits in the Power Sector." *Climate Policy* 6 (1): 49-72.

Stavins, Robert N. 1998. "What Can We Learn from the Grand Policy Experiment? Lessons from SO_2 Allowance Trading." *Journal of Economic Perspectives* 12 (3): 69-88.

Vihma, Antto, and Harro van Asselt. 2014. "The Conflict over Aviation Emissions: A Case of Retreating EU Leadership?" (Briefing Paper 150, Finnish Institute of International Affairs, Helsinki, Finland). http://www.fiia.fi/assets/publications/bp150.pdf.

Vivid Economics with Ecofys. 2014. "Carbon Leakage Prospects under Phase III of the EU ETS and Beyond." (Report, Department of Energy and Climate Change, UK). https://www.gov.uk/government/uploads/system/uploads/attachment_data/file/318893/carbon_leakage_prospects_under_phase_III_eu_ets_beyond.pdf.

Vogt-Schilb, Adrien, S. Hallegatte, and C. de Gouvello. 2014. "Long-Term Mitigation Strategies and Marginal Abatement Cost Curves: A Case Study on Brazil." *Climate Policy* 15 (6): 703-23.

Weitzman, Martin L. 1974. "Prices vs. Quantities." *Review of Economic Studies* 41 (4): 477-91.

Weitzman, Martin L. 1980. "The 'Ratchet Principle' and Performance Incentives." *Bell Journal of Economics* 11 (1): 302-8. http://ideas.repec.org/a/rje/bellje/v11y1980ispring p302-308.html.

Wood, Peter John, and Frank Jotzo. 2011. "Price Floors for Emissions Trading." *Energy Policy* 39 (3): 1746-53.

World Bank. 2014. "State and Trends of Carbon Pricing." Washington, DC, World Bank Group. http://documents.worldbank.org/curated/en/505431468148506727/State-and-trends-of-carbon-pricing-2014.

A Comment on "Reforming the EU ETS: Where Are We Now?"

Polona Gregorin[1]

In 2015, the Commission presented a legislative proposal on the revision of the EU Emissions Trading System (ETS) for the 2021–2030 period (phase IV). This followed the agreement on "back-loading" and "market stability reserve" measures to strengthen the system.

The paper provides a timely and stimulating perspective on these recent and ongoing discussions on reforming the EU ETS, which is a cornerstone of EU policy to combat climate change. More and more countries are putting in place carbon pricing mechanisms similar to the EU ETS and deciding on the same issues that the European Union has needed to decide on when developing and improving its own system, making this type of analysis relevant well beyond the European context.

The paper considers and analyzes three challenges of the EU ETS, concerned with a weak carbon price signal, the scope of the system and over-allocation of free allowances to industry. A number of the issues that the report focuses on as essential are indeed those that have also been at the center of the European Commission proposals to reform the system. These are reflected in proposed improvements, such as avoiding possible over-allocation by focusing the allocation of free allowances on the sectors at the highest risk of relocation of their production outside the European Union, updating benchmark values for free allocation to capture technological progress in different sectors, and making the system more flexible by better taking into account output increases or decreases.

What makes the paper different from many other academic papers on the subject is that it takes into due account political reality of the policy-making process. This is particularly valuable since, if earlier proposals concerning the ETS are any indication, it can be foreseen that the Member States in the Council and the European Parliament, who decide on such EU legislation, may find it challenging to find a common position on the most politically sensitive aspects of the proposal.

Policy development namely has to be informed by political feasibility, as well as by experience. For example, that is why, in its proposal for a revision of the EU ETS, the Commission has opted to follow the mandate of the European heads of state and government (in their conclusions of October 2014) and to continue to work with the instrument that has proven to effectively address the risk of carbon leakage in the first two phases of the system, i.e., free allocation of emission allowances, instead of border adjustment measures.

I look forward to the authors taking their work on the proposed solutions to the next level. Some of the solutions require deeper analysis to flesh out how they would work and what their impacts would be in practice. Following the legislative proposal for the revision of the EU ETS, the next stage is to address the sectors not covered by the ETS after 2020. This could be also an interesting subject for the authors' future work. I look forward to their contributions, which I am sure many policymakers would read with great interest.

Note

1. The views expressed in this article are the author's and do not necessarily correspond to those of the European Commission.

2 Agreeing on an EU ETS Price Floor to Foster Solidarity, Subsidiarity, and Efficiency in the EU[1]

Ottmar Edenhofer, Christina Roolfs, Beatriz Gaitan, Paul Nahmmacher, and Christian Flachsland

Key Points for Policymakers

- The EU Emissions Trading System (EU ETS) has provided neither credible incentives for long-term investments in low-carbon technologies nor strong near-term mitigation incentives.
- Low EU ETS allowance (EUA) prices and the heterogeneity of the EU Member States (MS) have led to a patchwork of national climate policy across MS, with variable and unequal policy stringency.
- Under the current EU ETS design these national policies do not achieve additional emission reductions within ETS sectors. Instead, they reduce the EU ETS carbon price and reallocate carbon emissions to MS with weaker national climate policies.
- A price floor for EUAs combined with appropriate transfers (the redistribution of EU ETS revenues) allows for the heterogeneity of MS within the multilevel policy structure of the European Union to be addressed.
- While the economic literature suggests using optimal transfers across MS to achieve efficiency when a quantity (ETS) or price instrument is employed, the implementation of optimal transfers may not be feasible. Nevertheless, there are other transfer schemes that can improve upon the EU's solidarity and subsidiarity—two well-established EU normative design principles—and the EU ETS' economic efficiency.
- A numerical exercise is provided to quantify the cost effects of the EU ETS price floor proposal within the European power sector.

1. Introduction

Taking into account the heterogeneity of EU Member States (MS), this chapter proposes an EU Emissions Trading System (ETS) price floor as a key element of an EU ETS reform. It links economic efficiency to the

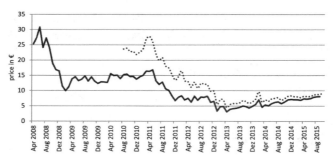

Figure 2.1
Evolution of EUA price (solid line) and EUA future contracts for the year 2020 (dotted line)
Sources: Data for EUA prices for the year 2008 are taken from ECX EUA Futures, Continuous Contract #2, ICE (Quandl 2015b). EUA prices from 2009 to 2015 are based on the
settlement prices at the secondary market, EEX (2015). Future contract prices for the year
2020 are taken from the settlement prices in December 2020, ICE (Quandl 2015a).

EU's principles of solidarity and subsidiarity, and illustrates the cushioning effect of an ETS price floor on intra-ETS leakage. While the price
floor's stabilization effect is also identified in chapter 1, this chapter
provides an analysis of the role of fiscal transfers to enhance the MS'
agreeability of introducing a price floor.

The EU Emissions Trading System (EU ETS) has not yet provided
credible incentives for long-term investments in low-carbon technologies. Its credibility has suffered since the year 2008 because the emission cap has been consistently above the EU ETS sectors' carbon
emissions for which the financial crises that started in the second half
of the 2000s are blamed for. The subsequent decline in EU ETS allowance (EUA) prices from mid-2008 onward, as depicted in figure 2.1,
triggered an ongoing and remarkable debate about reforming the
EU ETS. EU policymakers attempted to fix the EU ETS by implementing a back-loading provision[2] and the market stability reserve (MSR).[3]
Both measures focus on shortsighted fixes of the carbon price decline:
they temporarily remove EUA surpluses from the market. However,
the EUAs that were temporarily removed will be returned to the market
at some point in the future, leaving the cumulative cap (the aggregate
supply of permits) unchanged. It was also decided to increase the
Linear Reduction Factor—reflecting the annual reduction of the cap—
from 1.74 percent to 2.2 percent per year, thereby reducing the cumulative EU ETS cap. This has not had a major effect on the EUA price.
While there is no clear consensus about the core problems of the EU ETS
and the best response options to effectively address them, it is likely
that back-loading and the MSR will be insufficient (Knopf et al. 2014).

The debate on structural EU ETS measures launched by the European Commission (EC 2012) is still unresolved and opens a window of opportunity for a debate on long-term reform.

In addition to concerns about a lack of the EU ETS' credibility, fundamental questions about the coordination of regulatory authorities have been raised. In particular, there is a lively debate about whether MS' climate polices undermine the cost effectiveness of the EU ETS (IPCC 2014). EU MS have implemented a diverse national climate and energy policies[4] with varying stringencies, which affect carbon emissions. To illustrate these different stringencies, we derive an aggregate effective carbon price using the OECD's estimated effective carbon prices for Denmark, France, Germany, and the United Kingdom for different sectors.[5] Based on climate and energy policies, the OECD's study estimates the net social cost paid for each unit of emissions abated for various sectors and countries.[6] We weight the OECD's estimated sectoral prices according to the given sector's share of aggregate emissions in each country. Data on sectoral emission shares is taken from the European Environment Agency (EEA 2013). The result is depicted in figure 2.2. For the sectors and countries we consider, Germany has the highest effective carbon price of 53€/tCO$_2$e, followed by Denmark, the United Kingdom, and France, with respective effective carbon prices of 46, 42, and 25€/tCO$_2$e. The variety of instruments implemented across MS and the effective carbon prices presented here indicate that MS prioritize emission mitigation objectives differently and prefer distinct means to pursue those objectives.[7]

The heterogeneity of the EU MS[8] has led to different willingness to pay (WTP) for abatement as reflected in national climate policies. If the different WTP for abatement had been anticipated and taken into account in the design of the EU ETS, current national polices would not have a weakening effect on the EU ETS. Given the evolution of MS policy choices and lessons learned on the interaction among the EU ETS and national policies, it is pressing to revisit and discuss fundamental EU ETS design features.

We base our analysis on two normative design principles that are well established within the European Union—the principle of solidarity[9] and the principle of subsidiarity.[10] We use well-known theoretical arguments to conclude that the current EU ETS does not satisfy these principles. We point to solutions provided by economic theory that would help to make the EU ETS more compatible with these principles. We claim that a price floor for EUAs combined with appropriate transfers enables the heterogeneity of MS within the multilevel policy

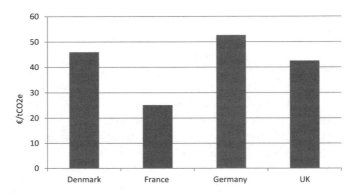

Figure 2.2
Estimated effective carbon prices by country derived from the electricity, transport, pulp and paper, and cement sectors
Source: Calculation based on a study by the OECD (2013) and weighted according to the sectoral share of emissions data from the year 2010 (EEA 2015).

structure of the European Union to be accounted for, while also allowing the principles of subsidiarity and solidarity to prevail. A first-best outcome and an optimal policy design will not be implemented by self-interested MS. It is therefore used as the socially optimal benchmark—a normative focal point—for our analysis. However, an EU ETS supplemented with a carbon price floor and an appropriate transfer scheme[11] is consistent with the self-interests of the MS such that no Member State is harmed and at least some MS are made better off. This policy design approach promises to be a win-win strategy for all MS.

The chapter is organized as follows. In section 2, we review previous findings about shortcomings of the current EU ETS price. In section 3, the interaction between heterogeneous MS and EU policies is discussed; in particular the effect on carbon prices. Two normative design principles and one implementation rule are subsequently suggested, taking into account the second-best reality of EU policy-making. In particular, we argue that the introduction of a carbon price floor is a promising proposal for EU ETS reform. Section 4 illustrates the effects of an EU ETS price floor by means of numerical simulations for the EU power sector. Section 5 states our conclusions.

2.   The Main Shortcomings of the Current EU ETS Price Signal

Recent economic literature on climate change favors the use of a carbon tax (price) or hybrid system (a quantity-based instrument with price stability provisions) over a pure quantity-based instrument such as an ETS without price stability provisions (e.g., Cramton et al. 2015). Those kinds of policy instruments are expected to deliver a more stable price signal and are economically superior to a pure ETS in terms of the ability to avoid price volatility, emission leakage effects, and uncertainty about economic costs (Goulder and Schein 2013; Philibert 2009). However, taxation power in the European Union is limited—the collection and redistribution of direct taxation is a sovereign right of MS.[12] If an EU carbon tax were going to be implemented, it would require a unanimous vote, whereas an ETS requires a two-thirds majority vote (Talus 2013). In practice, this has meant that the quantity-based ETS was the only politically feasible carbon pricing instrument at the time of its inception (Skjærseth and Wettestad 2010; Talus 2013).[13] An ETS price floor implemented as an auction reserve price (as done in the Californian ETS) should not be considered a tax in legal terms but builds on the ETS' political feasibility.

Another line of argumentation focuses on the ongoing price decline of the EU ETS which causes specific credibility challenges. Reasons for the EUA price decline are analyzed by Koch et al. (2014; 2016). They find that the global economic recession, renewable support schemes, the inflow of carbon credits, and gas and coal prices can only explain about 10 percent of the price decline in the EU ETS over the 2008–2013 period. They conclude that policy events have a strong influence on EUA price formation and suggest that controversial debates by EU policymakers as well as EU parliament votes—particularly over back-loading—have destabilized the long-term expectations of investors.

Not surprisingly, the low price of futures contracts for the year 2020 indicates that traders anticipate only a modest long-term scarcity of emission permits in the market (see figure 2.1). Neither back-loading nor structural reform proposals like the MSR promise to change this expectation, as they only shift the release schedule of a constant cumulative EUA budget over time. Elsewhere it has been extensively discussed why a price floor—potentially complemented by a price ceiling, thus yielding a price corridor—at the EU level would help to stabilize price expectations and support long-term credibility (Knopf et al. 2014; Philibert 2006; Wood and Jotzo 2011). Since carbon and energy pricing have a positive impact on clean technology investments (Copenhagen Economics 2010; Eyraud et al. 2011), the low EUA prices from mid-2008 onward together with low prices for future contracts lack the intended incentives for EU-wide clean technology investments.

Even in the presence of the EU ETS, MS continue to implement and modify various forms of national energy and climate policies (Strunz et al. 2015; Talus 2013). These additional policies suggest that some MS would rather pursue either a less or more stringent climate policy than is available through the EU ETS. For example, Poland threatened to withdraw from EU climate policy altogether,[14] demonstrating its wish for less stringent climate policy. On the other hand, Germany, the United Kingdom, and Sweden have implemented policies demonstrating a wish for more stringent climate policy. Germany implemented the Renewable Energy Act to foster the German energy transition *(Energiewende)*. The United Kingdom established the Climate Change Levy, consisting of inter alia a carbon price support rate for EUA. It functions as a national price floor with a current level of $18£/CO_2e$ (HM Revenue & Customs 2014).[15] Sweden established a general carbon tax in 1991, but it made exemptions to some sectors after the EU ETS implementation (OECD 2014).[16] Despite these efforts toward more stringent climate policies, national climate policies act to weaken the EUA price as the demand for allowances from MS with more ambitious climate polices decreases (Böhringer et al. 2008).

In the following section, we extend the debate about EU ETS reform by considering the heterogeneity of MS. The current EU ETS is supposed to equalize marginal abatement costs[17] across MS. This can only be efficient without the presence of any unilateral MS policies (Williams 2012). Additionally, the equalization of marginal abatement costs among MS does not account for the federal-like structure between the European Union and its heterogeneous MS, in which EU and MS policies coexist. Instead, climate policy at the EU level could be set in a similar fashion as the EU tax minima for value-added tax in alcohol, tobacco, and energy products. For these, the European Union sets required minimum rates for MS, but they have the flexibility to set higher rates if they wish to for fiscal or other reasons (EP 2014). In the climate context, an EU ETS price floor would not hold back those MS that wish to price emissions more aggressively.

The existence of EU minimum rates in other regulatory domains raises the question of whether the European Union's vertically divided regulatory regime and the MS' heterogeneity are sufficiently considered in the design of the EU ETS, and if improvements are conceivable. The MS' heterogeneity has largely been ignored in the EU ETS design, though income heterogeneity is addressed to some extent by certificate allocation provisions.[18] As a result, the simultaneous interaction between the EU ETS and MS climate policies will continue to distort the functioning of the EU ETS. The policies implemented by individual MS reduce the EUA price and increase the effective national carbon price in the respective MS. Because the cap remains constant, they do not achieve emission reductions. Fixing the EU ETS will be required to ensure an effective, efficient, and ambitious European climate policy. Otherwise, there is a risk that EU climate policy will become further fragmented, ineffective, and costly, and consequently deteriorate over time.

3. Guiding Principles for EU ETS Design with Heterogeneous Member States

In this section we explore the implications of MS' heterogeneity on the EU ETS price design. For this purpose we consider two types of MS' heterogeneities. First, MS can differ in income levels. This can stem from differences in factor endowments such as physical capital and human capital, access to fossil resources, and technological differences. In the face of income disparities, the optimal provision of climate change mitigation requires specific transfers (see section 3.1). The use of transfers within the context of climate change has a direct link to the principle of solidarity as described by Hilpold (2015). He relates the EU solidarity principle to the use of transfers to achieve a common goal. Second, MS can be heterogeneous in terms of their preferences for environmental quality and/or how they are affected by climate change. For example, EU countries might expect different effects on their populations from climate change-induced heat waves, droughts, and flooding. Taking these preferences into account plays a fundamental role in the fulfillment of the EU subsidiarity principle (see section 3.2).

3.1 Efficiency, Transfers, and Solidarity

Traditional wisdom suggests that, by equalizing the cost increase from reducing a unit of emissions (marginal abatement cost, or MAC) across emission sources, emissions trading always achieves efficiency[19] (Coase 1960). However, in the presence of unequal income across countries, a uniform carbon price that equalizes MACs across countries may not be efficient. For example, richer countries may be able to afford more stringent national climate policies. The efficiency of MAC equalization across countries was first challenged and refuted by Chichilnisky and Heal (1994), who showed that if a poor country gains more from increases in private consumption than a rich country, the poor country's WTP[20] for mitigation is lower relative to that of the rich country. For expository reasons, let us consider the case of a poor country in Asia in which a large portion of its population suffers from malnutrition. In that country the gain from increasing private consumption (in particular, food) should be much higher than the gain of a developed country in Europe from increasing private consumption. In such a case, the poor country's WTP for mitigation is lower and hence it should pay less for emissions mitigation than a developed country in Europe. Despite smaller income gaps among EU MS, similar effects resulting from unequal income levels across countries matter within the European Union. Crucially, Chichilnisky and Heal (1994) demonstrate that an efficient solution to this situation features different MACs across countries. If, however, MACs across countries were to be equalized under an ETS, optimality would require specific transfers from richer to poorer countries.

Optimal Abatement If the optimal transfers are not implemented, Chichilnisky and Heal (1994) show that poorer countries should set lower MACs than richer countries. They find that an efficient outcome is one in which a country's MAC equals the ratio of the sum of social gains from emission reductions across all countries relative to the social gain from larger private consumption in the respective country. Since countries benefit differently from increasing private consumption, MACs must not necessarily be equalized to achieve efficiency. In such a situation, different carbon prices for each country are an institutional pre-condition for social optimality. However, national carbon prices could lead to a more nationalized and fragmented European climate policy, which would undermine future cooperation within Europe.

Optimality Under an ETS To counteract the fragmentation of European climate policy, a uniform carbon price seems preferable to differentiated national carbon prices. However, a uniform carbon price requires a specific transfer scheme since, without transfers, an ETS imposes MAC equalization across countries but is not efficient. As indicated above, this equalization is not efficient as long as the social gain from increasing private consumption is not equal across countries. Chichilnisky and Heal (1994) point out that optimality within an ETS that employs a uniform carbon price can only be fulfilled by using a transfer scheme that equalizes the social gain from increasing private consumption (*SGIPC*) across countries. Thus, since poorer countries gain more than richer countries from increasing private consumption,

---

Box 2.1
Design Principle 1. Efficiency, Transfers, and Solidarity
A uniform emissions price at the EU level must be supplemented with appropriate transfers to ensure economic efficiency. The current EU ETS design in which marginal abatement costs are equalized across all MS is not per se efficient. Efficiency is only obtained if rich MS provide sufficiently large transfers to poorer MS. Such transfers enable higher levels of consumption in poorer MS—hence complying with the EU's solidarity principle—while significantly increasing the poorer MS' willingness to pay for mitigation. If the transfers cannot be implemented, rich MS need to have higher marginal abatement costs and therefore abate relatively more than poor MS.

---

poorer countries must receive transfers leading to the equalization of the *SGIPC* for all countries. In the face of large income differences across countries, significant transfers must occur.

In the current EU ETS, two general types of transfers exist. The first is the redistribution of EU ETS auction revenues to MS. In 2013, 40 percent of all EUA were auctioned for a total auction revenue of about €3.6bn (EC 2015d). Of these revenues, 88 percent were distributed in proportion to historical emissions across MS. Ten percent of the auction revenues were channeled to less wealthy EU MS to promote investments dedicated to carbon intensity reduction and for adaptation to climate change (EC 2013; 2015a; 2015a). The remaining 2 percent (the "Kyoto bonus") were allocated to nine EU MS that had reduced their emissions by at least 20 percent of their Kyoto Protocol base year or period level by 2005.[21] Second, the value of the remaining 60 percent of all EUAs were transferred to firms. If firms are transnational, then it is not clear whether the MS' population is the full beneficiary of this type of transfer, nor whether the transfer can address differences in wealth as would be needed to equalize the social gains from increased consumption across countries.[22]

If we consider the EU MS' per capita gross domestic products as a wealth indicator, we can conclude that differences across MS are rather large. Thus, transfers of 12 percent of the total EUA auction revenues to less wealthy MS are probably insufficient to achieve optimality. In section 3.3, we provide estimates for transfers that would lead to EU ETS optimality (the equalization of the gain from increasing private consumption across EU MS) based on Chichilnisky and Heal's analysis. Box 2.1 summarizes this section and embeds its findings in a design principle.

3.2   National Preferences and Subsidiarity

The analysis in the previous section focused on income differences and on one common goal (climate change mitigation). We now address the use of multilevel climate policies driven by heterogeneous MS' preferences. Heterogeneous preferences can arise due to differing effects from multiple emission externalities, i.e., climate change and air pollution, as well as differing priorities for environmental quality. Even if information about transboundary and global effects of carbon emissions were perfectly available to regulators at all regulatory levels, MS authorities typically only care for the well-being of national inhabitants. By contrast, an overarching regulating layer, such as the European Union, considers the well-being of all inhabitants of all MS, and is better equipped to provide global public goods such as climate change mitigation. In the following section, we focus on the interaction of multilevel regulation for cases in which MS have heterogeneous preferences. Addressing this type of heterogeneity in the context of multilevel policies is important because, as clarified below, it plays a fundamental role in the fulfillment of the EU subsidiarity principle (see also Oates 1972, 2011).[23]

Heterogeneous Preferences and Strategic Member States   A study by Williams (2012) analyzes interactions between government layers in which both sub-level (MS) and top-level (EU) regulating authorities are allowed to regulate emissions simultaneously. He finds that if the top-level regulator implements an ETS, additional MS' climate policies become either ineffective or may even result in additional costs for the multilevel regulatory system. To attain efficiency with an over-arching ETS, MACs across MS must be equalized and optimal transfers have to be set. However, if MS implement additional policies, MACs can differ. Williams shows that within an over-arching ETS there is no transfer from the top-level regulator to the MS that can achieve efficiency as long as MS policies are present. Instead, since the ETS cap is fixed and the ETS price adjusts as MS unilaterally cut emissions leading to increased emissions in other MS (intra-ETS leakage), the top-level ETS cancels out all unilateral abatement efforts.[24] Williams also finds that a carbon tax implemented by the top-level regulator is superior to an ETS. This occurs because the top-level and sub-level prices are additive, while quantity instruments are not as the stricter cap is always binding.[25]

Box 2.2

Design Principle 2. Member States' Preferences and Subsidiarity

Implementing an emissions' price instrument at the EU level—either by an EU ETS price floor or an EU carbon tax—is consistent with the principle of subsidiarity. With a price-based instrument at the EU level, national policies can prosper as companion policies of the EU ETS. It allows effectively accounting for the MS' heterogeneous preferences without undermining the EU policy. In contrast, purely quantity-based instruments at the EU level—such as the current EU ETS—would not only make it harder for ambitious MS to become frontrunners with respect to climate policy but would even render their national efforts fruitless.

More specifically, it would be preferable for the European Union to implement an EU-wide carbon tax to address emission leakage effects among MS, and for MS to set national taxes for regulating local emissions externalities and/or local preferences. Reflecting Chichilnisky and Heal's (1994) findings, the multilevel system eventually achieves optimality if the carbon taxes at the two different levels are supplemented by optimal transfers. Based on Williams's argument, a uniform EU carbon price combined with MS' carbon prices and optimal transfers can lead to an efficient outcome. On the contrary, the use of a pure ETS—as opposed to one with a binding price floor—precludes the achievement of an efficient outcome, because MS cannot be prevented from implementing national climate polices.

In a similar line of research, Roolfs et al. (2016) find that a carbon price set by the top-level regulator in addition to MS' policies can approximate the first-best outcome, if the top-level regulator employs optimal transfers. They analyze the potential of a top-level regulator to set a union-wide carbon price in coexistence with strategic MS policies while the top-level regulator anticipates how MS' carbon prices react to the top level's carbon price. If non-optimal transfers are available, they identify the price floor level that at least comes closer to the first-best outcome while making all MS better off. Box 2.2 summarizes this section and embeds its findings in a design principle.

Design Principle 1 and 2 consider different bases for the heterogeneity of MS (income levels and preferences) but lead to a common result: in a multilayered policy regime, a price instrument implemented at the top level more efficiently allows for heterogeneity to be addressed as long as optimal transfers are employed. However, optimal transfers derived from economic theory are often unviable for policymakers. In the next section, we propose a pragmatic rule that does not achieve the first-best outcome, but can find consensus across MS such that some MS are better off, while also ensuring that other MS' well-being remains at least at their original level (Pareto-improvements).

3.3   Institutional Design in a Non-Optimal World

The aforementioned design principles are normative focal points derived within an economic, theoretical setting. However, the optimal implementation of both principles may prove difficult in the real world. This may be due to enforcement constraints, to the difficulty or impossibility of overcoming the free-rider behavior of self-interested actors, and/ or—as will be discussed next—to the political infeasibility of the transfers that would be necessary to lead to the optimality of an EU ETS.

Building on Chichilnisky and Heal's (1994) findings, we derive the optimal transfers needed to make the EU ETS efficient. To do so, we assume that (a) each country's well-being is influenced similarly by private consumption, and (b) an upper-level regulator such as the European Union weighs all countries equally.[26] Given these assumptions, equalizing the social gain from increasing private consumption across countries requires that all countries have an equal level of private consumption. To estimate the transfers needed to equalize consumption levels across EU MS, we use private consumption expenditure data (WDI 2015) in purchasing power parity U.S. dollars (PPP$) for the year 2010. Our objective is to find transfers that enable the EU's population the same level of per capita consumption while making aggregate consumption equal to observed data. The transfer per person in each Member State is the gap between the EU's and each Member State's per capita consumption levels. Based on consumption data in the year 2010, figure 2.3 shows optimal per capita transfers (per person) across all EU MS that would equalize EU per capita consumption. A negative number indicates that a respective country is not a receiver but it is instead a donor. The population of Luxembourg, as the richest in the European Union, would be the largest donor (with a negative transfer, a net payment of PPP$7,819 per person). Luxembourg's population is followed by the populations of Austria, the United Kingdom, and Germany, with respective negative per capita transfers of PPP$4,370, PPP$3,470 and PPP$3,101. The populations receiving the largest transfers would be those living in Bulgaria, Latvia, Estonia, and Romania. The estimated optimal transfers serve to demonstrate the magnitude of the difference in consumption levels across MS. The difference in consumption levels has a large implication for the individual WTP for climate change mitigation.

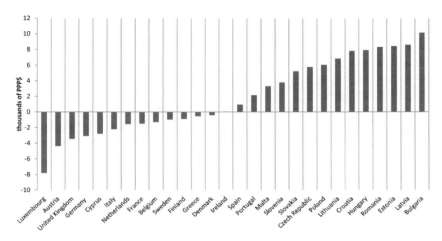

Figure 2.3
Optimal transfers per *person* according to private consumption in the year 2010 in thousands of dollars of purchasing power parity (PPP$)

Figure 2.4 indicates the aggregate optimal transfers per Member State (the per capita transfers multiplied by the population of each Member State). Transfers of the size depicted in figure 2.4 are very unlikely to be politically feasible. At the same time, current EU ETS transfers equal to 12 percent of the revenues from the EUA auction (0.432bn€ in 2013) seem insufficient.

Since a theoretical, first-best outcome of a pure ETS with optimal transfers is very likely to be politically infeasible, we propose the consideration of second-best options.[27] One such case that is particularly useful is a second-best world in which changes in the EU ETS design make a Member State better off, while also ensuring that other MS' well-being remains at least at their original level (this is compared to a case in which only MS implement climate policies in a decentralized, uncoordinated setting). From a welfare perspective, this ensures that the joint implementation of climate policies creates winners, while also guaranteeing that there are no losers.

In contrast to the normative framework described in sections 3.1 and 3.2, we now consider results from a study that analyzes a setting in which: (a) optimal transfers are not viable; (b) a multilevel policy regime is already established; and (c) a uniform price signal is set at the top level and each Member State sets its own carbon price. This starting point is more similar to the current EU ETS in which the EUA market intends to deliver a uniform price signal to all MS, while MS set additional

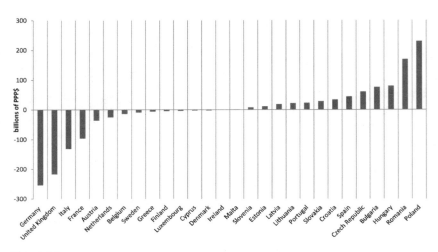

Figure 2.4
Optimal transfers per *country* according to private consumption in the year 2010 in billions of dollars of purchasing power parity (PPP$)

climate policies and transfers are given as discussed in section 2. In a comparable setup and with heterogeneous MS, Roolfs et al. (2016) identify MS' carbon prices and a range of top-level uniform carbon prices, including a price floor level, combined with simple transfers[28] that make all countries better off compared to a decentralized setting.

When income heterogeneity is considered, Roolfs et al. find that equity-based transfers can put a disproportionate cost burden on the richest Member State. The richest Member State agrees to bear the cost burden of the top-level policy as long as its gain outweighs its costs. Based on the nature of the equity-based transfers, poorer MS carry no burden but benefit by internalizing the emission externalities and by a net income gain. Therefore, the tipping point for the feasibility of top-level policy becomes the consent of the richest Member State and is represented by a carbon price floor. Here, the carbon price floor is the carbon price level that leads to the highest well-being of the richest Member State. As long as the top-level regulator considers the carbon price floor, the top-level policy is compatible with the self-interest of all MS in the sense that all MS are better off.

Within the context of their model, Roolfs et al. (2016) show that the price floor based on the richest Member State's utility and in combination with equity-based transfers works as long as the wealth gap among poor and rich MS is not extreme. Since the price floor ensures that no

---

Box 2.3
Implementation Rule. Set a Price Floor and Provide Appropriate Transfers
A carbon price floor can help to address the challenges associated with the heterogeneity of MS while accepting a non-optimal world. With an EU ETS price floor, transfers must not necessarily be optimal to lead to welfare improvements for all MS.

Member State falls below the welfare level of the decentralized outcome, it also satisfies the principle of subsidiarity. Analogously, Roolfs et al. find that a price floor works for transfers based on the MS' historical emission levels. However, this transfer scheme—in contrast to equity transfers—can make all MS better off, and it does not always impose restrictions on wealth gaps. They conduct a similar analysis on heterogeneous preferences for emissions' externalities on MS' well-being, and find similar results. In box 2.3 we propose an implementation rule based on this section's findings by paying tribute to a non-optimal world.

4.   Illustration of the Effects of an EU ETS Price Floor

In this section, we provide a twofold sketch demonstrating that national climate policies will not undermine the efficiency of the EU ETS when a price floor is implemented (see also IPCC 2014; Goulder and Stavins 2011). We first give an illustrative description of the cushioning effect of a price floor. We then present results from the European power sector model LIMES-EU.

4.1   Cushioning Intra-ETS Leakage with a Carbon Price Floor

Consider a multinational ETS without MS policies. The ETS allowance price (p_{ETS}) is determined endogenously by the ETS market, such that MACs are equalized across all participants. Thus, the MS' emission levels (E_i, E_j) are determined by p_{ETS} (see figure 2.5). If Member State i prefers a lower national emission level E_i^* than the level that results from the ETS alone, its WTP for mitigation is above p_{ETS}. In order to obtain E_i^*, Member State i sets an additional national policy τ, which results in an effective national carbon price of p_{MS}, such that $p_{MS} = p_{ETS} + \tau$.

As soon as τ is implemented, Member State i's firms reduce their demand for allowances subject to p_{MS} and the ETS allowance price falls from p_{ETS} to p'_{ETS}. If Member State i wants to ensure that its preferred emission level (E_i^*) is reached, it can do so by adjusting its national

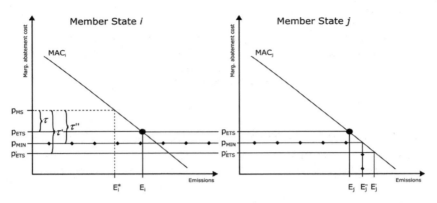

Figure 2.5
Illustration of the cushioning effect of intra-ETS leakage with a carbon price floor (p_{MIN})

policy (τ') by means of a so-called variable fee.[29,30] However, Member State j, which has implemented no additional national policy, also faces a decrease on the ETS price (from p_{ETS} to p'_{ETS}). This results in an increase in Member State j's emission level from E_j to E_j'. In effect, since the ETS cap is set exogenously, the additional national policy of Member State i has no effect on overall emissions as the emission allowances are used by Member State j's emitters (100 percent emission leakage).[31] From a multinational perspective, the national policy can be considered a disturbance. From a national perspective, the national policy may have beneficial side-effects (e.g., increased national revenues, reduction of local air pollution). However, it fails to reach the goal of total emission reduction due to the intra-ETS leakage effect.

The problem of the ETS price decline and the ineffectiveness of national policies can be cushioned by the implementation of an ETS-wide price floor, p_{MIN} (refer to figure 2.5, in which MS i now implements the variable policy τ''). Since the ETS price decrease is cushioned, Member State j faces p_{MIN}, which is lower than the initial ETS price (p_{ETS}) but above p'_{ETS}. Therefore, Member State j implicitly benefits from Member State i's policy due to the price decrease. However, the emission leakage effect triggered by the national policy disturbance in the ETS is weakened. The effective emission level of Member State j (E_j'') is above the initial emission level (E_j), but below the emission level without a price floor (E_j'). In the end, Member State i and j are both better off.

4.2 Implications for the European Power Sector: Numerical Simulation

In this section, our theoretical analysis is complemented with quantitative results from the long-term investment model for the electricity system of Europe (LIMES-EU). The model is a multi-country model[32] that simultaneously determines cost-minimizing investment and dispatch decisions for generation and storage and transmission technologies needed to serve future electricity demand and comply with future energy and climate policies. Its integrated approach, together with an intertemporal optimization in five-year steps from today until 2050, allows for the analysis of consistent and cost-efficient pathways for the future development of the European power system on both aggregate and national levels.

The optimal deployment of different electricity generation options strongly depends on future climate and energy policies at EU and national levels. We illustrate the effect of a European price floor plus additional emission reduction efforts in Germany. This is motivated by the current German discussion about how to reach national 2020 climate targets using additional unilateral policies (see, e.g., BMWi 2015). Our analysis is focused on the time span 2015–2030, assuming a common European carbon price from 2030 onward. In the present model framework, a price floor on carbon emissions leads to additional costs for the energy system. The revenues and redistribution (transfers) from carbon pricing are not considered in our numerical exercise.

Table 2.1 provides an overview of the policy scenarios analyzed. Three different European carbon price floors until 2030 are considered. In the baseline scenarios, the carbon price in Germany is equal to the level of an EU carbon price floor. For the policy scenarios, we implement a variable fee in Germany that raises the effective German carbon price to 20€/tCO_2, a price that is in line with the long-term EU decarbonization targets (EC 2011; Knopf et al. 2014).[33] In all scenarios, aggregate European emissions are constrained to be less than or equal to the emission budget that results from the different EU carbon prices (5, 10, and 15€/tCO_2) without an additional Germany policy. From 2030 onward, we consider four scenarios with carbon prices of 20, 25, 30, and 35€/tCO_2 that are effective for all European countries.

In order to reflect the energy policies currently in place, the nuclear phase-out in Belgium, Germany, and Switzerland as well as the German renewable energy expansion target are taken into account. Nuclear power investments in other countries are constrained to the expansions

Table 2.1
Policy Scenarios (all prices in euros per tCO_2)

Until 2030	Europe	Carbon price floor of €5/€10/€15
	Germany	No additional policy* or effective carbon price of €20
After 2030	Europe	Common European carbon price of €20/€25/€30/ €35 in 2030, subsequently rising by 5 percent per year until 2050
	Germany	No additional policy*

* If no additional policy is set, the German carbon price is equal to the European carbon price.

already under construction or planned and to the investments needed to replace depreciating capacities. As the future of carbon capture and storage (CCS) is highly uncertain, our policy scenarios are run both with and without the possibility of CCS investments. In total, this leads to 24 baseline scenarios without and 24 policy scenarios with an additional emission policy in Germany. Figure 2.6 summarizes the effects of such an additional policy on carbon emissions in Germany and in Europe on the whole.

The results show that an elevated German carbon price reduces German emissions in all policy scenarios (figure 2.6a). This is mostly due to an overall reduction in German electricity production (figure 2.6b). Replacing the missing domestic supply with electricity imports from neighboring countries results in an increase of emissions abroad. In most cases, however, the emission reductions in Germany outweigh the emission increases abroad, leading to an overall reduction of emissions across Europe—implying that it is the EU-wide price floor and not the cap that becomes binding. Figure 2.7 illustrates this effect in the year 2020 for a scenario with a common European carbon price of 30€/tCO_2 in 2030 and different price floors in the years prior to 2030. In these scenarios, the European-wide emission reductions vary between 0 and 0.67tCO_2 per ton of emission reduction in Germany. The reductions in German electricity production when there is an EU price floor of 5 or 10€/tCO_2 result from reductions in the use of lignite and hard coal, while the increase in neighboring countries is predominantly based on natural gas and renewables. The lower emission intensity of newly installed foreign power plants reduces the total European

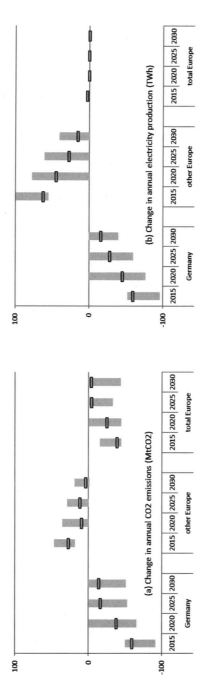

Figure 2.6

Change in (a) annual CO_2 emissions and (b) electricity production due to a higher CO_2 price in Germany

Note: The gray bar indicates the range over all scenarios and the outlined box indicates the median over all scenarios.

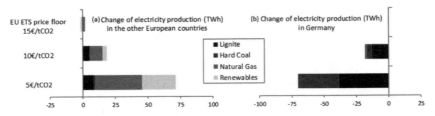

Figure 2.7
Change in annual electricity production (a) in European countries except Germany and (b) in Germany in the year 2020 due to a higher CO_2 price in Germany

Notes: Although the use of CCS is possible, it is not yet deployed in 2020 in these scenarios. The annual electricity production of nuclear power plants does not change in any of the three scenarios.

emissions. When there is a 15€/tCO_2 European price floor, the German carbon price of 20€/tCO_2 is not high enough to induce a considerable change in the electricity production pattern, nor in CO_2 emissions.

Overall, the results suggest that an EU-wide carbon price floor allows for the introduction of more ambitious national carbon prices with a net reduction effect on overall emissions. In our numerical model framework, such additional efforts increase total system costs. This increase in costs[34] depends heavily on the level of the European price floor. It varies between 12bn€ (in the case of a 15€/tCO_2 price floor) and 36bn€ (in the case of a 5€/tCO_2 price floor). For a price floor of 10€/tCO_2, costs incurred by the additional German climate policy are around 24bn€. Other scenario variations, e.g., the level of the common carbon price after 2030, have only a very limited effect on overall costs (i.e., +/−1bn€), with lower cost differences for higher future carbon prices. Our analysis for the German case can only serve as an illustration. Additional analyses focusing on other countries are needed and should be an interesting subject for further research.

4.3   Some Implementation Issues

There are several challenges that go beyond the scope of this chapter that are associated with the implementation and operation of a price floor in terms of the detailed design. An extensive analysis can be found in Wood and Jotzo (2011). For the operational implementation of a price floor, they suggest an auction reserve price (which is implemented in the California and Regional Greenhouse Gas Initiative ETSs), a variable fee (as implemented in the United Kingdom), or the buy-back of allowances by the regulating authority. To avoid excess allowances being sold at a price below the price floor, the regulator should be willing to buy back and cancel excess allowances at the level of the price floor, as pointed out by Goulder and Schein (2013). This would imply additional costs for the regulator. Another option to avoid buy-back necessities would be to use a price instrument only (no ETS) (Goulder and Schein 2013). For a detailed discussion on cancelling allowances, see, e.g., Kollmuss and Lazarus (2010). In terms of the newly proposed MSR, a price floor could also be used as a signal indicating when allowances should be withdrawn—i.e., when the ETS price floor is binding.

Some analysts might argue that an EU ETS price floor is unnecessary. Another decentralized alternative for MS with higher WTP for mitigation reduction is the unilateral purchase and retirement of allowances (P&RA). This procedure could be carried out in the current legal EU structure as EU responsibilities and the ETS design would remain unchanged. To express a significantly higher WTP for mitigation, MS (such as Germany or the United Kingdom) would need to purchase and retire significant amounts of EUAs. If huge amounts of EUAs were withdrawn and retired, the first effect that would be observed on the ETS market is an EU ETS price increase, due to a reduction in the total EUA effectively available. This procedure could result in dissent from other MS as they may face a higher ETS price that might not be compatible with their (comparably lower) WTP for mitigation. Therefore, compensation or side payments may become necessary. This brings back the question of transfer design and the role of transfer coordination. The role of coordination could be effectively carried out at the EU level if an EU ETS price floor and appropriate transfers are set. There are consequently two drawbacks to the P&RA. First, national funds need to be used as side payments to generate agreeability among MS on the use of P&RA. Second, the Member State that purchases and retires EUAs must use national revenues that could otherwise be used in other programs, including climate programs (Bianco et al. 2009), thereby causing budgetary disturbances. Given current fiscal pressures, it seems unlikely that a country would do this. A case in point is the United Kingdom, whose government is under intense political pressure to moderate fiscal austerity.[35] Therefore, it seems politically infeasible to divert revenues from the national budget to purchase EUAs, which would effectively divert revenues from the UK Treasury to allowance holders in other EU MS. In order to avoid the use of governmental revenues, a country could force companies to retire allowances as Germany attempted through the implementation of a "climate levy" (BMWi 2015). This might not affect the national budget but it hurts some MS due to a higher EU ETS price and causes the same problems as discussed above.

From an individual government's perspective, there are additional potential advantages of a price floor. A price floor not only ensures a more stable price signal for market-participants, but also more stable revenue flows for MS and EU ETS funds. If the carbon price floor is binding in the longer term, it can be a substitute for income and corporate taxation, ameliorating the effect on government revenues derived from tax competition (Heinemann et al. 2009) and counteracting distortionary effects of taxation. It can therefore be used as a more efficient source of public finance (Edenhofer et al. 2015). Sweden's environmental national policies exemplify the successful implementation of a carbon price[36] and the shift of the fiscal burden from labor to carbon emissions (OECD 2014). Parry et al. (2014) present an extensive analysis of multiple incentives—besides climate change mitigation—for countries to put a price on carbon emissions, subsequently extended to a discussion of climate regime design based on co-benefits by Edenhofer et al. (2015). Cramton et al. (2015) highlight that the commitment to a uniform multinational carbon price is less risky for individual countries than the commitment to a quantity instrument. They argue that future business-as-usual emissions and abatement costs are both highly uncertain. Due to these uncertainties, the financial risk for countries agreeing on quantity commitments becomes much larger than commitments to a price.

A carbon price floor can also entail benefits for the operation of the EU ETS market. Burtraw (2014), for example, emphasizes that a carbon price floor is a non-discretionary and transparent signal by policymakers about the level of climate policy ambition, which allows market participants to better anticipate future developments. Burtraw also points out that a price floor may be used as a signal for cap adjustments. The more often the price floor binds, the higher the likelihood that the cap was set too loose. As a result, the regulator would need to withdraw and retire allowances or tighten the future cap schedule more often. Therefore, a price floor explicitly and transparently addresses the objective implicitly intended by the MSR—stabilizing the ETS market. More importantly, if credibility about an ETS is lacking, as is the case in the EU ETS, the use of a carbon price floor would increase policy credibility as an additional signal and commitment by policymakers to a certain level of policy ambition.

5.   Concluding Remarks

This chapter proposes a price floor, in combination with appropriate—not necessarily socially optimal—transfers, as a key reform option for the EU ETS. A carbon price floor has additional advantages to stabilization effects. One such advantage that is often overlooked is the ability to address heterogeneity and the policies of MS in vertical regulatory structures like the European Union.

There may be gains from multinational climate policy when there is a multilayered governmental structure such as in the European Union. A pure ETS without optimal transfers cannot correctly accommodate MS' heterogeneity as it neglects differences in income and preferences on carbon emissions. The multilayered structure, however, facilitates a solution. An EU ETS carbon price floor, combined with appropriate transfers, can enable MS to implement national climate policies that are indeed effective. This does not necessarily imply additional changes in EU legislation in terms of an EU revenue system. For example, if allowances are auctioned at a price floor, MS can remain in charge of revenue collection. Transfer payments could be coordinated at the EU level while actual payments could be made bilaterally.

To conclude, this chapter identifies guiding design principles to reform the EU ETS and depicts why and how the heterogeneity of the MS should be considered. We point out efficiency shortcomings in the EU ETS design particularly in light of the heterogeneity of the MS. We connect economic theory to the solidarity principle and discuss why the traditional EU ETS as a pure cap-and-trade system—in which MACs are equalized—is not efficient per se. A higher WTP by MS and subsequent transfers from richer to poorer MS should play a role. To achieve social optimality, significant explicit transfers from richer to poorer MS would need to be deployed. In a model that departs from an EU ETS, differentiated carbon prices could be implemented in each MS, which would implicitly function as transfers. However, different national carbon prices could lead to a fragmentation of the EU climate policy damaging the cooperation among MS.

When embedded in a multilevel governmental system, a quantity-based instrument (such as an ETS) at the upper governmental layer leads to inefficient outcomes if it coexists with MS' policies. Hence, the current EU ETS is inconsistent with the principle of subsidiarity. The MS' policies distort the long-term optimal carbon price within the EU ETS. Therefore, we have suggested that an EU-wide price floor combined with optimal transfers for the EU ETS could approximate efficiency.

To cope with the MS' heterogeneity if neither optimal prices nor optimal transfers are attainable, we propose an EU ETS price floor as a useful tool. Besides the price stabilization effect, an EU ETS price floor allows willing MS to implement national climate policies without decreasing the dynamic efficiency of the EU ETS. It allows MS' policies to be integrated without undermining EU ETS-wide emission reductions. Our numerical simulations of the European power sector indicate that an EU ETS price floor ameliorates leakage within MS and can achieve additional EU-wide emission reductions of up to 50MtCO$_2$, if a Member State, such as Germany, also implements a carbon price.

Regardless of the benefits of carbon pricing, the window of opportunity for a debate on long-term reform has more far-reaching implications. The European Union can be considered a laboratory for multilateralism and lessons can be learned for implementing global climate policies (Goulder and Stavins 2011; Grubb et al. 2014). If the European Union succeeds with its EU ETS reform, it may prove wrong the accusations of "blame-and-burden" and instead shift attention toward the design of a common climate policy with mutual gains (Grubb et al. 2014). A failure of the EU ETS may send a negative signal about the plausibility of multinational cooperation to non-EU countries trying to implement an ETS.

The debate about EU climate policy and the EU ETS reform also interacts with the international climate policy process beyond the twenty-first Conference of the Parties (COP 21) in Paris. At the COP 21 the European Union and its MS committed to a 40 percent EU-wide GHG emission reduction by the year 2030 compared to 1990 levels (UNFCCC 2015). According to the EC's Impact Assessment document of alternative EU ETS reform options, these EU-wide GHG emission reductions would require EUA prices of 40€/tCO$_2$e in the year 2030, and 264€/tCO$_2$e in 2050 (EC 2014).

The agreement of the COP 21 feeds back into the need to reform the EU ETS. An improved coordination between EU and MS' climate policies is required to meet the EU's and MS' pledge of EU-wide GHG emission reduction. MS that currently seek to phase out coal-fired power plants, e.g., by unilateral carbon pricing schemes, do not achieve any additional emission reductions beyond the EU ETS cap (pricing schemes are already implemented in the United Kingdom and under consideration in Germany). Since coal phase-outs are pressing measures to meet the EU's reduction target, unilateral MS' initiatives should be empowered to accompany EU policy. Currently, MS policies function in the opposite direction. They weaken the EU ETS by lowering EUA prices. Low EUA prices jeopardize the achievement of the EU's GHG emission reduction target. As this chapter describes, an EU ETS reform that implements a price floor would allow the policies of ambitious MS to prosper as companion policies to the EU ETS and contribute to the EU-reduction target instead of weakening the EU ETS.

Socially optimal targets and policies may not be attainable, but as this chapter points out, coordination around an EU ETS price floor and appropriate transfers could at least enable policy reforms that support consensus across MS and increase the level of success of climate policy ambitions. These findings, just as they apply to a regional ETS, can also apply to international instruments for climate change mitigation.

Notes

1. We thankfully acknowledge helpful comments on a preliminary version of this chapter from Ian Parry, Karen Pittel, Michael Pahle, Kristin Seyboth, and Eva Schmid. Any remaining errors and flaws remain in the authors' responsibility. Financial assistance by the German Federal Ministry of Education and Research under grant agreement no. FKZ 03EK3523B (de.zentral-project) and by the European Union's Seventh Framework Program under grant agreement no. 308481 (ENTRACTE-project) is gratefully acknowledged. The conclusions expressed here do not necessarily represent the views of the above-mentioned institutions.

2. Auctioning of 900 million EUAs was postponed from the years 2014–2016 to 2019–2020.

3. The MSR mechanism withdraws EUAs from auctioning when a certain upper threshold of unused EUAs in circulation (allowance surplus) is exceeded and feeds these into the "market stability reserve." Once a lower threshold is triggered, these EUAs are re-released from the MSR.

4. For example, the UK's climate change levy, the German Renewable Energy Act (which includes subsidies to renewable energy production) and eco-tax, the Danish and Swedish fuel and carbon taxes, and a variety of funds for energy efficiency measures in various MS (Landis et al. 2012).

5. The sectors considered by the OECD study are electricity generation, road transport, pulp and paper, cement, and households' domestic energy use.

6. Note that the OECD's estimated effective carbon prices are based on specific calculations for different policies. It implies neither that all instruments considered (such as carbon taxes and feed-in tariffs) function in the same way, nor that they have the same effect on emission mitigation.

7. We stress that the estimates based on the OECD (2013) serve for illustrative purpose only. There are different methodologies available to calculate implicit carbon prices. A

discussion of alternative estimates of effective carbon prices can be found in OECD (2013).

8. The heterogeneity of the EU MS can be in terms of, e.g., economic development, environmental objectives, dependency on domestic polluting fuels, and concerns about vulnerability related to the import of energy fuels.

9. According to Hilpold (2015), the EU solidarity principle means that contributions (transfers) across MS or from the EU budget to MS are given with either (a) the hope of receiving counter-contributions at some point in the future or (b) the intent to pursue a common goal.

10. The subsidiarity principle defines the exercise of the EU's competences to be justifiable only if the European Union can improve on the MS' action (EP 2015).

11. We will specify how we define "appropriateness" later in this chapter.

12. See Lisbon Treaty and tax legislation in the European Union (EC 2015c; 2015b).

13. The claim that allowing special treatments, such as grandfathering, is only possible within an ETS is questioned by Goulder and Schein (2013), who argue that when using a carbon tax price, tax exemptions can achieve similar effects as those from grandfathering.

14. See, e.g., Garside (2015b; 2015a).

15. At the current exchange rate of 1.35, this accounts for approximately €25/tCO$_2$e in the year 2015 and €40/tCO$_2$e in the year 2020.

16. Under the Swedish carbon tax program, small industrial producers and agriculture and forestry sectors pay lower carbon taxes than do households (OECD 2014).

17. Roughly defined, the marginal abatement cost is the cost increase from reducing a unit of emissions.

18. For example, by assigning a higher proportion of certificates to Eastern European countries, in particularly Poland (Garside 2015b; EC 2013).

19. We refer to "efficiency" in terms of allocative efficiency, not to be confused with cost-effectiveness, which is sometimes also called "cost-efficiency."

20. See Sheeran (2006) for intuitive details on the modelling work of Chichilnisky and Heal (1994) and their consecutive work in Chichilnisky et al. (2000).

21. The beneficiaries of the "Kyoto bonus" are Bulgaria, the Czech Republic, Estonia, Hungary, Latvia, Lithuania, Poland, Romania, and Slovakia.

22. During phase I and II of the EU ETS, EUAs were granted for free (grandfathered) to industry and power companies. Many of these power companies are fully or partially state-owned. In such cases, it is likely that domestic consumers indirectly benefited from these free allowances. Additionally, a proportion of EU ETS emissions are generated by non-domestic and/or transnational firms, inside and outside of electricity production, in which case it is not necessarily the domestic consumers who benefited from the grandfathered allowances.

23. In addition to climate change externality considerations, there are other reasons why a uniform carbon price—which equalizes MACs across countries—may not be efficient. For example, some countries may wish to price emissions more aggressively for fiscal

reasons. If a country has a relatively mobile tax base with respect to broader fiscal instruments (e.g., due to a prevalence of informal markets, tax evasion), then implementing carbon prices may be a fiscal alternative to other taxes.

24. In a comparable setup, Santore et al. (2001) arrive at similar findings.

25. See also Goulder and Schein (2013) and Shobe and Burtraw (2012).

26. In technical terms we impose a separable utility function in which the consumption component is identical across countries. We also assume that an upper regulator such as the European Union equally weighs each country within a social welfare function.

27. Within this essay the EU ETS-transfer estimation only depicts *optimal* transfers. Estimates for other *appropriate* EU ETS transfers—those transfers that achieve (Pareto) improvements for all MS but not necessarily optimality—are subject to our ongoing research.

28. That is, equity-based transfers and transfers based on historical emissions.

29. If the Member State would not use a variable but a fixed fee, its price would drop below p_{MS}. We suppose that a Member State may anticipate the price drop effect and therefore adjust its policy to meet its preferred emission level. However, both instruments—a variable and a fixed fee—in general generate the same effects in this exercise. For a detailed discussion of a variable fee as a national price floor, see Wood and Jotzo (2011).

30. The mechanism is similar to the UK's carbon price floor for the EU ETS.

31. See also Goulder and Stavins (2012), who discuss the leakage effect in more detail.

32. The model version applied in this paper comprises 26 of the 28 EU MS plus Switzerland, Norway, and the Balkan region, and excludes Malta and Cyprus. Except for the Balkan region, all countries are represented as individual model regions. Transmission is modelled as a transport problem from the center of one region to the center of a neighboring region, with the maximum transmissible amount of electricity being restricted by the installed net transfer capacity. There are 14 different generation technologies and two different storage technologies represented in LIMES-EU. See Nahmmacher et al. (2014) for detailed model documentation.

33. The large model comparison exercise presented in Knopf et al. (2014) showed that a carbon price of at least €20/tCO$_2$ is needed before 2030 in order to cost-efficiently reach the long-term decarbonization targets by 2050.

34. The total system costs comprise the dispatch and investment costs of all generation, storage, and transmission technologies until 2050. They are discounted to today's values with a discount factor of 5 percent per year.

35. See, for example, Inman (2015).

36. In this case, it is a tax. However, it is a constant revenue stream—a feature of both a tax and a price floor.

References

Bianco, Nicholas, Jonas Monast, Tim Profeta, and Franz Litz. 2009. "Allowing States to Retire Allowances without Affecting National Allowance Prices: A Straw Proposal"

(Working Paper, World Resources Institute/Duke University Nicholas Institute for Environmental Policy Solutions). https://nicholasinstitute.duke.edu/sites/default/files/publications/allowing-states-to-retire-allowances-without-affecting-national-allowance-prices-a-straw-proposal-paper.pdf.

BMWi (Bundesministerium für Wirtschaft und Energie). 2015. "Eckpunkte-Papier, Strommarkt." *Bundesministerium für Wirtschaft und Energie.* http://www.bmwi.de/BMWi/Redaktion/PDF/E/eckpunkte-papier-strommarkt,property=pdf,bereich=bmwi2012,sprache=de,rwb=true.pdf.

Böhringer, Christoph, Henrike Koschel, and Ulf Moslener. 2008. "Efficiency Losses from Overlapping Regulation of EU Carbon Emissions." *Journal of Regulatory Economics* 33 (3): 299-317.

Burtraw, Dallas. 2014. "Commentary: Saving Europe's Key Weapon against Climate Change, 2014." *Resources for the Future* 187. http://www.rff.org/research/publications/commentary-saving-europe-s-key-weapon-against-climate-change.

Chichilnisky, Graciela, and Geoffrey Heal. 1994. "Who Should Abate Carbon Emissions?" *Economics Letters* 44: 443-49.

Chichilnisky, Graciela, Geoffrey Heal, and David Starrett. 2000. "Equity and Efficiency in Environmental Markets: Global Trade in Carbon Dioxide Emissions." In *Environmental Markets: Equity and Efficiency*, eds. G. Chichilnisky and G. Heal. Chichester, West Sussex, UK: Columbia University Press, 46-67.

Coase, Ronald H. 1960. "The Problem of Social Cost." *Journal of Law and Economics* 3: 1-44.

Copenhagen Economics. 2010. "Innovation of Energy Technologies: The Role of Taxes, No. 0036" (Taxation Studies, Directorate General Taxation and Customs Union, European Commission). http://ec.europa.eu/taxation_customs/resources/documents/common/publications/studies/taxation_energy_innov.pdf.

Cramton, Peter, Axel Ockenfels, and Steven Stoft. 2015. "An International Carbon-Price Commitment Promotes Cooperation." *Economics of Energy & Environmental Policy* 4 (2): 51-64.

EC (European Commission). 2011. "Energy Roadmap 2050—Impact Assessment and Scenario Analysis." *European Commission: Energy.* https://ec.europa.eu/energy/en/topics/energy-strategy/2050-energy-strategy.

EC. 2012. "The State of the European Carbon Market in 2012." COM(2012) 652 final. http://ec.europa.eu/clima/policies/ets/reform/docs/com_2012_652_en.pdf.

EC. 2013. "The EU Emissions Trading System (EU ETS) Factsheet." http://ec.europa.eu/clima/publications/docs/factsheet_ets_en.pdf.

EC. 2014. "A Policy Framework for Climate and Energy in the Period from 2020 Up to 2030. SWD(2014) 15 final." http://ec.europa.eu/smart-regulation/impact/ia_carried_out/docs/ia_2014/swd_2014_0015_en.pdf.

EC. 2015a. "EU ETS Auctioning." *European Commission: Climate Action.* http://ec.europa.eu/clima/policies/ets/cap/auctioning/index_en.htm.

EC. 2015b. "EU Tax Policy Strategy." *European Commission: Taxation and Customs Union.* http://ec.europa.eu/taxation_customs/taxation/gen_info/tax_policy/index_en.htm.

EC. 2015c. "The Lisbon Treaty and Tax Legislation in the EU." *European Commission: Taxation and Customs Union.* http://ec.europa.eu/taxation_customs/taxation/gen_info/tax_policy/article_6759_en.htm.

EC. 2015d. "Allowances and Caps." *European Commission: Climate Action.* http://ec.eur opa.eu/clima/policies/ets/cap/index_en.htm.

Edenhofer, Ottmar, Michael Jakob, Felix Creutzig, Christian Flachsland, Sabine Fuss, Martin Kowarsch, Kai Lessmann, Linus Mattauch, and Jan Siegmeier. 2015. "Closing the Emission Price Gap." *Global Environmental Change* 31: 132-43.

EEA (European Environment Agency). 2013. *Trends and Projections in Europe 2013—Tracking Progress towards Europe's Climate and Energy Targets until 2020.* Luxembourg: Publications Office of the European Union. http://www.eea.europa.eu//publications/trends-and-projections-2013.

EEA. 2015. "EEA Greenhouse Gas—Data Viewer." *European Environment Agency: Data and Maps.* http://www.eea.europa.eu/data-and-maps/data/data-viewers/greenhouse-gases-viewer.

EEX (European Energy Exchange). 2015. "Emissions Secondary Market." *European Energy Exchange: Environmental Markets.* https://www.eex.com/en/products/environmental-markets/emissions-secondary-market.

EP (European Parliament). 2014. "Indirect Taxation." *European Parliament: Fact Sheets on the European Union.* http://www.europarl.europa.eu/atyourservice/en/displayFtu.html?ftuId=FTU_5.11.3.html.

EP. 2015. "The Principle of Subsidiarity." *European Parliament: Fact Sheets on the European Union.* http://www.europarl.europa.eu/ftu/pdf/en/FTU_1.2.2.pdf.

Eyraud, Luc, Abdoul Wane, Changchang Zhang, and Benedict Clements. 2011. "Who's Going Green and Why? Trends and Determinants of Green Investment" (IMF Working Paper 11/296). https://www.imf.org/external/pubs/ft/wp/2011/wp11296.pdf.

Garside, Ben. 2015a. "BRIEFING: In or Out? Poland Approaches EU Climate Crossroads." *Carbon Pulse.* http://carbon-pulse.com/briefing-in-or-out-poland-approaches-eu-climate-crossroads.

Garside, Ben. 2015b. "Poland's Surging Opposition Seeks Talks on EU Emission Opt-out." *Carbon Pulse.* http://carbon-pulse.com/polands-surging-opposition-seeks-talks-on-eu-emission-opt-out-bloomberg.

Goulder, Lawrence H., and Andrew R. Schein. 2013. "Carbon Taxes Versus Cap and Trade: A Critical Review." *Climate Change Economics* 4 (3).

Goulder, Lawrence H., and Robert N. Stavins. 2011. "Challenges from State-Federal Interactions in US Climate Change Policy." *American Economic Review* 101 (3): 253-57.

Grubb, Michael, Heleen de Coninck, and Ambuj D. Sagar. 2014. "From Lima to Paris, Part 2: Injecting Ambition." *Climate Policy* 15 (4): 413-16.

Heinemann, Friedrich, Philipp Mohl, and Steffen Osterloh. 2009. "Who's Afraid of an EU Tax and Why? Revenue System Preferences in the European Parliament." *The Review of International Organizations* 4 (1): 73-99.

Hilpold, Peter. 2015. "Understanding Solidarity within EU Law: An Analysis of the 'Islands of Solidarity' with Particular Regard to Monetary Union." *Yearbook of European Law* 34: 257-85. http://dx.doi.org/10.2139/ssrn.2599725.

HM Revenue & Customs. 2014. "Carbon Price Floor: Reform and Other Technical Amendments." *Gov.UK: Business Tax—Policy Paper.* https://www.gov.uk/government/publications/carbon-price-floor-reform.

Inman, Philip. 2015. "UK Deficit Rises Steeply after Surprise Fall in Tax Receipts." *The Guardian.* http://www.theguardian.com/business/2015/sep/22/uk-deficit-rises-steeply-after-surprise-fall-in-tax-receipts.

IPCC. 2014. *Climate Change 2014: Mitigation of Climate Change. Contribution of Working Group III to the Fifth Assessment Report of the Intergovernmental Panel on Climate Change.* Cambridge, UK, and New York, NY, US: Cambridge University Press.

Kahn, Debra. 2015. "California Engaging in Carbon-Trading Discussions with Other Western States." *E&E Publishing.* http://www.eenews.net/stories/1060023751.

Knopf, Brigitte, Nicolas Koch, Godefroy Grosjean, Sabine Fuss, Christian Flachsland, Michael Pahle, Michael Jakob, and Ottmar Edenhofer. 2014. "The European Emissions Trading System (EU ETS): Ex-Post Analysis, the Market Stability Reserve and Options for a Comprehensive Reform." Nota di Lavoro 79, Fondazione Eni Enrico Mattei, Milan, Italy.

Koch, Nicolas, Sabine Fuss, Godefroy Grosjean, and Ottmar Edenhofer. 2014. "Causes of the EU ETS Price Drop: Recession, CDM, Renewable Policies or a Bit of Everything? New Evidence." *Energy Policy* 73: 676-85.

Koch, Nicolas, Godefroy Grosjean, Sabine Fuss, and Ottmar Edenhofer. 2016. "Politics Matters: Regulatory Events as Catalysts for Price Formation under Cap-and-Trade." *Journal of Environmental Economics and Management* 78: 121-39.

Kollmuss, Anja, and Michael Lazarus. 2010. "Buying and Cancelling Allowances as an Alternative to Offsets for the Voluntary Market: A Preliminary Review of Issues and Options" (OECD Environment Working Paper No. 21).

Landis, Florian, Oliver Schenker, Miguel Angel Toar Reanos, Christina Vonnahme, and Sonja Zitzelsberger. 2012. "An Overview on Current Climate Policies in the European Union and Its Member States." Centre for European Economic Research, ZEW Mannheim.

Nahmmacher, Paul, Eva Schmid, and Brigitte Knopf. 2014. "Documentation of LIMES-EU—A Long-Term Electricity System Model for Europe." Potsdam Institute for Climate Impact Research, Potsdam, Germany. https://www.pik-potsdam.de/members/paulnah/limes-eu-documentation-2014.pdf.

Oates, Wallace E. 1972. "An Essay on Fiscal Federalism." *Journal of Economic Literature* 37: 1120–49.

Oates, Wallace E. 2011. *Fiscal Federalism.* Cheltenham, UK: Edward Elgar Publishing Ltd.

OECD. 2013. *Effective Carbon Prices.* Paris, France: OECD Publishing. http://dx.doi.org/10.1787/9789264196964-en.

OECD. 2014. "Sweden—Highlights." *OECD: Environmental Country Reviews.* http://www.oecd.org/env/country-reviews/highlights.htm.

Parry, Ian, Chandara Veung, and Dirk Heine. 2014. "How Much Carbon Pricing is in Countries' Own Interests? The Critical Role of Co-Benefits" (CESifo Working Paper No. 5015). https://www.cesifo-group.de/DocDL/cesifo1_wp5015.pdf.

Philibert, Cédric. 2006. "Certainty Versus Ambition: Economic Efficiency in Mitigation Climate Change" (International Energy Agency Working Paper Series). http://philibert .cedric.free.fr/Downloads/rb_certainty_ambition.pdf.

Philibert, Cédric. 2009. "Assessing the Value of Price Caps and Floors." *Climate Policy* 9 (6): 612-33.

Quandl. 2015a. "ICE Futures Europe. ECX EUA Futures, Continuous Contract #2." https://www.quandl.com/data/CHRIS/ICE_C2-ECX-EUA-Futures-Continuous-Contract-2-C2.

Quandl. 2015b. "ICE Futures Europe. ECX EUA Futures, December 2020." https://www .quandl.com/data/ICE/CZ2020-ECX-EUA-Futures-December-2020-CZ2020.

Roolfs, Christina, Beatriz Gaitan, and Ottmar Edenhofer. 2016. "The Richest Wins Them All: Triggering Benevolent Hegemony by Federal Transfers." (Mimeo).

Santore, Rudy, H. David Robison, and Yehuda Klein. 2001. "Strategic State-Level Environmental Policy with Asymmetric Pollution Spillovers." *Journal of Public Economics* 80 (2): 199-224.

Sheeran, Kristen A. 2006. "Who Should Abate Carbon Emissions? A Note." *Environmental and Resource Economics* 35 (2): 89-98.

Shiell, Leslie. 2003. "Equity and Efficiency in International Markets for Pollution Permits." *Journal of Environmental Economics and Management* 46 (1): 38-51.

Shobe, William M., and Dallas Burtraw. 2012. "Rethinking Environmental Federalism in a Warming World." *Climate Change Economics* 3 (4): 33.

Skjærseth, Jon Birger, and Jørgen Wettestad. 2010. "Making the EU Emissions Trading System: The European Commission as an Entrepreneurial Epistemic Leader." *Global Environmental Change* 20 (2): 314-21.

Strunz, Sebastian, Erik Gawel, and Paul Lehmann. 2015. "Towards a General 'European-ization' of EU Member States' Energy Policies?" *Economics of Energy & Environmental Policy* 4 (2).

Talus, Kim. 2013. *EU Energy Law and Policy: A Critical Account*. Oxford: Oxford University Press.

UNFCCC. 2015. "EU Submits its Climate Action Plan Ahead of Paris 2015 Agreement." http://www4.unfccc.int/submissions/INDC/Published%20Documents/Latvia/1/LV-03-06-EU%20INDC.pdf.

Williams, Roberton C. 2012. "Growing State–Federal Conflicts in Environmental Policy: The Role of Market-Based Regulation." *Journal of Public Economics* 96 (11-12): 1092-99.

Wood, Peter John, and Frank Jotzo. 2011. "Price Floors for Emissions Trading." *Energy Policy* 39 (3): 1746–53.

A Comment on "Agreeing on an EU ETS Price Floor to Foster Solidarity, Subsidiarity, and Efficiency in the EU"

Jos Delbeke

The EU Emissions Trading System (EU ETS) is the flagship instrument of the EU's policy to combat climate change and the key tool for reducing industrial greenhouse gas emissions. The ETS is designed to be technology neutral, cost-effective, and to reinforce the functioning of the internal energy market.

The authors of the article argue that the EU ETS has not provided credible incentives for long- and near-term mitigation due to low allowance prices and heterogeneity between Member States, who have different willingness to pay for climate policies. The authors conclude that this had led to fragmentation of national policies, which would be ineffective in incentivizing additional emission reductions in the ETS sectors due to the overall unchanged cap. The authors propose that differentiated national policies, supplemented with an EU carbon price floor and redistribution mechanisms, would lead to a more effective outcome in reducing emissions. Differentiated national policies would undermine the cost-effectiveness of the EU climate policy. As an EU-wide and market-based instrument, the EU ETS allows companies in Europe to find the cheapest ways to reduce their greenhouse gas emissions or to pay others for whom it is cheaper to do so. With its flexible and technology-neutral approach it helps to ensure that the overall cost to society of reducing emissions is as low as possible. The ETS also creates an unprecedented level playing field for European companies, reinforcing the functioning of the internal market. Fragmented national policies would instead risk leading to a costly situation and creating unnecessary red tape. Differentiated policies would also hinder the creation of an international carbon market. The lack of a harmonized EU ETS policy would seriously undermine the efforts to link the ETS with emissions trading systems around the world and create a global level playing field. This, in turn, would perpetuate concerns about the risks of losing industry from Europe to other countries that do not pursue similar carbon-pricing approaches.

There are additional concerns with regard to setting up a carbon price floor in the ETS, as proposed by the authors. In 2012, the Commission published a report with different options on how to reform the ETS to address the surplus in the market. The introduction of a price management mechanism was one of the options.[1] However, there were several reasons for which a price management mechanism was not the agreed way forward and instead Member States agreed on the introduction of the market stability reserve. First, introducing a carbon price floor would require governance arrangements, starting with the political process to determine the appropriate level of such a price floor. This risks that the carbon price becomes a product of administrative and political decisions instead of the interplay of supply and demand on the market. As a result, this would make it more difficult to agree on ambitious European targets, as Member States that do not opt for additional national policies would strongly argue for keeping the carbon price floor as low as possible. Many stakeholders view as one of the key benefits of the ETS that the carbon price reflects the quantity of allowances and their relative scarcity. The carbon price adjusts over the business cycle; for instance, it will decline in a recession, thereby helping industries in difficult times. Additionally, a carbon price floor would potentially impose excessive costs on ETS participants and society in the case of technological breakthroughs, which would substantially lower the abatement costs. Finally, the introduction of a carbon price floor is the legal equivalent of the introduction of a carbon tax. In order to agree on a carbon price floor, the EU Member States would need to reach a unanimous agreement.

A more efficient approach to differentiated national policies is an EU-wide price signal with the appropriate solidarity elements, which would not undermine the efficiency of the EU ETS. This approach has been confirmed by EU Member States when, in October 2014, they endorsed the 2030 Climate and Energy Framework with the ETS as the main instrument of EU climate policy. The use of redistribution mechanisms in the ETS that reflect equity and solidarity have been key to secure endorsement by the Member States of an ambitious greenhouse gas target for 2030. Such mechanisms are already used in the current phase of the ETS and are also foreseen for the period after 2020, clearly recognizing differences between Member States in capacity to act. The distributional elements in a multi-country context have been instrumental in mobilizing support for a cap-and-trade system, while preserving an efficient market outcome.

The years since the ETS has been operational have demonstrated that building a well-functioning carbon market takes time. The EU ETS has evolved over time through the strong involvement and support of all actors. The experience and lessons learned in the European "policy laboratory" are valuable for international partners who are starting work on setting up their own carbon markets.

Notes

1. EC (European Commission). "COM(2012) 652 final." http://ec.europa.eu/clima/policies/ets/reform/docs/com_2012_652_en.pdf.

3   Under Pressure: European Electricity Markets and the Need for Reform

Nils-Henrik M. von der Fehr

Key Points for Policymakers

- Developing market design will allow for more responsiveness and flexibility of supply and demand.
- Coordinating generation and network expansion will ensure better balance between generation and network capacity.
- Integrating networks and system operations will increase the effective capacity of existing infrastructure.
- Facilitating market integration will take advantage of gains from trade.
- Strengthening European-level regulation will ensure a level playing field and better integration of electricity markets.
- Facilitating demand-side flexibility will better accommodate inflexible renewable generation.

1. Introduction

The European electricity market is under pressure, mainly due to ambitious renewables policies that have resulted in considerable market volatility, both with regard to quantities and prices. In this paper, I discuss how these developments challenge the current regulatory regime and the extent to which reform is needed in order to alleviate the pressure and ensure an efficiently working electricity market.[1]

Below I first provide a short background of recent events, as well as a brief introduction to electricity market regulation, before discussing a number of issues that these events have made increasingly relevant: networks, market integration and market design, demand management, and reserves. I end with a short discussion of governance issues before I conclude by elaborating on suggestions for reforms.

2. Recent Trends in European Electricity Markets

Ambitious renewables policies have in recent years resulted in large amounts of new generation capacity that have put a downward pressure on wholesale prices; for example, in Central Western Europe (Austria, Belgium, France, Germany, the Netherlands, and Switzerland), monthly average based-load prices fell from 50 EUR/MWh in the beginning of 2011 to 40 EUR/MWh at the end of 2014 (European Commission 2015b). Low wholesale prices, in combination with low prices of coal and carbon permits—the latter resulting from relatively generous emission targets and the economic downturn—have shifted the generation mix away from gas, toward renewables and coal; around 2010, the downward trend for solid fuels, and the upward trend for gas shifted, with solid fuels increasing its share of EU-28 generation from 24.7 percent in 2010 to 27.4 percent in 2012 and gas reducing its share from 23.7 to 18.7 in the same period. The share of renewables (including hydro, wind, solar, and biomass) has been steadily growing and reached 24.2 percent in 2012, mostly due to the expansion of wind and solar capacity (European Commission 2014). This development is particularly noticeable in Germany, where gas-based generation capacity is being mothballed, or closed down completely, whereas coal-based generation is experiencing somewhat of a renaissance; since 2010, generation from hard coal has been more or less constant, while the use of lignite was up by 7 percent to a share of 26 percent in total generation in 2014 (Agora Energiewende 2015). As a result, traditional generators, especially those relying on gas, are left with stranded assets while CO_2 emissions have been increasing.[2,3]

The expansion of renewables has not only put downward pressure on wholesale prices, but has also led to more price volatility. The intermittent nature of wind and solar power means that there is considerable variability in their supply; the variations are especially pronounced in the short run, within and between days, but there are also seasonal variations. As a result, there is additional need for flexibility, both on the supply and the demand side of the market (such as generation plants or consumption devices that can easily be adjusted up or down), to ensure overall balance of the system. The need for flexibility puts pressure both on wholesale markets and instruments available to system operators (such as automated response, balancing markets, and reserves).

This pressure is further enhanced by the geographic shift in supply. Investments in renewables are not evenly spread across Europe, but are concentrated to certain countries, such as Germany, Italy, and Spain, where renewables policies have been particularly aggressive.[4] Also, investment in renewables often takes place away from consumption centers, dictated by the availability of sites and weather conditions. Finally, the capacity that is being replaced is located in different areas than the new capacity. The geographic development of generation capacity has put further pressure on market instruments and system operations that aim to ensure balance in all parts of the market, especially since network capacity has not been adjusted in line with generation capacity; as a result, the frequency with which bottlenecks occur in the network has increased, and so has the frequency and magnitude of price differences between different areas, both within and between countries (see below).

While recent developments have had considerable distributional impact—for example, between electricity consumers who are faced with the cost of reforms and consumers who are not,[5] or between producers involved in renewable generation and producers relying on traditional thermal technologies—here I concentrate on efficiency issues. In particular, I base my analysis on the assumption that, given other policy considerations (e.g., environmental sustainability and security of supply), electricity market policy aims at cost efficiency, as well as a balance between the cost and benefits of supplying electricity.

Before discussing the implications of recent events, it may be useful to revisit the rationale for government regulation in electricity markets.

3. Aims and Consequences of Regulation

The electricity sector has a number of characteristics that hinder market forces from achieving a fully efficient performance; the sector has all sorts of what economists call "market imperfections." Such imperfections call for regulatory intervention, possibly with the help of fiscal instruments, to alleviate hindrances and improve performance.[6]

There are externalities, in the form of local and global environmental damages. Thermal generation emits various forms of gases, including CO_2, that contribute to global warming; in the European Union, around a quarter of CO_2 emissions originate from electricity generation (eea.europa.eu). Nuclear generation, and the storage of its waste, involves the risk of leakages of radioactive material. Hydro generation requires interventions in the natural environment, with the construction of dams and changes to natural waterways. And solar and wind generation, as well as the lines required to transport electricity, lay claim to areas and impact the visual characteristics of the landscape. Regulation aims to limit environmental damages and balance them against the (net) benefit of the energy produced (i.e., consumer benefits less supply costs).

There are also externalities within the industry itself, particularly in the form of network externalities. Due to the laws of physics that govern flows of electricity, power consumed or generated by a particular agent at a given point in the network affects flows throughout the entire system. As such, the behavior of individual consumers and generators have an impact on energy losses and the risk of violating network capacity constraints—which would lead to brownouts or blackouts—with direct consequences for other users of the system. Network externalities require regulatory intervention to ensure coordination of demand and supply so as to avoid system failures. In addition, regulation is called for to ensure coordinated expansion of consumption and generation capacity on the one hand and network capacity on the other.

Certain aspects of electricity have public-good characteristics. In particular, the quality of supply—that the voltage and frequency levels stay within limits so as not to damage electrical equipment—is of benefit to all users of the system. To ensure quality of supply, consumption and generation must be balanced at all times. This requires that centralized control is vested with a single agent—a system operator—who is given the power to intervene and ration the demand and supply of network users.

Certain parts of the electricity industry also constitute natural monopolies. The most obvious are the networks, where economies of scale rule out the possibility of parallel and independent infrastructures within a given area. Regulation is required to ensure that prices of network services reflect underlying costs, and that networks are built and operated in an efficient manner.[7]

While the characteristics of the electricity market call for regulatory intervention, such interventions are not always designed to address market imperfections directly. For example, rather than concentrating efforts on limiting emissions from thermal generation that contributes to global warming, regulation has to a large extent aimed at advancing cleaner alternatives, such as solar and wind power; the problem with this approach is that it misses some other opportunities for mitigating emissions, like shifting from coal to natural gas, or shifting from these fuels to nuclear and promoting reductions in demand for electricity. Also, rather than discouraging the use of electricity in order to reduce environmental damages, regulation has mainly been directed at increasing the efficiency of its use; however, these regulations do not promote other behavioral responses for reducing demand, such as turning down the air conditioner and switching off the lights. If one were serious about reducing demand, penalizing energy consumption—say, through higher excise taxes—would be more effective than implementing efficiency standards.

While there may be good reasons—political and otherwise—for such regulatory designs, they are not fully efficient in countering the imperfections of the electricity market and hence are either less effective and/or involve extra costs.

Although some regulatory interventions have, by intention, only limited regard for improving the performance of the electricity market, certain designs may perhaps best be characterized as political or regulatory failures. For example, investment in renewable technologies resulting from subsidies and other governmental support has not been matched by a corresponding expansion of networks from where this new electricity is generated to where it might be consumed—partly due to local opposition to new lines, but also to a lack of effective governance structures at the regional, national, and European level (see below)—with the consequence that networks have come under considerable strain. The comeback of coal at the expense of gas—to some extent explained by the fall in the price of coal relative to that of gas, but also from lax overall emissions restrictions that have kept prices of carbon permits low in the European Trading System (ETS)—seems unintended. Furthermore, the introduction of large amounts of intermittent capacities may drive out thermal capacity that is needed to ensure the balance between demand and supply. And national and regional regulatory interventions are not always well coordinated to ensure overall efficiency of the European electricity market, most often due to conflicting interests, especially concerning the sharing of costs and benefits across different jurisdictions, but also due to a tradition of national self-sufficiency in electricity supply; as a consequence, cross-border interconnecting capacities are not sufficient to ensure a fully integrated market.

Below, I turn to how regulatory design needs to be improved to tackle the pressure currently put on the electricity industry from policies aiming at the security and sustainability of energy supplies.

4. Networks

Generation and consumption of electricity is generally located in different places. This is partly out of necessity; for example, a hydro plant must be placed where there is (running) water and a wind farm where there is sufficient wind, which is not always near where consumers live and work. Furthermore, efficiency requires a certain scale—at least for some technologies, such as nuclear and thermal generation—which implies that a single plant of efficient scale can serve a large number of consumers, so that, especially in sparsely populated areas, the plant will necessarily be located at a distance from most consumers.

Networks provide the transportation of electricity from the site of generation to the site of consumption. Moreover, networks relieve the dependence of specific consumers on specific producers, and vice versa. In other words, when connected to a large network, consumers can, in effect, draw on many different sources of supply, while producers face many alternative consumers. This not only allows for competition—on both sides of the market—but also protects against shocks to demand and supply. For example, if a certain plant is unable to generate, another plant connected to the same network can take its place. Similarly, idiosyncratic variations in consumption at the level of individual network users tend to even out in a large network. A larger network therefore provides greater security of supply.

Renewables increase the need for network capacity. Since new generation is often located in different areas than old generation, and also away from consumption, new network capacity is required to transport power between generation and consumption sites. Furthermore, variation in the availability of renewables raises the benefits of aggregation of shocks, for example to exploit different weather conditions across regions or the different nature of technologies such as intermittent resources and adjustable hydro.[8]

Planning, investment, and financing of networks traditionally take place at the national or local level. However, many network projects involve two or more countries, either because the new line crosses national borders or because investments in some countries affect the power flows in other countries. Such projects have often been difficult to realize.

The EU Commission has taken various initiatives to promote network projects with an international dimension, such as the Ten Year Development Plan[9] and Projects of Common Interest.[10] These initiatives have had some success, but we are still far from eliminating all inefficient cross-border bottlenecks, as demonstrated, for example, by considerable and persistent price differences across markets (see the next section). Taking account of the fact that networks are truly interconnected, with the consequence that developments in one part of the network affect power flows not only in immediately neighboring parts but over the entire system, it would seem natural to vest responsibility for the transmission network at the European level.

A step toward a more overall perspective on transmission networks would be to allow for, or indeed encourage, integration of transmission network operators (TSOs). There are a few examples of TSOs that operate cross-border networks; for example, the Dutch TSO Tennet operates part of the German transmission network. However, there are a number of political and regulatory obstacles to mergers across national borders or the establishment of regional TSOs (e.g., the Dutch and German operations of Tennet are subject to different regulations). Removing such obstacles—for example, harmonizing the rules governing network and system operation—would be required in order to promote such developments.

Unlike traditional generation plants, renewable generation capacity is often connected to the network at low voltage levels. These parts of the network are typically constructed for distributing energy to consumers and often lack both the capacity and the characteristics to handle generation, at least in large volumes. The challenge requires new investments, different modes of operation, and more active demand-side management. While this challenge may be met with appropriate regulation at the local level, the general impression is that regulatory authorities have been relatively slow in adapting to the new situation facing distribution networks.

5. Market Integration

European electricity markets are only partially integrated, implying that the benefits from trade are not fully utilized. This is demonstrated by the considerable and persistent price differences across adjacent markets; for example, in the fourth quarter of 2014, average baseload wholesale prices varied from around 30 EUR/MWh in the Nordic region, via 35 EUR/MWh in the Austrian-Czech-German-Slovakian-Swiss region, 40 EUR/MWh in France, 50 EUR/MWh on the Iberian peninsula, and in Poland to almost 60 EUR/MWh in Greece, Italy, and the United Kingdom (European Commission 2015b). Given the cost of building networks, it would not pay to eliminate all bottlenecks and so price differences would exist even in a fully integrated electricity market; however, current price differences are clearly too large to be consistent with full integration. Moreover, the lack of integration also limits liquidity, reduces competition, and makes it difficult to take full advantage of the flexibility of resources across geographical areas.

The expansion of renewables strengthens the rationale for integrating markets, due to the resulting increase in price variability, greater price differences, and hence arbitrage opportunities across different marketplaces.

There is, in fact, no inherent reason that electricity markets should be divided along national borders. The Nordic countries have operated an integrated market for many years. In other parts of Europe—such as the Western European region, which includes Belgium, France, Germany, the Netherlands, and the United Kingdom—national markets have been coupled together, in the sense that these markets are cleared simultaneously so as to maximize power flows over interconnectors.

Indeed, market integration—in the sense of allowing for efficient trade in electricity—should be seen as independent of national borders; networks, not national borders, represent the ultimate restrictions on physical trade. As such, in the Nordic area markets are split according to characteristics of the underlying network infrastructure, not national borders. In other words, efficiency requires that delineation of markets—or bidding zones—should be based on physical capacity constraints, not institutional borderlines (assuming that institutions, including transmission and system operators, can adapt to the requirements of the market).

There is an on-going process of further coupling spot markets. The day-ahead power markets in northwestern Europe have been coupled as of 2014. It is expected that the intraday markets will follow soon, and that the process will subsequently be continued with the aim of coupling together all the markets of Europe.

The market-coupling process is based on voluntary cooperation between power exchanges, that is, the organized marketplaces. This is a difficult and cumbersome process, where many different interests will need to be aligned in order for the involved power exchanges to reach an agreement. The regulatory framework opens up the possibility that new marketplaces may be established, and, in particular, that a power exchange may offer trading opportunities in different national markets, in effect integrating these markets. It remains to be seen how this process will play out, but one can envisage a development toward one or more power exchanges that cover the entire European market.

So far, there has been very limited integration of other markets, including the balancing markets used by system operators to ensure quality and security of supply. While there is close cooperation between system operators in some regions, we are far from a situation with a fully efficient use of available balancing resources across Europe. System operators have traditionally had a national role and little incentive to widen their perspective (costs of balancing can be passed on to network users, so there is little gain for system operators from sharing resources; moreover, they risk the blame for imbalances spilling across borders). Also, the fact that system codes are not fully harmonized across countries means that it will likely take time before we see more integration of balancing markets.

6. Market Design

A good market design ensures that the overall balance of the system is secured in an economically efficient manner. This is achieved by, on the one hand, decentralized decisions of consumers and generators based on their individual costs and benefits, and, on the other hand, centralized intervention by the system operator when such is called for; specifically, since decentralized decisions may lead to imbalances or overload of network infrastructure—especially in unforeseen contingencies, such as plant failure or sudden changes in weather conditions—the system operator must intervene to restore balance and ensure that critical network limits are not exceeded. The growth in renewable generation capacity raises the question of whether the current market design can meet the challenge of intermittency.[11]

Any analysis of market design must take into account transaction cost, including costs associated with receiving and processing (price and other relevant) information, making bids and offers, setting prices, writing contracts, metering, settling contracts, and handling payments, as well as adjusting consumption and generation.

In theory—that is, in the absence of transaction costs—trade could take place continuously, in real time. In practice, transaction costs imply that in electricity markets transactions are conducted before actual delivery, time is divided into discrete market time units, contracts cover multiple market-time units, and contracts involve flexible volumes. Furthermore, transaction costs imply that there will be deviations (imbalances) between contracted and actual trade that necessitates balancing or rationing (by the system operator or others), in the form of curtailing, or ordering increases in, output or input of individual market participants.

The importance of transaction costs differs between consumption technologies, generation technologies, means of storage,[12] and agents of different size and diversification. Therefore, market participants should be allowed to choose between contracts of different types with regard to time between transaction and exercise of contract, length of market-time unit, duration of contracts (number of contract periods), whether the contract is for a fixed or a flexible volume, and the extent of rationing in specified contingencies.

In spot markets, gate closure is typically 12-36 hours in advance in day-ahead markets and one to two hours or less in intraday markets, mostly dictated by system-operation considerations.[13] A shorter time between transaction and exercise allows for better optimization of consumption and generation to real-time costs and benefits, but reduces liquidity when gate closure approaches.

Do larger volumes of renewables require a shortening of time between transaction and exercise? Weather conditions—especially wind and sunshine—are generally predicted with relatively high levels of accuracy, even hours beforehand, but exceptions do occur. So, perhaps gate closure should be revisited as the importance of renewables increases.[14]

The minimum market time unit—that is, the shortest duration of contracts—is typically one hour (although often shorter in balancing markets). A shorter time unit allows for more frequent price adjustments to reflect underlying market conditions and thereby reduces deviations from the average volume within a given period; however, a shorter time unit also increases the number of transactions. Do larger volumes of renewables increase variation in market conditions within current market time periods? Most variation occurs between and within days, not within the hour, although there is increasing variation within the hour also. So, perhaps the market-time unit should also be revisited.

Many market participants hold contracts with long duration on time-invariant terms, often with flexible volumes; this is especially true for (small) consumers and generators on special terms (such as feed-in tariffs). Shorter durations and less volume flexibility would increase sensitivity to market prices, reduce variation in actual volumes, and induce more active participation in short-term markets, but it would also raise transaction costs. One may ask whether larger volumes of renewables require contracts with shorter duration or less volume flexibility. The answer depends on the cost of metering and opportunities for (contracts for) curtailment of renewable electricity.

Rationing (balancing) of feed-in and withdrawal is warranted due to both imbalances within the (minimum) contract period and (unplanned) deviations from contracted volumes. Rationing is undertaken in many different ways, including by automatic frequency control, restrictions on ramping (the speed at which agents increase or reduce output or input of power to the network), activation of balancing reserve, demand-side management, and, as a last resort, by blackouts. An important question is whether larger volumes of renewables increase the need for rationing. This will depend on the possibilities for imposing ramping restrictions on renewable generation, demand-side management, and balancing reserves.

We have seen that the penetration of renewables may require changes to current market designs, to allow for better accommodation of these intermittent resources. If needed, one would expect that such changes will, to a large extent, result from the adaptation of market participants themselves—including operators of marketplaces and system operators—to changing market conditions.

Indeed, one could argue that market design should be left to the market itself, in the sense that market participants, through their expressed interests and actual choices, should be allowed to determine how the market is designed. After all, the market provides, first and foremost, a service to those who trade there.

Some marketplaces have indeed been set up and developed by market participants. For example, the Nordic market traces its history back to "clubs" of major generators trading energy surpluses and deficits on voluntary exchanges (these were typically hydro generators with fixed, long-term contractual supply obligations, which needed to adjust to varying availability of water).

There are also examples of power exchanges being established not by market participants themselves, but by independent market organizers or entrepreneurs. An example of particular interest is the entry of Nord Pool/NASDAQ in the UK market, which introduced direct competition between different exchanges within the same physical market. Decentralization of the design issue will lead to a suitable market design only if market participants—including those who own and operate marketplaces—are subject to the full costs and benefits of their decisions.

For example, operating a marketplace with a wide selection of products is more costly than a marketplace where only a narrow selection is available. Also, it is more costly to facilitate trade in some products than in others. In order for buyers and sellers to make optimal choices about which products to trade in, they need to face the costs of making products available on the market.

More generally, for market participants to face the true costs of their trading activities, fees, and other payments that participants have to incur must accurately reflect the costs of these activities. In practice, in some marketplaces participants do not bear the full costs of their choices. This is partly because the structure of fees does not reflect underlying costs—typically the fee structure is simplified relative to the cost structure—and partly because certain marketplaces or trading activities are, in effect, subsidized. In particular, fees on organized electricity markets (power exchanges) typically have a two-dimensional structure, with a fixed, annual fee and a variable fee per unit of energy traded. These fees are not related to the underlying structure of available products or other services offered (although there may be a relationship between the level of fees and what the marketplace offers).

It is not clear how strong these arguments are. Indeed, given the many examples of apparently well-functioning power exchanges in Europe, a number of which have been developed without direct government intervention or support, there do not appear to be compelling reasons why such markets would require specific support in order to thrive and adjust (when that is needed) as the amount of renewables increases. That is not to say that these markets are necessarily optimally designed or perform fully efficiently. One apparent difficulty is the (ab)use of market power or gaming by individuals or groups of market participants; while power exchanges typically have in place various measures to reduce such problems, including market surveillance and penalties for breach of trading practices, they are difficult to eliminate completely. However, given the fact that market organizers—and, indeed, traders themselves—have an interest in protecting the integrity of the market, they have incentives to curtail such problems and improve market performance.[15]

Another potential problem is ensuring that marketplaces contribute to the overall functioning of the electricity industry, particularly the quality and security of supply. By facilitating trade, markets help with balancing consumption and generation of electricity, but this is generally not enough to achieve the warranted real-time physical balance; such balance can be achieved only by a system operator with the necessary powers to intervene in the decisions of individual market participants. In order to help the system operator perform its task, close cooperation with marketplaces, especially power exchanges, is required. While such cooperation may in principle be based on voluntary agreements, in practice regulatory intervention is called for.

7.   Demand Management

The intermittency of renewables may be accommodated by greater flexibility on the demand side of the electricity market. As a popular saying has it: before, supply was adjusted to demand—now demand must adjust to supply.

Traditionally, the demand side of the market has been considered inflexible and with limited or no response to market prices. This is not entirely true; when market conditions are favorable, demand does respond to price.[16] However, under current market conditions, net benefits from demand management have been negative for most consumers; that is, the benefit from optimizing electricity consumption against price has not been sufficient to cover the cost of installing and operating the necessary technical equipment (in particular, real-time meters), with the consequence that few consumers have been involved in short-term demand management. New technology—in particular, "smart meters" and "intelligent devices" in the form of real-time meters, remote control of electrical appliances, and computer applications to optimize electricity usage—may change this and provide opportunities for enhancing demand management and flexibility; already we see examples around Europe of consumers who are, directly or indirectly, taking advantage of these opportunities to optimize their use of electricity.

First, new technology allows consumers to respond directly to short-term price variations. Smart meters provide real-time information about prices and other relevant statistics, making it possible for consumers to optimize their consumption over time. Furthermore, smart devices make it possible for consumption decisions to be automated; for example, heating and cooling equipment, such as water boilers, refrigerators, and freezers, may be adjusted by a pre-set computer program that optimizes temperature against price.

Second, demand management may be delegated to third parties. Consumers can enter into contracts with distributors, suppliers, or third parties, leaving these with the right to remotely control electricity consumption according to a specified agreement. For example, consumers can choose an interruptible-supply contract according to which heating and cooling devices will to be turned off with a certain frequency and for a certain length of time. The contractor (or "aggregator")—who will typically hold a portfolio of such contracts and hence will aggregate the contracted power from a range of individual consumers—will sell the regulated power on the market, as a balancing service.

Greater variation on the supply side of the electricity market due to the penetration of intermittent power not only increases the need for demand flexibility, but may also increase the incentive for demand management. Greater variation in prices—and higher premiums in balancing markets—provides an economic incentive, both for the individual consumer and for aggregators. Nevertheless, there appear to be a number of obstacles to the development of demand management on the warranted scale. These include the cost of equipment, transaction costs, and market regulations, which do not necessarily allow for the sort of contracting that would be required for efficient trading of demand-management services.

While a number of adjustments to market design are conceivable, it is not obvious that larger volumes of renewables warrant fundamental design changes, particularly when one takes into account the risk of increased complexity in an already quite involved design. However, there may be a need for further developing retail and wholesale markets and the extent to which they are utilized, including both the direct and indirect participation of consumers.[17]

It would appear that the flexibility problems currently experienced are mainly due to renewables being introduced too quickly for other adjustments to take place at a corresponding rate, including divestment of inflexible, and investment in flexible, consumption and generation capacity.[18] There is reason to believe that, given time, markets will deliver the required adjustments and flexibility without fundamental changes to the underlying design.

8. Reserves

Balancing reserves are needed to cover deviations between actual and planned volumes, or, alternatively, to balance the difference between demand and supply at any given point in time. Efficient balancing requires a mix of reserves with different response times, including primary reserves (with response times counted in seconds), secondary reserves (with response times in minutes), and tertiary control reserves (with even longer response times). Fast response is an important quality, but reserves with such qualities tend to be more costly to operate, at least over longer periods of time. In principle, as well as in practice, reserves on both the demand-side (i.e., electrical appliances such as industrial machinery and boilers that can be turned up or down when required) and supply-side (generation plants) are relevant.

Do larger volumes of renewable electricity increase the need for balancing reserves? The answer is yes, if deviations between actual and planned volumes—or between demand and supply—increase in (some) contingencies. If that is the case, the next question becomes: what kind of reserves?

The answer to the latter question hinges on the nature of variation (volatility) in renewable generation, including frequency, amplitude, and distribution over time. The nature of variation affects the need for flexibility of resources (reaction time), total amount of resources needed (difference between maximum and minimum output), and cost structure (fixed versus variable costs).

It would seem that renewables do not, first and foremost, have a strong impact on imbalances in the very short run. Both wind and solar output can be forecasted with high degrees of accuracy, at least up to a few hours before operation. The main worry has been related to the fact that renewable output may fall to very low levels, or disappear almost entirely, in certain circumstances: on a windless, rainy day there is very little output from either wind or solar power. It is especially in such circumstances that renewables impact the need for reserves.

The extent to which relevant resources are made available will, to a large extent, depend on market-based incentives, which determine the profitability of establishing and maintaining reserves. These incentives follow from the number of hours that reserve plants can be expected to operate (residual load duration), the price in operating hours (which again will depend on caps on market prices), and the existence of any fixed payments (for availability).

It is not obvious that incentives resulting from current market designs will be sufficient to bring forth the required reserves. In particular, the closure of gas-based generation plants—traditionally viewed as the most flexible part of the generation park—may be seen as a sign that incentives are not sufficient.

Nevertheless, the question of whether incentives are sufficient does remain open.[19] The wave of closure of traditional generation plants is a necessary and unavoidable consequence of the influx of renewable capacity and the consequent downward pressure on market prices. Although one may have sympathy with the owners of stranded assets, this in itself does not justify support to keep plants open for reserve purposes. However, it could be that plant closure—and lack of investment in alternative reserves—will eventually bring the market to a point where supply security cannot be guaranteed any longer. We are not there now, but if and when there are clear signs that we are heading in this direction, measures should obviously be put in place before such a point is reached.

More fundamentally, it is not obvious that the solution to imbalances caused by the intermittency of renewables lies on the supply side of the market.[20] Since, due to different weather conditions at any given point in time, the availability of wind and sun is imperfectly correlated across Europe, strengthening network capacities would allow for greater movements of power from areas with abundant supply to deficit areas; more efficient use of existing capacities, as well as the building of new interconnectors, will provide an important contribution to tackle imbalances. Furthermore, there is considerable potential for better demand-side management. A combination of new technologies, more accurate price signals and third-party management of power consumption on a commercial basis is likely to make the demand side of the market much more responsive to the availability of power.

9.   Governance: Institutions and Organizations

In Europe, regulation and operation of electricity markets has mostly been a national matter, with national regulators, (one or more) transmission system operators, and (mostly) national markets.

Admittedly, there is cooperation across borders, at various levels. Regulators meet in CEER (the Council of European Energy Regulators) and transmission system operators in Entso-E (the European Network for Transmission System Operators of Electricity). And the cooperation between power exchanges has been strengthened through the ongoing process of market coupling.

At the European level, DG Energy of the European Commission has responsibility for overall policy and regulatory framework while ACER (the Agency for the Cooperation of Energy Regulators) is responsible for regulatory oversight, with the possibility to intervene in certain areas.

It is not clear, however, whether this institutional structure is sufficiently strong to meet cross-border challenges, not to speak of developing consistent policies and securing full integration of the European electricity market.

The ambitious renewables policies pursued in some European countries, as well as other recent events, have highlighted the strong externalities—or spillover effects—between national markets; policies pursued in one country have a direct and substantial impact on the performance of electricity markets in neighboring countries. The externalities work through volumes and prices—with effects on both levels and volatility—but also affect system security; the strong loop-flow effects of intermittent generation have put heavy, and often unexpected, pressure on transmission infrastructure in general and interconnectors in particular. Tackling such externalities requires tight coordination and, indeed, cooperation.

The Nordic experience suggests that one can come a long way in developing a truly integrated electricity market without supranational institutions. The Nordic market has, to a considerable extent, been the result of cooperation between industry agents—in particular, the national TSOs—in a sort of bottom-up process; developments have been driven by consensus and a common understanding of the gains from integration, sanctioned, but rarely initiated, by political and regulatory authorities. However, it is also true that the process has been slowed, and sometimes even halted, by conflicting interests that could not be resolved through consensus; this is especially true for capacity expansions in the transmission network across national borders.

It would seem that similar difficulties arise in the European context; it is hard to develop an integrated market based on consensus. A recent example is the ongoing process of market coupling, which relies on the various power exchanges negotiating among themselves how to integrate their marketplaces; while the negotiations have provided some impressive results—an extent of integration that many would have seen as entirely unrealistic only a short while ago—it has nevertheless been a tortuous process. Undoubtedly, market coupling could have been introduced in a quicker and better fashion if supervised and conducted by institutions at a supranational level.

Thus, while various sorts of political obstacles may lay in the way of developing a better institutional structure at the European level, there do seem to be good reasons to try to overcome these.[21] The recent initiative to establish an "Energy Union" points to the need for coordination and cooperation also at the political level; indeed, much of the pressure currently put on the European electricity market is the result of political decisions and the solutions would, fundamentally, have to be political. However, stronger institutions at the European level—both regulatory and operational—would also seem to be required; it is hard to see how the current cross-border challenges in the electricity market can be resolved without supranational institutions with sufficient powers.

10. Conclusion

Given that the goal is to enhance the efficiency of the European electricity market, the above discussion points to a number of suggestions for policymakers and regulators, as well as for market participants themselves:

1. Develop market design. Overall, it does not seem that the increase in renewable generation poses a challenge to the design of European electricity markets that warrants fundamental reform. Nevertheless, various modifications—such as shortening of market time periods or bringing gate closure nearer to actual transactions—may well be called for, so as to accommodate the intermittent nature of renewables.
2. Coordinate generation and network expansion. The rapid expansion of renewable generation (and, indeed, the resulting closure of other generation capacity) has not been matched by a corresponding expansion of network capacity. Given the geographical concentration of much of renewable capacity, and its location away from consumption centers, new infrastructure, or better use of existing ones, is warranted.

3. Integrate networks and system operations. The rise of renewables has highlighted the need for better integration of transmission networks and system operations across national borders. Planning, building, and operation of a fully integrated electricity network all require close coordination across the entire European area. It may be that this can only really be achieved with a European TSO in place, although cross-border mergers of TSOs may provide a useful start.

4. Facilitate market integration. The intermittency of renewables leads to greater price variation and differences across the different marketplaces in Europe. There is an ongoing process of integrating these marketplaces, both with regard to day-ahead and intraday markets, that needs to be finalized. Moreover, one should aim for integration also of the different balancing markets run by system operators across Europe.

5. Strengthen European-level regulation. There is an apparent mismatch between an integrated European electricity market on the one hand and a non-integrated governance structure on the other. While much may be achieved by cooperation and consensus, it does seem that complete integration of the market requires integration of regulation also, in other words, a European regulator.

6. Facilitate demand-side flexibility. The demand side has traditionally been given little attention as a means to ensure flexibility and balance of electricity markets. This is now changing, due to both the need for further flexibility to deal with the intermittency of renewable power as well as the opportunities presented by new information technology. One would expect that demand-side flexibility—in the form of automated and self-controlled consumption and through markets for balancing services—will develop in response to new market conditions, but regulatory intervention, especially to remove barriers for market participation, may also be required.

While the above list is unlikely to be very controversial—and, indeed, certain developments along these lines are already taking place—some of the aims may be difficult to achieve. This is particularly true where cross-border cooperation is required, and especially so when reforms require not only administrative but political decisions. Nevertheless, if the aim is to relieve the pressure that the European electricity market is currently under, and to achieve a well-functioning, integrated market, such reforms would seem to be warranted.

Notes

1. The challenges to electricity market regulation have recently been put in a wider perspective by the European Commission's "framework strategy for a resilient Energy Union with a forward-looking climate change policy" (European Commission 2015a). See Boltz (2013) for a recent discussion of the challenges facing electricity market regulation in the European Union.

2. Pfaffenberger and Chrischilles (2013) provide a description and discussion of the recent "turnaround" in the German electricity market, the so-called *Energiewende*. See also Bauknecht, Brunekreeft, and Meyer (2013) for a more general discussion of the integration of renewables, with particular reference to the German experience.

3. Given that CO_2 emissions (for relevant sectors) are capped at the European level by the ETS quota, the larger German emissions have been accommodated by lower emissions elsewhere in Europe; the paradox nevertheless remains that a policy with a stated "green" intention has, at least within the country pursuing this policy most aggressively, led to the opposite result. The trend may have been broken, as German CO_2 emissions from electricity generation, which had increased from 294 million tons in 2009 to 317 million tons in 2013, fell in 2014 to 301 million tons, although most of the fall is explained by unusually low energy consumption due to mild weather (Agora Energiewende 2015).

4. Haas, Auer, Resch, and Lettner (2013) give an overview of the impact of renewable energy in European electricity markets.

5. For example, in Germany, the energy-intensive industry is exempt from the renewable-energy surcharge and has hence benefited from lower (wholesale) electricity prices; household consumers, however, have seen their electricity prices increase by, on average, 55 percent from 2006 to 2013, mostly due to the rise in the surcharge (Agora Energiewende 2015).

6. See Ranci and Cervigni (2013) for an introduction to the economics of electricity markets, including analyses of the need for, and implications of, government regulation.

7. Market power is not restricted to the natural monopoly parts of the electricity industry, but may constitute a problem also in parts where competition could, at least in principle, work well. There may consequently be a need for regulatory intervention—in the form of competition or antitrust policy—also in other parts of the industry, such as generation and supply. I do not pursue this issue here.

8. Knieps (2013) discusses the implications of renewable energy for efficient electricity networks, based on a disaggregated nodal-pricing theoretical framework.

9. EU legislation has mandated the European Network of Transmission System Operators (Entso-E) with the delivery of a biennial Ten-Year Network Development Plan (TYNDP), the first pilot of which was released in 2010 (entsoe.eu). The TYNDP identifies gaps in infrastructure from a European perspective and informs decision makers in Member States and other stakeholders about projects with a network-wide impact.

10. To help create an integrated EU energy market, the European Commission has drawn up a list of 248 projects of common interest (ec.europa.eu). These projects may benefit from accelerated licensing procedures, improved regulatory conditions, and access to

financial support totalling €5.85 billion from the Connecting Europe Facility between 2014 and 2020. The list of projects is to be updated every two years.

11. See Bertsch, Growitsch, Lorenczik, and Nagl (2012, 2013) for recent analyses of the penetration and impact of renewables in European electricity markets.

12. Storage of electricity may be direct, in the form of batteries, or indirect, in the form of water in reservoirs.

13. In Europe, decisions about market design have, to a large extent, been decentralised to market participants themselves, including those responsible for running power exchanges; while regulatory authorities may have been informed, market design has typically not been explicitly regulated.

14. The cost and benefits of changing gate closure, as well as some of the other potential changes to market design, remain open and the issue would have to be addressed by analytical research and, possibly, by trying out alternative designs to gain experience.

15. The presence of different trading places or platforms in a given market may make it more difficult to oversee market performance, given that each platform observes only a share of total trade. In such cases, cooperation between platforms, or the establishment of an independent entity, may be warranted to ensure market-wide surveillance.

16. Exactly how responsive electricity demand is to price is a subject of some controversy. A recent study, Valitov et al. (2014), estimates the price elasticity in the European Power Exchange (EPEX) day-ahead market for Germany and Austria to be -0.81 in 2010-2012, suggesting that price responsiveness may, at least in some places and under certain conditions, be substantial. More generally, we would expect price responsiveness of electricity demand to depend on time and place, as well as the underlying circumstances and the duration of the change.

17. The need for regulatory intervention to ensure incorporation of demand flexibility, in particular demand response, has recently been discussed by the European Commission (2013c).

18. Pfaffenberger and Chrischilles (2013) point to this as one of the main lessons from the German *Energiewende*.

19. Cervigni (2013) provides a thorough discussion of whether regulatory intervention is needed to ensure sufficient capacity reserves; see also Cervigni, Commisso, and Perekhodtsev (2013) and Pérez-Arriaga (2013).

20. The point that governments must look beyond generation to ensure generation adequacy is emphasized in a recent communication from the European Commission (2013b; see also European Commission 2013a).

21. Bertola et al., in their analysis of what they term the "European energy conundrum," provide a forceful argument in favor of such developments, starting from the observation that "the failure to achieve greater coordination reveals how the greater part of policy formation and preference accumulation primarily occurs at the national level" (2015, 51).

References

Agora Energiewende. 2015. "The Energiewende in the Power Sector: State of Affairs 2014—A Review of the Significant Developments and an Outlook for 2015." January 7,

Berlin, Germany. https://www.agora-energiewende.de/fileadmin/downloads/publika
tionen/Analysen/Jahresauswertung_2014/Agora_Energiewende_Review_2014_
EN.pdf.

Bauknecht, Dierk, Gert Brunekreeft, and Roland Meyer. 2013. "From Niche to Main-
stream: The Evolution of Renewable Energy in the German Electricity Market." In *Evolution of Global Electricity Markets: New Paradigms, New Challenges, New Approaches*, ed.
Fereidoon P. Sioshansi. London, UK: Academic Press.

Bertola, Giuseppe, John Driffil, Harold James, Hans-Werner Sinn, Jan-Egbert Sturm, and
Akos Valentinyi. 2015. *The EEAG Report on the European Economy: Blurring the Borders*,
No. 14, European Economic Advisory Group. CESifo Group, Munich, Germany.

Bertsch, Joachim, Christian Growitsch, Stefan Lorenczik, and Stephan Nagl. 2012. "Flexibility Options in European Electricity Markets in High RES-E Scenarios—Study on
Behalf of the International Energy Agency (IEA)." Institute of Energy Economics, University of Cologne, Germany.

Bertsch, Joachim, Christian Growitsch, Stefan Lorenczik, and Stephan Nagl. 2013. "Do
We Need an Additional Flexibility Market in the Electricity System? A System-Economic
Analysis for Europe" (Working Paper, Institute of Energy Economics, University of
Cologne, Germany).

Boltz, Walter. 2013. "The Challenge of Electricity Market Regulation in the European
Union." In *Evolution of Global Electricity Markets: New Paradigms, New Challenges, New
Approaches*, ed. Fereidoon P. Sioshansi. London, UK: Academic Press.

Cervigni, Guido. 2013. "Generation Capacity Adequacy in Europe: What Economic
Rationale for Capacity Remuneration Mechanisms?" CERRE (Centre on Regulation in
Europe) Study.

Cervigni, Guido, Andrea Commisso, and Dmitri Perekhodtsev. 2013. "Generation Capacity Adequacy." In *The Economics of Electricity Markets: Theory and Policy*, eds. Pippo Ranci
and Guido Cervigni. Loyola de Palacio Series on European Energy Policy. Cheltenham,
UK: Edward Elgar Publishing.

European Commission. 2013a. "Delivering the Internal Electricity Market and Making
the Most of Public Intervention." Communication from the Commission, November 5.

European Commission. 2013b. "Generation Adequacy in the Internal Electricity Market—Guidance on Public Interventions." Commission Staff Working Document, November 5.

European Commission. 2013c. "Incorporating Demand Side Flexibility, in Particular
Demand Response, in Electricity Markets." Commission Staff Working Document,
November 5.

European Commission. 2014. "EU Energy in Figures." Statistical Pocketbook 2014.

European Commission. 2015a. "Energy Union Package—A Framework Strategy for a
Resilient Energy Union with a Forward-Looking Climate Change Policy." Communication from the Commission to the European Parliament, the Council, the European Economic and Social Committee, the Committee of the Regions and the European Investment
Bank, February 15.

European Commission. 2015b. "Quarterly Report on European Electricity Markets." *DG
Energy* 7 (4).

Haas, Reinhard, Hans Auer, Gustav Resch, and Georg Lettner. 2013. "The Growing Impact of Renewable Energy in European Electricity Market." In *Evolution of Global Electricity Markets: New Paradigms, New Challenges, New Approaches*, ed. Fereidoon P. Sioshansi. London, UK: Academic Press.

Knieps, Günter. 2013. "Renewable Energy, Efficient Electricity Networks, and Sector-Specific Market Power Regulation." In *Evolution of Global Electricity Markets: New Paradigms, New Challenges, New Approaches*, ed. Fereidoon P. Sioshansi. London, UK: Academic Press.

Pérez-Arriaga, Ignacio J. 2013. "Generation Capacity Adequacy: What Economic Rationale for Support Mechanisms?" Issue Paper prepared for CERRE's Executive Seminar on "Europe's Wholesale Electricity Markets: Future Regulatory Perspectives and Challenges." Centre on Regulation in Europe, June 19.

Pfaffenberger, Wolfgang, and Esther Chrischilles. 2013. "Turnaround in Rough Sea—Electricity Market in Germany." In *Evolution of Global Electricity Markets: New Paradigms, New Challenges, New Approaches*, ed. Fereidoon P. Sioshansi. London, UK: Academic Press.

Ranci, Pippo, and Guido Cervigni, eds. 2013. *The Economics of Electricity Markets: Theory and Policy*. Loyola de Palacio Series on European Energy Policy. Cheltenham, UK: Edward Elgar Publishing.

Sioshansi, Fereidoon P., ed. 2013. *Evolution of Global Electricity Markets: New Paradigms, New Challenges, New Approaches*. London, UK: Academic Press.

Valitov, Niyaz, Sebastian Nielen, Werner Bönte, and Torben Engelmeyer. 2014. "Price Elasticity of Demand in the European Wholesale Electricity Market" (Working Paper, Schumpeter School of Business and Economics, Wuppertal).

A Comment on "Under Pressure: European Electricity Markets and the Need for Reform"

Georg Zachmann

In this comment I want to put Nils-Hendrik von der Fehr's article into the broader context of efficient electricity sector design. To do that, I will separate three types of efficiency: (1) static efficiency that implies the cost-optimal usage of the existing system; (2) dynamic efficiency, which relates to the buildup of the cost-optimal system; and (3) innovation efficiency, which relates to the optimal development of new technologies.

I will argue that the current European electricity system is very far from the efficiency frontier in all definitions. In regard to (1), coal plants are being used instead of gas plants,[1] consumers use too much electricity,[2] and individual power plant operation schedules are not always coordinated throughout Europe in the cheapest technically feasible way.[3] I would argue that such static inefficiencies are regrettable, but their monetary value is limited compared to the overall cost of the electricity system.

As for (2), as capital costs are the largest component of the cost of the electricity system and many installations (power plants, transmission lines, and energy-intensive appliances) have economic lifetimes of 20 years or more, getting the investment decisions right is what will drive the future cost of energy services the most. Public intervention has made it such that market signals play virtually no role in these investment decisions. Wholesale electricity prices and emission allowance prices have fallen massively, as investments were triggered outside the market. National renewables support schemes, support schemes for nuclear and coal, and an increasing number of national capacity mechanisms are driving investments in generation. The likely result is an inefficiently large portfolio of power plants that is geographically and technologically unbalanced—this will cause massive excess cost to European consumers. Network regulation is also national. While some countries prefer to underinvest, arguably to avoid becoming energy-transit countries, others have overinvested to enable more exports. The resulting network development is in any case far from an efficient European layout. Finally, electricity prices in the European Union vary widely between Member States and consumer groups. This is not a reflection of the cost of the corresponding services, but a political choice based on social and industrial policy considerations. Consequently, many of the customer investments in more energy-efficient appliances cannot rely on good price signals. At the same time, energy efficiency standards for individual products (e.g., the famous light bulbs) force buyers to invest more in energy saving than sometimes would be justified by the saved energy cost.

As the market signals that were supposed to coordinate European investment decisions were undermined by massive national interventions, we are currently in a situation where investment decisions are no longer coordinated between Member States, between technologies, between locations, and between different parts of the value chain. There is no rational reason to believe that investment decisions in the EU electricity sector are anywhere close to the optimal point.

Finally, in terms of (3), in the very long run, the cost of the energy system is strongly driven by innovation. Despite continuously growing energy demand and the extraction of most easily reachable fossil reserves during the last two centuries, energy cost did not explode because an endless series of new technologies (for exploration, production, transformation, and consumption) have been invented (Smil 2010). Technology development also reacts to scarcity—but here it is well-accepted that the public will intervene to resolve market failures. In this context, many of the technology-specific support schemes (for renewables, energy efficiency, etc.) might make sense, as they create the—otherwise absent—market-pull that drives innovation. But the issue is, again, how to allocate the resources between so many technology options, how to best support them, and when to stop support. So far, there is not even a theoretical answer to this question—let alone a translation into policy. But as Europe spends hundreds of billions of euros on corresponding innovation policies, it is clear to me that we invest too little into understanding better what works well, and what does less good. To sum up, the European electricity system is far from the efficiency frontier in terms of usage, investment, and innovation.

Nils-Hendrik von der Fehr essentially argues that current market designs would largely be able to cope with static inefficiencies. He suggests sensible improvements in terms of responsiveness and flexibility as well as an integration of network and system operation. Most importantly, he calls for better integrating of markets across borders. He rightfully argues that this requires stronger European institutions.

These are all important points and I fully support his suggestions—some of which go significantly beyond the currently conducted process of harmonization through developing European network codes. Nils-Hendrik von der Fehr rightfully stresses that electricity services are differentiated across time and location, and that good market designs take the constraints to shift electricity across time or across space into account.

In terms of dynamic efficiencies, he implicitly follows the line of the European Commission, that getting the internal market right—and some more investments in cross-border networks—will, in the longer term, also generate sensible investment signals. Given all the aforementioned national policy interventions, I am less optimistic that we will see efficient investment/divestment signals in the EU electricity market anytime soon.

I would argue that in achieving an efficient electricity sector design, Nils-Hendrik von der Fehr's suggestions would be important steps toward a market-based cost-efficient coordination of usage, investment and innovation decisions. But significant and politically highly sensitive additional steps would be needed to make this vision work. These include creating truly European markets that provide sensible price signals for all relevant dimensions of electricity services (energy, location, time, emission, and capacity), restricting government interventions into the fuel mix to negative preferences (e.g., no shale gas or no nuclear), and orienting network development plans toward maximizing the total long-term welfare at the European level (Zachmann 2013). In addition, support for specific technologies should be done at the EU level, follow the classic "state aid" test (targeted, proportionate, and limited in time and scope) and avoid unexpectedly devaluing private assets without compensation. Otherwise, Europe will end up with highly complex and intrusive regulations ensuring the optimal European dispatch of power plants, but be unable to reap the true benefits of a European electricity market in terms of better-coordinated investment decisions.

Notes

1. Arguably, the emission allowance price is below the external cost of carbon emissions—hence, the market receives no incentive to prefer less CO_2-intensive natural gas plants over coal plants.

2. Regulated electricity prices for final consumers and targeted exemptions from network cost or emission cost for industrial consumers in many EU countries make it such that electricity prices do not reflect the full cost of the service.

3. For example, inner-German re-dispatch ignores power plants outside the German borders that might provide this flexibility more cheaply.

References

Smil, V. 2010. *Energy Transitions: History, Requirements, Prospects*. Westport, CT, US: Praeger Publishers.

Zachmann, G. 2013. "Electricity Without Borders: A Plan to Make the Internal Market Work." Bruegel Blueprint Series 20, Brussels, Belgium.

4 Reforming the EU Energy Tax Directive: Assessing the Options

Ian Parry and Herman Vollebergh[1]

Key Points for Policymakers

- The economic efficiency case for raising tax floors for fuels covered by the EU ETD is nuanced. Some fuels may be undertaxed—for example, road diesel and natural gas for heating—though, according to some (but not all) environmental damage estimates, others may already be adequately taxed or even overtaxed (for example, gasoline).
- Recent (though subsequently withdrawn) proposals to reform the ETD would increase some tax minima, including those for road diesel and natural gas, while leaving the gasoline tax floor unchanged. This would represent a step in the right direction, though the climate, fiscal, health, and net economic benefits are limited.
- There are potentially much larger gains from extending tax minima to fuels (especially coal) currently covered by the ETS (particularly if the ETS cap is tightened to maintain allowance prices).
- Two-speed systems (with lower tax minima for low-income countries) may improve the political acceptability of reform, while sacrificing little in terms of climate benefits.
- The benefits from ETD reforms are highly sensitive to the environmental damages from fuel use. Our damage assumptions appear to be at the lower end of the bandwidth of uncertainty, suggesting that there is a potentially strong case for reviving reform of the ETD, whatever its exact structure.

1. Introduction

The EU Energy Tax Directive (ETD) sets minimum tax rates for fuels—including motor fuels, heating fuels, and electricity—that Member

States typically need to incorporate in their national tax systems. The ETD is motivated by concerns about the environment and energy dependence, as well as containing tax competition (e.g., the risk of one country setting excessively low tax rates to attract mobile tax bases from other countries). Taxes or similar pricing instruments are potentially the most efficient policies for meeting environmental objectives (e.g., Parry et al. 2014, chapter 3) and their revenues lessen the burden on the broader fiscal system (an especially important concern in these days of historically high fiscal pressures).

Recent proposals for amending the ETD[2] seek to more effectively promote EU goals for reducing CO_2 emissions and improving energy efficiency.[3] Currently (see below), tax minima for (on-road) motor fuels favor diesel (which has higher energy content per liter) over gasoline, and minima for heating fuels moderately favor coal (the most CO_2 and air pollution–intensive fuel) over other fuels. Most coal is exempted, however, as it is used by large installations for the production of electricity, which are covered by the EU Emissions Trading System (ETS)—these fuels are currently exempt from the ETD on the principle of avoiding overlapping instruments.

The reform proposals would replace the current structure of volume-based rates with a charge on each fuel's carbon content, as well as harmonize charges on energy content within on-road transportation fuels and within heating/off-road transportation fuels. The reforms (phased in over several years) would, most notably, increase tax floors for diesel and especially for natural gas, while leaving that for gasoline unchanged. Although, in light of the little progress made since 2012, the reform proposal was withdrawn by the new Commission in March 2015, the issue is likely to resurface at some point with pressure for better harmonization of carbon prices across fuels as the European Union makes progress on its commitments to cut greenhouse gases, as reinforced by the 2015 Paris Agreement on climate change.

Besides requiring minimum prices on CO_2 emissions (a global pollutant) across fuels (both outside and within the ETS) and countries, it is difficult to provide specific guidance on what additional tax minima at the EU level might be efficient from a broader economic perspective. Although energy use is associated with other environmental side effects (air pollution, road congestion, etc.), to a large extent these are national in scope, and impacts vary substantially with local factors, so tax-setting for these environmental effects is generally better left to Member States. And while tax competition warrants coordination, the severity of the problem varies across fuels and countries (e.g., competition is more intense for trucks crossing several borders on one tank of fuel than for cars) and quantitative evidence is lacking on efficient tax minima.

Rather than attempting to estimate the fully efficient set of minimum tax rates for the ETD (an analytically challenging task!), this paper seeks, more modestly, to identify promising directions for reform, relative to the current situation. To do this, we provide a quantitative framework, based on a spreadsheet tool (populated with data for 2012), illustrating trade-offs across a range of possibilities for ETD reform in terms of metrics of concern to policymakers—CO_2 emissions, revenue, health impacts, and net economic benefits (environmental benefits less economic costs). Some reform possibilities simply consider more aggressive versions of recent proposals; however, some more radical alternatives, designed to increase environmental effectiveness and political acceptability, are also evaluated.

One reform extends the proposed CO_2 component of the ETD to fuels covered by the EU ETS, thereby establishing a floor price under ETS emissions, some form of which is needed (see Hepburn and Teytelboym, this volume, and Edenhofer et al., this volume) in light of low and volatile emissions prices (recently hovering around €8 per ton of CO_2). In addition, given that an obstacle to ETD reform has been concerns about higher minimum taxes among newer (lower-income) Member States, another reform entails a two-speed system granting these states less stringent tax floors.

Although our numbers are illustrative (e.g., it is difficult to project how tax rates that are formally non-binding might respond to higher tax floors), three general themes emerge from the discussion.

First, directionally, the recent ETD reform proposals seem to make economic sense. The case for increasing gasoline and electricity taxes is debatable. According to some, though not all, assessments, gasoline excise taxes may already charge for environmental costs like global warming, local pollution, congestion, and accidents; cross-border tax competition is mainly localized; and taxes on vehicles (or in the longer term, kilometers driven) may be more efficient instruments for raising revenue (as their tax bases are generally less mobile). And higher electricity tax floors are poorly targeted at emissions. The case for increasing the diesel tax floor is, however, more compelling, given higher environmental costs than for gasoline, more intense tax competition, and the currently favorable tax treatment of diesel. Similarly, the current tax floor for natural gas is below levels needed to reflect environmental costs. Existing reform proposals would, however, have limited environmental and fiscal effects, cutting EU CO_2 emissions and air pollution deaths each by about 1.5 percent, while raising revenues averaging 0.2 percent of gross domestic product (GDP).

A second theme, on the other hand, is the greater environmental and economic benefits of extending the ETD to fuels covered under the ETS, or just to coal used by power generators, as well as the fiscal benefits from extracting rents that would otherwise go to holders of free ETS allowances. In either case, EU CO_2 emissions would fall by around 4-5 percent (with a tightening of the ETS cap to maintain current allowance prices), and air pollution deaths around 5-7 percent, while raising new revenue on average of around 0.5 percent of GDP and generating net economic benefits several times larger than confining ETD reforms to non-ETS fuels.

A third theme is that two-speed systems (where increases in tax minima for low-income countries are half those for other countries) need not sacrifice a great deal in terms of climate benefits—EU CO_2 emissions reductions are still around 90 percent or more of those when low-income countries are subject to the same tax floors as other countries.

In sum, there does not appear to be a huge amount at stake—in quantitative terms—in the reform of the ETD as recently proposed. Much more effective from an environmental, fiscal, and economic perspective would be an extension of the ETD to ETS fuels, most importantly coal, even if lower-income countries were granted less stringent tax floors.

The rest of the paper is organized as follows. The next section provides background on the current ETD and proposed changes, current energy use, and taxation across the European Union, and efficient design of energy taxes from a national and EU perspective. Section 3 suggests alternative reform possibilities and presents (based on the spreadsheet tool described in the appendix) rough calculations of the environmental, fiscal, health, and economic impacts of these reforms. Section 4 offers concluding remarks.

2.   Background

2.1   The Current and Proposed ETD: A Closer Look

Introduced in 2003, the ETD sets minimum tax rates for five motor fuels—gasoline, diesel, kerosene, liquefied petroleum gas (LPG), and natural gas—making a distinction between on-road and off-road uses.

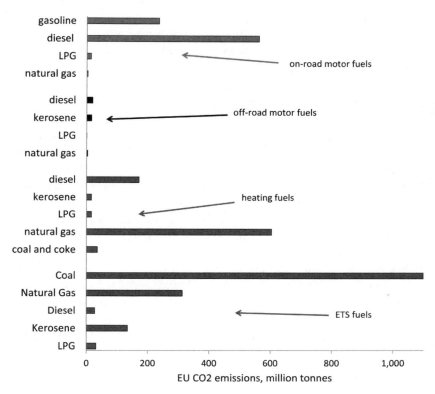

Figure 4.1
CO_2 emissions from ETD and ETS fuels, 2012
Source: See appendix B.
Note: Non-ETS fuels include on-road motor fuels, off-road motor fuels, and heating fuels.

Also covered are six heating fuels—diesel, heavy fuel oil, kerosene, LPG, natural gas, and coal/coke—as well as electricity.[4]

Figure 4.1 provides a sense of the importance of different fossil fuels in terms of their contribution to EU CO_2 emissions in 2012, along with emissions sources covered by the ETS (coal, natural gas, diesel, kerosene, LPG).[5] The discussion below is confined to the more important fuels from a CO_2 perspective—gasoline and diesel for on- and off-road motor fuels; diesel, natural gas, and coke/coal for heating fuels; and the five ETS fuels mainly used to generate electricity and for process heating in industry. Even combined, all the excluded fuels account for only 1.7 percent of EU-wide CO_2 emissions from fossil fuel combustion.

Currently, tax floors are generally set on a volume basis and recently proposed reforms (see table 4.1) would have changed them into taxes both on energy content—€9.6 per gigajoule (GJ) for on-road motor fuels and €0.15 per GJ for off-road motor fuels and heating fuels—and a charge of €20 per ton of CO_2 emissions.[6]

The tax minima for gasoline is currently €359 per 1,000 liters and the proposed ETD would leave this rate unchanged, but align other motor fuel taxes so that implied charges for CO_2 and energy content are the same as for gasoline. The net result would be to increase the (on-road) diesel fuel tax by 18 percent from €330 to €390 per 1,000 liters, or 8 percent higher than for gasoline (diesel fuel produces about 16 percent more CO_2 emissions per liter compared to gasoline, see OECD 2014). For on-road motor fuels, the proposed charge for carbon emissions would only represent a minor portion (about 13 percent) of the total tax minima (table 4.1).

For off-road diesel, the tax is much smaller at €57 per 1,000 liters, reflecting the much lower tax rate on energy content (lower tax rates might have some justification on environmental grounds to the extent that off-road vehicles such as tractors are driven on farms rather than contributing to road congestion, accidents, and urban pollution). Nonetheless, the proposed minima for off-road diesel would be 173 percent higher than the current minima.

In regard to heating fuels, the carbon charge accounts for around 90 percent of the proposed tax minima (table 4.1). Given relatively light, or in some cases zero, tax minima for these floors at present, the proposed floors still represent substantial increases in proportionate terms; for example, a 767 percent increase for natural gas. Member States are granted the option to exempt households from these taxes, though this possibility is not considered in the modeling below. For electricity, there is no change in the floor tax.

2.2 Current Energy Taxes

Table 4.2 shows, for a selection of ten Member States, the difference (in €/GJ) between energy taxes in 2012 and the proposed tax minima for 2018, a negative cell indicating cases where proposed floor increases would be formally binding. Floor increases are binding in some cases; for example, in four countries for non-road diesel and seven for natural gas for heating, and no countries for gasoline and electricity (where floor taxes do not change).

Table 4.1
Existing and Proposed Tax Floors for Energy Products

Sources: EC (2011a) and appendix B.

Notes: The proposed tax floors refer to those in EC (2011a, tables A–D), that were subsequently withdrawn in 2015. The rates shown for natural gas (heating and off-road motor fuels, coal and coke, and electricity) are the business rates (non-business rates are twice as high).

Energy product	Units	Comparison of current and proposed tax floors			Tax minima in €/GJ		Components of proposed floors		
		Existing EU law (since 2003)	Proposed (for 2018)	Percent change	Existing EU law (since 2003)	Proposed (for 2018)	CO$_2$-related €/ton CO$_2$	Energy-related €/GJ	Percent share of CO$_2$ charge in tax
On-road motor fuels									
Gasoline	€/1000 l	359	359	0	10.8	10.8	20	9.6	12.5
Diesel	€/1000 l	330	390	18	9.2	10.9	20	9.6	13.3
Kerosene	€/1000 l	330	392	19	9.1	10.8	20	9.6	13.0
LPG	€/1000 kg	125	500	300	2.7	10.7	20	9.6	11.3
Natural gas	€/GJ	2.6	10.7	312	2.6	10.7	20	9.6	10.4
Heating fuels and off-road motor fuels									
Diesel	€/1000 l	21	57	173	0.1	0.3	20	0.15	90.7
Heavy fuel oil	€/1000 kg	15	68	352	0.1	0.3	20	0.15	90.7
Kerosene	€/1000 l	21	56	168	0.1	0.3	20	0.15	90.7
LPG	€/1000 kg	0	65	na	0	0.3	20	0.15	89.1
Natural gas	€/GJ	0.15	1.3	767	0.15	1.3	20	0.15	88.2
Coal and coke	€/GJ	0.15	2	1,233	0.15	2.0	20	0.15	92.6
Electricity	€/MWh	0.5	0.5	0	0.2	0.2	0	0.15	0

Table 4.2
Difference between Current Tax (2012) and Proposed Minima (for 2018) for Some EU Member States
Source: EC (2011a) and appendix B.

Energy product	Austria	Bulgaria	Czech Republic	France	Germany	Hungary	Netherlands	Poland	Spain	United Kingdom
On-road motor fuels										
Gasoline	4.3	0.6	3.8	5.9	7.9	1.4	10.3	0.6	2.4	9.7
Diesel	0.9	-1.9	0.8	0.1	1.7	-0.3	0.9	-1.6	-1.0	8.3
Heating fuels and off-road motor fuels										
Diesel	2.8	-0.3	0.5	1.3	1.4	-0.3	-0.3	1.2	2.0	3.4
Natural gas	1.6	-1.3	-0.6	-1.0	0.2	-1.3	3.4	-1.3	-1.3	-1.3
Coal/coke	-0.3	-2.0	-2.0	-2.0	-2.0	-2.0	-2.0	-2.0	-2.0	-2.0
Electricity	4.0	0.2	0.2	6.4	20.4	1.3	2.0	1.2	2.3	0.2

Excise duty on motor fuels in the EU

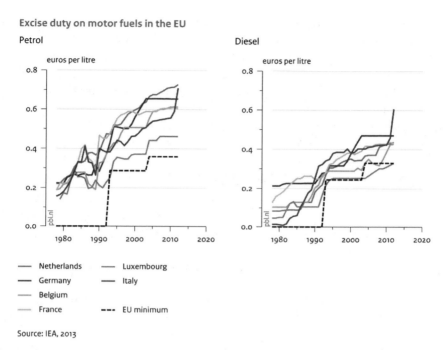

Source: IEA, 2013

Figure 4.2
Excise duty on motor fuels in selected EU countries, 1980–2015

However, table 4.2 provides only a lower-bound calculation of the impact of higher tax floors on tax rates. Economic theory suggests that tax floors can increase tax rates, even in countries where the rates are non-binding. The basic reason for this is the reduced threat of tax competition—countries might be emboldened to set higher tax rates in their own (fiscal or environmental) national interest with less risk of other countries poaching the tax base through cutting their own taxes.[7] Figure 4.2 provides some suggestive evidence for this. The modeling below takes an intermediate scenario between the cases when tax floors do and do not affect non-binding tax rates.[8]

2.3   Efficient Energy Taxation
This subsection discusses efficient energy taxation from an environmental and fiscal perspective, in each case exploring possible reasons to coordinate taxes at the EU level.

Environmental Considerations   *Climate change.* CO_2 is a global pollutant and international efforts to mitigate it have been hampered by the "free rider" problem (the reluctance of an individual country to incur mitigation costs when the climate benefits largely accrue to other countries). An EU-wide minimum CO_2 price, aligned to the global environmental cost of CO_2 emissions, makes economic sense (allowing individual countries to set higher prices if they wish to, for example, for domestic environmental, fiscal, or altruistic reasons). The appropriate value on CO_2 emissions is contentious, though for illustrative purposes below, a value of €25 per ton of CO_2 for 2012 is used.[9]

Other environmental impacts.   Fossil fuel energy use is also associated with other environmental side effects, or externalities, most importantly local air pollution and various externalities (e.g., congestion) from vehicles. These other impacts vary considerably across fuel products and countries and warrant additional tax measures rather than adjustments to CO_2 prices.

   As for air pollution, the main problem is elevated mortality risks to people breathing fine particulates (emitted directly during fuel combustion, or produced indirectly from chemical transformations in the atmosphere of other pollutants). WHO (2014) put outdoor air pollution deaths at 243,000 across the European Union in 2010, though mortality rates vary substantially across countries, from 0.1 annual deaths per 1,000 people in Finland and Sweden to 1.2 deaths per 1,000 in Bulgaria. These differences are due, for example, to differences in the intensity of coal and diesel use (the most polluting fuels), use of emissions control technologies (like sulfur dioxide scrubbers), and the density of populations exposed to emissions.

   Emissions released from tall smokestacks (e.g., coal plants) can be transported long distances, crossing national borders.[10] In principle, cross-border pollution calls for policy coordination, though involving only a limited number of affected countries. Emissions released closer to ground level (e.g., from cars or houses) tend to remain locally concentrated, limiting cross-border impacts. Local air pollution is therefore more efficiently addressed by national, or perhaps neighboring, governments, given that much of the damage occurs within national borders. Moreover, within the European Union, cross-border impacts are already taken into account through its air pollution policy.[11] Nonetheless, until polluters are fully charged for environmental damages through taxes or similar instruments (and recent estimates for the European Union suggest that this is not yet the case), reform of the ETD can still increase economic efficiency to the extent that there are unpriced local health benefits.

As regards other vehicle externalities, the main ones are congestion (costs that drivers impose on other road users through adding to delays on busy roads), accidents (risks drivers pose to pedestrians and other vehicle occupants and to third parties through property damages, medical costs, and so on), and wear and tear on the road network (mainly caused by vehicles with heavy axle weights). All of these externalities are better addressed through other measures than fuel taxes (e.g., de Borger and Proost, this volume), such as peak-period congestion fees and kilometer-based tolls on trucks related to their axle weight, and set at a national or sub-national level. Until these novel pricing instruments are comprehensively implemented, however, economic efficiency requires reflecting all these environmental costs in existing fuel taxes.[12] To the extent that ETD reforms push national fuel taxes up toward efficient levels, they yield net economic efficiency benefits, and vice versa if they push taxes (that are already excessive) further beyond the efficient level.

There are possibilities for cross-border externalities here as well—most notably, the external costs associated with truck driving may occur in countries other than where trucks re-fuel (and pay tax), given the long distances they can travel on a tank of fuel. But again, the ideal charges to reflect these cross-border externalities are highly location-specific and a minimum tax applied across the European Union would be a blunt instrument.[13]

Comparing existing and environmentally efficient fuel taxes. Figures 4.3-4.6 compare fuel excises in 2012 and (where applicable) ETD tax floors with some (albeit rough) estimates of efficient or "corrective" taxes needed to reflect external costs. The presented estimates are based on recent work by the IMF (methods underlying the quantification of externalities are summarized in appendix A). The absolute level of the estimates appears somewhat at the lower end of the uncertainty bound and should therefore be treated with care.[14]

As regards gasoline, the IMF estimates of corrective taxes (shown in figure 4.3) are typically between about €0.30 and €0.60 per liter, with congestion usually the biggest component, followed by traffic accidents, then carbon damages—a more modest €0.06 per liter—and local air pollution even less. For most countries, the efficient tax estimates

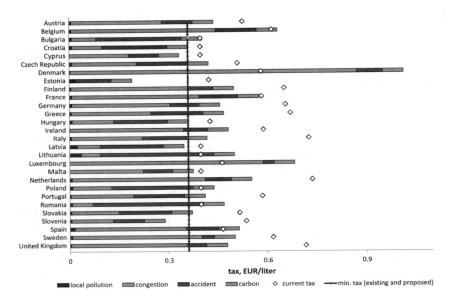

Figure 4.3
Corrective gasoline tax estimates and current taxes, EU countries, 2012
Sources: Parry et al. (2014) for corrective tax estimates (updated for inflation) and see below for current taxes.
Note: Local pollution damages for Luxembourg and Malta are not available from the data.

are in the ballpark of the ETD minimum rate (€0.36 per liter), or somewhat above it. However, existing taxes are significantly above the ETD minima and generally exceed corrective levels. This does not necessarily imply that fuel taxes should be reduced, given fiscal reasons for taxes and the fact that estimates of efficient taxes are imprecise and perhaps on the low side (see below), but it does at least suggest that a substantial increase in gasoline taxes (induced through a higher EU tax floor) is questionable on externality grounds.

For diesel fuel use (averaged across cars and heavier road vehicles), the corrective tax levels tend to be a bit higher than for gasoline, mainly because local air pollution costs are more substantial, and tax rates tend to be a bit lower, falling short of corrective levels in the majority of cases (figure 4.4). The case for increasing the tax floor for diesel on externality grounds therefore looks more compelling than for gasoline, particularly as the current floor is below that for gasoline.

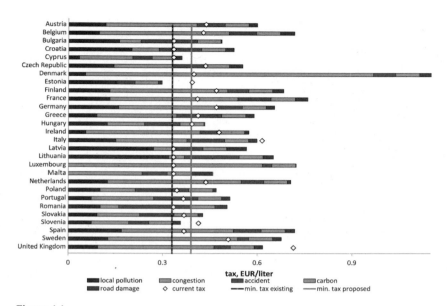

Figure 4.4
Corrective diesel tax estimates and current taxes, EU countries, 2012

Sources: Parry et al. (2014) for corrective tax estimates (updated for inflation) and see below for current taxes.

Note: Local pollution damages for Luxembourg and Malta are not available from the data.

As regards natural gas, the proposed increase would bring the tax minima much closer to levels warranted on environmental (mostly climate) grounds, though a number of countries already impose taxes exceeding the proposed floor (figure 4.5). Paradoxically, there is no tax floor for coal used in the ETS and where environmentally efficient taxes are much larger (figure 4.2) due to higher CO_2 emission rates per unit of energy (about 40 percent higher than for natural gas) and much higher air pollution emission rates. In fact, local air pollution costs exceed climate damages for the majority of countries, often by a substantial amount (especially in densely populated countries with limited deployment of air emissions control technologies). Countries do not generally impose excise taxes on coal, and implicit charges for CO_2 emissions through the ETS accounted for only about 30 percent of the assumed climate damages in 2012.

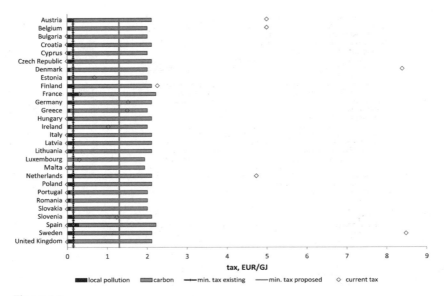

Figure 4.5
Corrective natural gas tax estimates and current taxes, EU countries, 2012

Sources: Parry et al. (2014) for corrective tax estimates (updated for inflation) and see below for current taxes.

Notes: Local air pollution is estimated for ground-level sources (e.g., households), though estimates for power plant emissions are similar. Local pollution damages for Luxembourg and Malta are not available from the data.

Fiscal Considerations   We begin here with some basic tax principles from a domestic perspective, and then consider tax competition issues.

Domestic revenue considerations.   One basic tax principle is that consumer goods, including residential electricity, heating, and passenger car fuels, are legitimate bases of taxation on fiscal grounds, but intermediate inputs, including industrial electricity and heating and truck fuels, are not. Taxing intermediate inputs at rates higher than those needed to reflect external costs would distort the way firms do business, causing them to use too little of the taxed input, and too much of other inputs, than would be efficient from society's perspective.[15]

Another principle is that all consumer goods should generally be taxed at the same ad valorem rate to avoid distorting relative consumer prices, and hence household choices over different goods, though there can be a case for additional taxation in specific cases. Without getting

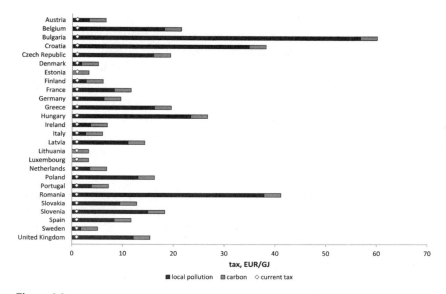

Figure 4.6
Corrective coal tax estimates and current taxes, EU countries, 2012

Sources: Parry et al. (2014) for corrective tax estimates (updated for inflation) and the coal tax is inferred from an ETS CO_2 price of €8 per ton.

Notes: Local air pollution damages are for power plant emissions. Estimates are not available for Estonia, Lithuania, and Luxembourg. Cyprus and Malta do not use coal.

into the technicalities, the case for additional taxation is potentially stronger if (up to a point) the product's tax base is relatively less mobile than tax bases for broader fiscal instruments. This can be the case if broader instruments cause a lot of distortion to economic activity (e.g., promoting black market activity, discouraging labor supply, causing tax-sheltering in housing, fringe benefits, or other tax-preferred activities).

These possibilities have been explored in the U.S. literature, with studies finding that on balance, fiscal considerations may warrant significant additional gasoline taxation beyond levels warranted by externalities (e.g., West and Williams 2007; Parry 2011). The estimates are imprecise, and could be somewhat higher or lower for different EU countries and for other energy products (depending, for example, on the specifics of countries' tax systems and behavioral responses to energy and broader tax changes), but the general point is valid: fiscal considerations may warrant setting excise tax rates on household energy products above levels needed to reflect external costs.[16]

On closer inspection, however, within the energy sector there are some taxes, like simple taxes on vehicle sales, vehicle ownership, or residential electricity, that have more immobile bases—and therefore are potentially even more attractive from a revenue-raising perspective than fuel taxes.[17] In fact, using just one tax instrument for two conflicting objectives sets up an inherent tension—the more environmentally effective the policy, the less revenue will be raised. This tension might be avoided by tailoring taxes on fuels to environmental objectives and taxes on vehicles and residential electricity to fiscal objectives. In fact, this is what many EU countries are already doing.[18]

Tax competition issues. A further complication, and one that may lead countries to set inefficiently low fuel taxes, is the potential for tax competition. National governments may be tempted to set taxes too low (from an international perspective) if this encourages domestic fuel purchases from cross-border sales, thereby appropriating some of the revenue base from other countries (without necessarily adding to domestic environmental costs).

The severity of tax competition varies across fuel products, however. Evers et al. (2004) find significant evidence of tax competition over diesel fuel within the European Union, not surprisingly given that trucks can drive 1,500-3,000 kilometers on a tank of fuel, allowing considerable flexibility over where to re-fuel. Tax competition for car fuels (gasoline and diesel) is generally less intense, given that most driving from a tank of fuel is contained within one country, though geographically small, landlocked states may have strong incentives to set lower tax rates to encourage cross-border purchases (see the example of Luxembourg in figure 4.2).

Summary The environmental case for substantially higher tax floors within the existing structure of the ETD is nuanced given that, according to estimates used here, current tax rates for gasoline exceed environmentally efficient taxes (though this is not a universal finding across studies). Current tax floors for diesel and natural gas, in contrast, are generally below levels warranted on environmental grounds. The degree of undercharging is most pronounced for coal—ironically, as coal use is mostly excluded from the ETD and also in the recent ETD reform proposals. Revenue-raising considerations may warrant some further taxation of household (but not industry) fuels, though other instruments are potentially more efficient from a fiscal perspective.

Conversely, tax competition suggests a stronger case for coordinating over taxes for intermediate fuels (for trucks) rather than household fuels (for cars), though solid analytical work quantifying the efficient level of the tax floor is lacking.

3.   Comparing Reform Possibilities

Leaving aside theoretical ambiguities in the case for higher EU energy tax minima, this section provides some quantitative sense of the environmental, fiscal, and economic welfare trade-offs across a wide spectrum of possibilities for reforming the ETD. We begin with the motivations for finding alternative options, briefly outline the methodology, and then present the results.

3.1   Motivation for Alternative Options

Eight options for reforming the ETD are considered, including four cases meant to roughly span the range of possibilities for different tax rate structures, but each done with and without a two-speed system involving increases in tax floors (relative to the current situation) that are 50 percent smaller for lower-income Member States than other states. Specific tax rate changes are discussed below and the focus in the results discussion is on effects aggregated to the EU level. All scenarios are based on data for 2012, comparing counter-factual situations for that year had different tax regimes been in place.

Lower-income Member States are defined as countries with per capita income below €15,000 in 2012. These include Bulgaria, Croatia, the Czech Republic, Estonia, Hungary, Latvia, Lithuania, Poland, Romania, and Slovakia. Collectively, these countries accounted for 19 percent of EU CO_2 emissions in 2012, so the emissions impact of granting them laxer tax floors will not be that dramatic. Their share of EU air pollution deaths is larger, however, at 51 percent, so relative differences in health outcomes between one- and two-speed reforms are more pronounced.

The four cases for higher tax floors include:

1. The recently proposed ETD (discussed in section 2 and indicated by comparing the fourth and third columns in table 4.1, or the sixth and seventh columns) by itself.
2. Establishing a €20 per ton charge on CO_2 emissions from ETS fuels, combined with (1). The key question here is how the ETS would be adjusted. We assume that the supply of allowances is reduced

accordingly to maintain the 2012 allowance price of €8 per ton on top of the new tax floor, implying a total price on ETS emissions of €28 per ton, which is equal to the (marginal) climate change damage we assume throughout this paper. If instead the supply of allowances is held fixed, allowance prices would (temporarily) drop to zero as the tax floor renders the ETS non-binding.[19]

3. A tax minimum of €3 per GJ for coal consumption across both ETS and non-ETS sectors, combined with (1). This is equivalent to (on average) a charge of about €28 per ton of CO_2 from coal use.[20] Again, ETS allowances are reduced to maintain the €8 per ton allowance price (on top of the coal tax).

4. Higher tax minima for the main road fuels, combined with (1). Specifically, the tax floor for gasoline is increased from €359 to €415 per 1,000 liters and the tax floor for diesel is increased from €330 to €450 per 1,000 liters.

3.2 Methodology

Appendix B provides details on the spreadsheet and data used to generate rough calculations of the impacts of alternative reforms. For each of the 28 EU member countries, 11 fuel use categories potentially subject to (changes in or new) tax minima are considered—three motor fuels (on-road gasoline, on-road diesel, and off-road diesel), three heating fuels (diesel, natural gas, and coal/coke), and five primary ETS fuels (coal, natural gas, diesel, kerosene, and LPG).

Changes in fuel taxes in response to higher tax floors are based on splitting the difference between two bounding cases, one in which taxes increase in line with tax minima only in those countries where rates are currently, or become, binding, and the other in which all tax rates increase by the same absolute amount as the increase in the floor tax. Tax changes are passed forward in higher fuel prices and fuels change according to simple assumptions about (long-run) fuel price elasticities (ignoring cross-price effects among fuels). The CO_2, health, revenue, and economic welfare impacts of these changes in fuel use are computed[21] and aggregated over fuel products and countries.

3.3 Quantitative Assessment

This section compares the reform scenarios described above in terms of their impacts, indicating the contribution of broad fuel groupings— motor fuels, other non-ETS fuels or heating, and ETS fuels. The numbers are useful in providing a broad sense of the impacts of different policy

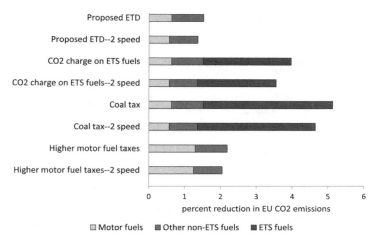

Figure 4.7
EU-wide CO_2 impacts of tax reforms, 2012
Source: Authors' calculations (see appendix B).

scenarios, though they should not be taken too literally (e.g., given uncertainty over parameters and how actual tax rates might respond to higher tax floors).

CO_2 Emissions   Figure 4.7 shows the percent reduction in EU-wide CO_2 emissions from alternative tax reform possibilities; that is, the reductions compared with actual 2012 levels had these higher tax floors been in place. To put the figures in perspective, actual CO_2 emissions in 2012 were 3,776 million tons, or nearly 10 percent below 1990 levels (the reference point for future emissions targets).

The proposed ETD reduces EU-wide CO_2 emissions by an estimated 1.5 percent, with two-fifths coming from reduced motor fuel consumption (i.e., diesel fuel as the gasoline tax floor is unchanged) and three-fifths from reduced heating fuel consumption (assuming, as noted above, no exemptions from tax increases). The higher motor fuel tax scenario pushes the CO_2 reductions up to 2.2 percent, though effects are limited.[22]

Achieving more substantial reductions in CO_2 emissions requires extending tax reforms to ETS fuels, either through directly pricing CO_2 or taxing coal—EU-wide CO_2 emissions are reduced by 4.0 percent in the former policy scenario and by 5.1 percent in the latter. Both of these extensions have a substantial effect on coal prices (given that coal is the most carbon-intensive fuel), and even though the price responsiveness

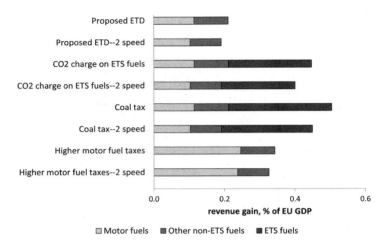

Figure 4.8
EU-wide revenue impacts of tax reforms, 2012
Source: Authors' calculations (see appendix B).

of coal is smaller than for road fuels, the EU-wide reduction in coal use is still 6 and 11 percent respectively.

Also noteworthy is that the two-speed structures allowing less stringent tax floors for lower-income members states do not sacrifice a large amount in terms of CO_2 reductions. Reductions are about 5-10 percent smaller than when all countries are subject to the same tax floors.

Revenue Figure 4.8 shows total revenues raised from the reform scenarios, expressed as a percent of EU-wide GDP (and accounting for any revenue losses from pre-existing fuel taxes from erosion of the tax base).

The proposed ETD raises revenues of 0.2 percent of GDP (averaged across the European Union) with about half coming from higher motor taxes and half from higher taxes for heating fuels. Extending the tax base to ETS CO_2 emissions more than doubles revenues, to 0.45 percent of EU GDP, while the scenarios with coal taxes and higher motor fuel taxes each raise revenues of 0.50 and 0.34 percent of GDP respectively. Aggregate revenues are 5-10 percent lower under the two-speed structures across the different scenarios, though proportionate impacts are bigger in low-income Member States (up to about 20 percent lower).

Health Impacts Figure 4.9 shows the percent reduction in premature air pollution deaths from fossil fuel air pollution.

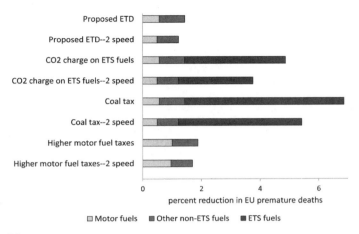

Figure 4.9
EU-wide health impacts of tax reforms, 2012
Source: Authors' calculations (see appendix B).

The proposed ETD has fairly modest health benefits—a reduction in air pollution deaths of 1.4 percent, with two-fifths coming from reductions in motor fuels and three-fifths from reductions in heating fuels. Heating fuels like natural gas do not really produce the pollutants (direct fine particulates and sulfur dioxide) that are especially harmful to human health, and although diesel fuel accounts for about 15 percent of premature air pollution deaths in the European Union, the proposed ETD only cuts diesel use by 4 percent. Again, extending the ETD to the ETS, or taxing coal, yields significantly bigger health benefits—4.9 percent and 6.9 percent, respectively—given that ETS coal accounts for two-thirds of air pollution deaths.[23] Under the two-speed scenarios, health benefits for lower income countries are typically around a third smaller than when they are subject to the same tax floors as other countries.

Economic Impacts   Finally, figure 4.10 illustrates the net economic welfare benefits from the policy reforms expressed as a percent of EU GDP. Net benefits are much larger, between 0.1 and 0.2 percent of GDP, when tax floors cover coal or ETS fuels. Again, this reflects the relatively large economic efficiency gains from taxing coal, the fuel where there is currently the largest discrepancy (by far) between the efficient level of taxation to charge for environmental costs and current taxation.

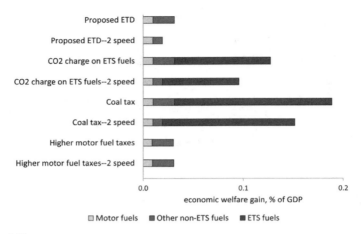

Figure 4.10
EU-wide economic welfare gains, 2012
Source: Authors' calculations (see appendix B).

4. Conclusion

The economic efficiency basis (as well as political support) for energy tax harmonization at the EU level remains unsettled. There is a clear case for minimum prices to reflect carbon emissions; however, this applies equally to fuels within the ETS (and not currently covered by the proposed ETD). There are important externalities (e.g., air pollution) besides carbon emissions, but their severity varies with local conditions and setting of tax rates is generally better left to Member States (with some additional coordination with the current EU air quality directive where needed). There are some tax competition issues (e.g., truck drivers re-tanking in countries where fuel prices are lowest), though quantitative estimates of efficient tax floors at the EU level are lacking.

Although the existing ETD reform proposals from 2011 would be a step in the right direction, illustrative calculations presented here suggest that the climate, fiscal, health, and net economic gains would be relatively modest. There are potentially much larger gains from extending tax minima to fuels (especially coal) covered by the ETS, though this would undermine the trading system (by driving allowance prices to zero) in the short run if the current emissions cap would not be adapted accordingly. Given the political challenges of reaching unanimity over common tax floors across the 28 EU Member States, policymakers might consider the possibility of two-speed systems with less stringent floors for lower-income states, and this would have a relatively modest sacrifice in terms of EU carbon emissions.

Finally, it should be noted that our estimates of the environmental costs of fuel use are at the lower end of the bandwidth of uncertainty that inherently surrounds such estimates. The case for a revival of ETD reform—whatever its exact structure—strongly increase with much higher environmental benefits from reform.

Appendix A: Methodology Underlying Environmental Damage Estimates

This appendix discusses the valuation of air pollution damages from stationary sources, and externalities from motor vehicles, developed in Parry et al. (2014) and used above to infer efficient fuel taxes (external costs are updated from 2010 to 2012 using the EU consumer price index).

Air pollution from coal and natural gas. The key air pollutant from a public health perspective is fine particulate matter ($PM_{2.5}$, with diameter up to 2.5 micrometers), which is small enough to penetrate the lungs and bloodstream. $PM_{2.5}$ can be emitted directly during fuel combustion, or formed indirectly through chemical reactions in the atmosphere involving sulfur dioxide (SO_2) and nitrogen oxides (NO_x).

Parry et al. (2014) assess damages from these pollutants for coal plants by first estimating "intake fractions"—the fraction of these emissions that are inhaled by exposed populations as $PM_{2.5}$. They begin with estimates (Zhou et al. 2006) of these fractions for the average coal plant in China, where these estimates account for exposure to people living up to 2,000 km from plants. Intake fractions are then extrapolated to other countries depending on the number of people living at different distance classifications from the average coal plant in that country relative to number of people living in those distance classifications in China. This is done by mapping data on the geographical location of coal plants in individual countries to very granular, spatial population data.

Intake fractions are then linked to mortality risks. Baseline mortality rates for diseases (e.g., lung cancer, heart disease, strokes) whose prevalence is potentially increased by pollution exposure are obtained for different countries from the World Health Organization's (WHO)

Global Burden of Disease (GBD) project. These baseline mortality rates are then related to evidence (again from GBD) on how the relative risk for each disease increases with the rate at which pollution is inhaled, to give health impacts per ton of emissions for the three air pollutants.

Health risks are then monetized using evidence from several hundred studies, compiled by OECD (2012), on how people in different countries are willing to give up income to reduce these risks. They find that each 1 percent increase in per capita income raises people's willingness to pay for health risk reductions by 0.8 percent and that, for the average OECD country, peoples' valuation of health risks implies a benefit of $3.7 million per premature death avoided. Parry et al. (2014) extrapolate this evidence to obtain health valuations at the individual country level.

Finally, environmental damages can be expressed per GJ of coal energy using country-level estimates of emissions rates per GJ—that is, the damage per GJ is the emission rate per GJ, times the damage per ton of emissions, summed over the three pollutants.

Parry et al. (2014) used the same approach to estimate air pollution damages per GJ of natural gas from power plants, though these damages are far more moderate as gas produces essentially no direct $PM_{2.5}$ and SO_2, and is also less NO_x intensive than coal. Air pollution damages for gas used in residences and industry were estimated in the same way as for motor fuels (see below) but, since the estimates are similar to those for gas power plants, the latter are used for all natural gas usage.

Vehicle externalities. Air emissions from motor fuel combustion are released close to the ground and tend to remain locally concentrated rather than being dispersed over large distances. For these fuels, Parry et al. (2014) extrapolate national average intake fractions for emissions in different countries from a large city-level database. Mortality effects and monetary damages are then inferred using the same procedures as above, and damages are expressed per liter of fuel use, based on country-level vehicle emission rates.

For the congestion component of corrective motor fuel taxes, Parry et al. (2014) start with average travel delay—the difference between the time taken to drive a kilometer at prevailing speeds and the time that would be taken at free-flow speeds—extrapolated to each country from a database containing 90 cities in different countries. Statistical regressions were used to relate travel delays to various transportation indicators at the city level, and then country-level delays were predicted using the regression coefficients and country-level data for the same transportation indicators.

Marginal delay (the delay one vehicle imposes on other vehicles) is taken to be four times the average delay, based on specifications that are commonly used by transportation engineers. Marginal delays are converted into passenger delays by scaling by car occupancy and are then expressed in monetary costs using the value of travel time that, based on reviews of empirical literature, is taken to be 60 percent of the market wage. Finally, marginal congestion costs are scaled back by a third, based on evidence suggesting that travel on congested roads (which is dominated by commuters) is less responsive to higher fuel prices than travel on uncongested roads. As discussed in Parry et al. (2014, ch. 5), there are a number of reasons why their overall approach might result in an understatement of congestion costs.

Parry et al. (2014) assess accident externalities by first breaking out country-level data on traffic fatalities into those assumed to reflect external risks (not considered by drivers), including pedestrian/cyclist fatalities and a fraction of fatalities to other vehicle occupants in multi-vehicle collisions, as opposed to risks that drivers take into account, including the risk of drivers killing themselves in single- and multi-vehicle collisions. Fatality risks are monetized using the same mortality values as used for pollution deaths. Other external costs (e.g., non-fatal injuries to pedestrians/cyclists and other vehicle occupants or medical/property damages borne by third parties) are extrapolated to other countries from a limited number of country case studies.

Lastly, Parry et al. (2014) measure the external costs of road damage by countries' spending on road maintenance, scaled back by 50 percent to make an adjustment for the role of weather in road deterioration.

Combined external costs from motor fuel use are summarized by corrective fuel taxes. For gasoline, corrective taxes are based on externalities from cars, and for diesel, on a weighted average of externalities from (diesel) cars and heavy vehicles with weights equal to the respective fuel shares of these vehicles. In computing corrective taxes, congestion, accident, and road damage, externalities are scaled back to take into account the fact that only about half of the tax-induced reduction in fuel use comes from reductions in vehicle kilometers driven (the other fraction comes from longer-run improvements in the average fuel efficiency of the vehicle fleet, which do not reduce these externalities).

Appendix B: Methodology and Data Sources for Assessing ETD Reform Possibilities

The modeling results discussed above are based on a spreadsheet tool populated, for the 28 EU member countries, with the following data:

- consumption of major fuel categories under the ETD and the ETS;
- prices for these fuels;
- fuel excises taxes;
- minimum tax rates under the current ETD and various scenarios for tax reform;
- CO_2 emission rates;
- premature deaths from air pollution attributed to different fuels;
- efficient fuel taxes to reflect environmental damages;
- fuel price elasticities; and
- miscellaneous data—GDP and exchange rates.

The spreadsheet calculates the change in tax for a particular fuel, in a particular country, implied by various reforms (see below). Any tax increases are assumed to be fully passed forward into higher prices for fuel users. In turn, fuel demand is reduced in response to higher prices according to fuel price elasticities, implying changes in CO_2 emissions, tax revenues, air pollution deaths, and economic welfare. These responses are meant to capture changes in fuel use after full adjustment—short-run dynamics (e.g., as the vehicle fleet turns over gradually in response to higher fuel prices) are beyond our scope, partly as they would require a far more complicated model. Cross-price effects (e.g., substitution from diesel to gasoline vehicles if tax reforms raise the price of diesel relative to gasoline) are also ignored, again because they would add considerable complexity, without affecting the general flavor of the results.

The spreadsheet uses data from 2012 (the latest for which data is available) and therefore looks at what would have happened had different tax scenarios been in place in that year (after full adjustment to those taxes). This avoids the need to make projections about future data inputs. All monetary figures are expressed in euros (converted, where needed, at market exchange rates in 2012).

Changes in fuel tax rates in different countries in response to changes in tax minima are obtained by splitting the difference (based on discussion in the main text) between two bounding cases. In the lower-bound case, taxes increase in line with increases in tax minima for countries/fuel products for which tax floors are currently, or become, binding (in cases where tax floors remain non-binding there is no change in the domestic fuel tax rate). In the upper-bound case, the tax on a fuel in each country increases by the same absolute amount as any absolute increase in the tax floor.

More details on the data sources and computations are provided below.

Fuel consumption. The model distinguishes, for each EU country, 11 fuel use categories. Outside of the ETS, there are three motor fuels—on-road gasoline, on-road diesel, and off-road diesel—and three heating fuels—diesel, natural gas, and coal/coke. And within the ETS sector there are five primary fuels—coal, natural gas, diesel, kerosene, and LPG. Six primary fuels were excluded from the calculations—various motor fuels (on-road LPG and natural gas, off-road kerosene, LPG, and natural gas) and LPG for heating, because the quantities are very small; for example, all these fuels in aggregate account for 1.7 percent of EU-wide CO_2 emissions. Changes in electricity consumption are not explicitly tracked, given no change in the proposed tax floor for electricity.

All fuel consumption is taken from the International Energy Agency (IEA) website and expressed in terra-joules.

Fuel prices. Fuel use is related to the fuel user prices, given by pre-tax prices plus excises.[24] The pre-tax prices are mostly obtained from OECD (2014a). In a few cases where data are unavailable (typically Bulgaria, Croatia, Cyprus, Latvia, Lithuania, Romania, and a greater number of countries for coal), a simple average of other EU prices is assumed. For the ETS fuels, prices for diesel, kerosene, and LPG are not available—the first two were proxied by diesel prices for heating and the last by natural gas prices for heating. Prices are expressed in euros per GJ.

Fuel excises. These are taken from OECD (2014a), converted into euros/GJ. In cases where data are not available, given that missing data are mostly for new EU members with relatively low rates, taxes are set equal to the lowest rate in other countries where data are available, or (for ETS fuels) assumed to be zero in cases where excises are uncommon.

ETD tax rates and reform scenarios.   Data sources for these tax rates are noted in the main text.

CO_2 emission rates.   For primary fuels, these were taken from Parry et al. (2014), based on factors calculated by the Institute for Applied Systems Analysis. Emissions factors are taken to be the same for a particular fuel product, regardless of its use (for a particular primary fuel product, there is essentially no variation in emission rates across countries). CO_2 emission rates for electricity by country (assumed the same for residential and industrial uses) are taken from IEA (2015).

Air pollution deaths.   These are taken from country-level estimates of deaths per unit of fuel use (which are the air pollution damages per unit of fuel use described in appendix A divided by the value per fatality).

Efficient fuel taxes.   These are estimates of fuel taxes needed to reflect CO_2, local air pollution and, in the case of road fuels, traffic congestion, accidents, and road damage (see appendix A).

Fuel price elasticities.   Fuel price elasticities are taken to be constant (rather than changing in response to changes in fuel prices), which is a standard assumption. Based broadly on the empirical literature,[25] price elasticities (for all countries) for road and heating fuels are taken to be -0.5, while elasticities for fuels covered by the ETS (most importantly, power generation fuels) are taken to be -0.25. Plausible alternative assumptions affect the results only modestly.

Miscellaneous data.   GDP and market exchange rates for 2012 are from IMF (2015).

Computing environmental, fiscal, and economic impacts. CO_2 emissions are simply calculated by multiplying the use of fuel in a particular country times the fuel's CO_2 emissions factor, and are aggregated over fuel products and countries. CO_2 emissions are re-computed in response to reductions in fuel use caused by different tax reforms and compared with the initial amount.

Revenue impacts are calculated in essentially the same way, except that fuel use is multiplied by the excise on a particular product. Reductions in revenues from pre-existing taxes, due to the erosion of the fuel tax base in response to new policies, are therefore taken into account. Revenue implications of changes in value-added tax (VAT) receipts are not included in these calculations.

Similarly, premature deaths are just deaths per unit of fuel product from Parry et al. (2014) (and taken as constant), times fuel consumption, aggregated over fuel products and countries. Again, health impacts are re-computed at the new distribution of fuel use in response to policy reform and compared with the initial number of deaths.

Economic welfare impacts are calculated by integrating the difference between the efficient fuel tax and the prevailing fuel tax over the reduction in fuel use induced by the tax change, and then aggregating over fuels and countries.

Notes

1. We are grateful to Mikael Skou Andersen, Karen Pittel, and Rozan Consten for very helpful comments and suggestions.

2. See, for example, EC (2011a; 2011b).

3. These goals include cutting EU greenhouse gas emissions by 20 percent by 2020 and 40 percent by 2030, and improving energy efficiency by 20 percent by 2020, all relative to 1990 levels (see Löschel and Oliver, this volume).

4. The ETD was the result of a long discussion on the introduction of an EU-wide carbon tax (Smith and Vollebergh 1993) and represents a much diluted version of earlier European Commission proposals (including COM (92) 226 and COM (95) 172).

5. Biofuels and biomass are excluded from our analysis, on the assumption that they capture as much CO_2 from the air as they release when being burned. The case for exemptions for biofuels and biomass—like biodiesel or waste incineration—may not be as strong as is often assumed, however, as they also strongly contribute to air pollution. See Vollebergh (1997) for early estimates of the overall environmental damage profile of both biodiesel and waste incineration.

6. The rate would be adjusted in the future to keep it in line with the ETS emissions price.

7. Kanbur and Keen (1993) provide the theoretical underpinnings for this and Evers et al. (2004) find suggestive evidence that tax floors increased diesel taxes, even in countries where the floor was not binding.

8. The focus here is confined to energy taxation. For an in-depth discussion of options for broader environmental tax reform in EU countries, see, for example, Hogg et al. (2014).

9. This value is broadly in line with central case estimates of the future global climate change damages per ton of CO_2 in U.S. IAWG (2013) and with starting prices for CO_2 emissions that are consistent (if applied globally) with containing mean projected warming to 2.5°C (e.g., Nordhaus 2013, 228). Efficient CO_2 prices ramp up at around 2-5 percent each year in real terms. More recent analyses, however, suggest that this (starting) value of the damage per ton is rather low. For instance, models that account for irreversibility and/or threshold effects are likely to add, at least, another €50 per ton to the current reference value (e.g., De Zeeuw and Van der Ploeg 2015).

10. However, a person's exposure to air pollution declines rapidly the further away they live from a pollution source. A study of China (Zhou et al. 2006), for example, estimates that someone living within 100 km from a coal plant inhales 86 times as much pollution as someone living 1,000-3,000 km away. At the same time, however, the contribution of many local air pollution sources also contributes to "background air pollution," which, in turn, exacerbates local health impacts everywhere. This is why, increasingly, air pollution coordination between global regions is called for.

11. Emissions of air pollutants in the European Union are restricted by the EU National Emission Ceilings Directive, which imposes national ceilings on emissions of air pollutants, without the possibility of bank or trade between the Member States.

12. Parry et al. (2014) discuss a simple formula for doing this, and apply it using country-level estimates of external costs.

13. Moreover, these cross-border spillovers will decline with the trend toward greater reliance on distance-based charging for trucks in the European Union, as the external costs caused by trucks occur in the country where distance-based taxes are levied.

14. A number of studies have estimated various environmental costs from transportation and energy in European countries, though these are not usually expressed in a form allowing for computation of efficient fuel taxes. One exception is Vollebergh et al. (2014), who provide a very involved estimate for the Netherlands, suggesting considerably higher corrective taxes than illustrated below. For some discussion, see, for example, Brandt et al. (2010), EXIOPOL (2011), Maibach et al. (2008), and NEEDS (2011). A valuable exercise (though one beyond the scope of this paper) would be to reconcile the different estimates that employ quite different methodologies and assumptions. In the meantime, the results from any one study should be treated with caution.

15. This issue is taken care of under normal procedures for value added taxes (VAT) where firms can claim rebates on VATs paid on intermediate inputs.

16. In this chapter we do not consider the potential role of using revenues from environmental taxes to reduce distortionary taxation such as those on wages (for a discussion in the EU context, see Kosonen and Nicodème 2009).

17. Electricity taxes have relatively immobile bases in the sense that (unlike for taxes on power generation fuels) they cannot be avoided by reducing fuel use per unit of generation, while simple vehicle taxes have immobile bases in the sense that (unlike for road fuel taxes) they cannot be avoided by driving vehicles less, or using fuel-efficient vehicles more intensively.

18. However, the European Union currently aims to phase out (sales) taxes on vehicles in order to improve the functioning of the internal market. Moreover, taxes on vehicles may provide an important second-best instrument to effectively price emissions like carbon. Recent evidence from a Dutch experiment with differentiated car sales taxes suggests that fuel (tax) price increases are much less effective in stimulating the purchase of small fuel-efficient cars (see Van Meerkerk et al. 2014).

19. Note that emissions can also be shifted over time due to the banking provision in the ETS that keeps allowance prices low for a (very) long period (for a detailed analysis, see Brink et al. 2015). Our assumption of allowance supply adaptation is equivalent to a so-called variable carbon tax option as currently applied by the United Kingdom.

20. Ideally, Member States would be allowed to vary this charge with local air emissions rates and population exposure, but this possibility is not considered here.

21. Economic welfare impacts are a partial equilibrium measure, reflecting environmental benefits less economic costs from changes in fuel use.

22. In this policy scenario, the proportionate changes in fuel prices for individual countries are around 5-8 percent for gasoline and 10-20 percent for diesel. Given the elasticity assumptions, these imply gasoline reductions of around 2.5-4 percent, and diesel reductions of around 5-10 percent.

23. Scaling coal taxes to smokestack air pollution emission rates would be significantly more effective as it would promote greater use of emissions control technologies.

24. For simplicity, VAT is excluded. Alternatively, this could be included for fuels consumed by households, with the excises also scaled by VAT rates, though the proportionate changes in fuel prices would be the same as calculated here.

25. See the summary in Parry et al. (2015).

References

Brandt, J., J. D. Silver, A. Gross, and J. H. Christensen. 2010. *Marginal Damage Cost per Unit of Air Pollution Emissions*. Roskilde: National Environmental Research Institute. Specific Agreement 3555/B2010/EEA.54131 Implementing Framework Contract Ref. No. EEA/IEA/09/002.

Brink, C., H. R. J. Vollebergh, and E. van der Werf. 2016. "Carbon Pricing in the EU: Evaluation of Different EU ETS." *Energy Policy* 97: 603-17.

de Borger, Bruno, and Stef Proost. 2015. "Tax and Regulatory Policies for European Transport—Getting There, but in the Slow Lane." In *Energy Tax and Regulatory Policy in Europe: Reform Priorities*, eds. I. Parry, K. Pittel, N. Anger, and H. Vollebergh. Cambridge, MA, US: MIT Press.

EC. 2011a. *Proposal for a Council Directive Amending Directive 2003/96/EC Restructuring the Community Framework for the Taxation of Energy Products and Electricity*. European Commission, Brussels, Belgium.

EC. 2011b. *Smarter Energy Taxation for the EU*. European Commission, Brussels, Belgium.

Evers, Michiel, R. A. de Mooij, and H. R. J. Vollebergh. 2004. "Tax Competition Under Minimum Rates: The Case of European Diesel Taxes" (CESifo Working Paper Series 1221, CESifo Group, Munich, Germany).

EXIOPOL. 2011. *A New Environmental Accounting Framework Using Externality Data and Input-Output Tools for Policy Analysis*. EU-funded Research Project. www.feem-project.net/exiopol/index.php.

Hogg, D., M. S. Anderson, T. Elliott, C. Sherrington, T. Vergunst, S. Ettlinger, L. Elliott, and J. Hudson. 2014. *Study on Environmental Fiscal Reform Potential in 12 EU Member States*. Final Report to DG Environment of the European Commission.

IEA. 2015. *World Energy Statistics and Balances*. International Energy Agency, Paris, France.

IMF. 2015. *World Economic Outlook Database*. International Monetary Fund, Washington, DC, US. www.imf.org/external/pubs/ft/weo/2015/02/weodata/index.aspx.

Kanbur, Ravi, and Michael Keen. 1993. "Jeux Sans Frontieres: Tax Competition and Tax Coordination when Countries Differ in Size." *American Economic Review* 83: 877-92.

Kosonen, Katri, and Gaetan Nicodème. 2009. "The Role of Fiscal Instruments in Environmental Policy" (CESifo Working Paper 2719, CESifo Group, Munich, Germany).

Löschel, Andreas, and Oliver Schenker. 2015. "On the Coherence of Economic Instruments: Climate, Renewables and Energy Efficiency Policies." In *Energy Tax and Regulatory Policy in Europe: Reform Priorities*, eds. I. Parry, K. Pittel, N. Anger, and H. Vollebergh. Cambridge, MA, US: MIT Press.

Maibach, M., C. Schreyer, D. Sutter, H. P. van Essen, B. H. Boon, R. Smokers, A. Schroten, C. Doll, B. Pawlowska, and M. Bak. 2008. *Handbook on Estimation of External Costs in the Transport Sector*. Produced within the study Internalization Measures and Policies for All External Cost of Transport (IMPACT), Version 1.1, Delft, CE, commissioned by European Commission DG TREN.

NEEDS. 2011. *New Energy Externalities Development for Sustainability*. EU-funded Research Project. www.needs-project.org

Nordhaus, William D. 2013. *The Climate Casino: Risk, Uncertainty, and Economics for a Warming World*. New Haven, CT, US: Yale University Press.

OECD. 2012. *Mortality Risk Valuation in Environment, Health and Transport Policies*. Paris, France: Organisation for Economic Co-operation and Development.

OECD. 2014a. *Energy Prices and Taxes, 4th Quarter 2014*. Organisation for Economic Co-operation and Development, Paris, France.

OECD. 2014b. *The Cost of Air Pollution—Health Impacts of Road Transport*. Paris, France: Organisation for Economic Co-operation and Development.

Parry, I. W. H. 2011. "How Much Should Highway Fuels Be Taxed?" In *U.S. Energy Tax Policy*, ed. Gilbert E. Metcalf. New York, NY, US: Cambridge University Press, 269-97.

Parry, I. W. H., C. Veung, and D. Heine. 2015. "How Much Carbon Pricing is in Countries' Own Interests? The Critical Role of Co-Benefits." *Climate Change Economics* 6: 1550019-1-26.

Parry, I. W. H., D. Heine, S. Li, and E. Lis. 2014. *Getting Energy Prices Right: From Principle to Practice*. Washington, DC: International Monetary Fund.

Smith, Stephen, and Herman Vollebergh. 1993. "The European Carbon Excise Proposal: A 'Green' Tax Takes Shape." *EC Tax Review* 2 (4): 207-21.

U.S. IAWG. 2013. *Technical Update of the Social Cost of Carbon for Regulatory Impact Analysis under Executive Order 12866*. United States Inter-Agency Working Group, Washington, DC, US.

Van der Ploeg, Frederick, and Aart De Zeeuw. 2015. "Climate Tipping and Economic Growth: Precautionary Capital and the Price of Carbon." Paper presented at the 2015 NBER Summer Institute (Environmental & Energy Economics), Cambridge, MA, US.

Van Meerkerk, J., G. Renes, and G. Ridder. 2014. "Greening the Dutch Car Fleet: The Role of Differentiated Sales Taxes" (PBL Working Paper 18, Den Haag, Netherlands).

Vollebergh, H. R. J. 1997. "Environmental Externalities and Social Optimality in Biomass Markets: Waste-to-Energy in the Netherlands and Biofuels in France." *Energy Policy* 25 (6): 605-21.

Vollebergh, H. R. J., E. Drissen, H. Eerens, and G. Geilenkirchen. 2014. *Milieubelastingen en Groene Groei Deel II: Evaluatie van Belastingen op Energie in Nederland Vanuit Milieuperspectief.* PBL Achtergrondstudies, 500229002, Bilthoven.

West, Sarah E., and Roberton C. Williams. 2007. "Optimal Taxation and Cross-Price Effects on Labor Supply: Estimates of the Optimal Gas Tax." *Journal of Public Economics* 91: 593-617.

WHO. 2014. *Public Health, Environmental and Social Determinants of Health.* World Health Organization. www.who.int/phe/health_topics/outdoorair/databases/en/.

Zhou, Y., J. I. Levy, J. S. Evans, and J. K. Hammitt. 2006. "The Influence of Geographic Location on Population Exposure to Emissions from Power Plants Throughout China." *Environment International* 32: 365-73.

A Comment on "Reforming the EU Energy Tax Directive: Assessing the Options"

Mikael Skou Andersen[1]

The EU's energy taxation directive (2003/96/EC) (ETD) was a landmark decision following more than a decade of negotiations on reforming its predecessor, the Taxation of Mineral Oils Directive (92/82/EEC). The ETD established new tax rate minima for a range of fuels and purposes, including for electricity. No doubt the prospect of EU enlargement from 2004 created the window of opportunity in which a compromise could be forged among old Member States, as did the perceived "race to the bottom" of tax rate reductions following fuel protests in France and Germany during the 2001–2002 spike in oil prices.

At the request of the European Council, the European Commission in 2011 proposed to amend the ETD to bring it more in line with the EU's energy and climate policy objectives. Key elements of the proposal were the introduction of a tax on CO_2 corresponding to the carbon price for ETS installations, improving on the cost-effectiveness of mitigation, and adjusted tax rates according to energy contents (gigajoule, GJ). Unfortunately, the proposal was soon stalled in Council negotiations, where unanimity is required, with resistance notably from Poland and Luxembourg, and according to some insiders, also from Germany, with its large diesel car industry. Following appointment of the Juncker Commission, the proposal was removed from the work program in early 2015.

Nevertheless, the principles of energy taxation proposed by the Barroso Commission continue to attract attention around Europe, and offer a long-term vision that is not without significance. France and Portugal, for instance, in 2014 introduced a tax on CO_2 linked to the stipulated carbon price for ETS installations, while Italy and Belgium are increasing the motor fuel tax for diesel, aligning it to petrol according to energy content. In the context of the EU's recovery effort, several Member States are receiving official country-specific recommendations to adjust their energy and transport-related taxes. In the context of the new security relationship to Russia, natural gas taxation is no longer a sacred cow in Central and Eastern Europe. Indeed, it is as if the proposed ETD amendments have a tailwind sweeping through Europe, triggering incremental adjustment.

The options for ETD reform offered in "Reforming the EU Energy Tax Directive: Assessing the Options" are based on principles comparable to and going beyond those of the 2011 ETD proposal, notably the taxation of non-ETS CO_2 and energy taxation according to energy content. The latter principle should be an eye-opener to several Member States that have paid little or no attention to the physical properties of energy products, maintaining from the oil crises of the 1970s considerably higher tax rates for mineral oils than for other energy products.

Still, the rationale of the options differ fundamentally from the ETD in that estimates of externalities provide a yardstick against which present country-specific tax rates are judged. In contrast ETD emphasis is on proper functioning of the internal market. Looming behind that is the European Union's lacking self-sufficiency and dependency on imports, providing a distinct rationale for curbing energy demand with taxation.

Leaving that aside, the options under assessment combine to produce a promising scenario: motor fuels are in their own class of energy content-related tax rates; the CO_2 tax component is applied to both non-ETS and ETS sectors; and finally, a specific penalty on coal, as the single most important fuel in generating carbon emissions and health damages from conventional air pollutants, is implemented.

Compared with the 2011 ETD proposal, these options would increase CO_2 reductions from 1.5 percent to 5.1 percent, while revenues would go up from 0.2 percent of GDP to 1.3 percent of GDP. The most dramatic effect is perhaps in reducing mortality from air pollution, where these options could provide a cut of 11.8 percent, considerably more than the 1.4 percent implied by the 2011 ETD proposal. The specific penalty on coal plays a key role for expected impacts.

The chapter rightly assumes that electricity tax rates are not a good candidate for adjustment, and might have mentioned the burdens of ETS and more importantly of feed-in tariffs for renewables. Tax rates for other energy products are calibrated on the implicit tax rate per GJ for electricity, though the lowest rate for business is the starting point, rather than the rate for households. As a result, the energy tax component of the options remains relatively modest for a range of energy products other than coal.

Is there a justification for energy taxation per se, other than emissions of carbon and air pollution? In view of the EU's energy efficiency objectives and supply crunch, a careful reading of ETD wording would suggest a reply in the affirmative. In contrast, the yardstick of externalities is not presently a legally accepted basis for taxation in the European Union, although externalities must be accounted for under other pieces of EU law.

The chapter provides estimates of external costs on the basis of the OECD's base value for the value of a statistical life (VSL). The OECD's approach starts from a VSL base value, which, in fact, is twice as high as the base value previously applied in EU analyses related to air pollution—though with the EU's value within the lower end of the OECD's uncertainty range.

Whereas in the European Union it is customary to estimate life years lost and monetize using VOLYs (value of life years), the chapter applies the U.S. Environmental Protection Agency's approach of counting mortality in gross figures. While this appears technical, it has, in fact, profound implications for the monetary estimates—there can be a factor of four between the EU's VSL-based and VOLY-based estimates (Schucht et al. 2015), and applying the OECD base value probably doubles estimates further. While this is a question of assumptions, it might not be fully persuasive to policymakers in a European context. In the technical realm, they might also raise questions about estimates according to air pollution modelling tools available in Europe (Bachmann 2015).

The specific tax on coal proposed in the chapter is important for the overall outcome, as discussed above, but the higher rate differs from that of other non-motor fuel energy tax products, which might not go down so well with nondiscrimination principles. Still, comparable results could well be obtained by taxing coal and other energy products according to their conventional air pollution emissions, while keeping the energy contents and CO_2 tax components fully harmonized. Sweden's SO_2 and NO_x taxes imply penalties on coal several times higher than for other fuels, providing the desired signal. Even if flue gas treatment is applied to control emissions, the costs involved are substantial and will help curb demand for coal. Several Member States[2] already have a legal framework for air pollution taxes in place, providing a good starting point (Hogg et al. 2015). Tax rate adjustments should reflect regional differences, as air pollution travels well beyond national borders, but would still provide domestic citizens significant health benefits in return.

Hence, future ETD options to be considered might have three components: energy taxation, carbon taxation, and taxation of air pollution (Andersen 2015). The energy and carbon elements, if modulated on the current electricity tax and ETS carbon price, will be sufficiently modest as not to constitute a challenge to low-income Member States—it is motor fuels that might be of concern. Hence, concerns will have to address how diesel and petrol can be taxed on a fair basis considering energy contents and emissions. The chapter makes an important contribution by showing that a slightly higher baseline than the current ETD will allow for a more general increase also in Member States that presently are above the existing minima, while still providing leeway for differentiation. In this context, the tank tourism for diesel could be reduced by shifting a smaller fraction of the diesel tax to surtaxes on the annual circulation tax for vehicles, as practiced for many years in Sweden and Denmark (Nordic Council 2014).

It follows from economic theory that externalities are the relevant yardstick for internalizing taxes. Yet with established approaches to account for external costs in Europe, estimates differ from the level suggested with American approaches, though we might see some convergence in methodologies in the years to come. Under the present circumstances in Europe, legal doctrines seem to have higher prominence than economic—and when the very framework of an EU energy taxation directive is acknowledged, energy-related taxation has indeed a purpose in its own right in creating a more level playing field for the internal market of energy products.

Notes

1. Financial support from Aarhus University's interdisciplinary research network on air pollution and health is acknowledged.

2. E.g., France, Italy, Poland, Czech Republic, Croatia, Bulgaria, Latvia, Estonia, Finland, Denmark, and Sweden.

References

Andersen, M. S. 2015. "Reflections on the Scandinavian Model: Some Insights into Energy-Related Taxes in Denmark and Sweden." *European Taxation* 55 (6): 235-44.

Bachmann, T. 2015. "Assessing Air Pollutant-Induced, Health-Related External Costs in the Context of Nonmarginal System Changes: A Review." *Environmental Science and Technology* 49: 9503-17.

Hogg, D., T. Elliott, L. Elliott, S. Ettlinger, T. Chowdhury, A. Bapasola, H. Norstein, L. Emery, M. S. Andersen, P. ten Brink, S. Withana, J.-P. Schweitzer, A. Illes, K. Paquel, I. P. Ventosa, and S. Sastre. 2015. "Study on Assessing the Environmental Fiscal Reform Potential for the EU28 (ENV D.2/ETU/2015/0005)." Final Report for European Commission, DG ENV. http://ec.europa.eu/environment/integration/green_semester/pdf/Eunomia%20EFR%20Final%20Report%20MAIN%20REPORT.pdf

Nordic Council of Ministers. 2014. *The Use of Economic Instruments: In Nordic Environmental Policy 2010–2013.* Copenhagen, Denmark: TemaNord.

Schucht, S., A. Colette, S. Rao, M. Holland, W. Schöpp, P. Kolp, Z. Klimont, B. Bessagnet, S. Szopa, R. Vautard, J. Brignon, and L. Rouïl. 2015. "Moving towards Ambitious Climate Policies: Monetised Health Benefits from Improved Air Quality Could Offset Mitigation Costs in Europe." *Environmental Science and Policy* 50: 252-69.

5   On the Coherence of Economic Instruments: Climate, Renewables, and Energy Efficiency Policies

Andreas Löschel and Oliver Schenker

Key Points for Policymakers

- The climate and energy policy in the European Union and its Member States is characterized by multiple targets and myriad (pricing and regulatory) instruments. All these instruments interact with each other. Most interactions lead to distortions and increase the costs of a given reduction in greenhouse gas (GHG) emissions.
- However, there might be additional targets that warrant complementary instruments as there are market failures (e.g., from knowledge spillovers) additional to the climate externality that make an adjustment of distorted incentives necessary. This provides a rationale for a policy mix.
- Nevertheless, the most important intervention is to price GHG emissions correctly (current prices are well below what is needed) and comprehensively across emissions.
- In any case, in order to be cost-efficient, additional policies need to be calibrated very well. This is extremely difficult as targets and market failures vary across technologies, markets, and time. Today's technology policy portfolio is putting too much emphasis on the deployment of existing technologies and not enough on research and development.
- Deployment policies can be justified by externalities inherent to this process. But these externalities are probably small and difficult to target. A feed-in premium is the preferable policy instrument to address this market failure. Such a scheme has clear advantages over a feed-in tariff scheme as it forces producers to respond to prices as a signal for scarcity.
- Adding new policy instruments therefore has to be done with the utmost reservation. Otherwise, the policy mix risks becoming a

policy mess. Moreover, innovation externalities might gradually vanish over time, requiring the progressive phase-out of complementary instruments next to carbon pricing.

1. Introduction

The climate and energy policy architecture in the European Union and its Member States is characterized by several targets and myriad instruments. Three main pillars constitute the European policy environment. The so-called 20-20-20 targets, defined in the EU Climate and Energy Package, were adopted in 2009. They consist of a 20 percent reduction in EU greenhouse gas (GHG) emissions relative to 1990 levels, a 20 percent share of renewables[1] in EU energy production, and 20 percent energy savings in comparison to a baseline projection by 2020. This triangle of targets has been iterated by the decision of the European Council on the 2030 Framework for Climate and Energy Policy that again defines targets in the similar three domains (European Council 2014). In 2030, GHG emission shall be at least reduced by 40 percent relative to 1990, renewables shall have a share of 27 percent in EU energy consumption, and there is also an indicative target for energy savings of 27 percent.[2]

Additionally, several EU Member States have their own targets, where targets and baseline years vary noticeably across countries (see table 5.1). For example, Denmark aims for a 34 percent GHG reduction in 2020. The United Kingdom targets an 80 percent GHG reduction by 2050. Germany has, by 2020, pledged to reduce its GHG emissions by 40 percent (relative to 1990), boost its share of renewables in electricity generation to 35 percent, and reduce (relative to 2008) its primary energy supply by 20 percent and total electricity consumption by 10 percent.

All of these targets interact. A higher penetration of renewable energy generation and energy efficiency reduces the emission of greenhouse gases, contributing to the emission reduction achievements.[3] Conversely, stringent policies to meet GHG reduction targets might increase the costs of energy, inducing a more efficient use of energy and contributing to the energy efficiency targets. At the same time, fossil fuel-based technologies might become more expensive, supporting the penetration of renewables in electricity, heat, and transport.

These interactions are crucial: in order to reach the respective targets cost-efficiently, policy instruments have to be chosen, implemented, and adjusted taking each other into account to minimize distortions.

Table 5.1
Climate and energy policy targets of the European Union and of select member states
Source: Landis et al. (2013).

	GHG Emissions	Renewable Energies	Energy Efficiency
EU	Reduction of 20% by 2020 and 40% by 2030 relative to 1990	20% in 2020, 27% in 2030	20% energy savings by 2020 compared to baseline, 27% in 2030
Denmark	Reduction by 34% in 2020 relative to 1990	35% in 2020, 100% in 2050	
France	Reduction of 40% by 2030 and 75% by 2050 relative to 2005	40% in 2030	Reduction in final energy consumption by 50% in 2050
Germany	Reduction of 40% by 2020 and 80% by 2050 relative to 1990	18% (35% in electricity generation) by 2020, 30% (50%) by 2030	20% energy savings by 2020 compared to baseline
UK	Reduction by 80% in 2050, derived from this: -50% by 2025 relative to 1990		

These instruments range from the cornerstone of the EU climate policy, the EU emission trading system (EU ETS), to Member State-specific fuel taxes. In order to increase the share of renewables different designs of feed-in tariffs and other renewable support policies have been implemented in the different Member States. The energy efficiency targets are also addressed by a broad set of instruments, ranging from labelling policies to minimum efficiency standards.

This paper discusses reasons and rationales for operating within a multi-dimensional target architecture and overlapping instruments, aims at identifying these interdependencies between instruments and targets, and proposes coherent renewables and energy efficiency policies that are part of a portfolio that contributes to an effective and efficient abatement of market failures in the energy sector.

The remainder of this paper is structured as follows: in the next section, we discuss briefly the current target architecture in the European climate and energy policy, the different layers of implementation, and the respective instruments to reach these targets. Then, we discuss from a more general point of view the rationales for such an instrument mix and supporting evidence for multiple instruments. With this knowledge at hand, we propose instruments and policy measures addressing renewables and energy efficiency investments that minimize distortions and interferences from interactions.

We conclude that there is indeed a rationale for a policy mix addressing different targets and a need for multiple policy measures that each address specific market failures. However, the current design of instruments in Europe needs some careful recalibration. The most important instrument is the price tag on GHG emission. The first priority should therefore be to set an economy-wide price for GHG emissions that reflects the damages it will provoke. The second priority is to correct market failures in knowledge generation and in the deployment of new renewables energy technologies as well as in energy efficiency-improving technologies. The size of these externalities depends on a large, difficult to estimate, and constantly changing number of factors. Getting the externality right and internalizing it correctly over time is difficult and accompanied with a constant risk of policy failure. However, there is empirical evidence for the need to rebalance efforts from deployment support policies of existing technologies to policies that support research and development (R&D) of new technologies. But even these externalities might vanish over time as knowledge spillovers become smaller and learning-by-doing effects diminish, reducing the scope for complementary instruments next to carbon pricing. So, policies addressing these externalities need to be adjusted and possibly even phased out over time.

2.   The European Climate and Energy Policy Architecture

2.1   Greenhouse Gas Emission Reduction Targets

In 2009, the European Union adopted a plan to reduce its emissions by 20 percent relative to 1990 in 2020. However, the EU-28 GHG emissions[4] in 2012 have already decreased by 19.2 percent relative to 1990, mainly due to the restructuring of the economies in Eastern European Member States and the economic decline due to the global financial crisis (EEA 2014). Figure 5.1 shows the GHG emissions of the EU-28 from 1990 to 2012.

In order to achieve this target and more stringent targets beyond 2020, it is anticipated that action will be taken both by individual Member States and on a pan-European level. Thus, the 20 percent GHG reduction target for 2020 and its update for 2030, a 40 percent GHG reduction target, is broken down into a target for sectors regulated under the pan-European instrument of the EU Emission Trading System (EU ETS). This covers the sectors of power and heat generation, energy-intensive industry, and commercial flights to and from the European Union, Iceland,

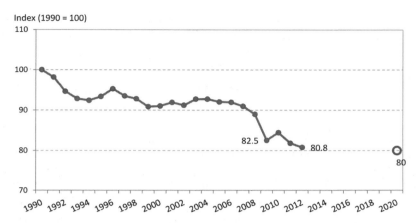

Figure 5.1
EU-28 GHG emissions, 1990–2012
Source: EEA (2014).

Liechtenstein, and Norway. Currently, the EU ETS covers about 45 percent of the EU's GHG emissions. The remaining emissions are subject to individual Member State actions in the remaining sectors of the economy such as transport (without intra-EU civil aviation), buildings, agriculture, and waste. As mentioned above, the multiple layers of emission reduction targets are supplemented with additional targets set by some Member States, in some cases legally binding, in some cases indicative.

This indicates how complicated the policy landscape is just in the domain of GHG emission reduction targets. An analysis of the International Energy Agency's (IEA) Policy and Measures database shows more than 110 active GHG reduction policies in force in the European Union and its Member States, without taking into account sub-national policies. The Member States' measures range from energy and fuel taxes to voluntary agreements with certain sectors in the economy. Of course, a simple counting of policies is per se not very informative regarding the stringency and coverage of the individual measures. However, the number of policies underscores the landscape's complexity, making it quite obvious that those policies cannot be analyzed individually but have to be put in perspective to each other.

We start by analyzing the coherence of policies in the other two domains of the EU energy and climate policy, the role of renewable energy and energy efficiency improvements, under the premise that reducing the emissions of GHG is the overarching target. This target architecture has been established for the restructuring of the energy supply in the context of the German energy transition by the German government (BMWi 2014) on the basis of the recommendations of the expert commission on the monitoring process (Löschel et al. 2014). Subsequently, we relax this premise and discuss its compatibility with other policy goals. All in all, we are looking for a policy portfolio that reduces overall policy costs.

2.2   Renewable Policies

There is a broad political and scientific consensus that renewable energy has to play an important role in the pathway to a low-carbon energy system. This materializes in the Renewable Energy Directive 2009/28/EC, which sets binding specific national targets for each EU Member State concerning the share of renewable energy by 2020, ranging from 10 percent in Malta to 49 percent in Sweden. They are also each required to have at least 10 percent of their transport fuels come from renewable sources by 2020. The achievement of these individual targets shall ensure that the European Union as a whole reaches a 20 percent share of energy from renewable sources by 2020. For 2030, the European Union aims for a share at least 27 percent renewables in the energy system (see figure 5.2). This target will not break down into national sub-targets as was the case in the target for 2020. This may create more flexibility for Member States, but it is still unclear how the Member States (beyond the EU ETS) will coordinate to ensure that the target will be met.

The first round of National Renewable Energy Action Plans submitted in 2011 to the European Commission in order to evaluate the pathway to the target showed a positive result: in 2012, 13 percent of the European energy consumption stemmed from renewable sources, rising from 8 percent in the year 2000. But as figure 5.3 shows, Member States differ substantially in the share of renewable energy in energy consumption in general and particularly in the weight of specific renewable technologies. However, the current economic situation might affect these plans negatively. Some countries, like Spain and the Czech Republic, have cut financial support for renewables.

Decisions are not taken on the EU level only; Member States have their own agenda. We draw again from the German example: the EU Renewables Directive sets for Germany a target of an 18 percent share of energy from renewable sources in 2020. In addition, the German government aims for a share of renewables in electricity generation of at least 35 percent in 2020 (and 50 percent in 2030). Other Member States have their own targets and sub-targets. This is reflected in around

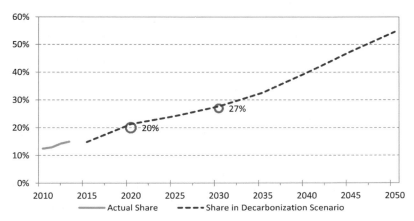

Figure 5.2
Share of renewables in gross final energy demand in the European Union
Sources: EEA (2015), EC (2011).
Notes: The solid line shows actual shares, and the dashed line shows the cost-efficient share in the Diversified Supply Technologies Scenarios of the EU Energy Roadmap 2050 that is consistent with an 80 percent GHG emission reduction in the European Union by 2050. The circles indicate legislated EU-wide renewable targets for 2020 and 2030, respectively.

275 policies and measures that are in place (either regulation of the European Commission or the individual Member States) to address renewable energy sources (IEA 2014). In the transport sector, almost all Member States have implemented a quota for biofuels in total fuel use.[5]

Three different types of instruments have been considered to incentivize either directly renewable energy supply in the electricity sector (RES-E) generation or support upstream industries that produce the necessary technologies: feed-in tariffs (FiTs), feed-in premiums (FiPs), and renewable portfolio standards (RPS). Recently, some Member States (e.g., Germany) have started to use auctions as a means to introduce some market-based incentives for renewables. Since auctions control the quantities under varying prices, the instrument is close in its characteristics to RPS. The idea is to introduce market-based incentives for renewables investors, instead of state-determined payments for every kilowatt-hour of green power fed into the system.

Most European countries draw on FiTs as the primary instrument in order to promote RES-E production. FiTs provide RES-E producers with long-term contracts that guarantee access to the grid at a fixed price that normally decreases over time. The remuneration generally differs among technologies, with higher payoffs for more expensive

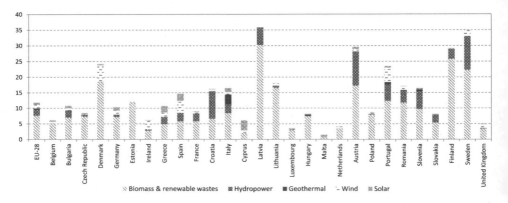

Figure 5.3
Share of renewables in gross inland energy consumption in 2013
Source: Eurostat (2015).

technologies such as photovoltaic energy and offshore wind energy. The stability of the cash flow makes it attractive for investors but can also generate huge bills for state budgets or electricity consumers if the scheme is "too" attractive. Since FiTs guarantee a fixed price, producers are immunized against price signals from electricity markets, potentially leading to market distortions from an unresponsive electricity supply.[6]

FiPs induce more responsiveness, but in return give less certainty for investors. FiPs provide an output subsidy per kilowatt hour of electricity produced, often differentiated by technology. Since producers face the wholesale price plus the subsidy, they have generally higher incentives to respond to demand and price changes, making markets more flexible. Denmark, for example, operates with such a scheme.[7]

RPSs are similar to non-technology-specific, uniform FiPs. RPSs define the minimum share for RES-E and create a market where the obligations to generate a certain amount of RES-E can be traded. Energy suppliers must purchase certificates or otherwise generate the necessary amount of RES-E. Such systems are used in several EU Member States, inter alia the United Kingdom and Sweden, but the characteristics differ in the details—sometimes, for example, treating different technologies differently.

FiTs, FiPs, and RPSs directly incentivize the generation of RES-E by downstream users of technology. Another important component of most policy portfolios is the support of R&D activities by upstream producers of RES-E technologies. On an EU-wide level, the NER300 program might serve as an example. This program is funded by the

Table 5.2
Renewable Support Policies in Germany, Italy, and the Czech Republic

Source: res-legal.eu (2015).

	Germany	Italy	Czech Republic
Electricity	FiT (FiP) for installations < 500kW (>500kW) in electricity, auctions (currently pilots, officially starting in 2017) investment subsidies	FiT for PV between 1 kW and 1 MW, FiP for other technologies, reduced VAT	FiT and FiP until end 2013
Heat and Cooling	Investment support	Investment support, tax reduction	Investments grants, exemption from real estate tax
Transport	Reduced tax rate for biofuels, biofuels quota	Biofuels quota	Reduced tax rate for biofuels, biofuels quota

sale of 300 million emission allowances from the New Entrants' Reserve (NER) set up for the third phase of the EU ETS and aims at supporting selected low-carbon energy demonstration projects. With the implementation of the 2030 Framework for Climate and Energy this program will be updated to NER400, having more allowances in its stock. Table 5.2 gives an overview on policies in three selected Member States: Germany, Italy, and the Czech Republic.

2.3 Energy Efficiency Target

The third EU target is a 20 percent improvement in the EU's energy efficiency. But it is actually defined as a 20 percent energy savings target compared to the projected use of energy in 2020. Under the 2030 Framework for Climate and Energy, an indicative energy savings target of 27 percent by 2030 has been enacted. This target will be reviewed in 2020 and might be adjusted to a 30 percent target by 2030. As in the case of the renewables target, there will be no Member State-specific sub-target and a coordination mechanism still needs to be designed.

This EU-wide target has not been translated into binding targets for Member States yet. The European Union has so far implemented only a fragmented set of single measures (such as the controversial ban of conventional light bulbs). According to the Commission's own last assessment, the European Union will achieve energy savings of around

Table 5.3
Selected energy efficiency policies in selected EU Member States

Source: Landis et al. (2013).

Ireland	France	Sweden
• Corporate tax incentives for energy efficient investments • Grants for home owners to improve insulation	• White certificate trading system for energy supplier • Bonus/penalty tax system to encourage purchase of energy efficient cars	• Electricity tax exemptions for energy efficiency investments • Labelling of buildings

18-19 percent in 2020 (European Commission 2014). But while the economic crisis contributed to this decrease in energy consumption, it has also negatively impacted energy efficiency investment decisions due to falling energy prices and uncertain returns of these investments. As a response, the Commission has adopted two new initiatives—the Energy Efficiency Plan and the Directive 2012/27/EU on energy efficiency, which establish a set of binding measures such as a given energy efficient renovation rate for governmental buildings—aiming at stepping up efforts toward the 20 percent target.

Also in this domain the target architecture is more complicated and contains several layers that include individual targets for Member States. Using the same example again, Germany has set a target of -20 percent primary energy consumption versus 2008, a 10 percent reduction in total electricity consumption, and a 10 percent decline in primary energy supply in the transport sector. All European efforts are reflected in more than 440 policies that are tabled as measures directed to improve energy efficiency (IEA 2014). Note that not all of these policies overlap with the EU ETS since many of the measures address sectors such as transport and buildings that are not included in the emission trading system. Table 5.3 illustrates some initiatives in a few selected countries.

3. A Complex Target and Instrument Architecture

3.1 Detrimental Overlaps of Policies

This brief assessment indicates how diverse the climate and energy policy landscape in Europe is. However, the question remains why the chosen architecture is as such. Basic economics tells us that if the goal is to reduce emissions in the most cost-effective way, it is necessary to equalize marginal abatement costs across sectors and implement one uniform price of carbon. All other instruments just cause distortions and excess costs by violating this principle. For typical examples of such distorting policies, consider policies that promote the deployment of carbon-free renewable energy technologies: if the target is binding, i.e., the renewable policy leads to a higher renewable share than the EU ETS alone would induce, the emission reduction target is not reached in a cost-effective way. Since the marginal abatement costs of installing additional renewables are greater than the costs of other abatement options such as fuel switches or demand reductions, the renewable target leads to excess costs relative to the case with an EU ETS as the only instrument—without additional GHG emissions reduction. Since marginal abatement costs are not fully equalized, the outcome of a policy portfolio is clearly detrimental. Moreover, an additional target for a minimum renewable share added to an existing ETS reduces the abatement pressure induced by the ETS and results in lower permit prices (Böhringer and Rosendahl 2010). Hence, a policy that aims at deploying renewables unintentionally promotes the most emission-intensive technology as it reduces their compliance costs. The choice of the instrument to promote RES-E technologies matters. Having the same renewable share target, RPS, FiTs, and FiPs, differ in their interaction with an ETS (Böhringer and Behrens 2015). The electricity price for consumers' responses is stronger upon the interaction of a RPS or an FiT with an ETS, but markedly lower if an FiP is combined with an ETS. For a given emission target the emissions constraint is the least binding under an FiP scheme since increasing wholesale price for electricity also causes higher remuneration for renewables. Hence, the net effect on consumer electricity price is smaller than with the other instruments.

There is also a dynamic dimension to consider. Prices for emission permits become more sensitive to changes in electricity demand if the ETS is combined with a minimum renewable share. The RPS in combination with an ETS under increasing electricity demand becomes less binding but puts relatively more pressure on the permit price (Flues et al. 2014). If policymakers value a clear and stable carbon price signal as crucial for encouraging long-term investments in low-carbon technologies, the combination of the two policy targets may have additional unintended negative consequences. Based on these arguments, the policy recommendation seems to be straightforward: scrap all other policies beyond the equalized carbon price. Studies indicate that such detrimental policy overlaps can cause significant costs: Boeters and

Koornneef (2011) show that the separate 20 percent target for renewable energy as a part of the EU climate policy for 2020 could create additional costs of up to 32 percent depending on the availability of low-cost technologies and the stringency of the renewable share target. Our policy note could end here.

But it is probably not that simple. There are indeed good arguments for applying more than one instrument, since instruments are not always only substitutes to a carbon price, i.e., supplementary policies.

3.2 Rationales for Multiple Policies

There are three potential rationales for complementary policies: (a) multiple targets, (b) market failures additional to the climate externality, and (c) regulation and policy failures (Sijm 2005). First, the use of multiple instruments has a rationale due to the existence of *multiple targets*. The goal to mitigate GHG is just one of many policy goals. As we know from Tinbergen (1952), several policy targets need a similar number of instruments. Hence, a simple justification for the application of multiple instruments can be provided by the existence of additional policy targets such as the consideration of energy security—policymakers want to reduce dependence on fossil fuel imports from unstable regions—that are affected differently by different GHG abatement options. The additional instruments thus have the aim to support the respective additional target.

Second, complementary instruments need to be applied because *market failures additional to the climate externality* make an adjustment of distorted incentives necessary (Bennear and Stavins 2007; Fischer and Prenonas 2010). Additional market failures may lead to insufficient demand for energy efficiency investments. These imperfections may arise due to the lack of credible information, landlord-tenant arrangements, or myopic behavior. Another market failure may arise due to the non-consideration of spillovers from knowledge and learning-by-doing on the benefits from new innovations in the energy sector. Because of this imperfect appropriation, the incentives for developing and deploying new technologies might be too low (Fischer and Newell 2008).

Third, regulation, policy failures, and imperfect information by regulators may make it necessary to implement supplemental instruments. Uncertainty about the future political valuation of emissions might make it necessary for a government to implement a subsidy of renewables as a supplementary policy instrument.[8] More generally, overlapping policies often arise from political constraints that limit the efficiency of a single policy (Bennear and Stavins 2007).

Taking all this into account it becomes clear that the analysis of policy interactions and multiple instruments has to take a step forward. The subsequent discussion of the European policy portfolio should be guided by the following questions: (1) How do policy instruments interact and influence each other's cost-efficiency and effectiveness (i.e., what the side effects of a particular intervention are)? (2) What justifies the use of additional instruments? (3) How might the discussed three rationales be addressed more comprehensively in the concrete policy setting? (4) What instruments shall be used? and finally, (5) What does all this imply for a successful implementation of the EU 2030 framework?

4. The Coherence of Renewable Policies

4.1 Complementary Renewable Policies: Addressing Additional Market Failures

The implementation of multiple climate and energy policy instruments can be justified by the existence of multiple market failures, which need to be addressed for an efficient market outcome. The most prominent of these market failures can be attributed to the knowledge generation in low-carbon technology industries. Even under a regime where carbon is priced according to its social costs, the dynamic incentives from such a carbon pricing system are not sufficient to exploit the full cost-reduction potential of low-carbon technologies.

Six major types of learning processes generate new knowledge: learning-by-doing (by the producers), learning-by-using (by consumers), learning from advances in science and technology, learning from inter-industry spillovers, learning by interacting, and learning-by-searching, where the last process is internal to the firm and related (mainly) to formalized activities (such as R&D) aimed at generating new knowledge (Malerba 1992). The literature focuses mainly on (a) knowledge spillovers from learning-by-doing and learning-by-using in the diffusion of RES-E technologies since future cost decreases from increasing cumulative production and use of these products are not taken into account by firms (Sorrell and Sijm 2003), and (b) knowledge spillovers from investments in R&D (learning-by-searching) since the benefits of R&D cannot be made fully private to the private provider of R&D. As modelling studies that take these externalities into account have shown, adding policy instruments that address these externalities in a cost-effective way might reduce the overall policy costs of tackling the climate change problem significantly.[9]

For a well-targeted policy, however, it is crucial to realize that the respective spillovers do not necessarily occur at the same stage in the supply chain. Rather, spillovers from learning-by-doing may occur upstream at the level of equipment production (wind turbines, photovoltaic [PV] panels) or downstream where other firms that install and manage the equipment also profit from learning-by-using. Spillovers from learning-by-searching, on the other hand, can mainly be attributed to the upstream technology developing sectors where most R&D activities accrue. Note that under the existence of such additional market failures, the additional instruments are complementary to a carbon price and do no harm since these instruments address other externalities. However, it is crucial that these instruments are targeted towards the right base and scaled to the size of the respective market failure. Moreover, learning spillovers vary over time and might diminish over time. In the following, we discuss briefly the evidence on the magnitude of these two externalities.

Learning-by-Doing and -Using   The idea that past experiences with technologies generate knowledge that helps to improve the technologies has a long tradition in economics (Arrow 1962). Such cost-reducing innovation can stem from two types of experiences. Learning-by-doing refers to experiences that are made within the production process, so that more produced units help firms to reduce the average cost per unit; for example, by incremental improvements in the production process that reduce waste in PV module production. Learning-by-using refers to gains that are generated from experiences by the subsequent use of the product. For example, engineers of offshore wind parks will learn from their experiences how to cope with corrosion in salty water.

A governmental intervention can be justified by the fact that this learning is not a purely private good but has a public good component since other technology users may also profit from the knowledge generated through cumulative experiences. A private technology applicant, however, will not take into account the societal benefits her experiences generate for other users, leading to an underuse of the technology compared with what would be a socially optimal usage. In a decentralized market economy, a policy intervention can correct this market failure and induce additional cumulative experiences, leading to cost reductions of the technologies. This argument is normally part of the justification why renewable technologies in Europe need to be supported. Accordingly, the 20 percent target of the European Union is a headline target for the European 2020 strategy for growth, since it contributes "to Europe's industrial innovation and technological leadership" (European Commission 2013a, 1).

An instrument that addresses the market-failure from "learning-by-experience" has to compensate the producer with the resulting marginal cost reductions stemming from the additional experience. This has not been taken into account by the producer privately. Thus, for a coherent RES-E policy it is crucial to understand (a) what the marginal cost reductions induced by an additional unit of output and its use are, and (b) to what extent this knowledge is a public good. Obviously, learning curve effects are not constant. Newer technologies tend to have a greater potential for cost reductions. The European Commission's (2013b) own assessment of potentials for cost-reductions for a portfolio of energy technologies, drawing on data from the European Commission's Strategic Energy Technologies Information System (SETIS), shows that potentials vary significantly between technologies. The global capacity of PV solar electricity systems increased in 12 years from 1.8 GW in 2000 to 100 GW at the end of 2012 (European Commission 2013b). PV systems became more than 50 percent cheaper over the last four years alone.

Under the simplifying assumption that capacity expansion is the sole driver of cost reductions, one can easily calculate the so-called learning rate, i.e., the cost-reduction as the cumulated installation volume doubles. For the period from 2001 to 2010, the learning rate of PV systems is estimated to have been around 14 percent (Kersten 2011). These learning rates vary over technologies and the maturity of technologies. An analysis of the deployment of windmills in the United Kingdom, Germany, Spain, and Denmark between 1986 and 2000 indicates a learning rate of 3.1 percent (Söderholm and Klaassen 2007). Therefore, there is evidence that increasing capacity reduces costs, which in turn helps to reduce the overall costs of the energy system decarbonization.

But in order to find an argument for policy intervention, it needs to be shown that this positive externality of experience is not fully private and is taken into account by the investors. Unfortunately, there is almost no evidence about the magnitude of such spillover effects from learning-by-doing and -using. In contrast to learning-by-searching, where spillovers are usually measured using patent-citation data, diffusion activities are often not patentable procedural knowledge. It is also unclear how far this procedural knowledge spills over spatially into other countries and markets. By end of 2014, Germany had around twice as much PV capacity installed compared to the United States. Evidence by Barbose et al. (2014) shows that the installation costs per Watt PV are in Germany only half as expensive compared to the United States, despite the fact that in both markets largely the same modules are used. Parts of these cost reductions might be explained by differences in regulation, competition, etc. Moreover, the causal direction between large installed capacities and low installation costs is not clear per se. However, this indicates that learning-by-using effects might help to cut costs in planning and installation of PV systems, increasing the competitiveness of this technology in the longer term.

To summarize, the magnitudes of learning-by-doing and -using externalities entail large uncertainties, although there is theoretically some evidence for the existence of this market failure. Conditional to the existence of such an externality, a FiP on top of the wholesale market price of electricity could be justified. The FiP should compensate the RES-E producer for the marginal cost reductions from the additional experience that becomes public knowledge. Since the additional experience is presumably decreasing over time, the FiP should also decrease over time. In a stylized model of the U.S. power sector, Fischer and Newell (2008) compute that the optimal FiP to compensate for learning-by-doing spillovers might be around 4 percent of the electricity price. This is quite small in comparison to typical subsidy rates, making it difficult to rationalize learning-based production subsidies for relatively mature RES-E technologies such as on-shore wind.

We propose an FiP instead of an FiT system because an FiT system leads to distorted supply incentives that are immune to price signals on the electricity market. A coherent policy portfolio has to take into account that volatile RES-E generation can cause further distortions due to grid congestion. It might eventually even become difficult to meet the load which endangers the stability of the grid. It is therefore crucial that RES-E producers also face price signals that reflect scarcity. However, the crucial question is the calibration of the FiP given nonconstant learning rates, which might change rapidly with the maturity of technologies. If the premiums are too low, they do not induce the necessary cost reduction since the market failure is not sufficiently corrected. But if deployment subsidies are too high, they have a negative effect on cost reductions as they induce renewables generators to choose high-cost sites and provide fewer incentives for cost cuts (Söderholm and Klaassen 2007). The latter seems more relevant given scant empirical evidence. It is important to note that such an RES-E diffusion policy which is strictly targeted to the correction of a market failure would—if properly calibrated—not cause distortions with other climate and energy policies, since such a policy is not a substitute but rather a complement to direct emission reduction measures in the power sector.

Learning-by-Searching   R&D investments are important to realize future cost reductions of RES-E technologies. They are necessary to make these technologies competitive, a precondition for a successful decarbonization of the energy system. But two market failures in the knowledge generation process prevent the uncorrected market economy from realizing the full potential of R&D (Jones and Williams 2000). First, innovators are not able to appropriate the entire surplus associated with their innovation. Second, present researchers "stand on the shoulders" of past researchers; that is, part of the output of R&D is knowledge that contributes to the capacity of others to innovate. Thus, the private return of investment in R&D is lower than the social rate of return. This justifies governmental intervention, for example by subsidizing R&D efforts.

There is evidence that the social rate of return per euro R&D investment is at least four times greater than private returns (Jones and Williams 1998). But the magnitudes of these spillovers differ between technologies (Otto et al. 2008). New and underdeveloped technologies benefit the most from R&D investments but also suffer from the highest spillover rates. They would hence need the largest subsidies. This is also consistent with empirical research that finds that the spillovers of RES-E technologies are significantly higher than spillovers of traditional fossil fuel energy technologies (Dechezleprêtre et al. 2013). A study of the wind industry finds a learning-by-searching rate of 13.2 percent between 1986 and 2000 (Söderholm and Klaassen 2007). This means that during this period, a doubling of the R&D efforts would have reduced technology costs by 13.2 percent. With a focus on the U.S. power sector, Fischer and Newell (2008) calculate that the optimal subsidy rate is around 50 percent for RES-E technologies in general. This evidence suggests that R&D subsidies are probably more

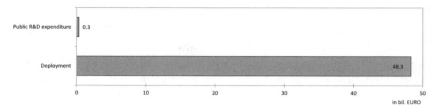

Figure 5.4
Deployment vs. R&D expenditure for wind and solar in 2010 in DE, ES, FR, IT, UK, and
CZ (in bil. EUR)
Source: Zachmann et al. (2014).

relevant for bringing down costs than learning-by-doing subsidies. However, the current spending on the two market failures is exactly the opposite: public spending on technology diffusion for wind and PV is two orders of magnitude larger than on R&D support. As figure 5.4 shows, in 2010, the five largest EU countries spent about €48 billion on deployment, but only €315 million on public R&D support for these technologies (Zachmann et al. 2014).

Public support addressing the two market failures needs to be better balanced, shifting resources to R&D support. The NER400 program, the successor program of NER300 that will be endowed with the revenue of 400 million carbon permits to support research, development, and demonstration activities of new renewable and CCS technologies, is a first step but likely not enough, in particular if EU ETS permit prices remain as low as they are now.

In any case, R&D support needs to be spent wisely by identifying technologies with large spillovers. Eventually, the technologies need to be taken up by the markets. Fischer (2008) reveals an additional policy interaction and argues that R&D investments in RES-E technologies need also moderate emission policies in place in order to become profitable. Additionally, renewable deployment policies tend to raise the return on R&D investments. Both policies addressing the two market failures that exist in the generation of knowledge for renewable technologies have then a general rationale: an FiP that directly incentivizes the generation of renewable energy, exploiting the full learning-by-doing potential, plus an R&D subsidy that equalizes social rates of return to private rates of return of R&D investments and internalizes learning-by-searching externalities.

It is again important to note that both externalities are complementary to a carbon price. Therefore, the implementation of policy instruments that address the two additional market failures does not lead to distortions but rather belongs to the optimal policy set of policies and leads to a cost-efficient mitigation policy. But in order to put this discussion into perspective, it is also crucial to stress that the most important regulation is the effort to get GHG emission prices right. As elaborated on above, there is indeed an economic rationale for multiple policy instruments. However, as several studies (see, e.g., Parry et al. 2003; Fischer and Newell 2008) show, correcting the emissions externality likely yields much bigger welfare gains than correcting the different knowledge externalities.

5. The Coherence of Energy Efficiency Policies

So far, our analysis has focused on policy intervention on the supply side of energy markets. In order to implement comprehensive interventions, we also have to take the demand side into account. Of course, every policy that affects the demand side has in equilibrium a supply side effect too, and vice versa. For example, if a policy reduces energy demand directly, less fossil fuel supply is needed to match demand, hence contributing indirectly also to security of the energy supply. However, it is important to point out that externalities from energy consumption such as the emission of greenhouse gases shall be addressed directly by pricing of the externality, for example through an ETS. But there might be additional market failures which motivate policy intervention specifically on the energy demand side to correct non-optimal investments.

The existence of market failures on the demand side is often derived from the observation that products with great potential for energy efficiency improvement—although seemingly cost-efficient—have not been embraced by consumers. The magnitude of this "energy efficiency gap" has been discussed extensively in the literature but remains heavily disputed (see, e.g., Allcott and Greenstone 2012). This "energy efficiency gap" is often assessed using the concept of maximizing physical energy efficiency as a benchmark. This generally does not coincide with maximal economic efficiency since energy efficiency measures come at a cost (Gillingham et al. 2009). In fact, the empirical size of the investment inefficiencies appears to be much smaller than the massive potential savings calculated in engineering analyses (Allcott and Greenstone 2012). There are numerous explanations for these differences. Geraden, Newell, and Stavins (2015) structure these explanations along the fundamental elements of cost-minimizing investments decisions.

For example, there are often unobserved costs not accounted for by the analyst, such as search and transaction costs. Studies often overlook that energy efficiency improvements may change the attributes of the product (e.g., lightning quality). Further, the heterogeneity of consumers is often ignored as well as the uncertainty regarding future energy savings.

Nevertheless, there is evidence that the "energy efficiency gap," although much smaller than suggested, exists. The insufficient uptake of energy efficiency potentials is explained through the existence of so called "market barriers" that hinder the adoption of energy-efficient technologies. Market barriers can be defined as any disincentives to the adoption or use of a good (Jaffe et al. 2004). These market barriers can be grounded on capital market failures that cause liquidity constraints, or they can be the result of split incentive structures, e.g., between landlords and tenants, and exist because of asymmetric and missing information. However, these barriers are often not market failures in the classical sense and include factors such as volatile energy prices. Shogren and Taylor (2008) classify these biases as "behavioral failures."

If behavioral and market failures exist they warrant correcting regulation to push energy efficiency investments closer to the social optimum. However, as these failures are grounded in very different sources, they also need to be addressed very specifically. If, for instance, missing and asymmetric information is identified as the main cause of lacking investment, the policy response should be either to provide this information to the consumers, for example through labelling or energy counselling, or to set regulatory measures such as building codes or standards. If up-front investments are required but consumers lack the necessary liquidity, the provision of credits might be advisable to enable consumers the financing of the energy efficiency measure. This is often done to incentivize the improved insulation of buildings, where several European state development banks provide credits below market conditions for this purpose. Finally, if the absorption of more energy efficient technologies is non-optimal due to "behavioral failures" and myopic consumers, subsidizing the purchase of energy-efficient technologies might seem to be the best instrument to push the absorption of energy-efficient technologies towards the socially optimal pathway. However, implementing a well-targeted utilization of such

subsidies is extremely difficult as it would require identifying investments with a carefully assessed cost-benefit ratio smaller than one
(such that all hidden costs are taken into account), which would not
have been realized without the subsidy.

It becomes immediately clear that efficiency policies need to be very
well-calibrated to ensure that they do not do more harm than good. It
is even more complicated as consumers are heterogeneous in the degree
of their investment inefficiencies. Subsidizing energy-efficient appliances, for example, changes relative prices for all consumers. While
these subsidies might improve welfare when targeted to consumers
subject to investment inefficiencies, they might cause distortions and
welfare losses when available to consumers not subject to such inefficiencies (Allcott and Greenstone 2012). It is therefore crucial to understand the proper calibration of the instruments before applying them.
The risk of doing more harm than good is large and policy failures
might easily outweigh the detrimental impacts of market failures in
energy efficiency. A careful approach would start with moderately
scaled policies that can be increased gradually if their assessment is
positive. Similar to policies that address knowledge externalities, it is
important to put energy efficiency policies in perspective with emission
pricing: The top priority is to price carbon emissions accordingly (Parry
et al. 2014). Relative to this, the welfare gains from correcting energy
efficiency market failures are modest.

6.   Conclusions for European Policy Making

We show that there is indeed a positive rationale for using a portfolio
of policies. The policy mix has to address the specific market failures
beyond the climate externality. It is crucial to stress that the most
important policy instrument to deal with GHG emissions is a price on
carbon that reflects the damages that the emissions provoke, mediating
mitigation actions economy-wide. It is therefore the first priority to fix
the EU ETS and have a clear and stringent carbon price in as many
sectors as possible. This makes low-carbon innovation more profitable
and energy efficiency measures more beneficial. One of the few climate
policy measures of the European Union that is not bound to a specific
target year is the linear reduction factor in the EU ETS that tightens the
cap annually. Until 2020, this factor is 1.74 percent and increases to 2.2
percent from 2021 onward in order to set the EU ETS on track with the
emission reduction of 40 percent by 2030. But the linear reduction factor

tightens the cap beyond 2030 even if policymakers are inactive. This provides a clear signal, which is important for the investment in long-term low-carbon technologies. But other instruments are also advisable to address additional market failures. These complementary instruments might reduce the long-term costs of decarbonization. Two market failures in the knowledge generation process hamper the market economy from realizing the full benefits of innovations.

First, learning-by-doing and learning-by-using externalities need to be addressed. Experience gained in the production and usage has a public good component because other technology users also profit from the generated knowledge. This market failure can be addressed with a market premium (or a renewable portfolio standard) on top of the wholesale electricity price that compensates RES-E producers for their contribution to the cost reduction. Such an FiP scheme has clear advantages over an FiT scheme since it forces producers to response to prices as a signal for scarcity. In any case, diffusion externalities might be small, and learning-by-doing—and probably learning-by-using even more so—externalities are difficult to target. Fischer and Newell (2008) compute, based on U.S. data, an optimal FiP of around 4 percent of the wholesale electricity price. This is much smaller than current subsidies for renewable technologies which are, depending on the technologies, often between 10 and 100 times larger.

Second, a learning-by-searching externality has to be considered, since the generation of knowledge through R&D is partly a public good. There is some empirical evidence that substantial spillovers exist. Moreover, R&D subsidies seem to be far more efficient in bringing down costs relative to learning-by-doing subsidies. However, the current public spending addressing the two market failures is the direct opposite. Public spending on diffusion of wind and PV has been two orders of magnitude larger than on R&D support. Spending that addresses these two market failures needs to be better balanced, reducing substantially the amount of subsidies for technology diffusion and shifting substantial resources to R&D support. In particular, beyond 2030, when the energy system needs to be on a track of becoming more or less carbon-free, technologies are necessary that are today in a very early stage of development. This requires additional efforts that cannot be achieved by a carbon price alone. When analyzing the demand side carefully, we can also identify market failures that hamper the uptake of energy-efficient technologies. However, these market failures are very specific and have particular effects on different consumers. Thus, successful policies need to be calibrated very well in order to reduce distortions. The risk of doing more harm than good is certainly high.

If it would be possible to calibrate policies such that they are able to address the market failures precisely according their first-best configuration, they would not cause distortions but would be part of the first-best instrument portfolio. However, policymakers often lack the information necessary to implement these first-best policy portfolios. This is even truer as renewable and energy efficiency policies operate in a world where a broad range of policy targets exists. These targets might be legitimate, but addressing these further goals cause distortions due to the interaction with existing instruments. Economists need to take this nth-best world into account in their assessments. The (societal) benefits of reaching additional goals have to outweigh the distortions from additional and interacting policy measures. Since this implicitly assumes that reaching one goal is more important than another, a societally defined ranking of goals is needed.

This paper has presented rationales, founded in economic theory, for utilizing a policy portfolio that contains several measures, each addressing a worthwhile goal. But in such a complex environment, policy interactions are not easily predicted; rather, surprising and unintended interactions might emerge. Moreover, innovation externalities might vanish over time, reducing the scope for instruments that complement carbon pricing. Therefore, new policy instruments have to be added with the utmost reservation because policy failures are a constant risk when designing extended policy portfolios. Otherwise, the policy mix risks becoming a policy mess.

Notes

1. The European Union defines energy from renewable sources as "energy from renewable non-fossil sources, namely wind, solar, aerothermal, geothermal, hydrothermal and ocean energy, hydropower, biomass, landfill gas, sewage treatment plant gas and biogases" (Directive 2009/28/EC of the European Parliament and of the Council of April 23, 2009).

2. The emission target was reaffirmed in the EU's Intended Nationally Determined Contribution for the UN climate conference in December 2015 in Paris.

3. Although this is not always as straightforward as it seems. Energy efficiency measures lower energy costs which can lead to higher energy demand, the so-called "rebound effect." New renewables may sometimes, depending on the structure of the energy market, replace other already installed low-carbon sources of energy. Energy efficiency measures might reduce the demand covered by low-carbon energy sources, leaving carbon emissions unaffected. See Borenstein (2012) for a discussion of these more specific issues.

4. All domestic GHG emissions without emissions from land use, land use change, and forestry, nor from international aviation and international maritime transport.

5. Note that biofuels are not always carbon-free. The Fuel Quality Directive regulates the carbon intensity of biofuels in the European Union. GHG emissions from biofuels must be at least 35 percent lower than from fossil fuels. This saving must increase to 50 percent in 2017 and to 60 percent for new installations in 2018.

6. For example, a typical rooftop PV system in Germany with 10-40 kW installed in July 2015 got about 12 c/kWh in the first month and decreased by 0.5 percent each month. At the same time, the average wholesale price for electricity was 3.5 c/kWh.

7. As an example, under this scheme, a Danish onshore wind plant commissioned after the beginning of 2014 received a guaranteed bonus of 0.25 DKK (approximately 3 c) per kWh for a certain number of load hours.

8. Because renewable investors are uncertain about the future profitability of their investments, see Hoel (2012). In the same vein, a renewable energy subsidy can be rationalized in a policy setting with volatile emission prices and a positive risk that the price drops to zero (Lecuyer and Quirion 2013).

9. See, for example, Fischer and Newell (2008).

References

Allcott, H., and M. Greenstone. 2012. "Is There an Energy Efficiency Gap?" *The Journal of Economic Perspectives* 26 (1): 3-28.

Arrow, K. 1962. "The Economic Implication of Learning-by-Doing." *Review of Economic Studies* 29 (3): 155-73.

Barbose, G. L., J. Seel, and R. H. Wiser. 2014. "An Analysis of Residential PV System Price Differences Between the United States and Germany." *Energy Policy* 69: 216-26.

Bennear, L., and R. N. Stavins. 2007. "Second-Best Theory and the Use of Multiple Policy Instruments." *Environmental and Resource Economics* 37 (1): 111-29.

Boeters, S., and J. Koornneef. 2011. "Supply of Renewable Energy Sources and the Cost of EU Climate Policy." *Energy Economics* 33 (5): 1024-34.

Böhringer, C., and M. Behrens. 2015. "Interactions of Emission Caps and Renewable Electricity Support Schemes." *Journal of Regulatory Economics* 48 (1): 74-96.

Böhringer, C., and K. E. Rosendahl. 2010. "Green Promotes the Dirtiest: On the Interaction between Black and Green Quotas in Energy Markets." *Journal of Regulatory Economics* 37: 316-25.

Böhringer, C., A. Löschel, U. Moslener, and T. F. Rutherford. 2009. "EU Climate Policy up to 2020: An Economic Impact Assessment." *Energy Economics* 31: 295-305.

Borenstein, S. 2012. "The Private and Public Economics of Renewable Electricity Generation." *Journal of Economic Perspectives* 26 (1): 67-92.

Dechezleprêtre, A., R. Martin, and M. Mohnen. 2013. "Knowledge Spillovers from Clean and Dirty Technologies: A Patent Citation Analysis" (Mimeo).

European Commission. 2013a. "Renewable Energy Progress Report, SWD (2013)102 Final." http://eur-lex.europa.eu/legal-content/EN/ALL/?uri=CELEX:52013DC0175.

European Commission. 2013b. "Energy Technology Developments Beyond 2020 for the Transition to a Decarbonised European Energy System by 2050." http://ec.europa.eu/energy/technology/strategy/doc/swf_2013_0158_en.pdf.

European Commission. 2014. "Energy Efficiency and its Contribution to Energy Security and the 2030 Framework for Climate and Energy Policy." Communication from the Commission to the European Parliament and the Council. http://ec.europa.eu/energy/effi ciency/events/doc/2014_eec_communication_adopted.pdf.

European Council. 2014. "Conclusions—23/24 October 2014." EUCO 169/14. http:// www.consilium.europa.eu/uedocs/cms_data/docs/pressdata/en/ec/145397.pdf.

European Environmental Agency. 2014. "Annual European Union Greenhouse Gas Inventory 1990–2012 and Inventory Report 2014." http://www.eea.europa.eu/publica tions/european-union-greenhouse-gas-inventory-2014.

Federal Ministry of Economic Affairs and Energy (BMWi). 2014. "The Energy of the Future—First 'Energy Transition' Progress Report." Summary. BMWi, Berlin, Germany. http://www.bmwi.de/English/Redaktion/Pdf/fortschrittsbericht-kurzfassung-en,pro perty=pdf,bereich=bmwi2012,sprache=en,rwb=true.pdf.

Fischer, C. 2008. "Emissions Pricing, Spillovers, and Public Investment in Environmentally Friendly Technologies." Energy Economics 30 (2): 487-502.

Fischer, C., and R. G. Newell. 2008. "Environmental and Technology Policies for Climate Mitigation." Journal of Environmental Economics and Management 55: 142-62.

Fischer, C., and L. Preonas. 2010. "Combining Policies for Renewable Energy: Is the Whole Less than the Sum of Its Parts?" International Review of Environmental and Resource Economics 4 (1): 51-92.

Flues, F., A. Löschel, B. J. Lutz, and O. Schenker. 2014. "Designing an EU Energy and Climate Policy Portfolio for 2030: Implications of Overlapping Regulation under Different Levels of Electricity Demand." Energy Policy 75: 91-99.

Gerarden, T. D., R. G. Newell, and R. N. Stavins. 2015. "Assessing the Energy-Efficiency Gap." Harvard Environmental Economics Program. http://dx.doi.org/10.2139/ ssrn.2554735.

Gillingham, K., R. G. Newell, and K. L. Palmer. 2009. "Energy Efficiency Economics and Policy." Annual Review of Resource Economics 1 (1): 597-620.

Goulder, L. H., I. W. Parry, R. C. Williams III, and D. Burtraw. 1999. "The Cost-Effectiveness of Alternative Instruments for Environmental Protection in a Second-Best Setting." Journal of Public Economics 72 (3): 329-60.

Hoel, M. 2012. "Second-Best Climate Policy" (Mimeo). Department of Economics, University of Oslo.

International Energy Agency. 2014. IEA Policies and Measures Databases. http://www.iea .org/policiesandmeasures/.

Jaffe, A. B., R. G. Newell, and R. N. Stavins. 2004. "Economics of Energy Efficiency." Encyclopedia of Energy 2: 79-90.

Jones, C. I., and J. C. Williams. 1998. "Measuring the Social Return to R&D." *Quarterly Journal of Economics* 133 (4): 1119-35.

Jones, C. I., and J. C. Williams. 2000. "Too Much of a Good Thing? The Economics of Investment in R&D." *Journal of Economic Growth* 5 (1): 65-85.

Kersten, F., R. Doll, A. Kux, D.M. Huljic, M.A. Görig, C. Breyer, J.W. Müller, and P. Wawer. 2011. "PV Learning Curves: Past and Future Drivers of Cost Reduction." *Proceedings of the 26th European Photovoltaic Solar Energy Conference*, September 5–9. Hamburg, Germany. https://www.eupvsec-proceedings.com/proceedings/dvd.html?TOC=26.

Landis, F., O. Schenker, M. A. Tovar Reaños, C. Vonnahme, and S. Zitzelsberger. 2013. "An Overview on Current Climate Policies in the European Union and Its Member States." ENTRACTE Report, Mannheim, Germany. http://entracte-project.eu/research/report-current-policies/.

Lecuyer, O., and P. Quirion. 2013. "Can Uncertainty Justify Overlapping Policy Instruments to Mitigate Emissions?" *Ecological Economics* 93: 177-91.

Lipsey, R. G., and K. Lancaster. 1956. "The General Theory of Second Best." *The Review of Economic Studies* 24 (1): 11-32.

Löschel, A., G. Erdmann, F. Staiß, and H. Ziesing. 2014. "Expert Commission on the 'Energy of the Future' Monitoring Process—Statement on the First Progress Report by the German Government for 2013." Summary. BMWi, Berlin, Germany. http://www.bmwi.de/English/Redaktion/Pdf/monitoringbericht-energie-der-zukunft-stellung nahme-zusammenfassung-2013,property=pdf,bereich=bmwi2012,sprache=en,rwb=true .pdf.

Malerba, F. 1992. "Learning by Firms and Incremental Technical Change." *Economic Journal* 102: 845-59.

Otto, V. M., A. Löschel, and J. Reilly. 2008. "Directed Technical Change and Differentiation of Climate Policy." *Energy Economics* 30 (6): 2855-78.

Parry, I. W. H., W. A. Pizer, and C. Fischer. 2003. "How Large are the Welfare Gains from Technological Innovation Induced by Environmental Policies?" *Journal of Regulatory Economics* 23 (3): 237–55.

Parry, I. W. H., R. C. Williams III, and L. H. Goulder. 1999. "When Can Carbon Abatement Policies Increase Welfare? The Fundamental Role of Distorted Factor Markets." *Journal of Environmental Economics and Management* 37 (1): 52-84.

Rodrik, D. 2008. "Second-Best Institutions." *American Economic Review* 98 (2): 100-04.

Shogren, J. F., and L. O. Taylor. 2008. "On Behavioral-Environmental Economics." *Review of Environmental Economics and Policy* 2 (1): 26-44.

Sijm, J. 2005. "The Interaction between the EU Emissions Trading Scheme and National Energy Policies." *Climate Policy* 5 (1): 79-96.

Söderholm, P., and G. Klaassen. 2007. "Wind Power in Europe: a Simultaneous Innovation-Diffusion Model." *Environmental and Resource Economics* 36 (2): 163-90.

Sorrell, S., and J. Sijm. 2003. "Carbon Trading in the Policy Mix." *Oxford Review of Economic Policy* 19 (3): 420-37.

Tinbergen, J. 1952. *On the Theory of Economic Policy*. Amsterdam, Netherlands: North-Holland Publishing Company.

Zachmann, G., M. Peruzzi, and A. Serwaah. 2014. "When and How to Support Renewables? Letting the Data Speak" (Bruegel Working Paper 2014/01).

A Comment on "On the Coherence of Economic Instruments: Climate, Renewables, and Energy Efficiency Policies"

Niels Anger[1]

The European Union is on track to meet the 2020 targets for greenhouse gas emissions reduction and renewable energy, and significant improvements have been made in energy savings thanks to more efficient buildings, products, industrial processes, and vehicles.

Nevertheless, experience with the current 2020 framework—the focus of the paper by Löschel and Schenker—indicates that while European and national targets can drive strong action by the Member States and growth in emerging industries, they have not always ensured market integration, cost-efficiency, and undistorted competition, inter alia due to the interactions among different climate and energy policies. I agree with Löschel and Schenker that, in principle, a main target for greenhouse gas emissions reduction implemented by a price on emissions represents the least-cost pathway to a low-carbon economy that of itself should drive an increased share of renewable energy and energy savings in the Union.

However, the paper by Löschel and Schenker also mentions additional targets as a rationale for complementary instruments. In this context, security of energy supply in particular should be considered as a further EU policy concern. For fossil fuels, the International Energy Agency projects an increasing EU reliance on imported oil from around 80 percent today to more than 90 percent by 2035. Similarly, gas import dependency is expected to rise from 60 percent to more than 80 percent. In 2012, Europe's oil and gas import bill amounted to more than €400 billion, representing some 3.1 percent of the EU GDP (European Commission, COM(2014)15). Policies designed to improve the Union's security of supply must follow a differentiated approach. Besides the diversification of supply countries and routes for imported fossil fuels, as well as improved interconnections of energy infrastructure within the European Union, declining EU oil and gas production makes further exploitation of sustainable indigenous energy sources, including renewable energy, a necessity. Greater efforts are also required to improve energy efficiency of the economy cost-effectively and to generate energy savings from the improved energy performance of buildings, products, and processes.

Against this background, the European Commission proposed a policy mix in the context of the 2030 Framework for Climate and Energy, which was adopted by the European Council in October 2014: a new reduction target for domestic greenhouse gas emissions of 40 percent compared to 1990, to be shared between the Emissions Trading System (ETS) and non-ETS sector, as the centerpiece of the EU's energy and climate policy for 2030—and as the EU contribution to the 2015 climate agreement under the United Nations Framework Convention on Climate Change in Paris (COP 21). The non-ETS target will be allocated among Member States through a revised effort-sharing decision in 2016. The greenhouse gas emissions reduction target is accompanied by coherent EU-level targets derived in function of the greenhouse gas emissions target: for renewable energy of at least 27 percent as well as for energy efficiency of at least 27 percent. The functional derivation and the EU-level nature of the 2030 energy targets ensures better coherence of the policy mix and more flexibility for Member States, thereby enhancing cost-effectiveness.

Alongside the 2030 Framework, the European Commission presented a proposal to reform the EU ETS. In particular, the agreement with Member States and the European Parliament on the introduction of a Market Stability Reserve, in place from 2019 on, will strengthen the ETS price signal. The reserve will address the current surplus of allowances and improve the system's resilience to major shocks by adjusting the supply of allowances to be auctioned. This is a crucial step to make the ETS ready to play its role as the main European instrument to achieve the 2030 greenhouse gas emissions target.

With its recent "Framework Strategy for a Resilient Energy Union with a Forward-Looking Climate Change Policy," the European Commission proposed for the first time a fully integrated approach to energy and climate policy along five interlinked dimensions: energy security, energy efficiency, internal energy market integration, decarbonization, and research and innovation. Besides delivering on the targets of the 2030 Framework for Climate and Energy, the Energy Union strategy thereby aims at further diversifying Europe's sources and supply routes of energy and supporting the development and deployment of low-carbon technologies by better coordinating and prioritizing research across the Union and promoting cooperation.

Promoting research and development, identified by Löschel and Schenker as a key action for addressing the externality of knowledge spill-overs, will require public support for developing the next generation of renewable energy technologies, together with energy storage; facilitating the participation of consumers in the energy transition through smart grids, smart home appliances, and smart cities; developing efficient energy systems and harnessing technology to make the building stock energy-neutral; and creating more sustainable transport systems that develop and deploy large-scale innovative technologies. The new Integrated Strategic Energy Technology (SET) Plan will support these efforts by promoting technologies with the greatest impact on the EU's transformation to a low-carbon energy system.

For the implementation of the Energy Union objectives, a European governance system will be put in place in order to deliver in particular the EU-level targets for renewable energy and energy savings in a manner that is consistent with attainment of national and European greenhouse gas targets and coherent with the wider principles of European energy policy—including the operation and further integration of the internal energy market and the delivery of a competitive, secure, and sustainable energy system.

At the core of the governance system are integrated national energy and climate plans for the period of 2021 to 2030. A transparent monitoring system will be based on streamlined progress reports by Member States, regularly assessing the implementation of national plans as well as key energy and climate indicators. The European Commission will assess collective progress made by Member States and, if necessary, propose policy measures to ensure the achievement of the Energy Union objectives, including the 2030 targets. The Energy Union also encourages closer regional cooperation on all five dimensions in order to achieve its objectives in a more cost-effective and secure way.

In summary, while the paper by Löschel and Schenker correctly points to potential inefficiencies of the 2020 framework, better coherence among EU energy and climate policy instruments, and increased cost-effectiveness in achieving policy targets are at the core of EU energy and climate policy development for 2030. These fundamental principles will be implemented by means of a solid and transparent

Energy Union Governance in close cooperation between the European Commission, Member States, and the European Parliament.

Note

1. The views expressed in this article are the author's alone and do not necessarily correspond to those of the European Commission.

6 Fiscal and Regulatory Instruments for Clean Technology Development in the European Union

Antoine Dechezleprêtre and David Popp

Key Points for Policymakers

- European countries currently emphasize technology deployment over direct R&D support. Current efforts on deployment should be augmented with additional public R&D support.
- Given that there is no evidence that we have hit diminishing returns to energy R&D funding, we recommend an increase of public R&D funding for low-carbon technologies. The IEA estimates that public R&D spending needs to at least double to achieve the substantial advancement of low-carbon technologies consistent with decarbonization.
- Increased funding should be gradual to avoid adjustment costs and should be supported by a long-term commitment. A doubling of public R&D expenditures over 10 years corresponds to what was observed between 2001 and 2011 and thus seems achievable.
- Assuming an average carbon price of €11/ton, directing ten percent of the revenues from auctioned EU ETS emissions allowances into low-carbon innovation would be enough to fund this doubling in public R&D funding in Europe over the next decade.
- Because emissions standards and permits markets favor innovation in technologies that are closest to the market, public R&D efforts should in contrast support the development of technologies further from the market that have a strong public good component, such as CCS, energy storage, smart grids, energy efficiency, and infrastructure for electric vehicles.

1. Introduction

On October 23, 2014, EU leaders adopted a commitment to reduce domestic greenhouse gas (GHG) emissions by 40 percent in 2030 relative to 1990. In 2012, GHG emissions were 19 percent lower than in 1990 at 4.5 Gt CO_2eq. The additional reduction thus represents a significant challenge. In order to achieve this objective (and further reductions beyond 2030) while meeting growing energy demand, significant changes in the mix of what existing technologies are used across Europe are needed. For this to happen at a reasonable cost for the economy requires decreasing the cost of clean technologies and developing new breakthrough technologies. This in turn depends on investment in innovation activities.

According to the last IPCC report, future investments in research, development, and demonstration (RD&D), both private and public, will be the determining factor for the cost of emissions reductions policies. For example, the unavailability of carbon capture and storage (CCS) technologies would substantially increase the cost of any climate change policy.[1] The influence of technology on costs moreover increases with the ambition of the climate change mitigation goal (IPCC 2014). Importantly, the diversity of energy uses, systems, resources, and national contexts means that addressing climate change and other environmental issues will require innovation across the whole range of existing and potential clean technologies. The cost of existing environment-friendly technologies, such as wind turbines and sulphur dioxide (SO_2) scrubbers, needs to be brought down so that they can be deployed on a large scale, while fundamental research needs to advance on the frontiers of technologies such as smart grids[2] or electricity storage, which lower the need for peak power generation. As a consequence, research and innovation is a key component of the EU energy policy, as demonstrated by the recent publication by the European Commission of a Roadmap on the Energy Union Integrated Strategy on Research, Innovation and Competitiveness.

Yet, despite these pressing challenges, European companies in the electricity production sector—the largest GHG emissions emitter in Europe, with 33 percent of European emissions in 2012—spend less than 1 percent of their turnover on innovation, against 10-15 percent in IT or pharmaceuticals (see figure 6.1), suggesting that incentives to conduct R&D of new or enhanced low-carbon technologies and their associated systems and processes are insufficient. This low intensity of

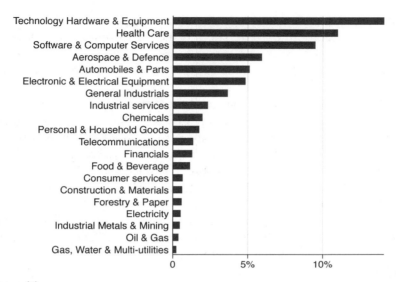

Figure 6.1
R&D expenditure by top 1,000 European companies in different sectors as a percent of revenue, 2012
Source: EU Joint Research Centre on Industrial Investment and Innovation, R&D Scoreboard 2013.

R&D in the electricity production sector has been associated with high development costs, long development timescales, homogeneity of the goods produced, and regulatory uncertainty. Importantly, the public sector does not seem to make up for the lack of private investment: public R&D expenditures in the energy sector in Europe represent less than 0.1 percent of GDP in almost all European countries and account for less than 5 percent of total public R&D expenditures on average.

The objective of this chapter is to investigate whether the current level of public support to environment-friendly technologies is sufficient to allow European countries to respond to the multiple challenges posed by climate change and other environmental concerns and to discuss the policy interventions that might be needed in order to drive forward clean energy technology investments in Europe. We first lay out the justifications for government support to clean R&D activity at the various stages of technology development, discussing particular features of clean technologies that justify policy intervention. We present empirical evidence for the impact of various policies on the development of clean technologies and use this to identify what the appropriate policy mix should look like. We present an overview of policies currently in place to support the development of clean technologies across Europe and compare the current policy landscape to the appropriate policy portfolio to draw some practical steps for policy reform.

Our analysis shows that the current low price of carbon in Europe is a major barrier to clean technology development. The new emissions commitments for 2030, as well as the planned market stability reserve, are steps in the right direction, but are unlikely to affect prices much in the next decade. Moreover, market-based policies such as the EU Emissions Trading System (ETS) favor technologies that are close to the market. The combination of low prices, political constraints on future emissions prices, and well-known innovation market failures justify strong policies directly targeted at clean technology development. Thus we recommend a gradual increase of public R&D funding for low-carbon technologies. The IEA has estimated that public R&D spending in OECD countries needs to at least double to achieve significant advance of low-carbon technologies. If possible, commitments to fund R&D should be long term (until at least 2030), just like carbon emission caps. Policy stability is important for companies, universities, and other research stakeholders to make long-term predictions on innovation needs. Revenues from auctioned carbon permits could provide a source of sustained funding for low carbon R&D with the necessary long-term commitment. In fact, directing 10 percent of the planned auctioned allowances revenues until 2025 to R&D funding would lead to the doubling of EU public R&D expenditures suggested above in 10 years. With 30 percent of global innovation activity toward low-carbon technologies currently occurring in European countries,[3] the European Union cannot just rely on other countries such as Japan or the United States to innovate and then transfer the technologies. Moreover, European countries have so far been clearly emphasizing technology deployment—especially for renewables—over direct R&D support. Yet, even as the costs of renewables begin to fall, technical barriers to deployment remain, suggesting that a greater emphasis on R&D is needed. In this respect, EU institutions and governments should focus their efforts on a broader portfolio of technologies that are central to any decarbonization pathway and have a strong public good component: CCS, energy storage, smart grids, energy efficiency, and infrastructure for electric vehicles. Since the benefits from subsidized R&D are much higher for Europe as a whole than for individual European countries, we call for a stronger involvement of

European institutions (such as the European Research Executive Agency, the European Research Council, or the Innovation and Networks Executive Agency) in public R&D in clean technologies. Finally, our analysis suggests that in a context of high general public spending, regulatory instruments, such as technological standards, may become increasingly attractive (relative to subsidy policies), provided they are tied to direct R&D support for technologies that have longer-term potential.

2. The Case for Government Intervention to Support Clean Technology Development

In this section, we explain why economic theory justifies public support for technology development, and particularly so regarding technologies with an environmental benefit. For climate change, examples of such technologies include alternative energy sources, capturing methane gas from landfills, energy storage, energy efficiency, smart grids, and CCS. Technological development is understood as encompassing not only upstream R&D activity but also technology deployment all the way to large scale commercial diffusion.

To consider the incentives (or lack thereof) that firms have to develop and deploy environmental technologies, it is useful to first consider the incentives faced for the development and deployment of new technologies in general.

2.1 The Main Stages in Technology Development

Technological change is a complex process, encompassing both the creation of new ideas (e.g., invention and innovation) as well of the diffusion and adoption of new technologies throughout the economy. Throughout this process, there is feedback between the various stages of technological change (see figure 6.2). For example, experience acquired during the commercialization process usually influences subsequent product innovation. Yet, at each stage, incentives, in the form of prices or regulations, affect the development and adoption of new technologies. These multiple levels of feedback in the innovation chain imply that if the right incentives are not in place at a given stage (in particular through public policies, as we will see below), this will have an effect on all stages.

Importantly, successful innovation requires an ecosystem, made up of the private sector (entrepreneurs, technology firms, capital), academia (research universities, technical training schools), and multiple

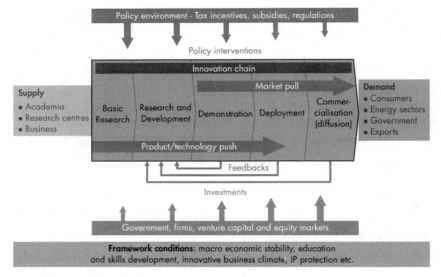

Figure 6.2
The main stages of technological development
Source: IEA (2008), adopted and modified from Grubb (2004).

government institutions (to ensure regulation, policy, and public funding). While not all European countries may individually possess a fully functioning innovation ecosystem, the European Union as a whole does possess all the ingredients necessary to carry out successful technological change, although some of the stages of technology development may be less relevant for some countries than for others. For example, it might be relevant for small or lower-income countries to focus on the diffusion stages of technological development and leave earlier stages to larger and more advanced economies.

2.2 The Rationale for Government Intervention to Support Innovation in Clean Technologies

At all stages of technological development, market forces provide insufficient incentives for investment in either the development or diffusion of environmentally friendly technologies. Economists point to two principal market failures as the explanations for underinvestment in environmental R&D. These market failures provide the motivation for government policy designed to increase such innovation.

A first market failure, which compounds innovation activity at all stages of clean technological change, is the traditional problem of environmental externalities. When pollution can be emitted freely, firms and consumers lack incentives to invest in the use of emissions-reducing and other environmentally friendly technologies. Thus, without appropriate policy interventions, the market for technologies that reduce emissions will be limited, reducing incentives to diffuse such technologies and hence to develop them in the first place. This underinvestment extends to technologies with both private and public benefits, such as energy efficient technologies that reduce a firm's costs as well as the resulting emissions from energy consumption. The market failure problem simply means that individuals and firms do not consider the social benefits of using technologies that reduce emissions, causing underinvestment in cleaner technologies. It is important to note that innovation activities are driven primarily by expectations about future environmental policies and the uncertainty surrounding future policies represents a clear barrier to technology development.

The second market failure[4] pertaining to clean technology development is the public goods nature of knowledge (see, for example, Geroski 1995), which impedes technological change at the R&D stage. In most cases, new technologies must be made available to the public for the inventor to reap the rewards of invention. However, by making new inventions public, some (if not all) of the knowledge embodied in the invention becomes public knowledge. This public knowledge may lead to additional innovations, or even to copies of the current innovations.[5] These knowledge spillovers provide benefit to the public as a whole, but not to the innovator. As a result, private firms do not have incentives to provide the socially optimal level of research activity. Economists studying the returns to research consistently find that knowledge spillovers result in a large difference between private and social rates return to R&D.[6] Typical results include marginal social rates of return between 30 and 50 percent. In comparison, estimates of private marginal rates of return on investments range from 7 to 15 percent (Hall et al. 2010). Since firms make investment decisions based on their private returns, the wedge between private and social rates of return suggests many socially beneficial research opportunities are being ignored by firms because they are unable to fully capture the rewards of such innovations.[7] Recent evidence (see box 6.1) further shows that knowledge spillovers are particularly high for clean technologies, suggesting that the wedge between private and social rates of return in environmental technologies might be particularly high.

Box 6.1
Knowledge Spillovers from Clean Technologies
Dechezleprêtre et al. (2013) investigate the magnitude of knowledge spill-overs from clean technologies in the electricity production and the transportation sectors and have found evidence that clean patents generate larger knowledge spillovers than the dirty technologies they replace. The magnitude of knowledge spillovers in clean technologies is comparable to those found in other emerging technological fields such as IT or nanotechnology. This means that underinvestment in innovation due to knowledge externalities might be particularly high for clean technologies (see figure 6.3). Moreover, while knowledge spillovers often have a strong local component, Dechezleprêtre et al. (2013) show that spillovers are highly prevalent across EU countries. While globally 50 percent of knowledge spillovers in clean technologies occur within the country of the inventor, this share is mechanically smaller for many European countries because of their small size: 25 percent for France, 17 percent for the United Kingdom, and 10 percent for the Netherlands. For Europe as a whole, however (i.e., considering Europe as a single entity), 61 percent of spillovers occur domestically. As such, coordination of EU research policy is theoretically justified and there is a strong case for European institutions—such as the European Research Executive Agency, the European Research Council, or the Innovation and Networks Executive Agency—to fund R&D, just like public R&D in the United States is funded by the federal government rather than by individual states.

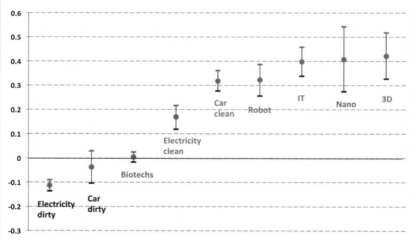

Figure 6.3
Knowledge spillovers from clean, dirty, and other emerging fields
Note: The y-axis indicates the difference in the intensity of knowledge spillovers, as measured by patent citations, between various technologies and the average innovation patented in the economy. For example, clean electricity technologies induce about 20 percent more spillovers than the average innovation.

A related market failure associated with technological change is learning-by-doing. It has been empirically demonstrated that production costs tend to decrease as the volume of production increases (Arrow 1962). Learning curve studies typically find faster learning for younger technologies, with estimates of learning rate revolving around 15-20 percent (so that production costs decrease by 15-20 percent for a doubling of production) for alternative energy sources such as wind and solar energy (McDonald and Schrattenholzer 2001). Hence, the early producers of a technology generate knowledge *through the production process* (and not through R&D activity). The extent to which this is a market failure depends on whether the benefits of learning spill over to other producers. For example, Nemet (2012) finds evidence of learning spillovers in California wind farms. This learning effect provides an incentive for producers to wait until the production costs have decreased. Similarly, there is evidence that product improvements often happen through producer-user relationships. This uncertainty over the benefits of a new technology, which resolves itself only through supply chain exchanges, creates an incentive for companies to wait until the technology has been developed by someone else (a "second mover advantage") even in the absence of knowledge spillovers.

The combination of the environmental market failure and the knowledge market failure creates the famous "double externality problem," whereby investment in clean R&D is doubly underprovided by the market, making policies to support clean technology development all the more necessary. However, the literature has identified many other potential market failures and barriers that compound private sector underinvestment in clean technologies at pre-commercial stages of development. In particular, even if problems associated with incomplete appropriability of the returns to R&D are solved, it may still be difficult or costly to finance such investments using capital from sources external to the firm. Information about the potential of a new technology is held by the innovator, creating a fundamental asymmetry of information that pushes investors to favor projects with least uncertain and short-term benefits (Hall and Lerner 2010). These imperfections in the market for capital decrease the incentives for financing technological development. Similarly, lock-in and path dependency of previous investments due to long-lived capital (like power plants), market power, network effects, and dominant designs impede technology development. These additional market failures (together with knowledge spillovers) underlie what has become known as the "technology valley of death" (for an extensive presentation of the issue, see Grubb 2013).

Of course, there are a wide variety of clean technologies, and different sets of market failures apply to different technologies. For example, knowledge market failures are highest in technologies that are newer, like solar PV, and that have wide applications across the board, like energy storage, while they are much smaller in magnitude in mature technologies such as hydro power (Dechezleprêtre et al. 2013). Hence, the case for policy support is stronger for the former types of technologies than for the latter, and support needs to be phased out as technologies mature.

3. Policies to Support Clean Technology Development

The combination of environmental externalities and knowledge market failures suggests two possible avenues through which policy can encourage the development of environment-friendly technologies: correcting the environmental externality and/or correcting knowledge market failures. Because knowledge market failures apply generally across technologies, policies addressing knowledge market failures may be general, addressing the problem in the economy as a whole. Examples include patent protection, R&D tax credits, and funding for generic basic research. Such policies focus on the overall rate of innovation—how much innovative activity takes place. In contrast, policies aimed specifically at the environment focus on the direction of innovation. Although the latter group of policies includes those regulating externalities, such as a carbon tax or cap-and-trade system, it also includes environmental and energy policies using more general R&D policy mechanisms with a specific focus on the environment, such as targeted government subsidies for the adoption of alternative energy and targeted funding for basic and applied research. As discussed below, such policies may be justified by differences in the returns to different types of R&D, or by evidence of behavioral anomalies that limit the diffusion of energy technologies.

3.1 Addressing the Environmental Externality
The Effects of Environmental Policy on Environmental Innovation
The existence of environmental externalities requires public policies that induce economic agents to "internalize" the benefits of environmental protection. Environmental policy tools are usually grouped

in two categories: market instruments, which establish a price on the externality (for example, a tax on carbon emissions or a cap-and-trade system), and command-and-control instruments, which impose limits on emissions of pollutants or require adoption of particular technical standards. By making polluting emissions costly, both types of environmental policies change the relative costs and benefits of competing technologies. For example, carbon taxes make coal relatively more expensive than natural gas. Renewable energy portfolio standards make alternative energy sources more attractive relative to carbon-based energy. Thus, policies that force agents to internalize environmental externalities encourage the diffusion of environmentally friendly technologies. In fact, studies addressing adoption of environmental technologies find that regulations dominate all other firm-specific factors in explaining the gradual diffusion of new technologies.[8]

Environmental regulation also encourages innovation. Because R&D is a profit-motivated investment activity, innovation responds to the change in the expected diffusion of technologies induced by environmental regulations. This notion of induced innovation (Acemoglu 2002; Acemoglu et al. 2012; Hicks 1932) provides the theoretical background for the vast empirical literature on the effect of policy and prices on environmental innovation. This literature—recently surveyed in Popp et al. (2010), Popp (2010b), and Ambec et al. (2013)—supports the conjecture of the induced innovation hypothesis and provides evidence on the magnitude of the effects. These studies, highlighted in box 6.2, show that both stricter environmental policies and higher energy prices encourage additional innovation on clean technologies, and that the innovative response to policy happens quickly. For example, much of the innovative response to higher (fossil fuel-based) energy prices occurs within five years or less. When looking at the innovative response to environmental regulation, rather than energy prices, the response time is even faster. Popp (2006a) finds an almost immediate innovative response to the passage of clean air regulations in the United States, Japan, and Germany. Similarly, figure 6.4, taken from Calel and Dechezleprêtre (2016), shows how the EU ETS has increased innovation activity in low-carbon technologies among regulated companies. The figure plots the patenting activity of firms regulated under the EU ETS with that of a control group of unregulated but similar firms selected through matching techniques. The control group represents what would have happened had the EU ETS not been implemented.

Box 6.2
Induced Innovation from Environmental Policy
Early studies of induced innovation from environmental policy (mostly for the United States) made use of pollution abatement control expenditures (PACE) to proxy for environmental regulatory stringency. Examples include Lanjouw and Mody (1996), Jaffe and Palmer (1997), and Brunnermeier and Cohen (2003). Each finds a significant correlation within industries over time between PACE and innovative activity. Renewable energy policies, which require the adoption of renewable energy technologies to generate electricity, have also been shown to incentivize innovation. Johnstone et al. (2010) find that patenting activity for renewable energy technologies, measured by applications for renewable energy patents submitted to the European Patent Office (EPO), has increased dramatically in recent years, as both national policies and international efforts to combat climate change begin to provide incentives for innovation. Dechezleprêtre and Glachant (2013) show that every 100 MW of new wind power capacity installed in OECD countries induces three new patented innovations globally.

Other studies examine the effect of changing energy prices on innovation, providing evidence on how innovation will react to higher energy prices resulting from regulation. Newell et al. (1999) show that the energy efficiency of home appliances available for sale changed in response to energy prices between 1958 and 1993. Suggesting the role that policy-induced technological change may play as climate policy moves forward, they find that energy efficiency in 1993 would have been about one-quarter to one-half lower in air conditioners and gas water heaters if energy prices had stayed at their 1973 levels, rather than following their historical path. Both Popp (2002) and Verdolini and Galeotti (2011) find similar estimates of the elasticity of energy patenting activity with respect to energy prices for alternative energy and energy efficiency technologies, with a 10 percent increase in energy prices raising energy patenting in the long run by 3.5 to 4 percent. Aghion et al. (2016) examine innovation activity by around 3,000 firms in the car industry and show that firms tend to innovate more in clean technologies (i.e., electric, hybrid, and hydrogen cars) and less in dirty technologies (i.e., internal combustion engines) when they face higher fuel prices. A 10 percent higher fuel price is associated with about 10 percent more clean patents and 7 percent less dirty patents.

Regulated and unregulated companies exhibit roughly comparable innovation activity before the introduction of the EU ETS, but they start diverging quickly after the new policy is put in place.

To sum up, there is ample empirical evidence that environmental regulations, by encouraging the diffusion of environmentally friendly technologies, affecting innovation activity further up the technology supply chain, and favoring R&D in clean technologies while discourag-

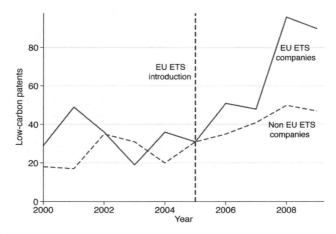

Figure 6.4
Low carbon innovation activity of EU ETS regulated companies compared with counter-factual scenario
Source: Calel and Dechezleprêtre (2016).
Notes: Around 3,000 companies regulated under the EU ETS are included in the sample. "Non-EU ETS companies" are a group of 3,000 European companies that are not regulated under the EU ETS but operate in the same country and the same economic sector and are comparable in size and innovation capacity to companies regulated under the EU ETS.

ing it in conventional (polluting) technologies. The impact on innovation appears both large and rapid. Thus, environmental regulations can help economies break away from a polluting economic trajectory and move to a "cleaner" one.

What Instruments Work Best? Studies on induced innovation provide some insight as to the pace of environmental innovation. Also important, however, is the nature of policies used to stimulate innovation. Policymakers have a range of instruments available to regulate environmental quality. Command-and-control regulations direct a specific level of performance. For instance, a performance standard sets a uniform control target for firms (such as pounds of sulfur dioxide emissions per million BTUs of fuel burned), but do not dictate how this target is met. Technology-based standards specify the method, and sometimes the actual equipment, that firms must use to comply with a particular regulation, such as by requiring that a percentage of electricity be generated using renewable sources. Market-based policies establish a price for emissions, either directly through the use of fees, such as a carbon tax, or indirectly through the use of permits that can be bought and sold among firms, such as in the U.S. SO_2 market or the EU's ETS for carbon.

Historically, economists have argued that market-based policies provide greater incentives for innovation. Market-based policies provide rewards for continuous improvement in environmental quality, whereas command-and-control policies penalize polluters who do not meet the standard, but do not reward those who do better than mandated (Magat 1978; Milliman and Prince 1989; Fischer et al. 2003). However, more recent research suggest that the effects are more nuanced. For example, standards can be of use when behavioral anomalies result in consumers paying little attention to the benefits of energy efficiency, as illustrated in box 6.3. Similarly, in a recent review, Vollebergh and van der Werf (2014) show that although standards are often viewed by economists as rigid and cost-inefficient command-and-control policy instruments, in appropriate conditions, standards are key complements to market-based instruments. For example, to promote the development of electric vehicles, charging stations must be in place. However, the private sector has little incentive to provide charging stations without existing demand from electric vehicles. In the case of such network externalities, clear technology standards provide guidance to firms as to the expected future direction of technology. However, these policy signals must be clear, or unintended consequences may result. See box 6.4 for an example.

Moreover, even among market-based policies, differences between policies matter. Johnstone et al. (2010) compare price-based policies to promote renewable energy, such as tax credits and feed-in tariffs,[9] to quantity-based policies, such as renewable energy mandates. Quantity-based policies, such as renewable energy certificates, favor the development of wind energy, as wind has the lowest cost and is closest to being competitive with traditional energy sources. As such, when faced with a mandate to provide alternative energy, firms focus their innovative efforts on the technology that is closest to the market. In contrast, direct investment incentives are effective in supporting innovation in solar and waste-to-energy technologies, which are further from being competitive with traditional energy technologies.

These results suggest particular challenges to policymakers who wish to encourage long-run innovation for technologies that have yet to reach market competitiveness. Economists generally recommend using broad-based environmental policies, such as emission fees, and

---

Box 6.3
The Energy Efficiency Paradox

A priori, energy efficiency and fuel-saving technologies should diffuse even without the aid of policy, as they do provide cost-saving benefits to the user. However, to the extent that fuel prices do not capture the external costs of energy use, such as carbon emissions, energy prices alone will not encourage a socially optimal level of adoption for energy efficiency technologies.

However, an important puzzle in the literature on energy technology diffusion is the notion that seemingly cost-effective energy-efficient technologies diffuse slowly, suggesting what has become to be known as an "energy efficiency paradox." To the extent that diffusion is limited by other market failures, policy measures that simply increase the economic incentive to adopt environmentally friendly technologies will be insufficient. In addition, policies focused directly on the correction of adoption market failures can be justified.

Several researchers have examined this energy efficiency paradox, offering explanations including consumers using high discount rates (Train 1985), credit-constrained consumers caring more about up-front costs than lifetime cost savings (Jaffe and Stavins 1994), agency problems such as in landlord/tenant relationships (Levinson and Niemann 2004), and uncertainty over future costs (Anderson and Newell 2004).

In addition to market failures, more recent research addresses potential behavioral anomalies that may affect the diffusion of energy efficient technology. This research combines psychology and economics, and notes cases where observed behavior differs from what traditional economic models predict. Gillingham and Palmer (2014) provide a review of studies on behavioral economics and energy efficiency and provide several examples of how behavioral economics can inform policy. For example, how choices are framed influences consumer decisions, suggesting that proper labelling of energy-efficient technologies matters. Inattention to future costs may cause consumers to undervalue energy efficiency (Allcott et al. 2014). However, Houde (2014) finds that while Energy Star labelling for energy-efficient appliances has positive net benefits, it also reduces consumers' incentives to gather information on energy costs and might therefore lower energy-saving activity. Attention to social norms, such as providing information on the energy consumption of neighbors, can increase energy conservation (e.g., Allcott 2011; Schultz et al. 2008). Similarly, Sallee (2014) argues that, given the time necessary to learn about the value of energy efficiency, in many cases it is rational for consumers to devote little attention to it. Such behavioral anomalies provide support for policies such as product labelling or minimum performance standards that reduce the burdens on consumers to seek out energy-efficient products.

---

letting the market "pick winners." This leads to lower compliance costs in the short run, as firms choose the most effective short-term strategy. However, this research suggests complications for the long run. Because

Box 6.4

Policy Signals and Innovations on SO_2 Scrubbers

Examples from the U.S. market for sulphur dioxide (SO_2) permits show the importance of clear policy signals to direct innovation. Popp (2003) compares innovation on SO_2 controls before and after the 1990 Clean Air Act (CAA) instituted permit trading. Before this Act, new plants were required to install a flue gas desulfurization (FGD) unit capable of removing 90 percent of SO_2. As a result, the innovations that occurred before the 1990 CAA focused on reducing the cost of FGD units, rather than on improving their environmental performance. After passage of the 1990 CAA, the nature of innovation changed, with a greater focus on improving the ability of FGD units to remove SO_2 from a plant's emissions. Similarly, Taylor et al. (2003) note that the scrubber requirement led to a reduction in patents on pre-combustion techniques for reducing SO_2 emissions, such as coal purification.

firms will focus on those technologies closest to market, market-based policy incentives do not provide as much incentive for research on longer-term needs. This suggests a trade-off: directed policies such as investment tax credits or technology mandates more effectively encourage the deployment of more expensive emerging technologies that are not yet cost-effective. However, this raises the costs of compliance, as firms are forced to use technologies that are not cost-effective. One possible solution here is to use broad, market-based policies to ensure short-run compliance at low costs, and use support for the research and development process to support research on emerging technologies. Thus, the focus is on continued improvement for emerging technologies, rather than on deployment of them.

Finally, the perceived stability of the policy is also important. Since expectations over future prices determine innovation, long-term regulatory consistency is crucial for new technology development (Held et al. 2009). For example, Butler and Neuhoff (2008) show how German feed-in tariffs stimulated overall investment quantity more than UK renewable energy quotas because the guaranteed revenues associated with FIT-reduced risks from the project investment. Similarly, the prices established by market-based policies must be sufficient to encourage innovation. Calel and Dechezleprêtre (2016) show that the effect of the EU ETS on innovation activity was concentrated at the beginning of the System's second phase, which saw a significant increase in the price of carbon on the market at about €30/ton CO_2 and an expectation that prices would remain at a high level in the foreseeable future. This suggests that the current level of carbon prices in the EU ETS combined with expectations of a low price in the next decade might be too low to provide sufficient incentives for technology development.

The Cross-Border Effects of Environmental Policies The European Union is composed of 28 countries, most of which are small and highly connected to their neighbors through trade relationships. Therefore, the impact of environmental policies across borders is of key importance for these countries. Two recent empirical papers look at this issue. Dechezleprêtre and Glachant (2014) study the effect of both domestic and foreign policies for the promotion of wind innovation. While both promote innovation activity, they find the marginal effect of policies implemented at home to be 12 times higher. However, since the foreign market is much larger than the domestic market across the sampled countries, the overall impact of foreign policies is on average *twice as large* as the overall impact of domestic policies on innovation. In other words, wind power policies induce twice as much innovation abroad than domestically.[10] Similarly, Peters et al. (2012) find that both domestic and foreign demand-pull policies are important for the development of solar PV technology. However, the overall impact of foreign countries is smaller than in the case of wind power, perhaps because barriers to international technology diffusion are larger in solar power.

These results provide a strong case for designing environmental policies jointly at the European level rather than at the Member State level. Indeed, the cross-country innovation spillovers might be viewed negatively from a narrow national perspective but are strongly positive from a global (or European) perspective. These results also constitute an incentive for Europe to push for strengthening of environmental regulation globally as this will encourage innovation in Europe by increasing the demand for clean technologies globally.

3.2 Addressing the Innovation Market Failures

The existence of knowledge market failures provides a rationale for public support to innovation. Note that there is no reason a priori to implement R&D policies targeted specifically at clean technologies. Positive externalities in knowledge production may be addressed by generic instruments, such as intellectual property rights protection and tax rebates for R&D activities that apply to all industries equally

(Schneider and Goulder 1997). Yet, in theory, public R&D expenditures and subsidies to private R&D activities should reflect the size of the external spillovers from the research (Goulder and Schneider 1999). Consequently, the optimal level of subsidies for clean R&D crucially depends on the magnitude of knowledge spillovers from clean technologies. The recent results from Dechezleprêtre et al. (2013), who show that spillovers from clean technologies are particularly large, suggest that specific support for clean innovation that goes beyond standard policies in place to internalize knowledge externalities is justified. As illustrated above, optimal subsidies for clean technologies are at least 20 percent to 30 percent higher than for the average innovation (and much higher still if the price of carbon is undercharged).

Public R&D Even when environmental regulations that encourage eco-innovation are in place, private firms will focus research efforts on technologies that are closest to the market. One of the particular problems faced with many climate-friendly innovations is the long timeframe from the initial invention to successful market deployment. Consider, for instance, the case of solar energy. Despite research efforts that began during the energy crises of the 1970s, solar is still only cost-competitive in niche markets, such as remote off-grid locations. This leaves a role for government-sponsored R&D to fill in the gaps, particularly in the case of climate change, where a diversified energy portfolio will be necessary to meet currently proposed emission reduction targets.

Government investment in R&D plays several roles. First, government R&D can help to compensate for underinvestment by private firms. Unlike firms, the government is in position to consider social returns when making investment decisions. In addition, government R&D tends to have different objectives than private R&D. Government support is particularly important for basic R&D, as long-term payoffs, greater uncertainty, and the lack of a finished product at the end all make it difficult for private firms to appropriate the returns of basic R&D. Thus, the nature of government R&D is important. For example, Popp (2002) finds that government energy R&D served as a substitute for private energy R&D during the 1970s, but as a complement to private energy R&D afterward. One explanation given for the change in impact is the changing nature of energy R&D. During the 1970s, much government R&D funding went to applied projects such as the ultimately unsuccessful effort to produce synfuels. Beginning with the

Reagan administration, government R&D shifted toward a focus on more basic applications. To avoid duplicating, and potentially crowding out, private research efforts, government R&D support should focus on basic research or on applied research whose benefits are difficult to capture through market activity. For instance, improved electricity transmission systems benefit all technologies, and will typically not reap great rewards for the innovator. Applied technologies whose costs are still high, such as solar photovoltaics, will also see less private investment, as firms focus on projects with greater short-term payoffs. In cases such as these, public R&D efforts will be important.

The uncertain nature of long-term research also makes government R&D valuable. In a situation where failure is more likely than success, but the successes will have great social value, government can bear the costs of a diversified R&D portfolio more easily than any one private firm. Consider, for example, the U.S. National Research Council's review of energy efficiency and fossil energy research at DOE over the last two decades (National Research Council 2001). Using both estimates of overall return and case studies, they concluded that there were only a handful of programs that proved highly valuable. Their estimates of returns suggest, however, that the benefits of these successes justified the overall portfolio investment. These uncertain returns also suggest that government research portfolios should be diversified, rather than try to pick winning technologies at early stages of development.

IP Systems As stated in the previous section, competitive markets under-incentivize innovation because of the public-good nature of ideas (Arrow 1962; Nelson 1959). Intellectual property rights (IPR), such as patents and copyrights, aim to incentivize innovation by allowing firms to capture a higher share of the returns to their research investments. Successful patent applicants are provided a temporary monopoly, lasting 20 years from the initial application date in the main patent offices (the United States, Europe, and Japan), in return for disclosing information on the innovation in the patent document, which is part of the public record. By granting this market power, IPR helps to mitigate potential losses from knowledge spillovers and encourage innovation. It is also supposed to help other inventors since innovation activity is cumulative in nature. Evidence shows that patents are effective in encouraging innovation in countries with high economic development, which would generally include all European economies, but that sectors that develop environmental technologies are not critically dependent on patent protection (see box 6.5).

Support to Private R&D   Another way for governments to help firms internalize the knowledge externalities associated with innovation is to directly subsidize firms for their innovation activities, through technology prizes, research grants (such as the public R&D funding discussed earlier), or R&D tax credits. In theory, subsidies to private R&D activities should reflect the size of the external spillovers from the research (Goulder and Schneider 1999).

Evidence on the effectiveness of R&D tax credits is mixed. Bloom et al. (2002) find evidence that tax incentives are effective in increasing R&D intensity. They estimate that a 10 percent fall in the cost of R&D stimulates a 1 percent rise in the level of R&D in the short run, and a 10 percent rise in R&D in the long run. More recently, Duguet (2010) and Czarnitzki et al. (2011) also find evidence that R&D tax credits lead to additional innovation output. Lokshin and Mohnen (2012) find that small firms (below 200 employees) have a larger cost elasticity of R&D than larger firms. One caveat is that the studies mentioned all analyze R&D subsidies or tax credits more generally, rather than R&D tax credits designed to promote cleaner technologies. Compared to direct

---

Box 6.5
Intellectual Property Rights, Innovation, and Technology Diffusion
Whether patents are effective in encouraging innovation is the subject of a vast literature. Economic theory does not provide a clear prediction in this respect. On the one hand, by allowing firms to capture a higher share of the returns from their R&D investments, IPR incentivize innovation. On the other hand, the possibility for inventors to charge a higher price may hinder the diffusion of new innovations, thereby reducing future innovation, which is cumulative in nature (for recent papers on this subject, see Moser 2013; Williams 2013; and Galasso and Schankerman 2015). Empirical studies provide mixed findings. For example, Moser (2005) constructs a data set of 15,000 innovations from a number of European countries that were displayed at two international fairs during the 19th century, and finds that the level of innovative activity in these countries was unaffected by the presence of a patent system. Park and Ginarte (1997) use data on 60 countries from 1960-1990 and an index of the strength of IP rights and find that the strength of IP rights is positively associated with R&D investment, but only in countries with above-median income (among which all European countries can be found) and not for less developed countries. Qian (2007) also finds that patent protection stimulates domestic innovation only in coun-

tries with higher levels of economic development, educational attainment, and economic freedom. Additionally, there appears to be an optimal level of intellectual property rights regulation above which further enhancement reduces innovative activities.

Note that the above studies focus on the effects of patents on innovation throughout the entire economy. An important finding from the empirical literature is that some sectors are more likely than others to react to patents by increasing innovation, because some products are more prone to imitation and more easily codified in a patent document. These include the pharmaceutical, biotechnology, medical instrument, and chemical sectors. In other sectors, patents are not perceived as an important means to protect innovation (Cohen et al. 2000). This has implications for environmental technologies, which for the vast majority do not belong to the sectors most dependent on patent protection.

Nonetheless, patents may be useful to address the imperfection in capital markets stemming from the asymmetry of information about the technology between the inventor and potential funders. Patents may be useful signals to investors that a startup firm has valuable assets even in the absence of a current profit stream. For example, Haeussler et al. (2009) find that European patent applications (but not grants) serve as an important signal to venture capital investors in German and British biotechnology firms. Similarly, Dechezleprêtre (2013) finds that programs to fast-track green patent applications have been particularly successful among start-up companies currently raising capital, for which a granted patent represents a valuable asset.

The impact of patenting on the diffusion of climate change-related technologies has recently become a subject of significant debate. It is certainly true that, conditional on an innovation having taken place, one would expect technology diffusion to be slower when IPR is in place, because monopoly power implies that the price of clean technologies will be higher. The role of demand for clean technologies cannot be overstated, however, and is consistent with results found elsewhere. In an oft-cited study on the role of IPR on pharmaceuticals, Attaran and Gillespie-White (2001) ask whether patents constrain access to AIDS treatments in Africa. They find that, even in African countries where patent protection is possible, few AIDS drugs are patented, as the markets for such drugs are too small to be of interest to multinational pharmaceutical companies. Rather than patents, they conclude that a lack of income, national regulatory requirements, and insufficient international aid are the main barriers to the spread of AIDS treatments in Africa. Similarly, with green technologies, one would expect demand (or the lack thereof) for clean technologies to be a primary constraint on international technology diffusion. The strengthening of environmental regulation across Europe is an important pre-condition to the diffusion of eco-innovations. Calls to weaken IPR for eco-innovations would likely have little impact on their diffusion.

public funding of R&D, firms applying for R&D tax credits retain control over the type of R&D projects they pursue. Thus, while tax credits may make marginal projects profitable, firms will still focus on projects with the greatest short-run returns (David et al. 2000). As such, tax credits may not be the best policy tool to promote new technologies that are not close to the market.

Williams (2012) provides a review of recent research on technology prizes. One failed example is a prize offered by a group of U.S. electric utilities for an energy-efficient refrigerator. While Whirlpool was able to develop a refrigerator meeting the required technical specifications, the model was not popular with consumers, and thus Whirlpool did not sell the necessary number of units to receive the prize. This illustrates one of the challenges for using prizes for promoting new energy technologies, as the risk of failure is borne by companies, rather than government. In the case of technologies for which consumer demand is likely to be low, monetary prizes will need to be sufficiently large to entice firms to take on these risks.

3.3   The Problem of Crowding Out Non-Clean Innovation
An important question for the macroeconomic impact of policies supporting clean technologies is whether policy-induced innovation activities in clean technologies come at the expense of innovation in other technologies. It is reasonable to assume that the supply of researchers in the economy is fixed in the short run, so that at the macroeconomic level new R&D activity in one technology should almost completely crowd out innovation in another technological field. This question of crowding out is raised in two recent simulations of climate policy. Using the ENTICE model, Popp (2004) begins with a base case that assumes one-half of new energy R&D crowds out other R&D. In this case, induced innovation increases welfare by 9 percent. Assuming no crowding-out, the welfare gains from induced innovation increase to as much as 45 percent, while assuming full crowding of R&D reduces welfare gains to as little as 2 percent. Gerlagh (2008) extends this work by separately modeling the choice of carbon-energy producing R&D, carbon-energy saving R&D, and neutral R&D. In such a case, it is carbon-producing R&D, rather than neutral R&D, that is crowded out by induced carbon-energy saving R&D. As a result, the impact of induced technological change is larger, with optimal carbon taxes falling by a factor of 2.

Box 6.6
Crowding Out Non-Clean Innovation

A few empirical papers have addressed the question of crowding-out of environmental R&D. Gray and Shadbegian (1998) find that more stringent air and water regulations had a positive impact on paper mills' technological choice in the United States, but that the increased investment on abatement technologies came at the cost of other types of productivity-improving innovation. Hottenrott and Rexhäuser (2013) find that regulation-induced environmental innovation crowds out R&D in other technologies, especially for small firms that are credit constrained. Popp and Newell (2012) use patent and R&D data to examine both the private and social opportunity costs of climate R&D. Looking first at R&D spending across industries, they find that funds for energy R&D do not come from other sectors, but may come from a redistribution of research funds in sectors that are likely to perform energy R&D. Given this, they link firm-level patent and financial data to take a detailed look at climate R&D in two sectors—alternative energy and automotive manufacturing—asking whether an increase in alternative energy patents leads to a decrease in other types of patenting activity. They find evidence of crowding-out.

Interestingly, the patents most likely to be crowded out by alternative energy research are innovations enhancing the productivity of fossil fuels, such as energy refining and exploration. This is consistent with the notion that any apparent crowding-out reacts to market incentives—as opportunities for alternative energy research become more profitable, research opportunities for traditional fossil fuels appear less appealing to firms. This is also in line with the result by Aghion et al. (2016) which shows that automobile companies react to increases in fuel prices by conducting more innovation in "clean" cars (electric, hybrid, and hydrogen) and less innovation in "dirty" (combustion engine) cars. Thus, while evidence of crowding out exists, those studies that are able to detail the types of R&D crowded-out suggest that it is dirty R&D that is reduced to make way for policy-induced clean R&D.

Thus, an important question is what types of R&D are replaced by an increased focus on clean technologies. Recent research, highlighted in box 6.6, suggests that there is evidence for a crowding-out effect, but that clean innovations tend to crowd out dirty innovations in the same sector. These results imply that the complementarity between technology policies and environmental policies is key to make sure that that clean innovation activity comes at the expense of innovation in dirty technologies and not of other socially valuable innovation.

It also suggests that any policy effort to accelerate innovation in clean technologies include a component to train new scientists and technical workers in order to increase the supply of qualified scientists in the long run. As an example, consider the experience of the U.S. National Institutes of Health (NIH), which supports biomedical research in the United States. The NIH budget has traditionally grown at a slow, steady pace. However, between 1998 and 2003, annual NIH spending nearly doubled, from $14 billion to $27 billion. Adjusted for inflation, this represents a 76 percent increase in just five years, and was nearly twice as high as the increase for the entire decade before. This rapid increase resulted in high adjustment costs. New post-doctorate researchers needed to be brought in to support research projects. Managing a larger budget entails administrative costs for NIH. Moreover, after this rapid doubling, research funds were cut, so that real NIH spending was 6.6 percent lower in 2007 than in 2004. This created a career crisis for the same post-doctorate researchers supported by the earlier doubling of support, as there was more competition for funds to start their own research projects. Moreover, scientists spent more time writing grant proposals. Because the probability of funding for any one proposal falls as the NIH budget falls, researchers submitted multiple proposals in the hope that one would succeed (Freeman and Van Reenen 2009). This NIH experience suggests that growth in clean R&D budgets should be slow and steady, allowing time for the development of young researchers in the field. The training of new scientists through graduate and post-graduate grants should be an important component of the overall public research funding approach.

3.4 The Appropriate Policy Mix

Combining Instruments The presence of several market failures requires the implementation of several policy instruments. Technology policies alone are irrelevant: if no carbon pricing is in place to create a market demand for technologies like CCS, no R&D will be conducted even with large research subsidies in place. Similarly, environmental policy cannot supplant the need for technology policy. Indeed, studies evaluating the effectiveness of these various policy options find that environmental and technology policies work best in tandem. Although technology policy can help facilitate the creation of new environmentally friendly technologies, it provides little incentive to adopt these technologies. For example, Popp (2006b) considers the long-run welfare gains from both an optimally designed carbon tax (one equating the marginal benefits of carbon reductions with the marginal costs of such reductions) and optimally designed R&D subsidies. While combining both policies yields the largest welfare gain, a policy using only the carbon tax achieves 95 percent of the welfare gains of the combined policy, whereas a policy using only the optimal R&D subsidy attains just 11 percent of the welfare gains of the combined policy in his model. While this model is a stylized representation of the global economy, and thus ignored barriers to diffusion such as those discussed in box 6.3, meaning it overstates (perhaps quite significantly) the portion of the welfare gains from the efficient tax/technology policy combination that can be achieved by the tax alone, it does highlight the key lesson that developing new clean technologies without providing incentives to use them will not be sufficient.

Fischer and Newell (2008) use a micro approach to study a broader set of policies, including those encouraging technology adoption, to assess policies for reducing CO_2 emissions, promoting innovation, and diffusing of renewable energy. Although the relative cost of individual policies in achieving emission reductions is sensitive to parameter values and the emission target, in a numerical application to the U.S. electricity sector, they find the ranking is roughly as follows: (a) emission pricing, (b) emission performance standard, (c) fossil power tax, (d) renewables share requirement, (e) renewables subsidy, and (f) R&D subsidy.[11] Nonetheless, an optimal portfolio of policies— including emission pricing and R&D—achieves emission reductions at significantly lower cost than any single policy (see figure 6.5). The benefits from more R&D are even able to compensate for the cost of the carbon tax. Gerlagh and van der Zwaan (2006) find an emission performance standard to be the cheapest policy for achieving various carbon stabilization goals. They note that the ordering of policies depends on the assumed returns to scale of renewable energy technologies. Fischer and Newell (2008) assume greater decreasing returns to renewable energy, due to the scarcity of appropriate sites for new renewable sources. Thus, an important question raised by Gerlagh and van der Zwaan (2006) is whether the cost savings from innovation will be sufficient to overcome decreasing returns to scale for renewable energy resulting from limited space for new solar and wind installations.

What is the optimal policy mix between technology-push and demand-pull? The answer to this question depends on the relative intensity of market failures associated with technology development, mainly knowledge spillovers and learning-by-doing. Recent papers attempt to disentangle the separate contributions of R&D and experience by estimating two-factor learning curves for environmental

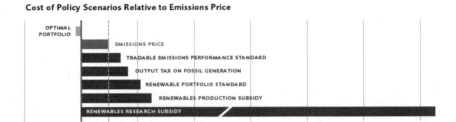

Figure 6.5
Cost of climate change policy under different policy scenarios
Source: Fischer and Newell (2008).

technologies. These two-factor curves model cost reductions as a function of both experience (learning-by-doing, or LBD) and R&D (learning-by-searching, or LBS). Söderholm and Sundqvist (2007) find LBD
rates around 5 percent and LBS rates around 15 percent, suggesting
that R&D, rather than learning-by-doing, contributes more to cost
reductions. However, these results are very sensitive to the model
specification, illustrating the difficulty of sorting through the various
channels through which costs may fall over time. Nemet (2006) uses
simulation techniques to decompose cost reductions for PV cells into
seven categories. Plant size (e.g., returns to scale), efficiency improvements, and lower silicon costs explain the majority of cost reductions.
Notably, most of the major improvements in efficiency come from
universities, where traditional learning by doing through production
experience would not be a factor. Learning from experience (e.g.,
through increased yield of PV cells) plays a much smaller role, accounting for just 10 percent of the cost decreases in Nemet's sample.

Fischer, Newell, and Preonas (2013) model the U.S. energy system
and determine the optimal distribution of public spending between
R&D support and deployment under various scenarios. They find that
the ratio of deployment spending to R&D spending does not exceed
one for wind energy in almost all scenarios. With extreme assumptions
on learning-by-doing this ratio goes to 6.5. The ratio of public spending
on deployment to R&D exceeds one for solar energy but not by much.
The ratio reaches 10-to-1 under the "high learning-by-doing" scenario.
As one can see, the optimal policy mix varies across clean technologies,
depending on their degree of maturity. The relative importance of
market pull vis-à-vis technology push decreases, as one moves from

technologies close to market competitiveness toward highly immature ones (Grubb 2004).

Acemoglu et al. (2014) develop a model of endogenous growth with clean and dirty technologies and characterize the optimal climate change policy. They show that the transition to clean technology is slow when dirty technologies are initially more advanced. They find that the optimal policy includes a very aggressive research subsidy for clean technology. With a 1 percent social discount rate, the optimal carbon tax is fairly low (representing 16 percent of the turnover of the carbon emitting sector), while research directed at clean technologies receives a 61 percent government subsidy (meaning that for every dollar of R&D spending, there is a 61-cent subsidy). With a social discount rate of 0.1 percent, carbon taxes are raised to 44 percent, but clean research subsidies are even more aggressive, at 95 percent. Moreover, they show that relying only on carbon taxes and not on research subsidies leads to large welfare losses. This is in line with the result by Acemoglu et al. (2012), which shows that optimal policy involves both carbon taxes and research subsidies, so that excessive use of carbon taxes can be avoided.

In sum, the studies cited here demonstrate that both demand-pull policies such as a carbon tax and technology-push policies such as R&D subsidies best work in tandem, with the appropriate balance between R&D support and other environmental policies depending on the maturity of the technology in question. One question that research has yet to address is what specific combinations of R&D and environmental policy instruments best encourage innovation in green technologies (Burke et al. 2016). This is a fruitful area for future research.

Optimal Public R&D Funding An important question for policymakers is how much government R&D money to spend on environment-friendly innovation. Here, however, economics provides less of an answer. Cost-benefit analysis provides a useful tool for ex-post evaluation of R&D spending, but estimating the potential benefits from new R&D spending is more difficult. Engineers are better suited to determine which projects are most deserving from a technical standpoint. Given the need for a diversified energy portfolio to address climate change, it is hard to imagine that there would not be enough deserving technologies for the research funding available. Rather, as suggested above, economic analysis suggests that the constraints for funding are likely to come from other sources, such as the pool of scientist and engineering personnel currently available to work on energy projects and how quickly the pool can grow. That is, the limits to how much we can spend come not from the number of deserving projects, but rather limits of the existing research infrastructure. It is worth pointing out, however, than recent models of climate policy show that the optimal policy heavily relies on research subsidies. For example, Acemoglu et al. (2014) suggest that 90 percent of all R&D expenditures in clean technologies should be funded by the government for a couple of decades, so that the productivity of clean technologies quickly catches up with that of dirty technologies. Moreover, recent IEA estimates suggest that achieving global energy and climate change ambitions consistent with a 50 percent reduction of energy-related CO_2 emissions in 2050 with respect to 2007 (the 2010 BLUE Map scenario) would require a twofold to fivefold increase in public RD&D spending (IEA 2010).

As regards what sorts of technologies should be priority for funding, European governments should focus on technologies have a strong public good component but are central to any decarbonization pathway. The goal is to avoid providing public support for research that the private sector would otherwise do on their own. This could include projects supporting long-term research needs where the payoff occurs farther into the future, as well as infrastructure that has a public goods component. Examples include CCS, energy storage, smart grids, energy efficiency, and infrastructures for electric vehicles.

4. Current Policies for Clean Technology Development in Europe

4.1   Policies Targeting Environmental Externalities

The EU ETS is Europe's flagship policy to address climate change. Beginning with an overall cap on EU carbon emissions, the European Union sets a national CO_2 emissions limit for each country. From this, the European Union specifies economic activities (such as burning of fuel or production of cement) that participate in trading of carbon permits.[12] As a result the EU ETS covers around 45 percent of the European Union's greenhouse gas emissions. As with any environmental policy, the effect of the EU ETS on innovation depends on the strength of the policy. Indeed, Calel and Dechezleprêtre (2016) show that the large positive impact of the EU ETS on low-carbon innovation coincided with the time at which carbon prices were highest at around €25-35/ton. Unfortunately, the EU ETS has been plagued from the beginning by over-allocation of permits (or the lack of a price stability

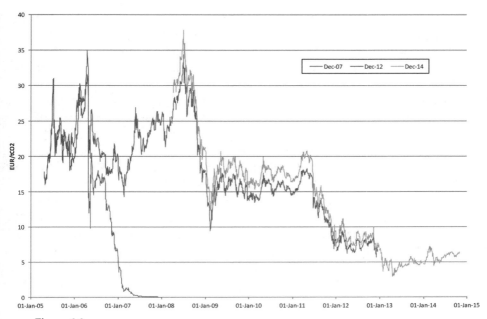

Figure 6.6
EUA Futures prices, 2005–2014
Source: Intercontinental Exchange.

mechanism). In addition, the economic downturn and the resulting contraction of production reduced industrial carbon emissions. As a result, permit prices are far below the level required to provide meaningful incentives for companies to invest in low-carbon technology development, with the price of futures on the European carbon market now at a record low (around €5/ton, see figure 6.6).

According to recent analysis by Thomson Reuters Point Carbon,[13] the European carbon market is likely to remain oversupplied with allowances for many years to come, despite the recent commitment to reduce greenhouse gas emissions by 40 percent in 2030, because of the accumulated oversupply in the market, which is expected to be in the order of 2.5 Gt in 2020. As a consequence, carbon prices are expected to remain low, at an average of €13/ton between 2015 and 2020 and an average of €24/ton from 2021 to 2030.

Thus, carbon prices are likely to remain at a low level for the next decade or so, and are unlikely to provide companies with strong incentives to conduct low-carbon R&D at the scale needed, especially since the EU ETS covers less than half of Europe's emissions. The Energy Tax Directive indirectly prices emissions outside the EU ETS by imposing minimum tax rates for energy products across the European Union, but the proposal to reform the Directive by imposing a €20 tax on emissions is currently stalled. Thus, policies to augment low carbon prices will be necessary to spur innovation during the next decade. For example, the United Kingdom introduced in 2013 a carbon price floor (CPF) starting at around £16 (€22) per ton of CO_2 and projected to reach £30 (€42) per ton of CO_2 in 2020. The CPF is made up of the price of CO_2 from the EU ETS and the carbon price support (CPS) rate per tCO_2, which ensures that the minimal price paid by power generator does not go below the CPF. The carbon price support rates for 2013–2014 is £4.94/t, rising to £9.55/t in 2014–2015 and £18.08/t in 2015–2016. The CPF is explicitly designed to provide an incentive to invest in low-carbon power generation. Of course, the UK carbon price floor is environmentally ineffective at the EU level where emissions are fixed by the EU ETS cap, unless the EU ETS is supplemented by a price floor. At present, this is highly unlikely.

4.2   Technology Policies

Public R&D Support   Public R&D spending plays a particularly important role in the energy sector. In 2011, the last year for which both private and public energy R&D data are available, European industry spent around €7 billion on energy R&D according to the EU Joint Research Centre on Industrial Investment and Innovation R&D Scoreboard 2013 (European Commission 2013), while European governments spent around €4 billion, according to IEA public R&D data. Although public energy-related R&D expenditures in European countries have increased significantly since 2005, after having stagnated at around €2 billion/year for almost a decade, they are still 30 percent below (in real terms) what they were in the early 1980s after the second oil shock. Moreover, while public R&D grew at an average annual rate of 8 percent between 2001 and 2011, it has seemingly started to decrease recently, perhaps as a consequence of falling energy prices which make the value of future energy savings smaller (see figure 6.7). Energy-related expenditures account for 4 percent of total government R&D in Europe, compared to over 10 percent in 1980. Meanwhile, environment-related expenditures account for 2.5 percent of total government R&D. However, there are important differences across countries, with France and Germany spending around 8 percent of their public R&D budgets on energy and environment issues, while the figure is only 4 percent in the United Kingdom (see figure 6.8). Overall, energy and

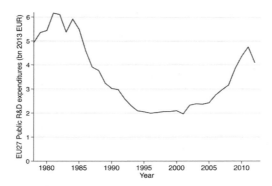

Figure 6.7
EU-27 public R&D spending in energy technologies (billion euros)
Source: IEA.

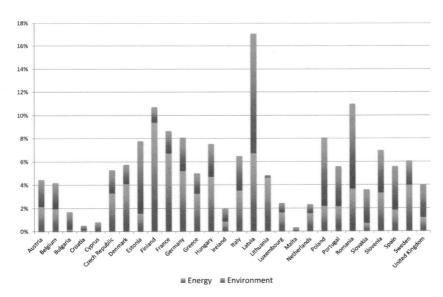

Figure 6.8
Share of public R&D expenditures toward energy and environment across EU-28 countries (2013)
Source: Eurostat.

environment appear to lag behind other research priorities such as health, space exploration, or defence (figure 6.9). Public R&D expenditures in the energy sector in Europe represent less than 0.1 percent of GDP in almost all European countries (see figure 6.10).

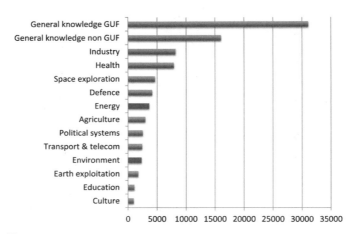

Figure 6.9
Distribution of public R&D expenditures in Europe across socio-economic objectives (2013)

Source: Eurostat.

Note: GUF = General University Funds. General knowledge non-GUF stands for "General advancement of knowledge: R&D financed from other sources than GUF."

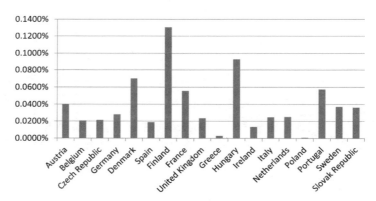

Figure 6.10
Public R&D expenditures on energy as a share of GDP (2011)
Source: IEA.

"Environment" relates to pollution control and includes atmosphere and climate protection; protecting the air; solid wastes; water protection; soil and phreatic water protection; noise and vibrations; the protection of species and their habitats; protecting against natural hazards; and radioactive pollution. "Energy" covers the production, storage, transportation, distribution, and usage of any type of energy and processes designed to increase efficiency in the production and distribution of energy. It includes energy efficiency; the capture and storage of CO_2; sources of renewable energies; nuclear fission and fusion; and hydrogen and gas.

Of the €4.7 billion of public expenditure in 2011, 30 percent went to energy efficiency, 25 percent to renewable energy (with biofuel, solar, and wind energy respectively accounting for 9 percent, 7.5 percent and 4 percent of the total), 22 percent to nuclear energy R&D, 10 percent to energy storage, and 6 percent to fossil fuels (including €123 million for CCS). Less than 2 percent (€90 million) was spent on electric cars, including batteries, motors, and infrastructure.

Importantly, the vast majority of public funding for clean energy technologies in Europe comes from national governments. European institutions play only a marginal role. For example, the estimated public (EU and national) RD&D investments dedicated to six technologies covered by the EU Strategic Energy Technology Plan[14] in 2010 reached €2.26 billion, out of which €2.02 billion were national funds and €0.24 billion (or 11 percent) were EU funds. A possible consequence of the primary involvement of national governments is the relatively low efforts dedicated to technologies that are further away from the market and have a very strong public good component, such as electricity grids and CCS. For example, in 2010, public R&D investments in wind and PV were around €900 million each, while for electricity grids and CCS they were €323 and €400 million, respectively (see figure 6.11). Yet the financing needs of technology development, as described in the SET-Plan roadmaps (European Commission 2009), have been established at €1-1.5 billion per year for CCS. Thus R&D support for CCS may be lower than what is socially desirable, especially given the potential for European CCS technologies to be deployed in China and other large industrializing countries.

True, the European Union has limited funding available to support clean technology development, with its budget capped at 1.05 percent of the EU-27's Gross National Income. However, an interesting source of additional funding comes from the revenues from auctioned carbon permits. The European Union created the NER300 program, which was funded by the sale of 300 million emission allowances from the New Entrants' Reserve (NER) set up for the third phase of the EU ETS. The aim of the program is to fund innovative demonstration projects in CCS and renewable energy. The allowances were sold on the carbon market and the money raised—€2.1 billion—is being made available to projects

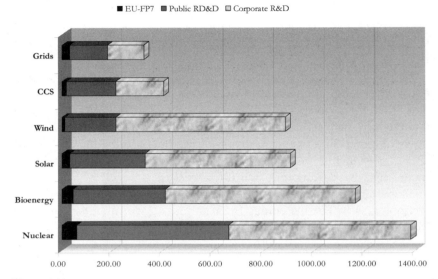

Figure 6.11
Estimate of public and corporate R&D by technology and source for the 6 SET Plan technologies (2010)
Source: European Commission.

as they operate. As part of their deliberations on the EU's Framework for Climate and Energy 2020–2030, European leaders recently mandated the creation of a successor program to NER300, "NER400," which would be initially endowed with 400 million carbon allowances. The new program would raise over €9 billion on the assumption of a carbon price of €23/ton.

The NER programs are interesting in that the auctioned carbon permits provide a source of sustained revenues that can be used for R&D support. Even though the price of permits is uncertain and volatile, committing a share of revenues to R&D support provides a signal to the private sector of long-term support. In contrast, temporary support programs to R&D are unlikely to be useful since, as explained above, R&D is by nature a long-term activity that necessitates some guarantee of sustained support. For example, in 2009 the European Commission implemented the European Energy Programme for Recovery (EEPR), which dedicated €4 billion to co-finance projects in the fields of gas and electricity infrastructure (€2.5 billion), offshore wind (€565 million), and CCS (€1 billion). To our knowledge all funded CCS projects have since then been abandoned because of the low carbon price on the market, suggesting that temporary R&D support programs are of little help and can even be counterproductive if they divert resources away from sustained R&D efforts.

Along with the NER programs, national governments can use auctioning revenues to support public R&D. Under the revised EU ETS Directive, at least 50 percent of auctioning revenues should be used by Member States for climate and energy-related purposes. Under the Monitoring Mechanism Regulation, Member States are requested to report annually on the amounts and use of the revenues generated. In 2013, the total auctioning revenues for EU countries reached €3.6 billion. From this, around €3 billion have been used for climate and energy-related purposes according to the European Commission, of which only €256 million (or 7 percent) have been dedicated to research (European Commission 2014). Between 2015 and 2020, around 6 billion allowances should be auctioned, or 1 billion per year on average. Thus, auctioning represents a potentially significant source of revenues to increase public R&D. For example, directing 10 percent of the planned auctioned allowances revenues until 2025 to R&D funding would lead to a doubling of EU public R&D expenditures in 10 years, similar to the one observed between 2000 and 2010.

Support to Private Research Many European countries have policies to subsidize private R&D expenditures. For example, in France, companies can deduct 30 percent of all R&D expenditures from profit taxes.[15] Most of these policies are technology-neutral, with a few exceptions. For example, Belgium has introduced a tax deduction of up to 15.5 percent of investments in R&D fixed assets if they have an environmental benefit.

At the European level, some policies are in place to facilitate access to finance for innovative firms. In particular, the European Commission and the European Investment Bank Group (EIB) have launched "InnovFin—EU Finance for Innovators," which includes guarantees for intermediaries that lend to SMEs, direct loans to enterprises, and advisory services. This scheme is expected to support up to €48 billion of final R&I investments.[16] The scheme is not targeted at any technology in particular, but is assuring financial support to the renewable energy and energy efficiency sectors.

Intellectual Property Rights Europe has a well-functioning patenting system. The European Patent Office makes it easier for applicants to file a patent across all European countries. Yet because of legal and translation costs, the cost of filing a patent in Europe is still relatively high. In the early 2000s, filing a patent cost around €5,000 in Japan, €10,000 in the United States, and €30,000 at the European Patent Office (Roland Berger Market Research 2005). Since January 2014, applicants have been able to apply for a "unitary patent" across Europe, which ensures uniform protection for an invention in 25 Member States (all EU Member States except Italy and Spain). The implementation of this new EU Patenting System is expected to substantially decrease patenting costs for innovators.

It is important to keep in mind that, as shown in the previous section, patents are likely to provide useful incentives for innovation in European developed economies, but not so much in many sectors where environmental technologies are actually being developed. Hence, changes in IP rights (either strengthening or weakening) would be unlikely to induce significant changes in innovation activity except in a handful of sectors, including, for example, biotechnology. However, programs to accelerate the examination of patents in clean technologies can be useful in helping start-up companies raise capital. Because proving that a patent application does cover a "green" technology is difficult, we do not however recommend restricting fast-track programs to green patents only, but instead recommend they be open to all patent applications.

Deployment Policies   As of 2011, every EU country has implemented at least one of the major support instruments toward renewable energy deployment (feed-in tariffs, feed-in premiums, tender schemes, or quota obligations). Among the major support instruments, feed-in tariffs schemes are clearly dominant, with 85 percent of countries implementing them in 2010 (Kitzing et al. 2012). Almost all countries have also implemented at least one supplementary support scheme: investment grants, fiscal measures (tax incentives, etc.), or financing support (loans, etc.). Among the supplementary support instruments, investment grants dominate.

Recent evidence indicates that European countries have put a strong emphasis on deployment policies compared with direct R&D support. A study by Zachmann et al. (2014) shows that the top six European countries spent €315 million in 2010 to support R&D in wind and solar power. The cost to society implied by the deployment of wind and solar technologies[17] that same year represented €48,300 million (see figure 6.12).

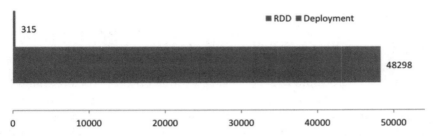

Figure 6.12
Public support to RDD vs. deployment in wind and solar energy in the top six European countries (2010)
Source: Zachmann et al. (2014).

5. Conclusion

Technological advances will play a crucial role in efforts to stabilize atmospheric greenhouse gas concentrations. As this paper demonstrates, well-designed climate policy can help shape the development of environment-friendly technologies. These policies must address multiple market failures pertaining to the environmental externalities of greenhouse gas emissions, knowledge spillovers, learning-by-doing, imperfections in capital markets, and other barriers. This requires a menu of policy options. Simply providing R&D support is not sufficient, as without environmental policy, there is little incentive to adopt clean technologies. At the same time, while broad-based environmental policies such as a carbon tax or cap-and-trade scheme provide an overall framework for emission reductions, this review suggests that other market failures remain important. Private firms will focus on technologies most likely to generate short-term profits. For instance, carbon taxes are likely to promote wind energy at the expense of solar, as wind is currently the most cost-effective renewable option. Similarly, because improving electricity transmission efficiency systems benefits all technologies, private innovators are likely able to capture only a small portion of the social benefits of such innovation. "Leaving it to the market" also picks a winner—markets will emphasize the lowest-cost technology, which might prevent the development of a broader portfolio of technologies. Long-term benefits, spillovers, and uncertain R&D returns all suggest a role for public R&D support, either through direct financing or targeted policy incentives. Finally, once technologies are available, additional policy support is needed to encourage diffusion. As the research on the energy efficiency paradox shows, even energy innovations with relatively short payback periods diffuse slowly. This suggests that simply getting the prices right through policies such as a carbon tax will not be sufficient.

As our review demonstrates, the European Union and national governments have adopted a set of policies to address these various market failures and lift the barriers to the development of clean technologies. These policies include the EU ETS, public R&D expenditures, support to private R&D and to start-up companies, a well-functioning IP system, and a range of policies to encourage the deployment of renewable energy technologies. While these policies are encouraging and go in the right direction, we suspect that the very low price of carbon on the EU ETS, which is projected to remain so for another decade, along with its partial coverage, is a major barrier to clean technology development in Europe. The new commitments for 2030 as well as the market stability reserve are steps in the right direction but have not had any influence on the price so far because of the vast amount of allowances currently on the market. Combined with the presence of innovation market failures and political constraints on high emissions prices, this justifies stronger policies targeted directly at technology development. Here we propose a series of reforms to the current policy landscape that could enhance clean innovation activities in Europe and help European countries tackle the challenges posed by climate change and other environmental issues.

Some Practical, Recommended Steps for Reform

1. While it is impossible to provide an "optimal" policy mix between R&D and deployment, it appears that European countries have been emphasizing technology deployment, in particular through feed-in tariffs for renewable energy production, over direct R&D support. This suggests that current efforts on deployment should be augmented with additional R&D support, such that in line with the recommendations below the marginal euro spent on clean technologies should go to R&D rather than deployment.

2. Given the scale of the climate change problem (and other environmental issues), the amount of money spent on R&D in clean technologies seems small, especially when compared with other equally important sectors such as health or defence. Public energy-related R&D expenditures in European countries are still 30 percent below what they were in the early 1980s and have decreased recently. There is no evidence that we have hit diminishing returns to energy

R&D funding, so at this point it is macroeconomic constraints on available funding that limit increases. The IEA estimates that public RD&D spending needs to at least double to achieve significant carbon emissions reductions. Thus, we recommend an increase of public R&D funding for low-carbon technologies.

3. This increase in funding needs to be gradual, however, because the supply of researchers in the society is fixed in the short run and expanding research in clean technologies involves training new scientists to avoid crowding out other socially valuable R&D. Ephemeral increases in clean R&D funding, like the 2009 EEPR programme, can be counterproductive as they divert resources away from steady research programs. A sustained 8 percent annual increase in funding leading to a doubling of public R&D expenditures in 10 years corresponds to what was observed between 2001 and 2011 and thus seems achievable.

4. We think that commitments to fund R&D should have a long-term component (until at least 2030), just like carbon emission caps. Policy stability is important for companies, universities, and other research stakeholders to make long-term predictions on innovation needs. To provide political credibility for a long-term commitment, revenues from auctioned carbon permits could provide a source of sustained funding for low carbon R&D. Directing 10 percent of the planned auctioned allowances revenues until 2025 to R&D funding would signal a commitment to long-term funding. Moreover, the European Union seems to be in a better position than individual European governments to make such long-term R&D commitments.

5. EU institutions and governments should focus their efforts on technologies that are central to any decarbonization pathway and have a strong public good component: CCS, energy storage, smart grids, energy efficiency, and infrastructure for electric vehicles. Compared to wind and solar power, these technologies have received relatively less support.

6. The low price of carbon on the market, combined with uncertainty over future policies, may make regulatory instruments, such as technological standards, attractive. However, because standards—just like emissions permits markets—are likely to favor technologies that are closest to the market, they too should be used in combination with direct R&D support for technologies that have longer-term potential.

Notes

1. Unavailability of CCS would increase the cost of a 450 ppm CO_2eq policy by a factor of 1.5 to 3.5 and of a 550 ppm CO_2eq policy by 20 percent to 70 percent (see Kriegler et al. 2014).

2. A smart grid is an electrical grid which includes a variety of operational and energy measures including smart meters, smart appliances, renewable energy resources, and energy efficiency resources.

3. See OECD online Patent Statistics, "Patents in environment-related technologies" section, at https://stats.oecd.org/.

4. This section draws heavily on Jaffe (2012).

5. Intellectual property rights, such as patents, are designed to protect inventors from such copies. However, their effectiveness varies depending on the ease in which inventors may "invent around" the patent by making minor modifications to an invention. See, for example, Levin et al. (1987).

6. Examples of such studies include Mansfield (1977, 1996), Pakes (1985), Jaffe (1986), Griliches (1992), Hall (1996), and Jones and Williams (1998). These studies typically construct a pool of "external" R&D available to a firm by weighting other firms' R&D by geographical or technological distance, and identify the effect of this external knowledge pool on firms' productivity.

7. A central problem in the spillovers literature is that firm performance is affected by two countervailing "spillovers": a positive effect from knowledge spillovers and a negative business-stealing effect from product market rivals. Bloom et al. (2013) incorporate these two types of spillovers and show that technology spillovers quantitatively dominate, so that the gross social returns to R&D are at least twice as high as the private returns even when taking product rivalry into account.

8. Examples include Kerr and Newell (2003) on the removal of lead from gasoline in the United States, Kemp (1998) on the effect of effluent charges on biological treatment of wastewater, Snyder et al. (2003) on the diffusion of membrane-cell technology in the chlorine manufacturing industry, and Popp (2010a) on NO_x pollution control technologies at power plants.

9. Feed-in tariffs, used in various European countries, guarantee renewable energy producers a minimum price for the electricity they produce for a limited period of time.

10. These results are valid on average across OECD countries but presumably differ with the size of the domestic economy.

11. Note that the analysis is confined to the power sector—presumably an economy-wide carbon price would be a lot more cost effective relative to other policies like renewable subsidies.

12. Activity-specific size criteria then determine which installations are included in the EU ETS. For instance, only combustion installations with a yearly thermal input exceeding 20 MWh are covered. In the absence of data on non-regulated installations it is not possible to determine fraction of emissions is produced by installations with input less than 20 MWh.

13. See http://www.commodities-now.com/reports/environmental-markets/18188-car bon-price-to-average-13-t-in-next-five-years.html.

14. Since 2008, the EU Strategic Energy Technology Plan (SET-Plan) has aimed to acceler-ate energy technology development and deployment across Europe. The implementation of the SET-Plan has led to the establishment of large-scale programs, called European Industrial Initiatives (EIIs), which bring together industry, the research community, the Member States, and the European Commission in risk-sharing partnerships aiming at the rapid development of key energy technologies at the European level. Six technologies have been identified as the focal points of the first EIIs: wind, solar (photovoltaics and concentrated solar power), electricity grids, bioenergy, CCS, fuel cells, and hydrogen and nuclear fission.

15. In 2011 this represented €5 billion in tax credits, i.e., 1.1 percent of the government budget and 0.2 percent of GDP.

16. See http://setis.ec.europa.eu/energy-research/content/eu-and-eib-group-jointly-pro vide-eur-48-billion-ri-investment-support.

17. Net deployment costs are calculated as the difference between the deployment costs and the net present value of the future electricity generated, so it does not only include direct support (e.g., loans, tax credits), but it also places a value on support mechanisms such as feed-in-tariffs and RPS.

References

Acemoglu, D. 2002. "Directed Technical Change." *Review of Economic Studies* 69: 781-809. doi:10.1111/1467-937X.00226

Acemoglu, D., P. Aghion, L. Bursztyn, and D. Hemous. 2012. "The Environment and Directed Technical Change." *American Economic Review* 102: 131-66. doi:10.1257/aer.102 .1.131.

Acemoglu, D., U. Akcigit, D. Hanley, and W. Kerr. 2016. "Transition to Clean Technology." *Journal of Political Economy* 124 (1): 52-104.

Aghion, P., A. Dechezleprêtre, D. Hémous, R. Martin, and J. Van Reenen. 2016. "Carbon Taxes, Path Dependency and Directed Technical Change: Evidence from the Auto Indus-try." *Journal of Political Economy* 124 (1): 1-51.

Allcott, H. 2011. "Social Norms and Energy Conservation." *Journal of Public Economics* 95: 1082-95.

Allcott, H., S. Mullainathan, and D. Taubinsky. 2014. "Energy Policy with Externalities and Internalities." *Journal of Public Economics* 112: 72-88.

Ambec, S., M. A. Cohen, S. Elgie, and P. Lanoie. 2013. "The Porter Hypothesis at 20: Can Environmental Regulation Enhance Innovation and Competitiveness?" *Review of Envi-ronmental Economics and Policy* 7: 2-22. doi:10.1093/reep/res016.

Anderson, S. T., and R. G. Newell. 2004. "Information Programs for Technology Adop-tion: The Case of Energy-Efficiency Audits." *Resource and Energy Economics* 26: 27-50. doi:10.1016/j.reseneeco.2003.07.001.

Arrow, K. J. 1962. "The Economic Implications of Learning by Doing." *Review of Economic Studies* 29: 155-173. doi:10.2307/2295952.

Attaran, A., and L. Gillespie-White. 2001. "Do Patents for Antiretroviral Drugs Constrain Access to AIDS Treatment in Africa?" *Journal of the American Medical Association* 286: 1886-92.

Berger, R. 2005. "The Cost of a Sample European Patent: New Estimates." Roland Berger Market Research, Munich, Germany.

Bloom, N., R. Griffith, and J. Van Reenen. 2002. "Do R&D Tax Credits Work? Evidence from a Panel of Countries 1979-1997." *Journal of Public Economics* 85: 1–31. doi:10.1016/S0047-2727(01)00086-X.

Bloom, N., J. Van Reenen, and M. Shankerman. 2013. "Identifying Technology Spillovers and Product Market Rivalry." *Econometrica* 81: 1347–93. doi:10.3982/ECTA9466.

Brunnermeier, S. B., and M. A. Cohen. 2003. "Determinants of Environmental Innovation in US Manufacturing Industries." *Journal of Environmental Economics and Management* 45: 278-93. doi:10.1016/S0095-0696(02)00058-X.

Burke, M., M. Craxton, C. D. Kolstad, C. Onda, H. Allcott, E. Baker, and R. S. J. Tol. 2016. "Opportunities for Advances in Climate Change Economics." *Science* 352 (6283): 292-93.

Butler, L., and K. Neuhoff. 2008. "Comparison of Feed-in Tariff, Quota and Auction Mechanisms to Support Wind Power Development." *Renewable Energy* 33: 1854-67.

Calel, Raphael, and Antoine Dechezleprêtre. 2016. "Environmental Policy and Directed Technological Change: Evidence from the European Carbon Market." *Review of Economics and Statistics* 98 (1): 173-91.

Cohen, W. M., R. R. Nelson, and J. P. Walsh. 2000. "Protecting Their Intellectual Assets: Appropriability Conditions and Why US Manufacturing Firms Patent (Or Not)" (Working Paper 7552, National Bureau of Economic Research, Cambridge, MA, US).

Council, N. R. 2001. *Energy Research at DOE: Was It Worth It? Energy Efficiency and Fossil Energy Research 1978 to 2000.* Washington, DC, US: The National Academies Press.

Czarnitzki, D., P. Hanel, and J. M. Rosa. 2011. "Evaluating the Impact of R&D Tax Credits on Innovation: A Microeconometric Study on Canadian Firms." *Research Policy* 40: 217-29. doi:10.1016/j.respol.2010.09.017.

David, P. A., B. H. Hall, and A. A. Toole. 2000. "Is Public R&D a Complement or Substitute for Private R&D? A Review of the Econometric Evidence." *Research Policy* 29: 497-529.

Dechezleprêtre, A. 2013. "Fast-Tracking 'Green' Patent Applications: An Empirical Analysis." ICTSD Programme on Innovation, Technology and Intellectual Property.

Dechezleprêtre, A., and M. Glachant. 2014. "Does Foreign Environmental Policy Influence Domestic Innovation? Evidence from the Wind Industry." *Environmental and Resource Economics* 58: 391-413.

Dechezleprêtre, A., R. Martin, and M. Mohnen. 2013. "Knowledge Spillovers from Clean and Dirty Technologies: A Patent Citation Analysis" (Grantham Research Institute on Climate Change and the Environment Working Paper No 151), 1-47.

Duguet, E. 2010. "The Effect of the R&D Tax Credit on the Private Funding of R&D: An Econometric Evaluation on French Firm Level Data." ERUDITE (Equipe de Recherche sur l'Utilisation des Données Individuelles en lien avec la Théorie Economique).

European Commission. 2009. "Commission Staff Working Document Accompanying Document to the Communication from the Commission to the European Parliament, the Council, the European Economic and Social Committee and the Committee of the Regions on Investing in the Development of Low Carbon Technologies." Commission Staff Working Document. Brussels, Belgium.

European Commission. 2013. *EU R&D Scoreboard: The 2013 EU Industrial R&D Investment Scoreboard*. Luxembourg: EU Law and Publications Office.

European Commission. 2014. "Commission Staff Working Document Accompanying the Document Report from the Commission to the European Parliament and the Council, Progress Towards Achieving the Kyoto and EU 2020 Objectives." Brussels, Belgium.

Fischer, C., and R. G. Newell. 2008. "Environmental and Technology Policies for Climate Mitigation." *Journal of Environmental Economics and Management* 55: 142-62. doi:10.1016/j.jeem.2007.11.001.

Fischer, C., R. G. Newell, and L. Preonas. 2013. "Environmental and Technology Policy Options in the Electricity Sector: Interactions and Outcomes." Resources for the Future Discussion Paper Series 13, Washington, DC, US.

Fischer, C., I. Parry, and W. Pizer. 2003. "Instrument Choice for Environmental Protection when Technological Innovation is Endogenous." *Journal of Environmental Economics and Management* 45: 523-45.

Freeman, R., and J. Van Reenen. 2009. "What if Congress Doubled R&D Spending on the Physical Sciences?" In *Innovation Policy and the Economy, Volume 9*, eds. Josh Lerner and Scott Stern. Chicago, IL, US: University of Chicago Press, 1-38.

Galasso, A., and M. Schankerman. 2015. "Patents and Cumulative Innovation: Causal Evidence from the Courts." *Quarterly Journal of Economics* 130 (1): 317-69.

Gerlagh, R. 2008. "A Climate-Change Policy Induced Shift from Innovations in Carbon-Energy Production to Carbon-Energy Savings." *Energy Economics* 30: 425-48. doi:10.1016/j.eneco.2006.05.024.

Gerlagh, R., and B. Van der Zwaan. 2006. "Options and Instruments for a Deep Cut in CO_2 Emissions: Carbon Dioxide Capture or Renewables, Taxes or Subsidies?" *The Energy Journal* 27 (3): 25-48.

Geroski, P. 1995. "Markets for Technology: Knowledge, Innovation, and Appropriability." In *Handbook of the Economics of Innovation and Technological Change*, ed. P. Stoneman. Oxford, UK: Blackwell Publishers, 90-131.

Gillingham, K., and K. Palmer. 2014. "Bridging the Energy Efficiency Gap: Policy Insights from Economic Theory and Empirical Evidence." *Review of Environmental Economics and Policy* 8: 18-38. doi:10.1093/reep/ret021

Ginarte, J. C., and W. G. Park. 1997. "Determinants of Patent Rights: A Cross-National Study." *Research Policy* 26: 283-301.

Goulder, L. H., and S. H. Schneider. 1999. "Induced Technological Change and the Attractiveness of CO_2 Abatement Policies." *Resource and Energy Economics* 21: 211-53. doi:10.1016/S0928-7655(99)00004-4.

Gray, W. B., and R. J. Shadbegian. 1998. "Environmental Regulation, Investment Timing, and Technology Choice." *Journal of Industrial Economics* 46: 235-56.

Grubb, M. 2004. "Technology Innovation and Climate Change Policy: An Overview of Issues and Options." *Keio Journal of Economic Studies* 41 (2): 103-32.

Grubb, M., J. C. Hourcade, and K. Neuhoff. 2013. *Planetary Economics: Energy, Climate Change and the Three Domains of Sustainable Development*. New York, NY, US: Routledge Publishing.

Haeussler, C., D. Harhoff, and E. Mueller. 2009. "To Be Financed or Not... The Role of Patents for Venture Capital Financing." Discussion Papers in Business Administration, Munich School of Management, Germany.

Hall, B. H., and J. Lerner. 2010. "The Financing of R&D and Innovation." In *Handbook of the Economics of Innovation*, vol. 1, eds., Bronwyn H. Hall and Nathan Rosenberg. Amsterdam: Elsevier, 609-39.

Hall, B. H., J. Mairesse, and P. Mohnen. 2010. "Measuring the Returns to R&D." In *Handbook of the Economics of Innovation*, vol. 2, eds., Bronwyn H. Hall and Nathan Rosenberg. Amsterdam: Elsevier, 1033-82.

Held, A., M. Ragwitz, and R. Haas. 2009. "On the Success of Policy Strategies for the Promotion of Electricity from Renewable Energy Sources in the EU." *Energy and Environmental Science* 17: 849-68. doi:10.1260/095830506779398849.

Hicks, J. 1932. *The Theory of Wages*. London, UK: Palgrave Macmillan.

Hottenrott, H., and S. Rexhauser. 2013. "Policy-Induced Environmental Technology and Inventive Efforts: Is There a Crowding Out?" ZEW-Centre of European Economic Research Discussion Paper.

Houde, S. 2014. "How Consumers Respond to Environmental Certification and the Value of Energy Information." National Bureau of Economic Research Working Paper Series No. 20019. doi:10.3386/w20019.

IEA. 2008. *Energy Technology Perspectives: Scenarios & Strategies to 2050*. Paris, France: IEA Publications.

IEA. 2010. "Global Gaps in Clean Energy RD&D: Update and Recommendations for International Collaboration." Report for the Clean Energy Ministerial. International Energy Agency, Paris, France.

IPCC. 2014. "Summary for Policymakers." In *Climate Change 2014: Mitigation of Climate Change. Working Group III Contribution of to the Fifth Assessment Report of the Intergovernmental Panel on Climate Change*, eds. O. Edenhofer et al. Cambridge, UK and New York, NY, US: Cambridge University Press, 1-31.

Jaffe, A. B. 2012. "Technology Policy and Climate Change." *Climate Change Economics* 3: 1–15. doi:10.1142/S201000781250025X.

Jaffe, A. B., and K. Palmer. 1997. "Environmental Regulation and Innovation: A Panel Data Study." *Review of Economics and Statistics* 79: 610-19. doi:10.2307/2951413.

Jaffe, A. B., and R. N. Stavins. 1994. "The Energy-Efficiency Gap: What Does It Mean?" *Energy Policy* 22: 804-10. doi:10.1016/0301-4215(94)90138-4.

Johnstone, N., I. Haščič, and D. Popp. 2010. "Renewable Energy Policies and Technological Innovation: Evidence Based on Patent Counts." *Environmental and Resource Economics* 45: 133-55. doi:10.1007/s10640-009-9309-1.

Kemp, R. 1998. "The Diffusion of Biological Waste-Water Treatment Plants in the Dutch Food and Beverage Industry." *Environmental and Resource Economics* 12: 113-36. doi: 10.1023/A:1016078930151.

Kerr, S., and R. G. Newell. 2003. "Policy-Induced Technology Adoption: Evidence from the U.S. Lead Phasedown." *Journal of Industrial Economics* 51: 317-43.

Kitzing, L., C. Mitchell, and P. E. Morthorst. 2012. "Renewable Energy Policies in Europe: Converging or Diverging?" *Energy Policy* 51: 192-201. doi:10.1016/j.enpol.2012.08.064.

Kriegler, E., J. P. Weyant, G. J. Blanford, V. Krey, L. Clarke, J. Edmonds, A. Fawcett, G. Luderer, K. Riahi, R. Richels, S. K. Rose, M. Tavoni, and D. P. van Vuuren. 2014. "The Role of Technology for Achieving Climate Policy Objectives: Overview of the EMF 27 Study on Global Technology and Climate Policy Strategies." *Climate Change* 123: 353-67. doi:10.1007/s10584-013-0953-7.

Lanjouw, J. O., and A. Mody. 1996. "Innovation and the International Diffusion of Environmentally Responsive Technology." *Research Policy* 25 (4): 549-71.

Levin, R. C., A. K. Klevorick, R. R. Nelson, and S. G. Winter. 1987. "Appropriating the Returns from Industrial Research and Development." *Brookings Papers on Economic Activity* 783. doi:10.2307/2534454.

Levinson, A., and S. Niemann. 2004. "Energy Use by Apartment Tenants When Landlords Pay for Utilities." *Resource and Energy Economics* 26: 51-75. doi:10.1016/S0928-7655(03)00047-2.

Lokshin, B., and P. Mohnen. 2012. "How Effective are Level-Based R&D Tax Credits? Evidence from the Netherlands." *Applied Economics* 44: 1527-38.

Magat, W. A. 1978. "Pollution Control and Technological Advance: A Dynamic Model of the Firm." *Journal of Environmental Economics and Management* 5: 1-25. doi:10.1016/0095-0696(78)90002-5.

McDonald, A., and L. Schrattenholzer. 2001. "Learning Rates for Energy Technologies." *Energy Policy* 29: 255-61. doi:10.1016/S0301-4215(00)00122-1.

Milliman, S. R., and R. Prince. 1989. "Firm Incentives to Promote Technological Change in Pollution Control." *Journal of Environmental Economics and Management* 17: 247-65. doi:10.1016/0095-0696(89)90019-3.

Moser, P. 2005. "How Do Patent Laws Influence Innovation? Evidence from Nineteenth-Century World's Fairs." *American Economic Review* 95: 1214-36.

Moser, P. 2013. "Patents and Innovation—Evidence from Economic History." *Journal of Economic Perspectives* 27 (1): 23-44.

Nelson, R. R. 1959. "The Simple Economics of Basic Scientific Research." *Journal of Political Economy* 67 (3): 297-306.

Nemet, G. F. 2006. "Beyond the Learning Curve: Factors Influencing Cost Reductions in Photovoltaics." *Energy Policy* 34: 3218-32.

Nemet, G. F. 2012. "Subsidies for New Technologies and Knowledge Spillovers from Learning by Doing." *Journal of Policy Analysis and Management* 31: 601-22. doi:10.1002/pam.21643.

Newell, R. G., A. B. Jaffe, and R. N. Stavins. 1999. "The Induced Innovation Hypothesis and Energy-Saving Technological Change." *Quarterly Journal of Economics* 114: 941-75.

Peters, M., M. Schneider, T. Griesshaber, and V. H. Hoffmann. 2012. "The Impact of Technology-Push and Demand-Pull Policies on Technical Change—Does the Locus of Policies Matter?" *Research Policy* 41: 1296-308. doi:10.1016/j.respol.2012.02.004.

Popp, D. 2002. "Induced Innovation and Energy Prices." *American Economic Review* 92: 160-80. doi:10.2307/3083326.

Popp, D. 2003. "Pollution Control Innovations and the Clean Air Act of 1990." *Journal of Policy Analysis and Management* 22: 641-60. doi:10.1002/pam.10159.

Popp, D. 2004. "ENTICE: Endogenous Technological Change in the DICE Model of Global Warming." *Journal of Environment Economics and Management* 48: 742-68. doi:10.1016/j.jeem.2003.09.002.

Popp, D. 2006a. "International Innovation and Diffusion of Air Pollution Control Technologies: the Effects of NO_x and SO_2 Regulation in the US, Japan, and Germany." *Journal of Environment Economics and Management* 51: 46-71. doi:10.1016/j.jeem.2005.04.006.

Popp, D. 2006b. "R&D Subsidies and Climate Policy: Is There a 'Free Lunch'?" *Climate Change* 77: 311-41. doi:10.1007/s10584-006-9056-z.

Popp, D. 2010a. "Exploring Links Between Innovation and Diffusion: Adoption of NO_x Control Technologies at US Coal-fired Power Plants." *Environmental and Resource Economics* 45: 319-52. doi:10.1007/s10640-009-9317-1.

Popp, D. 2010b. "Innovation and Climate Policy." In *Annual Review of Resource Economics, Volume 2*, eds. G. C. Rausser, V. K. Smith, and D. Zilberman. Palo Alto, CA: Annual Reviews, 275-98. doi: 10.1146/annurev.resource.012809.103929.

Popp, D., and R. Newell. 2012. "Where Does Energy R&D Come From? Examining Crowding Out from Energy R&D." *Energy Economics* 34: 980-91. doi:10.1016/j.eneco.2011.07.001.

Popp, D., R. G. Newell, and A. B. Jaffe. 2010. "Energy, the Environment, and Technological Change." In *Handbook of the Economics of Innovation, Volume 2*, eds. Bronwyn H. Hall and Nathan Rosenberg. Amsterdam, Netherlands: Elsevier B.V., 873-937.

Qian, Y. 2007. "Do National Patent Laws Stimulate Domestic Innovation in a Global Patenting Environment? A Cross-Country Analysis of Pharmaceutical Patent Protection, 1978-2002." *Review of Economics and Statistics* 89: 436-53.

Sallee, J. M. 2014. "Rational Inattention and Energy Efficiency." *Journal of Law and Economics* 57: 781-820.

Schneider, S. H., and L. H. Goulder. 1997. "Achieving Low-Cost Emissions Targets." *Nature* 389: 13-14.

Schultz, W. P., A. M. Khazian, and A. C. Zaleski. 2008. "Using Normative Social Influence to Promote Conservation Among Hotel Guests." *Social Influence* 3: 4-23.

Snyder, L., N. Miller, and R. Stavins. 2003. "The Effects of Environmental Regulations on Technology Diffusion: The Case of Chlorine Manufacturing." *American Economic Review* 93 (2): 431-35.

Söderholm, P., and T. Sundqvist. 2007. "Empirical Challenges in the Use of Learning Curves for Assessing the Economic Prospects of Renewable Energy Technologies." *Renewable Energy* 32: 2559-78.

Taylor, M. R., E. S. Rubin, and D. A. Hounshell. 2003. "Effect of Government Actions on Technological Innovation for SO_2 Control." *Environmental Science and Technology* 37: 4527-34.

Train, K. 1985. "Discount Rates in Consumers' Energy-Related Decisions: A Review of the Literature." *Energy* 10: 1243-53.

Verdolini, E., and M. Galeotti. 2011. "At Home and Abroad: An Empirical Analysis of Innovation and Diffusion in Energy Technologies." *Journal of Environmental Economics and Management* 61: 119-34. doi:10.1016/j.jeem.2010.08.004.

Vollebergh, H. R. J., and E. van der Werf. 2014. "The Role of Standards in Eco-innovation: Lessons for Policymakers." *Review of Environmental Economics and Policy* 8: 230-48. doi: 10.1093/reep/reu004.

Williams, H. 2012. "Innovation Inducement Prizes: Connecting Research to Policy." *Journal of Policy Analysis and Management* 31: 752-76.

Williams, H. 2013. "Intellectual Property Rights and Innovation: Evidence from the Human Genome." *Journal of Political Economy* 121 (1): 1-27.

Zachmann, G., A. Serwaah, and M. Peruzzi. 2014. "When and How to Support Renewables? Letting the Data Speak." Bruegel Working Paper 2014. http://bruegel.org/wp-content/uploads/imported/publications/WP_2014_01_renewables_.pdf.

A Comment on "Fiscal and Regulatory Instruments for Clean Technology Development in the European Union"

Claudio Marcantonini

The European Union has set very ambitious long-term GHG emission reduction targets: 40 percent by 2030 and 80-95 percent by 2050 compared with 1990 levels (European Council 2009; 2014a). This requires large investment in low-carbon technologies over a long period of time. Energy, transportation, and manufacturing are just some of the areas where significant technological development is needed. In this context, it is of primary importance to design and implement effective and efficient policies to develop clean technologies. This paper by Dechezleprêtre and Popp thoroughly describes the rationale for public support to technological development, accounting for the kind of policies already in place and the problems they address. The wide range of areas where technological development is needed and, as explained in the paper, the many different obstacles that render it difficult for the private sector to invest in innovation are such that a single policy cannot achieve the objective. Indeed, a portfolio of instruments is needed that should act at different levels (from basic research to market deployment) in a range of different areas. In the past ten years, the European Union has established a set of ambitious policies to support the development of low-carbon technologies. In this paper, to complement the work of Dechezleprêtre and Popp, I will comment on three key instruments of this package: direct support for research and development (R&D), the renewable energy policy, and the EU Emissions Trading System (EU ETS).

If the European Union wants to reach the abatement target, it needs to develop new low-carbon technologies; it is not enough, arguably, to simply focus on the improvement and deployment of current technologies. The first step toward new technologies is investing in R&D, beginning with basic research. As highlighted by a recent report from the Massachusetts Institute of Technology (MIT 2015), even in the area of solar energy, which has seen extensive investment in the past ten years, we still need significant R&D support into the development of innovative technologies. In this context, policies to support R&D are probably the most important policies to the development of low-carbon technologies. In particular, public funding for R&D is still needed, as basic research is mostly funded by the public sector and carried out in public institutions. Indeed, all the recommendations of Dechezleprêtre and Popp focus on improving R&D policies. The European Union has financed R&D for the development of low-carbon technologies through several funds and projects (among them Horizon 2020, the LIFE program, and the SET-Plan), and also through the Joint Research Centre, the in-house research facility of the European Commission (EC). The EU budget for R&D has continuously been increased. For example, in Horizon 2020, the main European funding program for research, the European Union will spend about €80 billion euros in the 2014–2020 period (EC 2013). This is about 30 percent more in real terms than the budget for FP7 (the previous funding program for research). Of this, more than 30 percent goes to projects related to climate change (EC 2014a).

However, despite this increase, EU funding represents only a small portion of the overall European investment in research, because most R&D is financed at the national level. The EU Member States agreed on the 2020 target of 3 percent of GDP for research spending at European level, combining public and private investment (EC 2010). This target has been translated into national targets that range from 1.21 percent for Greece to 4 percent for Finland and Sweden. The targets are non-binding and in 2014, the Member States invested, in total, only 2 percent of GDP in R&D (Eurostat 2015). There is the risk that the EU 2020 target will not be met, which is not surprising considering that non-binding targets are seldom reached. In this context, the recommendations of Dechezleprêtre and Popp to gradually and consistently increase funds for R&D, particularly from the public sector, are very positive. The EU institutions should also press and support Member States to reach their R&D targets. Moreover, within the EU energy and climate framework for 2030, and especially if the 2020 R&D target is not met, the European Union should define binding targets for R&D.

Regarding the European renewable energy policy, emphasis has been given to policy that deploy renewable technology in order to reach the 2020 renewable energy target, as highlighted by Dechezleprêtre and Popp. After years of policies aimed at supporting renewables, the European experience shows that it is not easy to strike the right balance between effectiveness and cost-efficiency for policies that provide direct incentives to technological deployment. In fact, on the one hand, the renewable energy policies (in particular, feed-in tariffs and feed-in premiums, which have been the most common renewable energy support in the European Union) were very effective in driving large investments into renewable energy technologies, especially for wind and solar. Such investments have significantly contributed to pushing down the cost of renewable energy in the European Union; as an example, the price of crystalline modules in Germany declined more than 50 percent in less than four years, from 2010 to 2014.[1] But, on the other hand, those policies turned out to be very expensive for consumers (in general, the cost of the policies is covered by a surcharge in the electricity bill). For example, in Germany, the renewable policy cost €23.6 billion in 2014 alone (BMWi 2014). As a result, some countries, such as Spain and Italy, have decided to drastically cut financial support, which has slowed down the deployment of renewable developments and created problems for the national renewable energy industry. In response, the EC recently produced new guidelines to help Member States to design more efficient public interventions in the field (EC 2014b). These guidelines represent an important step toward a more balanced renewable policy, promoting more flexible financial instruments that avoid overcompensation and a distortion of the energy market. The reduction of the renewable energy cost and a better design of the renewable policies should reduce the cost of those policies, which could facilitate the allocation of more resources for R&D.

Regarding the EU ETS, it supports technological development in two ways. Firstly, by pricing GHG emissions, it makes investment in high-carbon technology more costly. There is empirical evidence that the EU ETS supported investment in low-carbon technologies. In addition to increasing the patenting activity for regulated firms, as explained by Dechezleprêtre and Popp, there is also evidence that the EU ETS supported direct investment in GHG emission reduction technology, at least in Phase I (2005–2007) (Martin at al. 2016). However, the impact of the EU ETS on investment was lower than expected. In particular, it did not drive large investment in the power sector. This was caused by the low carbon price due to a high surplus of allowances. Currently, the price is around €8/tCO_2, well below €30, which is the assumed threshold at which the carbon price should generate enough incentive for substantial investment in abatement measures (KfW/ZEW 2015). In principle, this should not be a problem. A low carbon price is not a sign of the poor functioning of the carbon market[2] and, because the EU ETS emission cap linearly declines every year, the price will eventually increase. However, the carbon market, as any market, is far from being perfect, and may be subject to market or regulatory failures (Neuhoff et al. 2015). This could reduce the efficiency of the system and lead to underinvestment in low-carbon technologies in the short term. After a long debate, the EC decided to address the allowances surplus by increasing the stringency of the cap reduction from 2020 on, and by introducing a system to change the annual issuance of auctioned allowances based on the level of the allowance surplus (European Council 2014; EU 2015). The key characteristic of these measures is that they preserve the market-based principle of the EU ETS. It is hard to anticipate the impact of this reform on the carbon price (the history of the EU ETS shows that it is very difficult to predict the price). The Commission, in the base case scenario of a recent impact assessment (EC 2015a), assumed an average price of €25/tCO_2 for Phase IV (2020–2030), which is lower, but not much less than €30. In 2026, the Commission will review the system and, if needed, propose new changes.

The second way in which the EU ETS supports the development of technology is by investing revenue from the auctioning of the allowances. From Phase III (2013–2020), a large part of the allowance (more than 40 percent) has been auctioned. Most of the revenues (apart from the revenue used for the NER300 program) are held by the Member States, and the Commission cannot direct Member States on how to spend this money. According to the EU ETS directive, at least 50 percent of the revenue should be used for climate-related purposes, which explicitly includes funding R&D and development of renewable energy (EU 2009). However, this target is not binding. For the revenue collected in 2013 (about €3.6 billion), the Member States reported to the Commission that they collectively used, or planned to use, up to 87 percent of the revenue for climate and energy related purposes (EC 2014b). Yet few Member States reported how they used the revenue according to the type of action and it is not possible to know how much was really used for clean technological development. Only Germany, Denmark, and United Kingdom reported that they used a considerable part of the revenue for R&D (European Council 2014b). For Phase IV (2020–2030), the EC proposed amending the EU ETS directive, in which some of the new measures will be aimed at increasing the share of revenue for technological development. Besides extending the NER300 program with the NER400, two new funds should be created: the Innovation Fund, financed through €450 million of auctioned allowances for "innovative technologies to advance innovation in industry," and a Modernisation Fund financed with €300 million of auctioned allowances, which is specifically for the power sector and lower-income Member States. In addition to that, the Commission should also propose new measures to ensure that Member States invest the revenue of the auctioned allowances in clean technology. Experience shows that the most effective way is to have binding targets. One such target could be to direct a part of the revenue allowance to R&D, as suggested by Dechezleprêtre and Popp.

To conclude, in the past ten years, the European Union has developed a portfolio of ambitious policies that support the development of low-carbon technologies. However, the European experience has shown that it is not easy to design and implement successful and sustainable policies. As a result, the European Union has amended or reformed many of the policies introduced over this period. Indeed, the institutional complexity, the several levels of government involved, the changes to the external conditions, and the interaction between different policies and priorities make it difficult to design and implement an optimal portfolio of policies that attains the appropriate balance between effectiveness and cost-efficiency. The European Union is currently debating the new climate and energy policy for 2030, which goes under the name of the Energy Union (EC 2015b). One of the pillars of the Energy Union will be a "new strategy for Research and Innovation," particularly in the field of renewable energy, demand-side technologies, transport, and carbon capture and storage. As mentioned, some legislative action is already under way, and more is anticipated in the coming years. It is of primary importance that, for each policy, a system of regular monitoring and review is implemented, so that those policies can be improved and adapted to the changing conditions through a continuous learning-by-doing process. In this respect, the role of the EC in monitoring the application of the EU policies has been, and will remain, crucial.

Notes

1. See http://www.pvxchange.com.

2. The goal of the ETS is to reduce emissions at the lowest cost. Moreover, the ETS is countercyclical with respect to the economic activities: at times of economic crisis, the price is low, while during periods of growth, the price increases.

References

BMWi. 2014. "Renewable Energy Sources in Figures." National and International Development, 2013, German Federal Ministry for Economic Affairs and Energy.

EC. 2010. "Communication from the Commission, Europe 2020: A Strategy for Smart, Sustainable and Inclusive Growth." COM (2010) 2020 final.

EC. 2013. "Factsheet: Horizon 2020 Budget." http://ec.europa.eu/research/horizon2020/pdf/press/fact_sheet_on_horizon2020_budget.pdf.

EC. 2014a. "Report from the Commission to the European Parliament and the Council Progress Towards Achieving the Kyoto and EU 2020 Objectives." COM(2014) 689 final.

EC. 2014b. "Communication from the Commission, Guidelines on State Aid for Environmental Protection and Energy 2014-2020." 2014/C 200/01.

EC. 2015a. "Commission Staff Working Document Impact Assessment Accompanying the Document Proposal for a Directive of the European Parliament and of the Council Amending Directive 2003/87/EC to Enhance Cost-Effective Emission Reductions and Low Carbon Investment." SWD(2015) 135 final.

EC. 2015b. "Energy Union Package. A Framework Strategy for a Resilient Energy Union with a Forward-Looking Climate Change Policy." Communication from the Commission to the European Parliament, the Council, the European Economic and Social Committee, the Committee of the Regions and the European Investment Bank. COM(2015) 80 final.

EU. 2009. "Directive 2009/29/EC of the European Parliament and of the Council of 23 April 2009 amending Directive 2003/87/EC so as to Improve and Extend the Greenhouse Gas Emission Allowance Trading Scheme of the Community."

EU. 2015. "Decision (EU) 2015/1814 of the European Parliament and of The Council of 6 October 2015 Concerning the Establishment and Operation of a Market Stability Reserve for the Union Greenhouse Gas Emission Trading Scheme and Amending Directive 2003/87/EC."

European Council. 2009. "Presidency Conclusions of the European Council of 29 and 30 October 2009." 15265/1/09.

European Council. 2014a. "Conclusions of the European Council of 24 October 2014." EUCO 169/14.

European Council. 2014b. "Commission Staff Working Document Accompanying the Document Report from the Commission to the European Parliament and the Council Progress towards Achieving the Kyoto and EU 2020 Objectives." 15012/14 ADD 2.

Eurostat. 2015. "European Commission: Europe 2020 Indicators—Research and Development." http://ec.europa.eu/eurostat.

KfW/ZEW. 2015. "KfW/ZEW CO_2 Barometer 2015—Carbon Edition—Ten Years of Emission Trading: Strategies of German Companies." Centre for European Economic Research, Mannheim, Germany.

Martin, R., M. Muûls, and U. Wagner. 2016. "The Impact of the EU ETS on Regulated Firms: What Is the Evidence After Ten Years?" *Review of Environmental Economics and Policy* 10 (1): 129-48.

MIT. 2015. *The Future of Solar Energy.* Massachusetts Institute of Technology Energy Initiative, Cambridge, MA, US.

Neuhoff, K., W. Acworth, R. Betz, D. Burtraw, J. Cludius, H. Fell, C. Hepburn, C. Holt, F. Jotzo, S. Kollenberg, F. Landis, S. Salant, A. Schopp, W. Shobe, L. Taschini, and R. Trotignon. 2015. "Is a Market Stability Reserve Likely to Improve the Functioning of the EU ETS? Evidence from a Model Comparison Exercise." Climate Strategies, London, UK, February 2015.

7 Lessons from the U.S. Shale Gas Boom

Alan Krupnick and Zhongmin Wang[1]

Key Points for Policymakers

- Government policy, private entrepreneurship, private land and mineral rights ownership, and a number of other factors all helped generate the shale gas boom in the United States.
- With higher population densities and the cultural support for the precautionary principle, but without private ownership in mineral rights, Europe has found it difficult to obtain the social license to develop shale gas.
- While some of the environmental risks of shale gas development are no different than those with conventional gas exploitation, other risks are different in substance, scale, and location, and they are not all well understood.
- This paper explores a variety of policy approaches for cost-effective risk mitigation.
- The commitment of many European countries to reducing fossil fuel use relative to the United States helps the case for shale gas in the short run, but if energy production must be weaned off of fossil fuels in the longer term to meet global warming goals, there may be no conditions, short of carbon capture and sequestration, that permit long-term sustainability of natural gas in Europe.

1. Introduction

In the past decade, shale gas experienced an extraordinary boom in the United States, accounting for only 1.6 percent of total U.S. natural gas production in 2000, 4.1 percent by 2005, and an astonishing 40.4 percent by 2013 (Sieminski 2014). This remarkable growth has spurred interest in exploring for shale gas resources elsewhere. A number of countries,

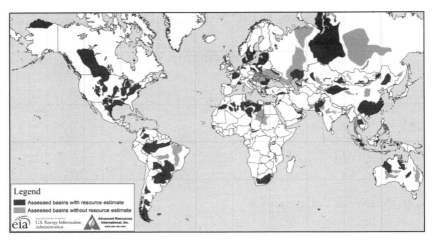

Figure 7.1
Map of basins with assessed shale oil and shale gas formations, as of May 2013
Sources: United States basins from U.S. Energy Information Administration and United
States Geological Survey; other basins from ARI based on various published studies.

including China, Mexico, Argentina, Poland, the United Kingdom, and
Australia, are beginning to develop their own shale gas resources
(figure 7.1). In contrast, some European countries (e.g., France and the
Netherlands) have banned or put moratoria on the activity, and
Germany is considering a bill that would effectively ban fracking for
at least five years with some testing permitted during that period.[2,3]

While no one can doubt that the United States has experienced a
shale gas boom, whether it has been sustainable from an environmental
perspective, i.e., whether the net economic benefits have been and will
continue to be worth the environmental damages it causes, is much
more controversial. Based on our review of the research on shale gas-
related externalities, we think the case can be made for sustainability so
far. It is less clear whether sustainability can continue with continued
rapid development, as operations encroach more on communities and
habitat, while concerns about the role of natural gas (and other fossil
fuels) in global warming grow. In this paper we lay out this thesis with
an eye toward the European experience, e.g., the question of whether
Europe has what it takes to have a shale gas boom and if this could
occur sustainably. We do not seek to answer this question; rather, we
have the more modest goal of setting up the proper arguments and
considerations and distilling some lessons for European policymakers.

Below we consider the causes of the U.S. shale gas boom and their possible applicability to Europe and then address the environmental risks associated with shale gas development. We follow with a look at alternative approaches to mitigate risk and then conclude.

2. What Caused the U.S. Shale Gas Boom?

For a real boom to occur in the private sector, high profitability, or at least the expectation of future high profitability, is a necessary ingredient. Our review (Wang and Krupnick 2014) suggests that a number of factors converged in the early 2000s—including technology innovations, high natural gas prices, favorable geology, private land and mineral rights ownership, helpful economic policies (e.g., open access to pipelines, favorable tax treatment), market structure, water availability, and natural gas pipeline infrastructure—to make it profitable to produce large quantities of shale gas in the United States. Some of the key technology innovations (e.g., slick water fracturing and microseismic fracture mapping) resulted from government research and development (R&D) programs and private entrepreneurship that aimed to develop unconventional natural gas, but other important technologies (e.g., horizontal drilling and three-dimensional seismic imaging) were largely developed by the oil industry for use in oil exploration and production. Indeed, without further government intervention, industry has been rapidly innovating to reduce costs and the time from starting to drill to completion.

The seed of the U.S. shale gas boom was planted in the late 1970s and early 1980s, when the U.S. government funded R&D programs and established tax credits (and incentive pricing) to encourage the development of unconventional natural gas in response to the severe natural gas shortage at the time. These policies were justified on the grounds that private firms lacked the incentive to make large, risky R&D investments, partly because it is difficult to keep new technologies proprietary in the oil and gas industry, where few technologies are patentable or licensable (NRC 2001), and because the operators act like general contractors rather than doing the work themselves. Also, in the early years, unconventional gas sources, due to their higher risks and lower returns, could not compete with conventional oil or gas sources for investment dollars. This partly explains why major international oil firms were essentially absent from early shale gas development. In addition, most U.S. natural gas producers were too small to have the incentive or capacity to do much R&D (Morgantown Energy Technology Center 1980). Government policies stimulated the development of shale gas in the Appalachian and Michigan Basins and helped develop some key technologies.

It was, however, the private entrepreneurship of Mitchell Energy & Development (Mitchell Energy, hereafter) that played the primary role in developing the Barnett play in Texas, and it was the successful development of the Barnett play that jump-started the shale gas boom. Government-sponsored R&D programs did not target the Barnett play, and tax credits had a rather limited impact on Mitchell Energy. Given that the argument for government interventions is that private firms lacked incentives, why did Mitchell Energy develop the Barnett play? Mitchell Energy had the need and the financial capacity. Later, the firm was also motivated by the potential to obtain large financial rewards from its innovations. The firm did this by leasing large tracts of land and the associated mineral rights at low prices and later selling the company—including not only its leases but also its innovations and expertise—at a higher price. This strategy, which is made possible by the private land and mineral rights ownership system in the United States, helps overcome the difficulty of monetizing technology innovations in the industry.

Needless to say, with mineral rights owned by the state throughout Europe, these economic advantages will be largely absent. On the other hand, with companies needing only to interact with a state government, rather than thousands of landowners, transactions costs would be greatly reduced relative to the U.S. experience. In addition, countries new to shale gas enjoy a major advantage over the United States in the early stage of the boom in that shale gas technologies are now much more advanced than they were in the early days of shale gas exploitation. The most important fracturing activities are concentrated in three worldwide oil and gas service companies.[4] So, the suite of U.S. technologies would be available for use in Europe. However, it is widely reported that companies are experiencing drilling costs in Europe that are far higher than those in the United States. One estimate for Europe (Ernst & Young 2013) quotes costs from $8-$12/MBtu relative to U.S. costs in the range of $3-$7/MBtu. Nevertheless, it took many years for operators to "get it right" and begin bringing costs down. With extensive drilling in Europe, the experience gained should bring costs down there as well.

2.1   Geology

Understanding the geology of the target reservoir is critical for deciding where to drill, how many wells to drill, and how to drill and stimulate wells. The geology of shale gas plays in the United States is by now well known, and the technologies to develop shale gas are mature, in the sense that there is little uncertainty about whether a set of wells can be profitable at a given price.

The biggest economic concern in Europe would be that the geologies are very different than those in the United States. Recently, the trade press has been rife with reports of exploratory well failures in Europe, e.g., in Poland, where geological conditions have frustrated fracturing attempts and caused at least three major oil companies to sell their holdings.[5] Industry consensus seems to be that it takes around 300 wells drilled before the geology of a play is understood well enough. In Poland, less than 20 have been drilled. One interpretation of the majors' exit is that the geology in Poland is so challenging that the existing technologies are far from being cost-effective. Another interpretation is that the incentive for the majors to drill is not strong enough: the potential return in the long run does not outweigh the short-run losses.

2.2   Land and Mineral Rights Ownership

Shale gas development in the United States has taken place primarily on private land, and the private ownership of land and mineral rights provided a key mechanism for firms that develop new technologies to obtain returns on their investments. The coupling of private land and mineral rights allowed natural gas firms to develop and test new technology, and then sell the lease (with access to mineral deposits) after demonstrating its potential. A key issue in Europe is whether firms would be able to secure large enough acreage positions at low enough prices to potentially reap the benefits of their R&D investments. However, given that mineral rights are owned by the states, securing such large positions is made even easier if governments are willing to cooperate.

2.3   High Natural Gas Prices

The wellhead price of natural gas had been largely deregulated in the United States by 1991. Mitchell Energy accelerated its development of the Barnett shale gas play in 2000 and 2001 partly because natural gas prices increased significantly in those two years (which coincided with

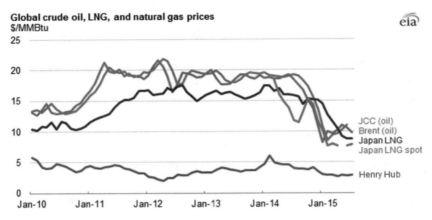

Figure 7.2a
Natural gas spot prices in the United States (Henry Hub) and Japan (both spot natural gas and LNG)
Source: https://www.eia.gov/todayinenergy/detail.cfm?id=23132.

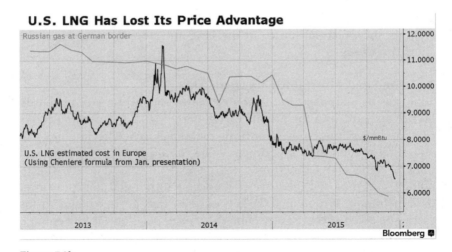

Figure 7.2b
Russian gas price at the EU border and U.S. LNG price
Source: http://www.bloomberg.com/news/articles/2015-12-31/five-questions-for-eur ope-s-gloomy-natural-gas-market-in-2016.

the California electricity crises), from an average wellhead price of about $2/thousand cubic feet (Mcf) in 1994–1999 to an average of $3.85/Mcf in 2000–2001. Natural gas wellhead prices decreased to an average of about $3/Mcf in 2002 but remained higher than $5/Mcf for most of the 2003–2008 period, briefly exceeding \$10/Mcf in 2008. Given the success of drilling and fracturing technologies, high natural gas prices imply that firms may realize significant profit margins from drilling shale gas wells. The prospect of high profit margins encouraged existing firms and new entrants to invest heavily in shale gas plays in the 2000s, which eventually drove down natural gas prices.

While current U.S. natural gas prices have been low since 2000 (around \$2/Mcf) and prices in Japan and Europe are coming down, because of transportation and liquefaction costs, Japan pays \$8.50/Mcf for LNG on the spot market while U.S. LNG sells for just \$6.50 in Europe (compared to Russian gas on the EU border selling for \$6/Mcf).

Of course, as we have seen for the United States, high natural gas prices can deliver an incentive to explore other options. Before deregulation, severe natural gas shortages occurred, reflecting firms' lack of incentive to explore and exploit new gas resources when the natural gas price was set below market value. Even with the recent drop in natural gas prices starting in 2008, production has barely slackened off, even at \$2/Mcf.[6]

While not a huge factor in the United States, concerns about the availability of natural gas at *any* price, or at far above market price as a result of political decisions—such as gas cutoffs from Russia—could well be important to European policymakers. Developing home-grown natural gas to diversify supply, even if somewhat more costly than LNG or Russian gas, could be justified.

2.4 Market Structure

The United States has thousands of natural gas firms, but it was a single independent natural gas firm—Mitchell Energy—that made large amounts of investments before shale gas development was proved profitable in 2002–2003. Mitchell Energy was small when compared with the major international oil firms, but it was large when compared with the typical natural gas firms. Wang and Xue (2014) find that over 650 natural gas firms had, by the end of 2012, drilled at least one well in six major shale gas plays—Barnett, Marcellus, Haynesville, Eagle Ford, Woodford, and Fayetteville—in the United States, but 60 percent of these firms drilled no more than five wells and the top 30 firms together drilled about 78 percent of the wells. Small natural gas firms do not have the financial or technical capacity to make the substantial risky investments that Mitchell Energy made. The major international oil firms had the capacity, but they did not have the incentive to do so: investments in conventional oil and gas fields (offshore or in other countries) were more profitable and less risky. Smaller operators are more willing to make risky investments because their owners have the chance to obtain extremely high returns for their risky investments. Surely the European set of such companies is much, much smaller than those in the United States.

2.5 Water Availability

Slick water fracturing of shale gas wells requires a few million gallons of water per well. In the United States, sufficient water has generally been available, although in some areas, shortages—and conflicts with farmers and other water users—are a growing concern. Thus, water availability may constrain U.S. shale gas production in some areas in the future (the California drought comes to mind), as well as production in other countries.

Figure 7.3 shows a water stress map overlaid with shale gas and tight oil plays worldwide,[7] with stress defined as the ratio of water withdrawals to available renewable surface water. This map is interesting because it actually shows the United States plays as being in some of the highest water stress areas in the world, while those of future competitors, such as Australia, Argentina, and even most European countries, seem to have lower water stress. The United Kingdom and Spain are the exceptions, where water stress appears to be high. Note, however, that water stress is highly site-specific, so such maps may be misleading. In addition, the industry is rapidly moving toward a recycling model, as well as toward use of briny water, which can dramatically reduce freshwater demand. Further, although this point goes far beyond shale gas development, where water prices are subsidized, which would include the western United States, a case can be made to remove them. Indeed, Schlumberger[8] makes the case that companies could greatly limit their use of freshwater if it were priced appropriately.

2.6 Natural Gas Pipeline Infrastructure

An extensive network of natural gas pipelines existed in the United States before shale gas became a major gas resource. Also important was the policy of open access to these interstate natural gas pipelines (as well as storage facilities) as a result of a series of Federal Energy Regulatory Commission orders in the 1980s and early 1990s. As a result of these orders, pipeline owners do not take ownership of the gas and have no stake in which company accesses their pipelines, a principle known as unbundling.

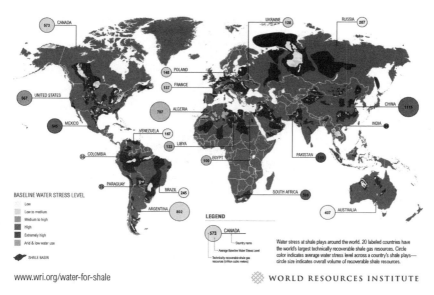

Figure 7.3
Water stress and shale gas plays, volume of technically recoverable shale gas in the 20 countries with the largest resources, and the level of baseline water stress
Source: World Resources Institute.

Even the United States, with its extensive network of gas pipelines, has recently experienced capacity shortages. Figure 7.4 shows that prices for natural gas at some local hubs in the Marcellus were significantly lower than Henry Hub prices, reflecting the lack of takeaway capacity in the Pennsylvania-Ohio (Marcellus-Utica shale) region. Countries without an extensive gas pipeline network will face a major hurdle in approving new pipelines at an appropriate speed. For existing pipelines, numerous questions must be resolved, including the control of pipeline access. A recent report (Ernst & Young 2013) states that not only is natural gas pipeline capacity largely decided by national governments in the European Union, but the existence of long-term capacity reservation contracts could make existing pipelines inaccessible for shale gas developers. Pipeline infrastructure becomes important as development of the plays proceeds, and it will be necessary for exploitation success in the longer term.

2.7 Capital Market

Some observers claim that the capital market has played an important role in pushing the shale gas boom forward. After the shale gas boom

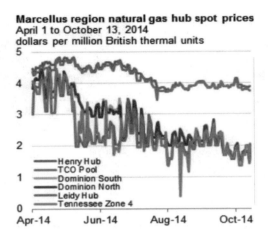

Figure 7.4
Local vs. Henry Hub prices as a result of transmission costs
Sources: U.S. Energy Information Administration and SNL.

took off, financial firms provided some natural gas firms with considerable capital to drill, facilitated many deals in which larger oil and gas firms bought out smaller firms engaged in shale gas drilling, and may have contributed to the recent oversupply of shale gas (Krauss and Lipton 2012). Mitchell Energy also relied on the capital market (e.g., conventional bank loans, public stock offering, public bond offering, and private placement) to raise funds to drill for oil and gas (Kutchin 1998). However, Mitchell Energy raised those funds not because of but despite its shale gas development that lost money for many years. The role of capital markets in the United States context is thus somewhat unclear, although the well-known short-term profit focus of Wall Street fits well with shale gas development, where, in contrast to conventional drilling, decline curves start higher, meaning that profitability comes faster (although they are far steeper, meaning production falls off more quickly). In Europe, shale gas faces greater uncertainty—while it is no longer an unproven resource elsewhere, it faces significant regulatory, geologic, and economic uncertainty. What this uncertainty means for capital markets, and for government investment and support, remains to be seen and will likely be highly variable.

2.8   Materials and Labor
Whether materials and skilled labor availability is sufficient in other countries is a potential issue. For instance, proppants (most often very

fine sand) are a necessary ingredient. In the United States, most of such sand comes from the upper Midwestern states. In some countries, such sand might have to be imported, raising its costs.

The necessary pipes, fittings, generators, computer equipment, rigs, etc., are not much different than those used for conventional drilling. The specialized drill bits, fracturing tubes, and other technologies can be easily imported if they are not available locally. However, if such equipment is not transferable due to differing regulatory requirements, then a shortage of critical equipment could occur (Ernst & Young 2013). Additionally, labor skills are less easily transferred to some countries, and labor shortages are a concern in some areas.

2.9 Other Factors
Additional factors contributing to U.S. shale gas development include the availability of underground injection wells for wastewater disposal; favorable topography; low population density above the plays; and a successful history of conventional oil and gas development. The latter two are particularly important for building a social license to operate (see below).

2.10 Another Take
One of the three fracking service companies (Baker Hughes) has produced their own comparison of the factors that could lead to a boom (see figure 7.5). The United States sets the standard, with mostly "green" signals for the seven criteria used to rate the likelihood of unconventional development booming. The above discussion offered a variety of positive elements for a boom, but at least an equal number of negative elements. The Baker Hughes assessment is even more pessimistic than ours, showing Europe with poorer conditions than the United States in all dimensions, including geology, infrastructure, land access, cost, water availability, and business environment, for overall commercial viability is rated far below that of the United States. Still, they take care to note that any significant production outside of the United States will take at least three to five years to develop and that many unknowns and market conditions will continue to evolve, meaning that international shale plays just now being looked at could come on line in a different environment (Rajan 2014).

2.11 Concluding Remarks on the Boom
In addition to the factors we noted above that could propel or stop a boom in shale gas development in Europe, there appear to us to be

Qualitative Assessment of International Unconventional Space

Dimension	U.S.	Canada	Argentina	MENA	China	Australia	Mexico	Europe	Russia
Resource Base									
Infrastructure/Logistics									
Public Policy, Land Access									
Development Cost									
Business Environment									
Upstream OFS									
Water Avail. and Management									
Overall Commerciality									

Poor — Good

Surya Rajan, Baker Hughes
37th IAEE/USAEE International Conference
June 17, 2014, New York City

Figure 7.5
Trends in fuel shares in total gross inland consumption of energy (EU-28)
Source: Eurostat (2015).

several more that deserve mention. One is the culture of precaution, energy security, and climate policy. The precautionary principle in Europe is a strong cultural feature: be sure something is reasonably safe before going ahead. In the United States, the dominant culture is "shoot first and ask questions later" (European Parliament 2012). The reticence about new technology (e.g., the European bans on GMOs) is made worse by the higher population densities in Europe and lack of private mineral rights to compensate those most likely to be harmed by shale gas development. As for energy security, Russian cutbacks on supplies to Ukraine raise European prices and raise fears of gas cutoffs to the EU countries. Such fears could give way to a more supportive public opinion toward "fracking." At the same time, the EU countries have been diversifying their sources of gas supply (e.g., the Southern Gas Corridor project and LNG import terminals in Poland and Lithuania), and Russia is dependent on European payments for natural gas for much of its revenue, encouraging a more sanguine view of energy security risks. Finally, we must mention the commitment of European countries to reducing fossil fuel use. Quite apart from the precautionary principle, the idea of promoting indigenous development of a potentially cheap fossil fuel may not sit well with a large segment of the European population (BIO Intelligence Service 2013). Indeed, if energy production must be weaned off of fossil fuels in the longer term to meet global warming goals, there may be no conditions, short of carbon capture and sequestration, which would permit long-term sustainability of natural gas in Europe.

3. Sustainably Developing Shale Gas: The Environmental Dimension

We now turn to a discussion of sustainable development and shale gas impacts more broadly. The development of shale gas resources entails risks to the environment, just as any resource extraction and processing activities would and just as the development of any form of energy would. The issue is whether shale gas resources are special compared to close substitutes in either having comparatively low risks or comparatively high risks relative to their costs to supply the market. Unfortunately, there are no studies that compare the full social costs (private plus environmental) of shale gas with other fuels. This is not surprising because many of the impacts, let alone their value, are poorly understood.[9] Below we have the more modest goal of discussing what is known and what is not well understood about various risks posed by shale gas development.

In general, potential risks from shale gas development have been comprehensively characterized, but not estimated. Krupnick and Gordon (2015) developed a risk matrix for upstream activities, identifying 264 risk "pathways" linking 15 development activities (e.g., site development) to seven classes of intermediate impacts (e.g., groundwater) from 20 classes of burdens (e.g., conventional air pollutants). These pathways cover routine risks. The authors also identified 14 classes of accident risks. They then had experts from the industry, NGOs, academia, and government choose from these pathways those with the highest priority for further regulatory or voluntary industry actions. Note that 12 of the top 20 routine risks are held in common by all four groups, another was identified by the self-selected "top" experts, and two of the top three accident risks are also held in common. Of the 15 consensus risk pathways, seven impact surface water, five impact groundwater, two impact air quality, and one leads to habitat

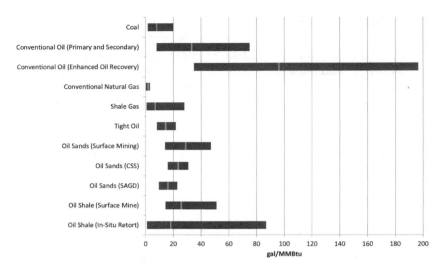

Figure 7.6
Ranges and averages of water intensity estimates in water-energy nexus literature
Source: Kuwayama et al. (2013).

disruption. Below, we address the salient risks so identified plus several others that have recently increased in concern.

3.1 Water Quantity

Shale gas development needs hydraulic fracturing and, in turn, the use of fracturing fluids and large quantities of water (3-5 million gallons per well). While hydraulic fracturing is occasionally used for conventional wells, the latter are in decline. As shown in figure 7.6 on a Btu basis, shale gas uses a lot more water than a non-hydraulically fractured conventional gas well, similar amounts to coal and far less than oil obtained through enhanced oil recovery and secondary oil using water flooding. The latter two, enhanced oil recovery and secondary oil, are used in 79.7 percent and 20.1 percent of total crude oil output (Kuwayama et al. 2013).

However, risks are related to the amount used and the amount present. Kuwayama et al. (2013), drawing on Freyman and Salmon (2013), find that areas of high shale gas activity overlap areas of high water stress in some areas of the United States and conclude that the timing (seasonality) and location of withdrawals (from small or large water bodies) are critical for assessing damage potential.

For countries with gas resources and chronic water scarcity (such as the Tarim Basin area in northwestern China), shale gas development presents obvious challenges. Many countries subsidize water use, creating distortions that will result in too much water being used overall. Even if water is priced at its marginal delivery costs, it will not necessarily (and surely rarely) be priced temporally and spatially to reflect low-flow externalities on water-dependent ecosystems (Kochhar et al. 2015).

3.2   Surface Water Quality

Surface water bodies can be affected by runoff, spills, and liquid wastes treated and released from wastewater treatment plants. Olmstead et al. (2013) find that for Pennsylvania, sediment runoff from well infrastructure (including roads) affects stream quality, as do emissions from outfalls. However, they find no statistically significant effect of spills of fracking fluid or produced water on streams and rivers. There is a significant literature on these topics (Entrekin et al. 2011; Ferrar et al. 2013; Olmstead et al. 2013; States et al. 2012; Vidic et al. 2013; Warner, Christie, Jackson, and Vengosh 2013; USEPA 2015). Enforcement data need to be analyzed further in order to figure out how often and to what magnitude spills are occurring. Ultimately, surface water quality impacts depend on the care taken to treat and dispose of liquid wastes.

3.3   Groundwater Quality

Groundwater is potentially affected in many ways, including leakage through faulty casing and cementing around the well bore; leakage to groundwater from upward migration of fracturing fluids and other produced water through the fractures themselves; leakage through existing fractures in the rock that are intersected through the fracturing process; and leakage through existing and abandoned well bores that are similarly compromised through the fracturing process.

The most contentious debate is whether fracturing itself can result in pollution of groundwater by methane or substances in produced and flowback water. Industry analysis shows that the fractures do not move above capping rock so such releases do not occur. Some studies offer evidence of such pollution from methane from deep underground sources (Osborn et al. 2011), but these studies have been heavily criticized (Schon 2011). USEPA (2015) was a major study on the extent that water wells are polluted from shale gas development, concluding that there were no systemic effects.

In contrast, there seems to be little debate that problems in well cementing and casing can cause pollution of aquifers from all oil and gas drilling, while the scope of this problem is unknown, at least to the public and researchers. Confidentiality agreements between the companies and landowners limit this potential source of information about well water pollution.

More, and better, information and research on risks to groundwater are critically needed. The enormous public concern about polluting groundwater and the lack of reliable information about these risks have powered concerns over development (for survey results in this area, see Siikamaki and Krupnick 2014).

3.4 Local Air Pollution

Air pollution is an inevitable by-product of shale gas development activities, with the amount depending on emissions controls and the regulatory system. Many of the activities associated with shale gas development—such as site development, water transport, the pumping of fracturing fluids, and processing the gas to remove water and natural gas liquids—generate "conventional" air pollutants through the burning of diesel and other fossil fuels. These conventional pollutants primarily include volatile organic compounds, diesel particulates, and NO_2. Many types of toxic releases are also possible.

There are several studies showing violations of air quality standards attributable to shale gas development and other oil and gas development activities in the West (Lyman and Shorthill 2013; Rieman 2013; Schnell et al. 2009; Stoechenius and Ma 2010). And as noted below in the health section, public health professionals are concerned about the short-term symptoms and long-term morbidity associated with air toxic releases wherever oil and gas development is taking place. Nevertheless, these activities are sufficiently short-term and place-specific (in areas with low population density) that major public health issues related to air pollution are unlikely, in our judgment. Where population densities are far larger than the United States, public health risks could be correspondingly larger, however.

3.5 Global Warming

One of the most contentious areas of debate is whether lifecycle greenhouse gas (GHG) emissions from shale gas (and conventional gas) are lower than the other fossil fuels they potentially substitute for—coal and oil. Numerous studies provide estimates of comparative lifecycle CO_2 equivalent emissions, with general agreement that natural gas is superior from a CO_2 perspective. The debate is about the role gas itself (as methane) plays in global warming, when emitted either intentionally (venting) or through leaks (fugitive). One issue is the amount of production that is vented and fugitive, another is the amount of fugitive emissions from other stages in the gas lifecycle, and another is how one accounts for the relatively short-lived life of methane in the atmosphere when it can contribute to global warming—whether the IPCC standard 100-year lifetime assumption is appropriate or the 20-year lifetime assumption often used as an alternative. There is agreement, however, that when methane is in the atmosphere its global warming potential is far greater than that of CO_2 (34 times greater with a 100-year horizon and 84 times with a 20-year horizon).[10] To summarize the current state of knowledge, some of the most recent literature using bottom-up approaches suggests that vented and fugitive emissions are low enough (below 3 percent of production) that natural gas's global warming potential is below that of coal (Allen et al. 2013). At the same time, the top-down literature, such as that using satellite and airplane data, finds much higher fractions—from 3 to 17 percent (Schneising et al. 2014). The global warming potential of natural gas relative to diesel and gasoline is even closer than that to coal, where the break-even leak rate for the former is only around 1 percent of natural gas production.

Of all the environmental issues, the contribution of the natural gas life cycle to global warming probably poses the greatest challenge to sustainability. In the relatively short run, industry needs to show conclusively that fugitive and leaking methane have been brought under tight control. In the United States, the EPA has developed several regulations in this regard and some in the industry have been developing their own voluntary program called One Future. The Environmental Defense Fund (2014) shows that about 20 percent of methane emissions from natural gas activities could be reduced at negative costs by, for example, using a new type of valve (and the cost offset by selling the gas that would otherwise be lost). In the longer term, sustainability of shale gas development is in doubt because most models show that fossil fuels cannot be in the mix (without carbon capture and sequestration [CCS]) if aggressive stabilization goals are pursued (McJeon et al. 2014; Brown et al. 2009). As Brown et al. (2009) show, however, the shale gas revolution has the potential to reduce the costs of attaining more modest carbon reductions.

3.6   Habitat

The fragmentation of habitat by wells, roads, pipelines, and ancillary equipment is a potential risk pathway that shows up as one of the RFF consensus pathways for further government regulation or voluntary industry actions (Krupnick and Gordon 2015). Such land use changes can make it more difficult for ecosystems to provide essential ecosystem goods and services, ultimately affecting public health, the economy, and social benefits (Slonecker et al. 2012).

There are two primary effects: patch shrinkage (smaller areas for species to live) and edge effects (disturbances to habitat from roads, cleared areas, etc.) with few studies conducted to document such effects. Certainly the potential for effects is high when well density is high. Johnson et al. (2011) from the Nature Conservancy estimate land conversion for pipelines and rights-of-way in Bradford County, Pennsylvania. They estimate that 1.65 miles of pipeline is needed per drilled well and conclude that between 120,000-300,000 acres will be affected by pipeline construction, which is much larger than the land required for natural gas infrastructure (Johnson et al. 2011).

Therefore, areas of the world with highly valued and endangered habitat are questionable for intensive oil and gas development, where roads, well pads, and pipelines are needed.

3.7   Community Impacts

There are numerous ways in which shale gas development can affect local communities beyond environmental impacts. In the risk matrix, we list noise, crowding, and visual degradation, which we categorize as "intermediate impacts." In the sections below we will discuss "final impacts" of crowding and growth, such as traffic accidents, health effects, and property value changes. Increased crime, overloaded schools, and the like, can also be classified as final impacts. In our view, one should think of these impacts as those that would occur with any major industrial development in rural communities, except that these developments arise from many small "plants" rather than from one or a few very large ones. Perceived impacts are as important as real ones, as perceptions affect behavior in property markets (Muehlenbachs and Krupnick 2014), as well as mental health.[11]

Local communities stand to benefit economically from shale gas development, but are also likely to bear the brunt of environmental and health damages. Where those trade-offs are and how a community feels about them, as well as what the operators and the government are attempting to do to ameliorate community concerns, are all important factors to consider in whether a given area is a good candidate for development.

3.8 Induced Seismicity

Areas with seismic concerns and without other viable means to dispose of liquid wastes from shale gas development are probably not good candidates for development. Research showing the probabilities of seismic events of different magnitudes as a function of added wastes would help in making those decisions. Seismic impacts have attracted significant press coverage, but the academic literature strongly leans to the view that seismic impacts from fracturing per se are trivial and that impacts from liquid injection into wells designed to accept such wastes, while of more concern, are still not a major issue because quake magnitudes have mostly been small. The USGS and state agencies continue to study earthquake records in Oklahoma (which experienced a 5.3 quake on the Richter scale and much more frequent quakes as oil and gas development has ramped up) and believe that wastewater disposal is a contributing factor (USGS 2013).

3.9 Final Impacts

The host of impacts discussed above—water quality and quantity changes, air quality changes, etc.—may be desirable to avoid in their own right, but our society is concerned primarily about their final impacts: on human and ecological health. We discuss the literature on these final impacts below.

Human Health Impacts   There are literally thousands of studies that relate changes in pollutant concentrations in the environment—ozone or fine particulate concentrations, for instance—to human mortality and morbidity risks; in this instance, however, we were only interested in those that could specifically relate changes in pollution concentration to shale gas development activities. There are at least three published studies (Adgate, Goldstein, and McKenzie 2014; Health Effects Institute 2015; and Public Health England 2014) that review the literature on public health risks from shale gas development. Adgate et al.

state that "no comprehensive population based studies of the public health impacts of unconventional natural gas operations have been published." The Health Effects Institute (2015) discusses potential impacts and develops a research agenda, but offers few definitive findings. Public Health England ruled out concern for radon exposure and indeed, exposure to all Naturally Occurring Radioactive Materials (NORMs), but on the basis of very little evidence from exploratory wells in the United Kingdom and on the assumption that proper waste handling techniques are followed.

In a provocative study, Hill (2012) estimated infant health impacts linked to shale gas drilling in the Marcellus shale region, using observed infant birth weights to mothers living near unconventional gas drilling sites from 2003-2010 in Pennsylvania. Hill concludes that low birth weights were 25 percent more common in mothers who lived within 1.5 miles of gas development. The same research team is doing a similar study in Colorado and finding similar results (Hill 2013). We expect another upcoming study by Janet Currie (Princeton University) and coauthors to similarly examine the impacts of hydraulic fracturing on infant health. The key issues here are whether there are factors correlated with shale gas development activities over time and space that are the true cause of these impacts and, if shale gas development is really the cause, through what specific channels these effects are occurring (e.g., through stress or toxic exposures).

RFF is also conducting research in this area; Muehlenbachs and Krupnick (2014) estimate the relationship between shale gas development in Pennsylvania over space and time and truck traffic and the frequency and severity of traffic accidents, with severity measured according to whether serious injuries or death resulted. The preliminary analysis reports around 100 excess accidents per year in Pennsylvania over the counties with greater than 20 wells developed, which further translates into nine and 12 excess mortalities and morbidities, respectively.

In developing countries where baseline health, particularly of infants and the old, is already compromised, the added burden created by shale gas development must be carefully weighed against economic benefits. In general, the health impacts are not well known, so fear of these effects is another driving force behind public opposition.

Ecological Health In addition to human health, shale gas development has the potential to impact ecological and animal health, the latter particularly in agricultural settings. Considering animal health, many scientific studies have focused on one specific impact on a species following exposure to natural gas and natural gas production chemicals, or other aspects of the development process. For instance, Waldner et al. (1998) studied the impact of a natural gas leaks on the productivity of beef cattle. While some authors conclude that exposure to gas drilling operations can have serious health effects on farm animals, Waldner found that there was no correlation with herd calf mortality and the distance from a gas leak (1998).

There are potentially direct effects of shale gas development on species, some of them endangered or threatened. For instance, the Sierra Club and others petitioned the Bureau of Land Management against leasing land for oil and gas development in California because it would further endanger the endangered/threatened kit fox, blunt-nose leopard lizard, California condor, and mountain plover (Center for Biological Diversity 2011).

The USFWS concluded that drilling in sagebrush habitat "poses a serious threat" to the greater sage-grouse (U.S. Fish and Wildlife Service 2010). And Taylor et al. (2012) found that "if [oil and gas] development continues, future viability of the already small sage-grouse populations in northeast Wyoming will be compromised." What is particularly interesting about this study is the observation that chance occurrences, such as an outbreak of West Nile virus, can wipe out a population already reduced by energy development (Taylor, Naugle, and Mills 2012).

Other Impact Categories   In addition to the impacts examined above, economists and risk analysts generally recognize some additional categories (Frohlich and Brunt 2013; Kim 2013) that may be broadly classified into external impacts on markets and non-market impacts. External effects on marketed commodities associated with shale gas development could include damages to agricultural productivity (say, from increased water scarcity or pollution), tourism (say, from habitat damages), and other industries that put a high premium on the use of high quality water, such as breweries. The non-market side includes recreational damages (such as those suffered from habitat reduction, loss of hunted populations, loss of forested area available for hiking and camping, etc.).

3.10   Conclusion on Risks

In the United States, shale gas development was off and running without much assessment of whether it posed any additional risks relative to conventional gas development (i.e., "shoot first and ask questions later"). With the most prominent exception of New York (and several other states, such as Maryland), most state regulators simply assumed that their extensive regulatory system and various federal regulations would be protective. Coupled with industry standard practices and the generally positive experience with conventional gas exploitation, few red flags were raised.

As the spotlight grew on shale gas development along with the growing number of wells, the social license to operate of the industry became the watchword of groups both opposed to and supportive of further development. That is, there came to be a recognition that the risks of further development had to be both better understood and more transparently mitigated for the industry to have the endorsement of the general public.

As the foregoing discussion shows, while some of the risks of shale gas development are no different than those with conventional gas exploitation, other risks are different in substance, scale, and location, and they are not all well understood. Only after they are well-understood can the question of reasonable mitigation be enjoined (unless mitigation means a ban!). Until then, the public will continue to mistrust the industry and question whether the economic benefits of shale gas development are worth the risk. Given the attitudes of the European public about environmental protection (particularly the western European countries) and their embrace of the precautionary principle, the bar to obtain a social license to operate is probably higher than in the United States.

4.   Mitigating Risks: Regulations, Best Practice, Liability, and Information Provision

Amidst all of these potential impacts of shale gas development, there have certainly been significant regulatory responses in the United States, as well as attempts by the industry to define best practices that, in some cases, exceed regulatory requirements (a good example is the list of best practices developed by the Center for Sustainable Shale Development).[12] Also potentially important for mitigating risks in the United States is the liability system that induces companies' good behavior, as well as attempts by government and other institutions to increase transparency and data availability. In this section, we explain each of the four approaches to mitigating risks.

4.1 Regulation

Regulation is defined to include any of the many regulatory tools available to the federal government and states—command-and-control, case-by-case permitting, performance standards, and other tools. Although these tools differ in important ways, all are valid forms of regulation, and none is necessarily less stringent or effective than the others.

In the United States, outside of federal lands and offshore production, oil and gas drilling and other extractive industries have historically been and still are regulated primarily by state governments. However, federal authority over some parts of shale gas development is significant, particularly regarding the protection of air, surface water quality, and endangered species. The federal government also issues regulations in its capacity as a landowner. In some cases, municipalities, too, have an important role, in zoning decisions, for instance.

The rapid expansion of shale gas development in recent years (along with tight budgets) has challenged state regulators to keep pace. Many states regulate shale gas development primarily or exclusively with older regulations written before unconventional drilling became common, though these regulations are not necessarily inadequate. Rapid expansion creates a dynamic regulatory environment and may be a significant factor in the high degree of heterogeneity we observe among state regulations of the same element, such as setback restrictions (how far away a drill pad must be location from a stream or building) or the required thickness of pit liners (Richardson et al. 2013).

As implied above, the challenges for regulating shale gas are somewhat different than those for regulating conventional gas extraction. One set of challenges is in the federalism dimension—the appropriate levels of government to regulate various parts of the extraction process. Greater possibilities for community disruption from shale gas exploitation is one set of challenges and leads to a presumption that local governments should be taking a larger role than they would in a conventional resource case. In addition to the technical reasons for community disruptions, the location of the shale gas plays in areas that were previously more rural in character but with relatively high populations, e.g., Pennsylvania, have added to risks.

Another set of challenges is regulating the disclosure of fracturing fluids. Regulation of this wholly new area has been controversial from the start. It is fair to say that because of public opposition to fracking, disclosure requirements have been a targeted area for state and federal regulation.

In general, using regulation presents a host of challenges, including choices about the type of regulation (command and control versus performance based), the stringency of the regulation, and the degree and type of monitoring and enforcement activities, choices that all together determine the regulation's success.

In the European context, the federalism issue likely comes down to whether the European Union or the individual countries regulate activities, but local governments might also want to play a role. As in the United States, because political and regulatory conditions are so different across countries, it is difficult to imagine the European Union making "one size fits all" policies for all countries, except for methane emissions, which are a global pollutant. As noted above, the European Union has already decided not to issue general regulations applicable to shale gas development. Many countries in Europe are closely watching regulatory activities by the United States, conducting study tours and writing reports (see, e.g., the UK's Royal Society 2012 report; Germany's Federal Environment Agency 2014 report; and the numerous European Commission and Parliament reports) to position themselves to write up-to-date regulations, if decisions are made to permit development.

4.2   Best Practices: Voluntary Industry Behavior

Voluntary behavior can take several forms, from companies trying to improve technologies and procedures to minimize risk (or better apply technologies and procedures already in place) to individual institutions or collaborations supporting efforts to codify best practices or model behaviors for the sector. Some efforts are led by industry groups, whereas others bring together nongovernmental organizations, industry, and other stakeholders. The main question is: what is the appropriate role for best practice guidelines (voluntary behavior by industry) versus government regulation? Are they substitutes, in the sense that stringent best practices may pre-empt or reduce the need for regulation, or complements, in the sense that they guide industry to superior performance to meet the spirit of the regulation by going beyond the letter?

In general, best practices have the advantage over regulation of setting a higher bar, but doing so in ways that industry participants find immediately acceptable. The disadvantage is that they are voluntary and may be so flexible and general that they do not lead to real environmental improvements. There is also a tension with best practice efforts in that industry participants are concerned that their voluntary practices not become regulated practices. In a European context the line between regulation and best practice may be fuzzier than in the United States, where adversarial interactions between the regulator and the regulated are the rule.

4.3 Liability

Although virtually all public discussion of the risks of shale development in the United States revolves around the proper role for regulation, it is arguably liability, not regulation, that is the most important driver of operator practices aimed at reducing risks—and this would probably remain the case under even the most ambitious proposals for more extensive regulation. Indeed, hydraulic fracturing and shale drilling litigation has rapidly increased since 2009 (Kurth et al. 2011).

Options for improving the liability system are relatively underexamined. Olmstead and Richardson (2014) explore several possibilities, organized broadly around principles in Shavell (1984). These options include (a) reducing information asymmetry among regulators, operators, and the public; (b) creating financial or insurance mechanisms to ensure that operators can make good on liability claims; (c) designing stronger financial responsibility requirements; and (d) moving to reduce the cost and complexity of class-action suits to reduce the ability of operators to escape liability for disparate harms. Information disclosure rules are also useful in that they enable actual and potential victims to find out about harms, identify responsible parties, and establish causation in litigation.

A successful use of the liability system as a mitigation tool is evidenced in Pennsylvania, where rules were written to make operators presumed liable for groundwater pollution near their wells unless the firms conducted groundwater testing to determine the state of the groundwater before they drilled. This approach—using the liability system and making guilt the default—has reportedly led to a dramatic increase in pre-drilling groundwater testing. While having obvious advantages, the use of lawsuits and the court system to mitigate risks can lead to very high transactions costs that, in some cases, would be borne by relatively poor people.

We are not experts on the use of the liability system as a substitute for regulations in Europe so cannot comment further, except to say it may be a fruitful area for further research if shale gas development appears imminent.

4.4   Information Provision

Requiring that information on polluting behavior be provided to the public has a long tradition in U.S. risk mitigation history, dating back to the U.S. EPA's Toxic Release Inventory,[13] requiring industry to list its toxic emissions.

For shale gas development, provision of information on fracturing fluids has been the most controversial issue, and protests have led those supplying the fracturing recipes to develop "greener" versions and induced the U.S. Department of Energy to help finance the creation of the FracFocus[14] website to act as a voluntary repository of chemical composition data. In this area, and considering all types of information, greater clarity is still needed on whether and exactly what additional data will quell the calls for more information. The clamor from Europeans for transparency would undoubtedly be even louder.

5.   Conclusion

In considering the export of the U.S. shale gas boom to Europe, one must be fairly pessimistic. Most of the resource-rich countries will have basic disadvantages relative to the United States, although the $4-$5/Mcf cost of liquefying LNG, transporting and regasifying it offers some economic headroom where imported LNG rather than piped gas is the marginal gas. In countries where citizens have significant influence over the government and particularly where mineral rights are held by the state instead of by individuals (almost all countries), the social license to operate will be difficult to obtain. In other countries, lack of key inputs, pipelines, and other infrastructure and high development costs may preclude development for some time. And, if energy production must be weaned off of fossil fuels in the longer term to meet global warming goals, there may be no conditions, short of economic carbon capture and sequestration, which permit long-term sustainability of natural gas in Europe.

Notes

1. Resources for the future, Krupnick: Krupnick@rff.org; Wang: Wang@rff.org. We thank Jan Mares, Paul Joskow, and Ian Parry for helpful comments.

2. See http://www.reuters.com/article/us-germany-fracking-idUSKBN0MS3PE201504 01/.

3. The European Commission decided in January 2014 to not issue binding environmental regulations for shale gas development, although future developments may still occur. See Glowacki and Henkel (2014) for associated legal discussion.

4. In addition to Schlumberger, Halliburton and Baker Hughes are considering a merger, which would reduce these dominant industry players to two.

5. See, for instance, Bloomberg News (10/14/2014), http://www.bloomberg.com/news/2014-10-09/fracking-setback-in-poland-dim-hopes-for-less-russian-gas.html.

6. See http://www.eia.gov/todayinenergy/detail.cfm?id=25832.

7. See http://www.wri.org/water-for-shale.

8. Presentation of Robert Kleinberg, Schlumberger, Colorado School of Mines, October 29, 2014.

9. However, see Siikamaki and Krupnick (2014), who estimate preferences for reducing given risks of shale gas development in monetary terms, using stated preference techniques.

10. See http://thinkprogress.org/climate/2013/10/02/2708911/fracking-ipcc-methane/.

11. Whether these impacts are all additive and all externalities could be debated. For instance, property value impacts likely reflect risk preferences related to a variety of other impacts, both real and perceived.

12. See www.sustainableshale.org.

13. See http://www2.epa.gov/toxics-release-inventory-tri-program/.

14. See http://fracfocus.org/.

References

Adgate, J. L., B. D. Goldstein, and L. M. McKenzie. 2014. "Potential Public Health Hazards, Exposures and Health Effects from Unconventional Natural Gas Development." *Environmental Science and Technology* 48 (15): 8307-20.

Allen, D. T., V. M. Torres, J. Thomas, D. W. Sullivan, M. Harrison, A. Hendler, S. C. Herndon, C. E. Kolb, M. P. Fraser, A. D. Hill, B. K. Lamb, J. Miskimins, R. F. Sawyer, and J. H. Seinfeld. 2013. "Measurements of Methane Emissions at Natural Gas Production Sites in the United States." *Proceedings of the National Academy of Sciences* 110 (44): 17768-73.

BIO Intelligence Service. 2013. "Analysis and Presentation of the Results of the Public Consultation 'Unconventional Fossil Fuels (e.g., Shale Gas) in Europe.'" Final Report Prepared for European Commission DG Environment.

Brown, S. P. A., A. J. Krupnick, and M. A. Walls. 2009. "Natural Gas: A Bridge to a Low-Carbon Future?" *Resources for the Future*, Issue Brief 09-11.

Center for Biological Diversity, Los Padres Forest Watch, and Sierra Club. 2011. "RE: Protest of BLM's September 14, 2011 Competitive Oil and Gas Sale." http://www.bio logicaldiversity.org/programs/public_lands/energy/dirty_energy_development/oil_ and_gas/pdfs/Monterey_Lease_Sale_Protest_7-15-2011.pdf.

Entrekin, S., M. Evans-White, B. Johnson, and E. Hagenbuch. 2011. "Rapid Expansion of Natural Gas Development Poses a Threat to Surface Waters." *Frontiers in Ecology and the Environment* 9 (9): 503-11.

Ernst & Young. 2013. "Shale Gas in Europe: Revolution or Evolution?" EYG No. DWO317.

European Parliament. 2012. *Resolution of 21 November 2012 on the Environmental Impacts of Shale Gas and Shale Oil Extraction Activities. 2011/2308 (INI).* http://perma.cc/NJS7-RGRD.

Federal Environment Agency. 2014. "Environmental Impacts of Hydraulic Fracturing Related to the Exploration and Exploitation of Unconventional Natural Gas in Particular of Shale Gas." Umweltbundesamt: Dessau-Roßlau, Germany.

Ferrar, K. J., D. R. Michanowicz, C. L. Christen, N. Mulcahy, S. L. Malone, and R. K. Sharma. 2013. "Assessment of Effluent Contaminants from Three Facilities Discharging Marcellus Shale Wastewater to Surface Waters in Pennsylvania." *Environmental Science and Technology* 47 (7): 3472-81.

Freyman, M., and R. Salmon. 2013. "Hydraulic Fracturing and Water Stress: Growing Competitive Pressures for Water." Ceres Report, Boston, MA, US.

Frohlich, C., and M. Brunt. 2013. "Two-Year Survey of Earthquakes and Injection/Production Wells in the Eagle Ford Shale, Texas, Prior to the $M_W4.8$ 20 October 2011 Earthquake." *Earth and Planetary Science Letters* 379 (2013): 56-63.

Glowacki, J., and C. Henkel. 2014. "Hydraulic Fracturing in the European Union: Leveraging the U.S. Experience in Shale Gas Exploration and Production." *Indiana International & Comparative Law Review* 24 (133): 1-48.

Health Effects Institute. 2015. "Strategic Research Agenda on the Potential Impacts of 21st Century Oil and Natural Gas Development in the Appalachian Region and Beyond." HEI Special Scientific Committee on Unconventional Oil and Gas Development in the Appalachian Basin. Boston, MA, US (October).

Hill, E. L. 2013. "Shale Gas Development and Infant Health: Evidence from Pennsylvania" (Charles H. Dyson School of Applied Economics and Management Working Paper 2012-12).

Johnson, N., T. Gagnolet, R. Ralls, and J. Stevens. 2011. "Natural Gas Pipelines—Excerpt from Report 2 of the Pennsylvania Energy Impacts Assessment." *The Nature Conservancy—Pennsylvania Chapter.* https://www.nature.org/ourinitiatives/regions/north america/unitedstates/pennsylvania/ng-pipelines.pdf.

Kim, W. Y. 2013. "Induced Seismicity Associated with Fluid Injection into a Deep Well in Youngstown, Ohio." *Journal of Geophysical Research: Solid Earth* 118 (7): 3506-18.

Kochhar, K. et al. 2015. "Is the Glass Half Empty or Half Full? Issues in Managing Water Challenges and Policy Instruments." IMF Staff Discussion Note, Washington, DC, US.

Krauss, C., and E. Lipton. 2012. "After the Boom in Natural Gas." *The New York Times,* October 20.

Krupnick, A., and H. Gordon. 2015. "What the Experts Say about the Environmental Risks of Shale Gas Development." *Agricultural and Resource Economics Review* 44 (2): 106-19.

Kurth, T. E., M. J. Mazzone, M. S. Mendoza, and C. S. Kulander. 2011. "American Law and Jurisprudence on Fracking." Haynes and Boone, LLP, Washington, DC, US.

Kutchin, J. W. 1998. *How Mitchell Energy & Development Corp. Got Its Start and How It Grew: An Oral History and Narrative Overview.* The Woodlands, TX, US: Mitchell Energy & Development Corp.

Kuwayama, Y., S. Olmstead, and A. Krupnick. 2013. "Water Resources and Unconventional Fossil Fuel Development: Linking Physical Impacts to Social Costs." Resources for the Future Discussion Paper 13-34, Washington, DC, US.

Lyman, S., and H. Shorthill. 2013. "2012 Uintah Basin Winter Ozone & Air Quality Study." Document No. CRD13-320.32. Utah State University, Vernal, UT, US.

McJeon, H., J. Edmonds, N. Bauer, L. Clarke, B. Fisher, B. P. Flannery, J. Hilaire, V. Krey, G. Marangoni, R. Mi, K. Riahi, H. Rogner, and M. Tavoni. 2014. "Limited Impact on Decadal-Scale Climate Change from Increased Use of Natural Gas." *Nature* 514: 482-85.

Morgantown Energy Technology Center. 1980. *Unconventional Gas Resources: A Research Program in Cooperation with Industry to Reduce the Uncertainties Associated with the Size of the Resources and the Methods of Extraction.* DOE/NBA—3008922, Morgantown, WV, US.

Muehlenbachs, L., and A. J. Krupnick. 2014. "Shale Gas Development Linked to Traffic Accidents in Pennsylvania." *Resources for the Future* 185: 6-7. http://www.rff.org/RFF/Documents/RFF-Resources-185_Infographic.pdf.

National Research Council (NRC). 2001. *Energy Research at DOE: Was It Worth It? Energy Efficiency and Fossil Energy Research 1978–2000.* Washington, DC, US: National Academy Press.

Olmstead, S., and N. Richardson. 2014. "Managing the Risks of Shale Gas Development Using Innovative Legal and Regulatory Approaches." Resources for the Future Discussion Paper 14-15, Washington, DC.

Olmstead, S. M., L. A. Muehlenbachs, J. S. Shih, Z. Chu, and A. J. Krupnick. 2013. "Shale Gas Development Impacts on Surface Water Quality in Pennsylvania." *Proceedings of the National Academy of Sciences* 110 (13): 4962-67.

Osborn, S. G., A. Vengosh, N. R. Warner, and R. B. Jackson. 2011. "Methane Contamination of Drinking Water Accompanying Gas-Well Drilling and Hydraulic Fracturing." *Proceedings of the National Academy of Sciences* 108 (20): 8172-76.

Public Health England. 2014. *Review of the Potential Public Health Impacts of Exposures to Chemical and Radioactive Pollutants as a Result of the Shale Gas Extraction Process.* PHE-CRCE-009.

Rajan, S. 2014. "International Shale Development: Prospects and Challenges." Presented at the 37th IAEE/USAEE International Conference, New York, NY. www.usaee.org/usaee2014/submissions/presentations/Rajan%20-%20International%20Shale%20Development%20NYC.pdf.

Richardson, N., M. Gottlieb, A. J. Krupnick, and H. Wiseman. 2013. "The State of State Shale Gas Regulation." Resources for the Future, Washington, DC.

Rieman, J. L. 2013. "Air Pollution Impacts and Implications." Presented at the Governor's Policy Forum on Shale Energy Development, Broomfield, CO, US, September.

Royal Society and the Royal Academy of Engineering. 2012. "Shale Gas Extraction in the UK: A Review of Hydraulic Fracturing." The Royal Society, London, UK.

Schneising, O., J. P. Burrows, R. R. Dickerson, M. Buchwitz, M. Reuter, and H. Bovensmann. 2014. "Remote Sensing of Fugitive Methane Emissions from Oil and Gas Production in North American Tight Geologic Formations." Earth's Future 2 (10), 548–58.

Schnell, Russell C., Samuel J. Oltmans, Ryan R. Neely, Maggie S. Endres, John V. Molenar, and Allen B. White. 2009. "Rapid Photochemical Production of Ozone at High Concentrations in a Rural Site During Winter." Nature Geoscience 2: 120-22.

Schon, S. C. 2011. "Hydraulic Fracturing Not Responsible for Methane Migration." Proceedings of the National Academy of Sciences 108 (37): E664.

Shavell, S. 1984. "A Model of the Optimal Use of Liability and Safety Regulation." The Rand Journal of Economics 15 (2): 271-80.

Sieminski, A. 2014. "Outlook for U.S. Shale Oil and Gas." Presentation at IAEE/AEA Meeting, Philadelphia, PA, January 4. http://www.eia.gov/pressroom/presentations/sieminski_01042014.pdf.

Siikamäki, J., and A. Krupnick. 2014. "Information and the Willingness to Pay to Reduce Shale Gas Risks." Contributing Paper to the 5th World Congress of Environmental and Resource Economists, Istanbul, Turkey.

Slonecker, E. T., L. E. Milheim, C. M. Roig-Silva, A. R. Malizia, D. A. Marr, and G. B. Fisher. 2012. "Landscape Consequences of Natural Gas Extraction in Bradford and Washington Counties, Pennsylvania, 2004–2010." USGS Open-File Report 2012-1154.

States, S., G. Cyprych, M. Stoner, F. Wydra, J. Kuchta, L. Casson, and J. Monnell. 2012. "Bromide, TDS, and Radionuclides in the Allegheny River: A Possible Link with Marcellus Shale Operations." Presented at the Pennsylvania Section–American Water Works Association's (PA-AWWA) 63rd Annual Conference, Hershey, PA, US, April 2011.

Stoeckenius, T., and L. Ma. 2010. "A Conceptual Model of Winter Ozone in Southwest Wyoming." Wyoming Department of Environmental Quality, Cheyenne, WY. http://deq.state.wy.us/aqd/Ozone/WDEQ_03conceptModel_Report.pdf.

Taylor, R., D. Naugle, and L. S. Mills. 2012. Viability Analyses for Conservation of Sage-Grouse Populations. BLM Contract 09-3225-0012, Number G09AC00013.

U.S. EPA. 2015. "Assessment of the Potential Impacts of Hydraulic Fracturing for Oil and Gas on Drinking Water Resources (External Review Draft)." U.S. Environmental Protection Agency, Washington, DC, EPA/600/R-15/047.

U.S. Fish and Wildlife Service. 2010. Proposed Rule to 50 CFR Part 17: Endangered and Threatened Wildlife and Plants; 12-Month Findings for Petitions to List the Greater Sage-Grouse (Centrocercus urophasianus) as Threatened or Endangered. Department of the Interior, FWS-R6-ES-2010-0-0008-B2.

USGS. 2013. "Earthquake Swarm Continues in Central Oklahoma" (Press Release). http://www.usgs.gov/newsroom/article.asp?ID=3710&from=rss#.VFjzPcnTAWU.

Vidic, R. D., S. L. Brantley, J. M. Vandenbossche, D. Yoxtheimer, and J. D. Abad. 2013. "Impact of Shale Gas Development on Regional Water Quality." *Science* 340 (6134).

Waldner, C. L., C. S. Ribble, and E. D. Janzen. 1998. "Evaluation of the Impact of a Natural Gas Leak from a Pipeline on Productivity of Beef Cattle." *Journal of the American Veterinary Medical Association* 212 (1): 41-8.

Wang, Z., and A. J. Krupnick. 2014. "A Retrospective Review of Shale Gas Development in the United States: What Led to the Boom?" Resources for the Future Discussion Paper 13-12, Washington, DC.

Wang, Z., and Q. Xue. 2014. "The Market Structure of Shale Gas Drilling in the United States." Resources for the Future Discussion Paper, Washington, DC.

Warner, N. R., C. A. Christie, R. B. Jackson, and A. Vengosh. 2013. "Impacts of Shale Gas Wastewater Disposal on Water Quality in Western Pennsylvania." *Environmental Science & Technology* 47 (20): 11849-57. doi:10.1021/es402165b.

A Comment on "Lessons from the U.S. Shale Gas Boom"

Bert Saveyn[1]

The shale gas boom in the United States during the last decade has been remarkable, and perhaps hydraulic fracking comes as close as one could get to a disruptive technology—well-known from the digital sector—in a traditional industrial activity like the fossil fuel sector where it has caused a paradigm shift in the United States. However, one could wonder whether we are witnessing a long-lasting breakthrough of a new technology or whether some specific conditions have fostered a particular steep increase. In other words, have all lessons from the U.S. shale boom been learned yet?

Krupnick and Wang emphasize the private ownership of mineral rights in which investors and innovators obtain returns on their investments as a decisive driving mechanism for the take-off of shale gas in the United States. Neighborhood effects influencing the behavior of these private owners may be one reason why—once the technology was in place and operational—the shale gas exploitation has shown an unprecedented steep take-off. The fact that a single project could involve hundreds of landowners or more (individuals, families, etc.) may trigger various kinds of competition. It may create some hype (as was the case nationally and internationally some years ago) and some owners may sign up because the neighbors did. Others may decide to sign up to counterbalance the risks of their own shale gas endowments being affected by the drilling activities of the neighbors. Very little is known of the long-lasting effects of nearby activities and on the longer term, the remaining gas may be diffused and leaked to the neighbors. A typical fracking happens about 2,500m under the ground with a horizontal shaft about 2km long. Property rights this deep underground may not be so easy to control and enforce. People may feel the urgency to jump on the "shale gas train" when it hurtles past, but the decline curves of shale gas are particularly steep and new wells have to be drilled constantly.

That means that the shale gas business and its infrastructure is not there to stay forever but will have to move on to new locations in a couple of years. These shale gas activities may never ever return and the shale gas that has not been extracted yet is there to stay. In addition, in locations where ownership of the minerals is separated from the ownership of the surface of the land, leading to a dual ownership of portions of the real estate, the exploitation may lead to conflicts among the various owners, and here shale gas exploitation may become a handbook example of a negative externality to the land surface owners and the local communities. States like Texas and Ohio recently have overruled municipalities and limited the regulation of oil and gas exploitation to the state authorities in order to counteract mounting local opposition toward the scale of drilling activities (e.g., Denton, Texas).

Another question is whether the shale gas boom is environmentally sustainable. Krupnick and Wang suggest that fracking and shale gas exploitation may be linked to various environmental problems that may be site- and exploitation-dependent. A lot is still not fully understood or estimated. In the best case, these types of pollution are well-managed and can be mitigated, but it is unlikely that fracking is ever going to become sustainable (sensu strictu) from an environmental point of view (but the same applies for conventional gas and oil projects).

Additionally, one can wonder whether shale gas reserves are sufficiently large, such that the shale gas supply is sustained in the long term. Currently, the common assumption is that the "shale gas revolution" is a game changer in the energy market and the EIA (2013) assesses that gas production will grow up to 2040 and beyond. These high gas production levels would guarantee a long-term low gas price in the United States and many businesses and power companies are investing accordingly. Moreover, export facilities are being constructed to enable the United States to ship liquefied natural gas abroad. Inman (2014), however, questions this assumption and states that the EIA's estimates may be too optimistic. A recent study for Texas with a high spatial resolution finds substantially lower estimates. The consequence could be that the shale gas growth will only continue for about a decade with a steep decline soon afterward. In this case, gas prices in the United States will rise significantly, affecting all gas-dependent investments. As forecasts are so uncertain for the United States, which rely on very detailed data for tens of thousands of shale gas wells, it remains to be seen how reliable the forecasts are on a global scale.

Is the shale gas revolution economically sustainable? In the two decades before 2000, natural gas prices in the United States were relatively stable and showed relatively few fluctuations. Prices started to increase after 2000, and important price spikes could be observed (e.g., in 2001, 2003, 2005, and 2008). By 2010, the gas prices levelled off to a lower level about twice as high as the long-term pre-2000 price. Hence, the shale gas boom may have developed during a period with above long-term pre-2000 prices. Since mid-2014, however, the crude oil price has shown a steep decrease down to -60 percent compared to the first half of 2014, while in mid-2015 the crude oil price is still about 40 percent below their highest price levels just a year earlier. Also, the gas price has declined substantially since 2014. The downturn has caused the oil and gas industry to pull back from drilling expensive new wells, but less-costly production continues. As a result, some recent forecasts even foresee a decline of U.S. natural gas production in 2016, which was something unheard of just one year ago. Part of the decline is due to associated gas production from oil wells. Other forecasts, however, merely see in 2016 a slowdown of growth and consider this a correction of what could be considered an overheated market before the oil slump in mid-2014.

What about shale gas in Europe? The 28 Member States of the European Union are estimated to have 472 trillion cubic feet (tcf) of technically recoverable shale gas resources (based on EIA 2013). So far the shale gas boom has not reached Europe. Many different reasons may underlie this. Population densities in Europe are, on average, higher than in the United States. This may complicate the chances for a "social consensus" as many types of environmental impacts are likely to be more directly felt by a larger group of people. Alternatively, some blame the ownership of the state of the mineral rights, but on the other hand, energy companies have only to negotiate with one single partner instead of many hundreds as in the case of the United States. Further, in a country such as Poland, which has the largest estimated reserves in the European Union (148 tcf), and where the government and public opinions are (relatively) in favor of shale gas explorations, the recent evolutions have been disappointing, with reduced new resource estimates (EIA 2013) and companies abandoning the exploration because of dropping energy prices and the discovery of more difficult geological formations. France has the second largest reserve in the European Union (137 tcf) but imposed a moratorium on fracking in 2011, possibly partly inspired by the "precautionary principle." The remaining reserves (187 tcf) for the European Union are shared among about ten Member States. Even long-time producers of conventional gas, such as Denmark (32 tcf of reserves), the Netherlands (26 tcf), and the United Kingdom (26 tcf), have rather limited reserves and the prospect of extraction look rather dim. The Netherlands extended in July 2015 its moratorium for commercial extraction until 2020. The Dutch debate is influenced by the damage to real estate caused by small earthquakes in the Groningen area due to conventional gas extraction. On June 29, 2015, Lancaster County in the United Kingdom voted to deny permission to frack two sites after two small earthquakes hit the area; there is also a fear of excessive traffic and noise and the prospect that the exploration activity may cumulate into the industrialization of the countryside. In Denmark a project close to Copenhagen was abandoned in May 2015 as the shale gas supply was too thin to justify further investigation, and the exploration in Jutland was halted by the authorities as an unapproved chemical was used.

As things stand now, an EU shale gas boom may not happen very soon. However, the shale gas reserves in the European Union (if any) are there to stay, and with lower exploitation costs, better technology, and possibly higher gas prices, any future exploitation may be even more profitable. The deployment of shale gas infrastructure could be achieved rather quickly, given the existing extensive network of natural gas conducts in the European Union. Moreover, if kept underground the EU's shale gas may get an option value as it can be used as a back-stop technology for periods with severe gas supply shocks. However, in order to estimate the size of this option value, at least a few shale gas projects may need to take place in the region. Without actual exploration drilling and hydraulic fracturing tests the size of the shale gas potential is unknown. However, if companies do exploration projects and they are successful, then they may also want to produce the natural gas immediately.

Note

1. The views expressed are purely those of the author and may not in any circumstances be regarded as stating an official position of the European Commission.

References

EIA. 2013. "Technically Recoverable Shale Oil and Shale Gas Resources: An Assessment of 137 Shale Formations in 41 Countries Outside the United States, June 2013." http://www.eia.gov/analysis/studies/worldshalegas/pdf/fullreport.pdf.

Inman, Mason. 2014. "Natural Gas: The Fracking Fallacy." *Nature* 516 (4): 28-30. http://www.nature.com/polopoly_fs/1.16430!/menu/main/topColumns/topLeftColumn/pdf/516028a.pdf.

8 Tax and Regulatory Policies for European Transport: Getting There, But in the Slow Lane[1]

Bruno De Borger and Stef Proost

Key Points for Policymakers

- External cost concepts have been successfully introduced in policy thinking.
- There is too much emphasis on climate and energy objectives in the transport sector and too little emphasis on other objectives (congestion relief).
- Modal split objectives (e.g., minimum shares for public transport) are not good policy objectives; they should not be used to judge policies.
- The transition from high fuel taxes to distance charges has begun for trucks, but the charges need to be differentiated according to place and time. The same transition will also develop for cars, as soon as implementation costs have been reduced and public acceptance has been improved.
- The costs and benefits of EU-wide transport policies depend on the response of member countries in setting local policy instruments right, conditional on what the EU framework allows.
- The EU policy priorities should be:
  - to allow and promote the progressive substitution of high diesel and gasoline taxes by other car and truck user charges that depend on place and time.
  - to scale back overambitious implementation of biofuel and electric car policies and re-orient resources to R&D into cleaner vehicles.
  - to efficiently regulate distance charges for trucks.
  - to assure an unbiased assessment of infrastructure investment needs.

- Member countries' priorities should be:
    - to move away from high vehicle ownership and fuel taxes to local congestion charges; the extra burden on motorists might be offset by scaling back vehicle excise taxes.
    - to complement the introduction of road pricing with peak-load pricing for public transport.

1.   Introduction

This policy paper will concentrate on road transportation, and more specifically on the role of road transport pricing, taxation, and regulation. We do not limit the discussion to the energy and environmental implications of transport policies, but take a broader perspective. The reason for this is that transportation policies are designed to tackle all major external costs of transport; these not only include the external costs of pollution, but also the externalities associated with congestion and accident risks. Therefore, emphasizing energy use and pollution while ignoring other external costs seems undesirable. We do focus only on road transport; policies that focus on other transport modes and on competition policy issues will be discussed only occasionally. We also largely disregard endogenous location of activities, which is an important long-term dimension of urban development.

We know from the analytical literature what reforms are most needed in the area of road pricing and taxation. The most important tax on transport users is a high-energy excise tax; however, although climate change and local pollution are important, the most dominant externality in transportation is congestion (mainly in urban areas). To more effectively mitigate congestion, a reform is required where we partially move away from fuel and vehicle taxes toward car and truck user taxes that depend on place and time of use. Making this policy switch acceptable and implementing such pricing policies at the right policy level are among the main policy challenges for the near future.

A brief overview is as follows. In section 1, we start by putting in perspective the different policy issues, the main external costs, the policy objectives, and the main tax and regulatory instruments currently used. Moreover, we briefly review EU policy developments over the last 20 years. The next sections focus on passenger transport (section 2) and freight transport policies (section 3), respectively. A final section concludes our discussion.

2.   Main Policy Issues and Developments over the Past 20 Years

Over the last 50 to 60 years (from the 1958 Treaty of Rome onward), a process of EU integration and enlargement from six member countries to the current 28 countries took place. For the transport sector, this integration has strongly increased the volume of both freight and passenger transport; road transport is by far the dominant mode. The integration has necessitated competition policies for the freight transport sector (for example, allowing trucks to operate in all countries), some fuel tax harmonization for diesel and gasoline to curb tax competition,[2] and regulation of toll regimes to avoid overcharging of through traffic. Moreover, as transport equipment and services are important inputs in production, these two markets have been deregulated and opened up for competition, and they have been re-regulated to achieve EU-wide environmental objectives like climate change and air pollution.

2.1   Transport Activity and Its External Costs

Table 8.1 puts the relative importance of different transport modes and their external costs in perspective. A brief overview of how these figures were calculated is given in the accompanying appendix. As already noted, road transport is still the dominant mode of transportation with a market share of some 75 percent for passengers and 72 percent for inland freight transport.[3] Airplanes, cars, and trucks use almost exclusively oil products and are the most carbon-intensive vehicles in the transport sector.

The figures reported in table 8.1 imply a wide range of estimated external costs of transport in Europe. For climate, we opted to use a relatively low external cost estimate of 25 euro/ton of CO_2. To put this estimate in perspective, industry is confronted with ETS prices in the range of 5 to 20 euro/ton of CO_2. Car and truck users pay—via gasoline and diesel taxes—a carbon tax of the order of 200 to 300 euro/ton of CO_2.[4]

For passenger transport, we distinguish urban and medium- to long-distance transport. In urban areas, the most important marginal external cost of car use is congestion, followed by climate change, other environmental externalities, and accident risks. Apart from the car, the main alternative urban transport modes are public rail and bus service.

Table 8.1
Relative importance of different modes and external cost estimates

Source: All values are taken from the EU Handbook of External Cost (2014), except for climate damage; here a value of 25 euro/ton was used—and there is a strong variation for all estimates.

| | Passengers (€ct/vkm for cars and buses and €ct/tkm or pkm for rail and air) | | | | Freight (€ct/vkm for trucks and €ct/tkm for rail) | | |
| | Urban (20%) | | Medium to long distance (80%) | | Local | Medium to long distance | |
	Cars (70%)	Other (30%)	Cars (80%)	Rail, air (20%)	Trucks (100%)	Trucks (72%)	Rail, ship, pipeline (28%)
External climate cost	0.8	2.1 (bus)	0.5	Air 0.4 €ct/pkm Rail 0.1 €ct/pkm	1.5	1.1	
External air pollution and noise cost	4.3	21.4 (bus)	0.1		37.9	2.0	
External accident cost	0.3		0.1-0.2		1.1	0.8-1.2	
External marginal congestion cost	0.6-242.6	1.2-576.3 (bus)	0-139.2		0-703.5	0-403.8	
Wear and tear infrastructure cost	0.8	2.7 (bus)	0.2	0.2 €ct/tkm (rail)	0-7.9	0-105.0	0.2 €ct/tkm (rail)
Oil dependency	x			Air	x	x	
Economies of density		x		x			x

The major external cost of urban public transport is crowding among public transport users.[5]

For medium- to long-distance transport, the externalities of car use are less important than in urban areas, as there is less population exposure to air pollution and less road congestion. The most important externalities are still congestion and climate change. As mentioned before, rail and bus are the main alternatives to car use. But for medium- and long-distance transport, it is well known that bus and rail service faces economies of density problems. Whenever demand is low, the low frequency that is offered makes the public transport modes unattractive. Additional users allow the frequency to be increased, implying an external benefit for all existing users due to smaller average waiting times at stops or more convenient service. Apart from yielding economies of density, additional users also allow public transport companies to benefit from economies of scale, lowering average costs per passenger kilometer. Finally, for long-distance travel, high speed rail (HSR) and air transport are the most important alternatives to the car. In the European Union, rail is mostly offered by the public sector, while air transport is privately offered. In terms of externalities, per passenger kilometer air is more carbon intensive than rail.

Turning to freight transport, for short distances there is hardly an alternative for road transport. For medium- to long-distance freight movements, and depending on local circumstances, rail and inland waterways are the main alternatives. Both are slower, but they cause less external costs per ton-kilometer.

One of the main recent issues in EU transport policy is the large oil dependency of car transportation—oil use accounts for 90 percent of fuel used by cars. In the European Union (White Paper 2013), this is considered to be problematic for two reasons. First, there is an important import bill as the oil is largely imported. Second, the sector becomes highly vulnerable to oil supply shocks. However, for economists who believe in the benefits of trade based on comparative advantage, a large import bill is not really an issue. The European Union is already among those federations with the highest consumption taxes for oil products, and these can be seen as import taxes that alter the terms of trade. The import bill argument is therefore open to question. Furthermore, the oil shock and unreliability argument is also not an entirely convincing basis for decreasing oil dependency. Note that since 1973 the European Union has not experienced a real rationing of oil supply (Kilian 2008); in fact, price shocks were often generated by demand rather than supply shocks. Emergency stocks and growing non-OPEC supply (non-conventional oil from North America) further limit the risks of politically motivated supply interruptions.[6]

Of course, one can also argue for a carbon-neutral transport sector. This is a very drastic move that only makes sense when there is a globally binding international climate agreement. With such an agreement one avoids the risk that the reduced use of oil by the European Union will give oil reserve owners incentive to sell oil at discount prices to the rest of the world, so that the carbon neutral EU transport sector has no net emission effect. The Paris agreement of December 2015 is an important but very modest step toward a worldwide binding climate agreement, as it lacks the necessary sanctions for non-compliance (Nordhaus 2015).

2.2 Policy Objectives and Policy Instruments

The choice of policy instruments at the European level has to be seen historically as a gradual reform process, starting from purely national policy priorities, and ideally converging to an EU-wide optimum. The European Union has defined policy objectives and preferred policies in a series of Green and White Papers.[7] Over the past 20 years there has been a strong re-orientation of the objectives formulated. In the 1992 White Paper, the main focus was still on integrating the EU economies by lowering transport costs and liberalizing the trucking industry. In 1995, a new focus came into play: next to regulation, transport pricing was suddenly considered as an important additional instrument. Transport taxes could be used not only to generate tax revenues but also to stimulate transport users to make better decisions regarding transport mode, the type of vehicle used, and when and where to make trips. Evidence was presented that "there is a significant mismatch between prices paid by individual transport users and the costs they cause—both in structure and in level" (European Commission 1995). For the first time, there was reference to the external costs of car and truck use, including congestion, and to solutions like road tolls in congested areas, differentiated fuel taxes to reflect differences in air emission rates between gasoline and diesel vehicles, etc. That getting the prices right was now stated as an explicit priority was a de facto revolution in the transport community, and the following White Papers turned the clock somewhat backward. For example, the 2001 White Paper again put more emphasis on quantitative objectives (such as a specific minimum share of public transport) and on the financing of new infrastructure.

From 2011 onward, the reduction of carbon emissions and oil dependency and the promotion of renewables became additional focuses of EU transport policy. In the most recent White Paper (European Commission 2013), a European alternative fuel strategy (biofuels, electric vehicles) was presented. The main justifications for this strategy are oil import dependency, the deficit in the EU trade balance (up to 2.5 percent of GDP), and the oil price hikes. These were "driven by speculation" according to the EU document and were estimated to cost $50 billion per year in additional import costs (Com(2013)17 final). The idea presented was that the promotion of alternative fuels would boost growth in Europe. Moreover, they are considered necessary to reach the official EU-wide objective of a 60 percent reduction of carbon emissions in 2050 (compared to 1990) and to reach the air quality objectives.

Summarizing the main policy lines (see the 2011 and 2013 White Papers), we now have three main objectives:

• Resource efficiency (less carbon intensity, less oil dependency, electro-mobility).
• A strong emphasis on promoting public transport for passengers (rail and bus in urban areas, and high speed rail for longer distances), and promoting rail and inland waterways for freight.
• A European multimodal transport information, management, and payment system.

These policy objectives are often translated into quantity or market share objectives such as "50 percent of urban mobility should be carbon-free in 2030." Operationalization of the objectives is often achieved using regulations and infrastructure subsidies at both the European Union (for example, car emission standards) and Member State levels (for example, subsidies for electric car refueling infrastructure).

Table 8.2 presents the main instruments used for taxing and regulating road transport. The most important instruments currently used are still fuel taxes on cars (gasoline and diesel) and on trucks (diesel). For cars and light vans, fuel taxes are complemented by EU fuel efficiency standards imposed on deliveries of car manufacturers to EU customers and by lower Member State taxes, or even subsidies, for other fuels (biofuels, natural gas, electricity). The fuel efficiency standards apply to the weighted average of new cars put on the market by each manufacturer. Despite the high subsidies, the share of other fuels is still very low: biofuels are blended with conventional motor fuels and their fuel share is less than 5 percent. The number of electric vehicles and natural gas

Table 8.2
Main instruments used for taxing and regulating road transport

Policy Instrument	Cars	Trucks
Gasoline excise	Yes	
Diesel excise	Yes	
Tax and subsidies for other fuels	Lower tax (LPG) or subsidy (electricity)	
Vehicle purchase and ownership taxes	In function of value, sometimes in function of CO_2 emissions and often with a surcharge on diesel cars	Eurovignette is fixed sum per year that is function of axle weight and Euro norm
Parking charges	In most cities	
Distance charging	No	Germany, Austria, Poland, Slovenia, etc.
Toll roads	France, Italy, Spain, Portugal	
Road pricing by time of day and by place	London, Stockholm, Milan, Goteborg	No
Fuel efficiency regulations	Yes	Small vans only
Conventional emission regulations	Yes	Yes

vehicles makes up less than 1 percent of the new vehicle fleet. Returning to table 8.2, most countries also tax vehicle purchases and ownership, but the tax formulas differ widely among countries. Moreover, in almost all urban areas, parking charges are used as an instrument to ration parking demand by non-locals and locals. Parking charges have progressively replaced permits, parking time restrictions, and other regulations. They are currently not used to curb congestion, although they could be. Moreover, work-related parking is often subsidized. Finally, only a few cities (London, Stockholm, and Milan) have implemented some limited form of road pricing in function of place and/or time of use. Motorway tolls have been used to finance motorway construction in some countries (historically France, Spain, and Italy).[8]

In those countries where there are no infrastructure tolls, taxes on trucks are complemented more and more by additional infrastructure payments in the form of daily or yearly passes (vignettes) that are unrelated to distance, or by charges related to distance. The infrastructure charges are also a function of the infrastructure damage (by differentiation according to axle weight) and environmental parameters of trucks. In addition, all fuel purchases (including excises) for trucks and cars are subject to VAT; however, firms will not pay the VAT, as fuel is an intermediate input.[9]

Quantitative policy objectives have the advantage of being easy to monitor, but they also have important disadvantages. First, the cost and benefits of reaching the objective are uncertain. Since Weitzman (1974), economists have preferred price instruments, as they can better deal with uncertainty over future (e.g., energy and technology) costs. This is true even more so when the EU objectives are implemented country by country, where the costs of meeting these objectives can vary considerably across countries.

Of course, in terms of policy instruments, the European Union is limited to its domains of competence: climate policy, international transport, and competition policies (vehicle and fuel standards, markets for public transport). Urban and regional policy issues like congestion and local public transport do not fall within EU competence.

National and EU decision processes differ. National decision processes vary across member countries and usually involve a majority in Parliament; often, they also require a qualified majority over regions. These processes can be slow, but they seem to work. At the EU level the procedure is more complex. First, for tax measures, unanimity is required, while other measures require a qualified majority only. Second, initiatives are usually taken up by the Commission, but they need to pass a double hurdle: the Council of Ministers and approval by the European Parliament. Finally, most regulations need to be implemented by the Member States. Therefore, the process is lengthy and can be difficult. A famous example is the "Eurovignette" directive that regulates the charging of trucks. The initial proposal was made by the Commission in 1999, based on a Green Paper of 1995. There was a demand by the European Parliament and the Council to have a better and more generic directive in 2006, and the new Eurovignette directive was only voted in 2011 (Weismann 2013). It is therefore no surprise that many member countries took national initiatives to implement new charges for trucks before the final directive was voted on.

3. Evaluation of Pricing and Regulation Policies for Passenger Transport

We start this section with an appraisal of the current instruments used toward car transport. Then we look into the possibilities of using new pricing instruments for controlling car use. Finally, we briefly discuss policies that might complement the use of novel car pricing instruments. Specifically, we focus on pricing and supply of public transport, and we point at the relation between transport and labor market policies. Note that we do not discuss various technology-driven supply policies (information sharing, self-driving cars, support to car-sharing systems and peer-to-peer transactions, multi-modal integration, etc.) that will definitely become more important in the future. We also ignore the innovation incentives of the pricing and regulation policies we review. These are discussed in more detail in chapter 6 of this volume.

3.1 Successes and Failures of the Current Instruments Used for Car Transport

For car transport, most countries rely primarily on a combination of fuel taxes, vehicle purchase or ownership taxes, and regulatory measures to achieve two main objectives: addressing external costs of car use, and raising tax revenues in an equitable way. Intra-country and international cross-border shopping limits the spatial variation of the gasoline and diesel tax. Moreover, this tax does not differentiate in terms of time of use. Hence, these instruments are poorly suited to addressing some of the external costs, especially congestion. But of course, there are many more ways to control externalities, and other policy instruments apart from fuel taxes could help. The most commonly used other instruments to control externalities are tax policies toward alternative fuels, purchase and ownership taxes on vehicles, and standards on vehicles (air pollution standards, fuel efficiency standards—or equivalently CO_2 emission rates—and safety standards).

In what follows, we consecutively deal with the gasoline tax, the taxation of fuels that substitute for gasoline (diesel) taxes on vehicle purchases or annual ownership taxes, the regulation of car emission policies, and specific policies to stimulate the purchase of alternative fuel and electric vehicles. We do not discuss some other types of regulations such as specific safety regulations for road use (for example, drunk driver penalties and speed regulations).

The Gasoline Tax If countries use the gasoline tax as the main instrument to address all externalities of car use, the tax should be in line with the following expression, to which one can add a margin for revenue raising:[10]

Fuel tax/liter = carbon damage/liter + γ (marginal external congestion, accidents, air pollution costs per veh km) (km/liter)

In this expression, γ is the fraction of the fuel reduction from reduced vehicle use in response to the tax. As just mentioned, the externality component can be augmented by an additional margin to capture the revenue raising function of the tax.

To understand the above expression, first note that the most straight-forward element is the carbon damage, because there is a proportional relationship between carbon emissions and fuel use. We know carbon damage per ton should in principle be uniform over all sectors of the economy; based on recent estimates, in the European Union it could be of the order of 20-25 euro/ton of CO_2 (this boils down to 0.06 euro per liter for gasoline and 0.07 euro per liter for diesel). Second, internalizing other externalities with a fuel tax requires a correction factor γ (γ < 1) that takes into account the share of fuel reduction that is due to reduced driving rather than to more fuel-efficient cars. As other externalities are related to distance rather than to fuel use, this component of the fuel tax wants to stimulate reduced driving rather than improvements in average fleet fuel efficiency. What complicates matters is that, whereas climate damage is independent of the location of the carbon emissions, the external cost of other externalities depends on location: accident externalities, congestion, and air pollution all vary by time and place.

Of course, a further complication is that there are many other ways to reduce such other externalities than through a reduction in total mileage: vehicles can be cleaner and safer; drivers can be more cau-tious; they can drive at other times and/or take other routes. Although the EU Handbook on External Costs is an important step forward, there is an obvious need to sharpen the external cost estimates, and to show how to apply them in more precise optimal tax formulas. There are two particular priorities. First, we need to know more concretely what the level of marginal congestion costs is and how it reacts to vehicle volume in a network. Second, we need to have a better understanding of the conventional air pollution externalities, and we need to know what the main differences between gasoline and diesel cars are.

Taxation of Fuels that Substitute for Gasoline   Before turning to the use of other instruments, it is instructive to study the taxation of fuels that substitute for gasoline. The most important substitutes are diesel, LNG, CNG, biofuels, and electricity. There is no reason to apply a different taxation principle to substitutes of gasoline than to gasoline itself. Europe has a strong penetration of diesel cars, and this evolution is a matter of intensive debate. When we apply the same tax principle as above to diesel cars, there is clearly a need for a higher tax per liter on diesel than on gasoline. Although, of course, diesel and gasoline cars produce the same mileage-related externalities, there are three reasons for this. First, the carbon emission per car-kilometer is slightly lower, but other air pollution damage is higher for diesel than for gasoline; the net effect implies slightly higher external costs per kilometer for diesel. Second, the main reason why the diesel tax per liter should be higher is that a diesel car drives some 20 percent more kilometers with a liter of fuel than a gasoline car. Hence, to internalize the same mileage-related externalities, one needs a higher tax per liter on diesel Despite these simple principles, many EU countries continue to tax diesel fuel at a lower rate than gasoline, where diesel advantage can be up to 50 cent/liter compared to gasoline. Third, a kilometer driven by a diesel car also tends to produce more conventional pollution than does a gasoline car. Of course, diesel is also used by trucks so that diesel taxes are a compromise between car and truck use. In the case of cars, one can easily bring in other specific tax instruments for diesel cars (purchase or registration taxes) to correct for too low diesel fuel taxes.[11] But these are much less efficient second best taxes, as diesel fuel use by cars will still not be sufficiently taxed. Not surprisingly, the tax treatment of diesel implies that diesel cars have a large market share in many European countries (see figure 8.1).

Finally, the same tax principle given above also holds for biofuels and electricity. However, for these fuels one can advance a learning-by-doing argument to justify a more favorable tax treatment until these vehicles have more substantial fleet penetration.

Vehicle Purchase and Ownership Taxes   Other instruments that have been used intensively are vehicle purchase and ownership taxes. Different member countries have been using these instruments for environmental and tax revenue objectives in widely different ways (for example, registration taxes often depend on CO_2 characteristics, but they do so according to very different formulas). Moreover, there is a large variation in the level of these taxes. For example, although many (but not all) member countries have a VAT on vehicle purchases, a registration tax, and an annual vehicle tax, the level of the registration tax varies between zero and more than 100 percent of the purchase price.

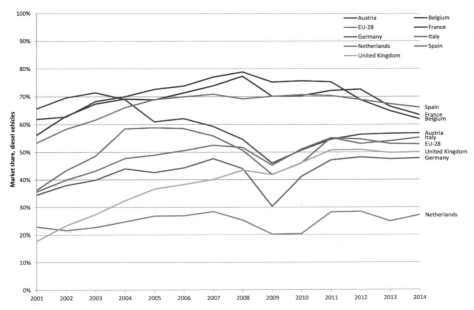

Figure 8.1
The share of diesel in new car sales in selected countries (2001–2012)
Source: Taken from the European Vehicle Market Statistics Pocketbook (ICCT 2013).

In what follows, we illustrate the variety of car ownership policies by focusing on Denmark and the Netherlands—countries that have a tradition of high ownership taxes to cope with car externalities and that have recently fundamentally reformed their tax system. Both countries favored high purchase and registration tax policies to discourage car ownership, particularly of large cars. For example, in Denmark, owners pay up to a 200 percent purchase tax on a car. Revenues from non-fuel taxes on cars were equal to 1.5 percent and 1.2 percent of GDP in Denmark and the Netherlands, respectively, compared with an average of 0.5 percent for the European Union as a whole. To put this into perspective, fuel taxes represent some 1.4 percent of GDP, on average.[12] The efficiency and equity effects of these high non-use tax policies have not yet been analyzed very thoroughly. Considering equity, ownership taxes of course tend to discourage car ownership but, even if this tax is progressive in the value of the car, the net equity effects are not obvious. They depend, among other factors, on how ownership of different car types varies across the income distribution. As for efficiency, there is strong evidence that high purchase taxes on new cars may induce postponing car replacement, leading to rather old car fleets and high pollution. This was the

Box 8.1

The Wrong Tax Reform in Denmark

First, consider the tax reform in Denmark; this consisted of moving from the existing system toward a strong feebate system. Munk-Nielsen (2014) documents how the reform, introduced in 2007, gave rise to a strong switch to more fuel-efficient vehicles. To illustrate its implications, take as example a fuel efficiency improvement from 6.25 l/100 km to 5.25 l/100 km. This gives a feebate of 1,560 euro or, using a mechanical calculation, a subsidy of the order of 1,000 euro/ton of CO_2. Based on a detailed modeling exercise, Munk-Nielsen derives a more precise estimate of the cost of the system for the Danish car market as a whole, taking into account the rebound effect and the other external costs of driving. He arrives at a subsidy of 1,545 euro/ton of CO_2 saved. This makes the system very inefficient compared to CO_2-saving efforts in other economic sectors (e.g., recent CO_2 prices in the EU Emissions Trading System have been below 5 or 10 euro per ton). In addition, the focus on CO_2 reduction led to an increase on the share of diesel cars in the new car stock in Denmark from 5 percent to 40 percent. This is difficult to justify, given the higher air pollution damage of diesel cars.

case in Denmark and the Netherlands (see boxes 8.1 and 8.2), until both countries recently reformed their purchase tax systems. High recurrent taxes on car ownership do not have this disadvantage.

Besides Denmark and the Netherlands, several other countries, including France and Germany, have used a scrappage scheme in the period 2008-2010. The net effect on CO_2 was low or even negative (D'Haultfoeuille, Givord, and Boutin 2013) and, if one does not account for the macro-economic stimulus, this program was costly.

In view of the policies implemented in European countries, it comes as no surprise that CO_2 emissions declined substantially over the past decades (see figure 8.2). However, the above discussion makes clear that this reduction was achieved at a huge economic cost, and that more efficient policies (sticking to fuel taxes or more efforts in non-transport sectors) might have generated the same savings in emissions at much lower cost.

Regulation of Air Pollution and Carbon Emissions   One of the most effective additional instruments to control the environmental externalities of car use is the regulation of emissions of traditional air pollutants. The Auto-oil program of the European Union regulated the emissions of new cars and the quality of fuel. This regulation was efficient in tackling traditional pollutants in the sense that, by installing additional

Box 8.2
The Netherlands: Another Costly Tax Reform
From table 8.1, we know that the external costs of a car are strongly related to car use and not to the ownership of a car, so there is a lot of room for tax reforms that substitute high purchase and ownership taxes by user taxes. The Netherlands tried to use this opportunity in 2006 to transform the purchase and ownership taxes into road user taxes, a reform that did not go through (see the next section). Instead, in the period 2006–2010, the Dutch government changed the structure of the purchase tax from a tax based on the value of the car to a progressive CO_2 tax. An example may illustrate the implications. Take the substitution of a 13.3 l/100 km car by a car consuming 10 l/100 km. This gives a reduction of the purchase tax of 12,500 euro and, using again a purely mechanical calculation, it implies a saving of 5.2 tons of CO_2. This leads to a cost of 2,403 euro/ton of CO_2. Of course, for more fuel-efficient vehicles the progressive tax will be smaller, but the cost is still of the order of 1,000 Euro/ton of CO_2. Moreover, according to van Geilenkirchen et al. (2014), the net saving of CO_2 emissions is much smaller than previously indicated due to the rebound effect. Taking this into account, they estimate that the tax reform leads to CO_2 savings of only 0.1 percent in the short run and 1 percent in the long run. The Dutch tax reform did avoid the promotion of diesel cars, but instead it strongly promoted the purchase of hybrid cars: in 2009, hybrid cars represented 4 percent of new car sales in the Netherlands, compared with a market share of less than 1 percent in the rest of the European Union (ICCT 2013).

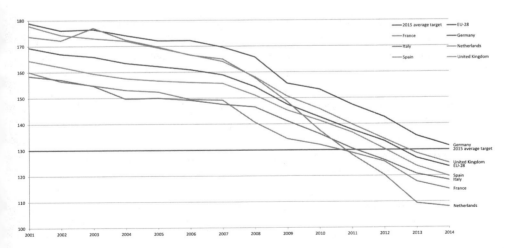

Figure 8.2
Average CO_2 emission (test cycle) for new passenger cars (vertical axis) in several member countries

Source: ICCT (2013).

equipment at relatively low cost, emissions could be reduced by a factor 5 to 20 (Calthrop and Proost 2003). The efficiency of the more recent and more stringent emission standards for traditional air pollution is more controversial, and serious doubts remain on the efficiency of the regulation of air pollution by diesel cars. For example, the NO_x standard of 2009 requires a maximum emission of 0.18 g/vehkm in the test cycle while the real emissions could be four times higher (ICCT 2013). With more strict emission limits and increasing marginal abatement costs, it pays to fine-tune the performance of the car specifically for the test cycle and to leave out of the test the engine load regimes that constitute real-world driving (e.g., uphill driving, acceleration on a ramp, or positive accelerations from a standstill). This results in an ever larger difference between test cycle emissions and the real emissions. On the positive side, emissions rates are maintained (at least partially) over vehicle life through periodic inspections programs.

Fuel efficiency regulation for cars to reduce CO_2 emissions is a more costly objective for several reasons. First, there is no technical measure, like a catalytic converter or the use of fuels with a lower sulfur content that can reduce carbon emissions by a factor 5 to 20, as was the case for traditional air pollutants. Second, there is already an important carbon tax; it is called a gasoline tax. The gasoline tax (amounting to some 200 euro/ton of CO_2) is much higher than the carbon tax or the carbon abatement cost in other sectors of the economy (note that the price of tradable emission permits for CO_2 has varied between 5 and 30 euro/ton of CO_2). The simple reason is that the gasoline tax also serves to raise revenues and to internalize other externalities. For these reasons, too much fuel and CO_2 saving is undesirable. We are already pushing very hard on CO_2 reductions through high fuel taxes and (to varying degrees) vehicle taxes related to CO_2 emissions—so additional incentives on top of these through CO_2-per-km regulations are likely to be very costly.

The standard case in favor of a fuel efficiency standard to reduce CO_2 emissions is twofold. One argument often invoked by the European Union is that of myopic consumers. However, the evidence to support the argument is mixed at best. For example, Grigolon, Reynaert, and Verboven (2014) show that when EU consumers make car purchase decisions, they take into account close to 90 percent of the effect of fuel prices. Moreover, even if they were myopic, jointly considering myopia and externalities implies that fuel efficiency standards could still be outperformed by fuel taxes (Parry, Evans, and Oates 2014).

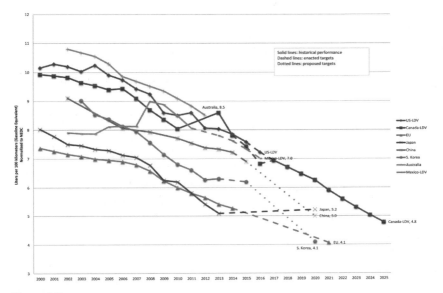

Figure 8.3
Fuel economy performance, and planned and prospective fuel economy standards, selected countries

Source: ICCT (2011).

A second argument in favor of efficiency standards is that they require, for the same total CO_2 savings, more technological progress than a tax instrument, and this technological element spills over to the rest of the world (Barla and Proost 2012; Dechezlepretre and Popp 2014). The latter argument would be in line with the EU's voluntary climate policy: the European Union is indeed a world leader in terms of fuel efficiency (see figure 8.3). But if we want to have a successful transfer of technology, we may need to re-orient our technology standards toward less ambitious targets, as other countries have less ambitious climate objectives and do not want to pay for fancy, super-efficient technologies (Eliasson and Proost 2014). Finally, does the world really benefit from the EU's efforts to make diesel cars more fuel efficient?

Alternative Fuels and Electric Vehicles As part of the EU Climate and Energy Policy, there was a directive pushing for the use of biofuels (bio-ethanol and bio-diesel made from biomass) and the promotion of electro-mobility. The most successful country in introducing biofuel cars was Sweden, where a subsidy program increased the market share (in new car sales) of flexible fuel cars from 8 percent in 2006 to 22 percent in 2008 (ICCT 2008). Huse (2014) analyzed the Swedish Green Car Rebate in great detail. This program gave a subsidy of 1,300 to 1,500 euro for the purchase of a medium-size flexible-fuel car, a car that could run on gasoline and on biofuel (ethanol) or other less CO_2-intensive fuels.[13] In addition, the program was lenient in terms of the fuel efficiency of flexible-fuel cars. As it is easy and cheap to turn a standard car into a flexible-fuel car, the consequence was that suppliers very quickly offered flexible-fuel car variants, but in a less fuel-efficient version.[14] Consumers could arbitrage between gasoline and biofuels and, when oil prices dropped, end up using a lot of gasoline. The final result was an expensive subsidy program, achieving a high share of flexible-fuel cars, but with a low environmental effectiveness. Similarly, it would be no surprise that the current stimulus for electro-mobility is, with present technologies, also not a very cost-effective option to reduce carbon emissions (see Crist 2012).

It is useful to turn to the implications of fuel efficiency standards and subsidy programs for more fuel-efficient cars for the manufacturers. As they are bound by an average standard on the sales of new cars in Europe, any incentive by one country to impose more fuel-efficient cars implies that a manufacturer can afford to sell less fuel-efficient cars in other countries. Two other particularities of the fuel standard are worth mentioning. The first is that the average fuel efficiency does not take into account the expected mileage; this gives too large a weight to electric vehicles, as these are typically used for short trips. The second issue is that there is a widening gap between the theoretical measurement of fuel consumption defined in the standard and effective fuel consumption. The ICCT (2013) reports an additional real world consumption of fuel that was of the order of 7 percent in 2001, but it has increased to 20 to 25 percent in 2011, the reason again being the fine-tuning of performance for a specific test cycle. Thus, the way the current standard is formulated is becoming less and less realistic.

Summing Up Summarizing, the main instruments used by the European Union to tackle externalities are high fuel taxes and fuel efficiency standards; in this regard, it has been a forerunner compared to other parts of the world. High fuel taxes have been a second-best instrument to correct several externalities at the same time. The stringent fuel efficiency standard has been eroding the effectiveness of the high fuel tax. Some Member States, overestimating the benefits of gasoline savings, have launched very costly subsidy programs for even more fuel efficiency, or to promote the use of alternative fuels. Promotion of alternative fuel vehicles may benefit from technical compatibility standards (as argued by Vollebergh and van der Werf 2014), because these allow network effects and reduce costs. But the European Union has imposed costly minimum market shares and is lagging behind in agreeing on technical compatibility standards.

3.2   Acceptability of New Instruments for Pricing Cars
We discuss consecutively urban congestion pricing, low emission zones, parking, and paying for motorway use.

Urban Congestion Pricing   For a long time, all big cities tried to implement "standard" instruments, such as offering cheap and extensive public transport services and charging high prices for parking, in their effort to reduce externalities. These instruments did have some effects, but they failed to solve congestion problems; moreover, they were expensive.[15] Singapore was the first city to implement some form of congestion pricing. Now many cities in the European Union are potentially interested in new price instruments to curb congestion, but very few also implement them. Cities that did introduce new pricing instruments include London (2003), Stockholm (2007), and Milan (2012); Goteborg introduced one in 2014.[16] London has implemented zonal pricing; Stockholm and Milan have implemented cordon tolls with prices varying by the time of day. In a cordon pricing system, road users pay only when entering the zone, but trips within the zone are free. In zonal pricing systems, one also pays for trips within a given zone. Many more cities were tempted and quite a few organized referenda about the issue, but they never implemented the new instrument. Although the European Union seems to be the world leader in the implementation of some form of road pricing, the question remains of why only a few cities took the final step. This may seem surprising, because careful analysis of the experience in the different cities shows that the implementation of these road pricing measures have been welfare-improving, provided that the revenue has been used productively (see Anas and Lindsey 2012).

Several lessons can be drawn from the available experience. First, the design of road pricing systems is very important for the net welfare effect. For example, Stockholm was more efficient than London, because the system had lower transaction costs and more finely differentiated charges.[17] Second, a striking feature is that only a small share (25 percent)

Box 8.3

The Political Economy of Road Pricing

De Borger and Proost (2012a) analyze the political economy of road pricing, using a model of policy reform. Road users have an initial majority, but they are uncertain about the individual costs of switching from car use to public transport, or of foregoing the trip altogether. They show that this uncertainty implies a high expected substitution cost, and that it is likely to lead to a negative expected benefit for initial car drivers. Assuming that non-drivers also share in the collected toll revenues, car drivers perceive high expected substitution costs and low revenue from toll charges before introduction of road pricing, because they have to share toll revenues with non-drivers. After implementation, uncertainty is resolved and the decisive car user (being close to the median) will see lower substitution costs, and may vote in favor ex post. The result is that a majority may vote against road pricing ex ante, although a majority would have been in favor after its introduction. The analysis further shows that fewer voters are against road pricing when toll revenues are used to subsidize public transport than when they are redistributed to all voters. Moreover, if the total number of peak trips is price-inelastic, one way to limit the toll level and still obtain the same total welfare gain is to subsidize public transport, as it is mainly the net price difference between road use and public transport that drives the modal shift. In addition, this strategy prevents that revenues are shared with those that do not travel. The results of the paper are consistent with a number of recent empirical observations on efforts to introduce road pricing, including the systematic rejection of road pricing in referenda, the more favorable attitudes toward road pricing after than before its introduction, and tying the toll revenues to support public transport.

---

of the suppressed car trips switched to public transport; the rest of the trips disappeared due to more car sharing, combining trips, or simply foregoing the trip. A third conclusion from the analysis of the experience in London (Transport for London) and in Stockholm (Eliasson et al. 2009) is that more people were in favor of the road pricing system after it was introduced (ex post) than before its implementation (ex ante). Box 8.3 deals with this puzzle.

In sum, there have been several successful road-pricing experiences in EU cities over the last 10 years. It is expected that more will follow soon, and that this will be an important policy development for the next decade. There are two important questions for this development, besides toll rates and time differentiation. First, what is the best form this road pricing should take: cordon pricing around the city or zonal pricing? This will depend on the geography of the city and the distribution of trips. Second, is the introduction of new instruments best organized as a bottom-up or as a top-down process? Top-down initiatives ("national road pricing") at the level of the federal government were discussed in the Netherlands and in the United Kingdom, but they were not accepted. The top-down schemes can avoid one region exploiting its local monopoly power by overcharging trips by non-residents. However, the disadvantage of top-down schemes is their lack of flexibility to adapt to changes in local circumstances. Moreover, acceptability is more difficult because federally imposed differentiated pricing runs the risk of regional discrimination.[18] The schemes that were implemented (in London, Stockholm, and Milan) are all bottom-up. The risk of monopoly pricing in local schemes can be overcome by constraining the use of the revenues.[19,20] Of course, one could also construct a dual system involving elements of congestion charging by both national and sub-national governments (note that the present combination of fuel taxes and parking charges is also a dual system).

Low Emission Zones   Closely related to road pricing is the proliferation of Low Emission Zones in Europe. The EU directive makes cities and regions responsible for implementing sufficient measures to reach the urban air quality guidelines. A large number of cities (for example, more than 40 in Germany alone, as well as Milan) took this air quality directive seriously (although enforcement is weak or non-existent) and implemented a variety of measures to comply with the objectives. These measures consisted of either banning the most polluting cars or enhancing public transport supply. According to Perry and Wolff (2011), the banning of polluting cars was effective and welfare-improving, while the extension of public transport supply was not. De Borger and Proost (2013) have studied low emission zones and various other externality-reducing measures in an urban environment (for example, traffic lights, speed bumps, bypass roads, etc.). They show how the initiatives taken by cities can very well lead to inefficient policies: overzealous implementation of traffic lights and speed bumps and insufficient investment in ring roads are good examples of poor local policies.

Parking   Cities have long been using parking charges. High parking charges can be a second-best measure to curb excessive car use in cities. Economists have been slow in picking up this instrument, but it has its function. Contrary to road pricing, this instrument is widely accepted. New technological developments and better modelling can increase its efficiency. Of course, efficient parking pricing has to be place and time dependent. The technology to implement such systems is available. For example, in part of San Francisco there is electronic monitoring of parking occupancy, and prices are adjusted regularly to achieve a given occupancy rate (say, 90 percent).

Paying for Motorway Use Several countries have installed tolling systems to pay for their motorway infrastructure. The tolls have been used mainly to generate revenues, but some motorways have started to implement time- and place-dependent tolls. Those countries that have not yet implemented tolling systems on their motorways are now tempted to also charge foreign cars by using vignettes. Switzerland was the first to do so, and other countries will follow; for example, Germany plans to introduce a vignette per day, month, or year in 2016. These vignette systems can be differentiated by type of car (as in the clean car zones in Germany), but they are not differentiated by distance, by time or by place of driving. The main function of these vignettes is therefore to make foreign users pay for the local infrastructure, because domestic car owners are often compensated by an equivalent reduction of local car taxes. Of course, such vignettes are relatively poor instruments to tackle congestion.

Summing Up In the longer term, we need higher transport prices in congested urban areas, and possibly lower prices in rural areas. This means that the function of gasoline taxes, managed by central government, will be eroded slowly by higher congestion charges and by parking charges that will most likely be set by local governments. The implications of this ongoing evolution for tax levels, environment, infrastructure funding, and intergovernmental transfers are still to be studied.

3.3 Complementary Public Transport Policies

In dense EU metropolitan areas, public transport has a high market share that can be well over 50 percent of passenger-kilometers. But in many cities this comes at a high cost, as cost recovery is low (often below 50 percent of the operation costs). Parry and Small (2009) find that high operating subsidies for public transport in large cities (London, Los Angeles, and Washington, DC) can be justified on the basis of second-best arguments. Subsidies allow exploitation of scale economies due to increased frequency (which reduces waiting times at stops), higher route density (reducing average user cost of accessing the system) and increased load factors (reducing average operating cost). But the most important justification for the high subsidy is that 50 percent of the extra public transit trips attracted by the higher subsidy reflect trips that would have otherwise been made by car. In practice, many cities have implemented high public transport subsidies, but, unfortunately, only a small share of the extra demand has come from former car users.[21] The result has been an important congestion problem in public transport in some cities. With a cost recovery of less than 50 percent, funding additional capacity is difficult. In addition, most cities do not yet differentiate their public transport fares in function of time of day and place in the network. Even without implementing road pricing for cars, it seems that many cities could benefit from an increase of public transport fares in the peak period (for an illustration for Paris, see Kilani, Proost, and Van der Loo 2014).

Public transport can not only be made more attractive by lower prices, but also by improved quality. This requires investments in trams, metros and high speed rail (HSR). Some countries do have a tradition of high-quality public assessment (including the United Kingdom, Sweden, the Netherlands, and France), but in many other countries such investments have not been assessed by a traditional cost benefit analysis (CBA). It turns out that many large transport projects are not justified according to traditional CBA methods. For urban transport, there seems to be a systematic preference for expensive trams, which is quite likely unjustified (see Tirachini, Hensher, and Jara-Diaz 2010). For medium- to long-distance transport, some high speed rail projects are difficult to justify. Several of the projects on the Trans European Network priority list that were eligible for additional EU funding also have a poor social rate of return (Proost et al. 2013). This illustrates the importance of detailed ex ante evaluation of large-scale investment projects. In this respect, it is encouraging to note that there has been recent progress in assessment techniques that better take into account agglomeration economies and regional effects (see Teulings, Ossokina, and De Groot 2014).

What the appropriate public transport policies are depends on whether or not new pricing instruments for passenger cars are introduced. For example, the introduction of road pricing makes differentiated (in space and time) public transport fares more desirable (with higher peak fares). Moreover, the benefits of public transport investment depend on which car pricing instruments are introduced.

Percentage of benchmark captured by tax system

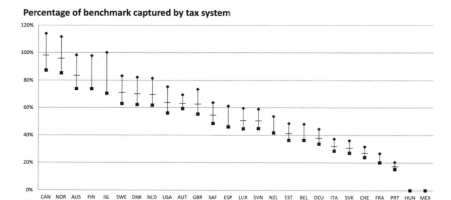

Figure 8.4
Share of the benefits of a company car that is fixed in 2012
Source: Harding (2014).

3.4 Complementary Labor Market Policies

Although detailed analysis of such policies are outside the scope of this paper, some countries have developed labor market policies that have strong—and sometimes very adverse—implications for the transport sector.

One example is the large implicit subsidy many European countries provide to company cars (see Guttierez and Van Ommeren 2011; De Borger and Wuyts 2011). This is illustrated in figure 8.4 (Harding 2014), where the proportion of the taxed benefits of a company car is reported for OECD countries. In many EU member countries, less than 50 percent of the (private) benefits of a company car are taxed. Although high labor taxes are probably the main reason for their existence, subsidies for company cars are often defended on the basis of their presumed environmental benefits. Company cars are, on average, more fuel efficient than the average car in the stock, because they are much younger than the average car and benefit often from specific fuel efficiency standards. However, these subsidies are well known to raise car traffic, mainly (but not exclusively) for commuting purposes, and they distort car ownership decisions. Moreover, the environmental benefits are highly doubtful, as the increase in kilometers compensates for the lower emissions per kilometer and as is already covered by other environmental policies in place (Copenhagen Economics 2010). The estimated welfare cost of subsidies to company cars is therefore large, and a drastic reduction of the implicit subsidy has been suggested to raise efficiency of the transport sector (see the references given above).

Another related example is the tax deductibility of commuting expenses in many EU countries. This deductibility can be justified under some conditions once new pricing instruments (road pricing) are introduced, but they reduce welfare at current taxes on car use (Van Dender 2003; De Borger 2009).

4. Pricing of Trucks

In this section, we turn to pricing policies for road freight transport. The share of trucks in freight transport has been growing over the years to 72 percent, while the rail share has been decreasing slowly to 17 percent in 2012.[22] There are two developments we want to highlight. First, the way trucks are charged is changing rapidly in the European Union; second, the European Union is pursuing a vigorous policy to decrease the modal share of road freight transport.

4.1 From Fuel Taxes to Distance Charges

Almost all EU countries charge excises for diesel fuel used by trucks. Because trucks can cover 1,000 to 2,000 kilometers with a single tank, countries or regions engage in fuel tax competition. The difference in distances covered implies that tax competition is much more important for trucks than for cars. Evers, de Mooij, and Vollebergh (2004) studied a panel data set for 17 countries (1978–2001) and estimated how countries react to the diesel excise taxes set in neighboring countries. They found strong evidence of tax competition: when neighboring countries increase their fuel excise tax by 10 percent, an average EU country increases its tax by 2 to 3 percent. Within the European Union, some smaller countries chose a strategy of low excise taxes to make international haulers fuel up in their country; Luxembourg is the most obvious example. This behavior has brought the European Union to negotiate a minimum level of excise taxes. In 2012, Germany charged an excise of $0.589/liter, while Luxembourg charged the EU minimum of $0.343/liter (IEA 2013). Evers et al. (2004) further found that the imposition of minimum tax rates has increased overall excise levels, but has not decreased the intensity of tax competition. Next to diesel excise taxes, EU Member States that did not use tolls on their motorways, were allowed to charge additional fees for road use in the form of a vignette (annual, monthly, or daily fixed payment per vehicle). This Euro-vignette had to be non-discriminatory, and it was to be based on the actual infrastructure costs[23] (see Vierth and Schleusser 2012). Over time its use was extended so that it could also charge for environmental costs.

Technological progress in charging techniques caused several countries facing through traffic to introduce distance-based charging. Switzerland (not an EU member) replaced its vignette system in 2001 with a kilometer charge that charged trucks much more than before. The neighboring countries followed: Austria (a transit country parallel to Switzerland) in 2004, Germany in 2005 (although it wanted to start earlier), the Czech Republic in 2007, Slovakia in 2010, and Poland in 2011. Other countries (for example, Belgium) are preparing distance charges as well. Some other EU countries already had a tolling system for most of their motorways (France, Italy, and Spain). This mainly serves to cover infrastructure costs, with the restriction in France that an un-tolled alternative (viz., national roads) has to be available.

The different charging systems in place for trucks in Europe (see figure 8.5 for the situation in 2012) show a clear pattern, in that the introduction of distance charges were geographically strongly correlated. The Member States in the center of Europe tend to use distance-based charges, while states further from the center use vignettes or no charges at all (apart from fuel taxes). This is no surprise, because countries still engage in tax competition and react to the introduction of higher kilometer charges in neighboring countries (De Borger, Proost, and Van Dender 2005).

There are four interesting features to note about the transition from vignettes to distance-based charges. First, distance-based charging has generated a lot more revenue than the vignettes it has replaced. In Germany, distance charge revenues were 6.5 times larger than the revenues of the Eurovignette (Vierth and Schleusser 2012). One of the reasons the vignette revenues lagged behind was that it is a system common to five countries, and unanimity is required for updates to capture inflation and to include environmental costs. Second, the distance charging schemes discriminate much more in function of conventional air pollution than do the Eurovignette systems. Third, as noted in the theoretical literature, kilometer charges imply the risk of tax exporting to foreign users (see Kanbur and Keen 1993; De Borger et al. 2005). Fourth, the system will lead to an equilibrium with high km-taxes and low diesel taxes (see box 8.4).

If one compares the distance charges between countries, one finds that Switzerland charges 10 times more per kilometer than most other EU countries. Austria also charges significantly more than the others. Of course, although infrastructure costs may be higher in these coun-

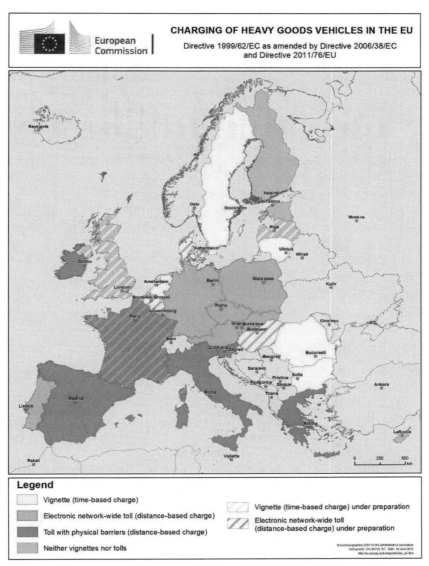

Figure 8.5
Different types of truck pricing in the European Union
Source: European Commission (2011).

tries, the main reason is the strategic position of Switzerland as a transit country. Austria is also a transit country but it is on a slightly less interesting route, and it is bounded by the EU cap on truck charges, while Switzerland is not. Finally, note that the transaction

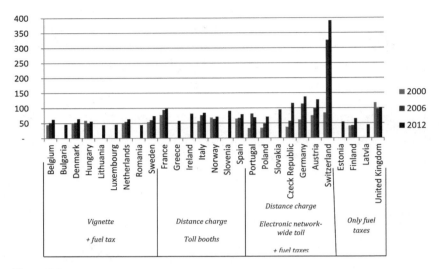

Figure 8.6
Total charges in euro for a standard domestic haul of 400 km by a 40-ton truck (charging policy as of 2012)

Source: Data taken from ITF (2013); regrouped by Mandell and Proost (2015).

costs associated with a distance-based system vary between 10 and 20 percent of the revenues (see Hamilton and Eliasson 2013), probably much larger than those for fuel excise taxation.

Figure 8.6 gives the total charges and taxes for a standard domestic haul in several OECD countries. The charges have increased strongly over the last 10 years. The countries with the lowest charges are those countries that have no tolls or distance charges.[24]

The European Union has, to some extent, anticipated that the introduction of distance charges in transit countries may lead to charges that are too high. The EU constitution does not allow discriminatory charges, but this is no guarantee against overly high truck charges in transit countries. It therefore requires that distance charges for trucks have to be based on external costs, but the estimation of external costs requires a lot of interpretation. For this reason, the distance charges are capped by the European Union on the basis of average infrastructure costs. When road congestion is an important external cost, and one has constant returns to scale in infrastructure extension, this cap can guarantee efficient pricing. This is due to the combination of two mechanisms. First, when tolls equal the marginal external congestion costs, they will pay for road infrastructure costs in the presence of constant returns to scale in road capacity. The second mechanism is that a gov-

---

Box 8.4
The Transition from Fuel Taxes to Kilometer-based Charges.
Mandell and Proost (2015) analyze this transition and find that distance charges are very contagious, but that the replacement of diesel taxes by distance charges is not necessarily welfare-improving. The outcome will depend on the availability of additional instruments to tax diesel cars and on whether or not the distance charges are finely tuned to external costs.

Consider first the case where diesel excises are used only for trucks, while cars are taxed using other instruments. In the Nash equilibrium, the diesel taxes can then be lower or higher than the external and infrastructure costs of trucks. The taxes will typically be low in countries of equal size with intensive tax competition. When countries differ in size, a low tax results in the small country, confirming results from the literature (Kanbur and Keen 1993). It is found that when distance charges also become available and their implementation costs are low, then all countries will adopt distance charges for trucks, and fuel taxes are driven to the bottom. The distance charges will all be higher than the external cost. One expects this to be the case, for example, when there is tolling on a serial corridor used by international traffic and where several governments tax traffic within their jurisdiction. As long as the different governments do not fully incorporate the consumer surplus of international traffic, tolls will be larger than the external cost (De Borger, Dunkerley, and Proost 2007). Moving from diesel taxes to distance charges can therefore be welfare-decreasing.

Consider next the case where fuel taxes are used to tax not only trucks but also diesel cars. If there are no distance charges, the fuel tax will have to balance the optimal taxation of diesel cars and trucks. As only one instrument is used, the tax will be a weighted average of external costs of diesel cars, trucks and margins on international trucking. Tax competition can again increase or decrease the tax, but diesel use by cars is typically less vulnerable to tax competition. The result will be that the diesel tax in one country reacts less strongly to tax changes in a neighboring country. Imagine that distance charges are now introduced for trucks. Both countries will use distance charges and fuel excises. The sum of distance charges and fuel excises will be higher than the external cost for trucks, and diesel tax tends to be lower than the external costs of diesel cars. Again there is no guarantee that the introduction of distance charges will improve the welfare effects of pricing.

---

ernment that wants to maximize the benefits for its local users and cannot discriminate against foreigners will implement the federally optimal policy. Adding the obligation to spend the toll revenues on road infrastructure forces the local government to implement optimal policies, so that there is no need for the federal regulator to know the external congestion costs (Van der Loo and Proost 2013).

Finally, note that the distance charges for trucks have up to now mainly been used as a simple distance toll with some environmental differentiation. They can become much more effective when they are more closely geared to the external costs of congestion, local air pollution, and accidents.

4.2 Complementary Policies

The EU policy line for freight contains ambitious modal share objectives. This requires additional investments but also better integration of international rail freight operations. Progress on the integration of rail freight operations (interoperability, etc.) has been slow. As observed before, many of the investment projects that were considered a priority did not pass the CBA test (Proost et al. 2013).

The introduction of more competition in rail freight services by the vertical divestiture between infrastructure and operations has been slow as well, despite the fact that the expected welfare benefits from increased competition are likely to outweigh the extra transaction costs. The latter are estimated to amount to just 2-3 percent of total costs (Merkert, Smith, and Nash 2012).

5. Conclusion

The European Union has succeeded in making Member States accept external costs as a basis for transport tax policies. As the available policy instrument set was up to now mainly restricted to fuel taxes and fixed taxes for vehicle ownership, suboptimal policy developments were the result. There has been too large an emphasis on climate issues leading to a strong focus on fuel saving and on development of alternative fuels, which has eroded the fuel tax base and the effectiveness of fuel taxes to address road traffic externalities, particularly congestion.

With the rising congestion pressures on urban roads and public transport systems, Europe needs a fiscal reform in the transport sector. The reform consists in replacing, to a large extent, the fuel tax instrument by a set of distance taxes that vary by place, time, and type of vehicle. New and potentially better instruments are being introduced for trucks under the form of distance-charging and for cars under the form of congestion-charging. Distance-charging for trucks is at present mainly geared to revenue and environmental objectives and is therefore lacking the right focus. Congestion-charging for cars has the correct emphasis on congestion but needs to work on its public acceptance and on its transaction costs. Dealing with congestion will be necessary if one wants cities to continue to be the engine of economic growth.

Appendix to Table 8.1

Unless otherwise noted, all external cost information is based on the EU Handbook on External Costs of Transport (2014).

External Climate Cost (Tables 35, 36, 38 in the Handbook)
A CO_2 damage cost of 25 euro per ton was used instead of the 90 euro per ton (based on avoidance costs) of the EU Handbook. The former estimate is more in line with the cost of reducing CO_2 in other sectors of the economy. The category "urban" in the Handbook corresponds to "urban" and "local" in table 8.1, while the categories "rural" and "motorways" in the Handbook are classified as "medium to long distance" in table 8.1. The values of climate costs for type Euro-5 vehicles (cars, trucks) of medium size are shown in the table. For air transport, the values for medium flight distance (1,000-1,500 km) are used.

External Air Pollution and Noise Cost (Tables 17, 20, 28 in the Handbook)
The calculation method focuses on the monetary valuation of the explicit impact that the emissions have on human health, environment, and economic activity. The effect of emissions is constructed taking into account diffusion and dose-effect relationships as well as valuation of statistical years of life lost and health impacts. The values are obtained by adding the air pollution and noise cost. We use the values of Euro-6 and medium-sized vehicles (cars, buses, and trucks) in our table. Using the bottom-up approach, the noise costs vary greatly according to time of day and density of traffic. We take the upper bound of noise costs, which are the noise costs of thin traffic at night, from the 2008 version of the Handbook, updated for the change in overall price levels in the European Union.

Again, the category "urban" in the Handbook corresponds to "urban" and "local" in our table 8.1, while the categories "rural," "suburban," and "motorways" in the Handbook are classified as "medium to long distance" in our table 8.1.

External Accident Cost (Table 12 in the Handbook)
External accident costs are those social costs of traffic accidents, which are not covered by risk-oriented insurance premiums. Therefore, the level of external costs depends on the level of accidents and on the insurance system (on whether there is experience rating or not, and on

what is covered by insurance). The most important accident cost categories are medical costs, production losses, material damages, administrative costs, and the so called risk value as a proxy to estimate pain, grief, and suffering caused by traffic accidents in monetary values. Mainly the latter is not covered properly by the private insurance systems. The values are corrected for underreporting of the number of injuries in some EU countries.

The categories "car" and "HGV" in the Handbook correspond to "cars" and "trucks" in our table 8.1, respectively. "Motorway" and "other non-urban roads" are classified as "medium to long distance" in our table 8.1.

External Marginal Congestion Cost (Table 9 in the Handbook)

The external cost is the additional cost imposed by a user of the road network on all other users of the road network. The EU Handbook estimates of congestion costs are derived from the UK estimates based on the aggregated approach of the FORGE model, using nominal GDP per capita and the average exchange rate between the euro and the British pound for 2010. The FORGE model distinguishes several congestion bands based on the volume to capacity ratio, but no EU data on the traffic shares in each bands are available. So instead of averages across congestion bands or road and area type, we give ranges of the external congestion costs.

The categories "urban—main roads, other roads" and "metropolitan—main roads, other roads" in the Handbook correspond to "urban" in our table 8.1, while the categories "rural" and "metropolitan—motorways" in the Handbook are classified as "medium to long distance" in our table 8.1.

Wear and Tear Infrastructure Cost (Tables 48 and 51 in the Handbook)

Marginal road infrastructure costs correspond to the increase in road maintenance and repair expenditures that are induced by higher traffic levels. Heavier vehicles tend to cause more damage to the roads, whereby the degree to which an increase in weight leads to higher damage follows a power law.

The categories "other truck roads" and "other roads" in the Handbook correspond to "urban" in our table 8.1, while the category "motorways" in the Handbook is classified as "medium to long distance" in our table 8.1.

Notes

1. We thank Ian Parry for several rounds of detailed suggestions, and Herman Vollebergh, Kurt Van Dender, and the participants of the CESIfo/EC/IMF/PBL conference on "Energy Tax and Regulatory Policy in Europe: Reform Priorities and Research Needs" (Munich, November 2014) for useful comments on a first draft. We are grateful to Chau Man Fung for research assistance.

2. Although fuel tax floors imposed at the EU level through the Energy Tax Directive are generally not binding, economic theory and causal evidence suggest they increase tax rates even in countries where they are not binding (as countries react to a reduced risk of tax competition). See, for example, Parry and Vollebergh (this volume).

3. All data are based on the Statistical Handbook of the EU for 2014.

4. The carbon tax = excise + VAT on excise for motorfuels. In Belgium on October 1, 2015, and using 2,344 kg CO_2/liter of gasoline and 2.7 kg CO_2/liter of diesel, this amounts to "carbon taxes" of 318 euro/ton of CO_2 for gasoline and 192 euro/ton of CO_2 for diesel.

5. This is not represented in table 8.1.

6. For example, for the United States, Brown and Huntington (2010) suggest that the costs (not taken into account by the private sector) arising from the vulnerability of the macro-economy to oil price volatility are not especially large.

7. Several different White Papers have been published: the 1992 White Paper (market opening), the 2001 White Paper ("European Transport Policy for 2010: Time to Decide"), the 2006 White Paper ("Keep Europe Moving: A Transport Policy for Sustainable Mobility"), the 2011 White Paper ("Roadmap to a Single European Transport Area: Towards a Competitive and Resource Efficient Transport System"), and the 2013 White Paper ("Clean Power for Transport: A European Alternative Fuels Strategy").

8. Large toll roads are these days also found in Portugal, Slovakia, Slovenia, Poland, and Austria (ITF 2013).

9. VAT rates are not applied to all modes of transport. In several EU countries, there is no VAT on aviation, rail, or public bus services.

10. See Parry et al. (2014) for details and an application to many countries in the world.

11. Countries often "compensate" the lower diesel tax by imposing higher annual vehicle and ownership taxes on diesel car owners. For a formal numerical simulation model analyzing the optimal taxation of diesel and gasoline car ownership and car use, see De Borger and Mayeres (2007).

12. Taken from the EU-Transport Pocket Book 2013. The data are for 2011; they are labeled as "Environmental taxes as % of GDP—transport (non fuel)."

13. Huse (2014) reports an emission reduction of 45 percent when gasoline is replaced by ethanol from sugarcane production. Of course, there are many other environmental issues associated to the production and use of biofuels than CO_2 emissions; these are not discussed here.

14. These happened to be often large, home-produced Volvos.

15. A few papers have made a systematic (but very simplified) comparison of the relative welfare gain of different instruments to address externalities in a city. Proost and

Van Dender (2001) find that public transport optimization as the only instrument can achieve only some 30 percent of the maximum welfare gains that could achieved by a combination of pricing of cars and public transport. Basso and Silva (2014) find similar results for London; for Santiago de Chile, where buses are the dominant transport mode, they find, not surprisingly, that a policy focusing on reserved bus lanes is as good as road pricing. For non-urban transport, De Borger and Mayeres (2007) illustrate the huge welfare loss of using pricing instruments that are not time-differentiated.

16. The Goteborg toll was not accepted by the public in a referendum. It was nevertheless accepted by the local parliament, mainly because it allowed benefiting from national investment funds that match the toll revenues.

17. Transaction costs consist of the pure administration costs of a payment scheme (ranging from 10 to 50 percent of total revenues) and of the effort and time costs for users that are associated to the payment. The administration costs of a payment scheme consist of an important part of enforcement costs (identifying number plates of cars, checking whether they paid or not, sending invoices, etc.). There may be an important learning effect here.

18. In the Netherlands, there was a political majority for transforming the high fixed car charges into smarter user charges, but one of the reasons the majority broke down is the regional differentiation of the charges.

19. In London, the revenues served mainly to finance public transport. In Stockholm, the toll revenues were used for additional road infrastructure in the region. In Goteborg, the toll revenues were used for a new rail tunnel under the city.

20. See De Borger and Proost (2013) for a theoretical comparison of the two schemes and an analysis of the constraints on federal and local schemes that can improve the outcome.

21. There is good evidence for Stockholm, where the cross-price elasticity for bus is rather low, about 0.1 (Borjesson, Fung, and Proost 2015). Van Goeverden et al. (2006) report results on the introduction of free busses in Hasselt (a town in Flanders) and found that some 15 percent of the new bus users would have used a car if public transport was not free.

22. Inland freight activity by mode (EU 2014).

23. See directive 1999/62/EC followed by directives 2006/38/EC and 206/103/EC.

24. Ireland (high fixed charges per truck) and the United Kingdom (high fuel charges) are the exceptions.

References

Alcott, H., and M. Greenstone. 2012. "Is There an Energy Efficiency Gap?" *Journal of Economic Literature* 26 (1): 3-28.

Anas, A., and R. Lindsey. 2011. "Reducing Urban Road Transportation Externalities: Road Pricing in Theory and in Practice." *Review of Environmental Economics and Policy* 5 (1): 66-88.

Barla, P., and S. Proost. 2012. "Energy Efficiency Policy in a Non-Cooperative World." *Energy Economics* 34 (6): 2209-15.

Basso, L. J., and H. E. Silva. 2014. "Efficiency and Substitutability of Transit Subsidies and Other Urban Transport Policies." *American Economic Journal: Economic Policy* 6 (4): 1-33.

Borjesson, M., C.-M. Fung, and S. Proost. 2015. "Should Busses be Subsidized in Stockholm?" (Mimeo).

Brown, S. P. A., and H. G. Huntington. 2010. "Estimating U.S. Oil Security Premiums" (Discussion Paper 10-05, Washington, DC: Resources for the Future).

Calthrop, E., and S. Proost. 2003. "Environmental Pricing in Transport." In *Handbook of Transport and the Environment*, eds. D. A. Henscher and K. J. Button. Oxford, UK: Elsevier.

Copenhagen Economics. 2010. "Company Car Taxation" (Working Paper 22).

Crist, P. 2012. "Electric Vehicles Revisited—Costs, Subsidies and Prospects" (ITF Discussion Paper 2012-03). http://www.internationaltransportforum.org/jtrc/Discussion Papers/DP201203.pdf.

D'Haultfoeuille, X., P. Givord, and X. Boutin. 2013. "The Environmental Effect of Green Taxation: The Case of the French 'Bonus/Malus.'" *Economic Journal* 124: F444-80. doi: 10.1111/ecoj.12089

De Borger, B. 2009. "Commuting, Congestion Tolls and Non-Competitive Labour Markets: Optimal Congestion Pricing in a Wage Bargaining Model." *Regional Science and Urban Economics* 39 (4): 433-48.

De Borger, B., and I. Mayeres. 2007. "Optimal Taxation of Car Ownership, Car Use and Public Transport: Insights Derived from a Discrete Choice Numerical Optimization Model." *European Economic Review* 51: 1177-204.

De Borger, B., and S. Proost. 2012a. "A Political Economy Model of Road Pricing." *Journal of Urban Economics* 71 (1): 79-92.

De Borger, B., and S. Proost. 2012b. "Transport Policy Competition between Governments: A Selective Survey of the Literature." *Economics of Transportation* 1: 35-48.

De Borger, B., and S. Proost. 2013. "Traffic Externalities in Cities: The Economics of Speed Bumps, Low Emission Zones and City Bypasses." *Journal of Urban Economics* 76: 53-70.

De Borger, B., and B. Wuyts. 2011. "The Tax Treatment of Company Cars, Commuting and Optimal Congestion Taxes." *Transportation Research B* 45: 1527-44.

De Borger, B., F. Dunkerley, and S. Proost. 2007. "Strategic Investment and Pricing Decisions in a Congested Transport Corridor." *Journal of Urban Economics* 62: 294-316.

De Borger, B., S. Proost, and K. Van Dender. 2005. "Congestion and Tax Competition in a Parallel Network." *European Economic Review* 49: 213-40.

Dechezlepretre, A., and D. Popp. 2014. "Fiscal and Regulatory Instruments for Clean Technology." Paper Presented at the CESifo/EC/IMF/PBL Conference on Energy Tax and Regulatory Policy in Europe: Reform Priorities and Research Needs, Nov. 13-14, CES-IFO.

Eliasson, J. 2014. "The Stockholm Congestion Charges: An Overview" (CTS Discussion Paper 2014/7).

Eliasson, J., and S. Proost. 2015. "How Sustainable is Sustainable Transport?" *Transport Policy* 37: 92-101.

Eliasson, J., L. Hultzkranz, L. Nerhagen, and L. S. Rosqvist. 2009. "The Stockholm Congestion Charging Trial 2006: Overview of Effects." *Transportation Research A* 43 (3): 240-50.

European Commission. 1995. "Towards Fair and Efficient Pricing." COM(95) 691.

European Commission. 2006. "Keep Europe Moving: Sustainable Mobility for Our Continent." Directorate-General for Energy and Transport, Brussels, Belgium.

European Commission. 2011. "Roadmap to a Single European Transport Area: Towards a Competitive and Resource-Efficient Transport System." Directorate-General for Mobility and Transport White Paper, Brussels, Belgium.

European Commission. 2013. "Clean Power for Transport: A European Alternative Fuels Strategy." COM(2013) 17 final.

European Commission. 2014. *EU Transport in Figures Statistical Pocketbook.* doi: 10.2832/63317.

Geilenkirchen, E., G, Renes, and J. van Meerkerk. 2014. "Vergroening van de Aanschafbelasting Voor Personenauto's. Effecten op de Verkoop van Zuinige Auto's en de CO_2-uitstoot" (PBL Report 970, the Hague, Netherlands).

Grigolon, L., M. Reynaert, and F. Verboven. 2014. "Consumer Valuation of Fuel Costs and the Effectiveness of Tax Policy: Evidence from the European Car Market" (CES Discussion Paper 14.34).

Guttiérez-i-Puigarnau, E., and J. van Ommeren. 2011. "Welfare Effects of Distortionary Company Car Taxation." *International Economic Review* 52 (4): 1105-22.

Hamilton, C., and J. Eliasson. 2013. "Costs and Benefits of the European Directive on Road Tolling Interoperability." *Transportation Research C* 30: 221-38.

Harding, M. 2014. "Personal Tax Treatment of Company Cars and Commuting Expenses: Estimating the Fiscal and Environmental Costs" (OECD Taxation Working Papers, No. 20, OECD Publishing). http://dx.doi.org/10.1787/5jz14cg1s7vl-en.

Huse, C. 2014. "Fast and Furious (and Dirty): How Asymmetric Regulation May Hinder Environmental Policy." Paper Presented at the Conference on the Future of Fuel Taxes, CTS-KTH, Stockholm, Sweden, September.

Hylen, B., J. Kauppila, and E. Chong. 2013. "Road Haulage Charges and Taxes" (Discussion Paper 2013-08, International Transport Forum, Paris, France).

ICCT. 2013. *European Vehicle Market Statistics Pocketbook.* International Council on Clean Transportation, the Hague, Netherlands.

Kanbur, A., and M. Keen. 1993. "Jeux Sans Frontières: Tax Competition When Countries Differ in Size." *American Economic Review* 83: 877-92.

Kilani, M., S. Proost, and S. van der Loo. 2014. "Road Pricing and Public Transport Pricing Reform in Paris: Complements or Substitutes." *Economics of Transportation* 3: 175-87.

Kilian, L. 2008. "Exogenous Oil Shocks: How Big are They and How Much Do They Matter for the US Economy?" *The Review of Economics and Statistics* 90 (2): 216-40.

Mandell, S., and S. Proost. 2016. "Contagious Truck Distance Charges Drive Fuel Taxes to the Bottom." *Journal of Urban Economics* 93: 1-17.

Mayeres, I., and S. Proost. 2013. "The Taxation of Diesel Cars in Belgium—Revisited." *Energy Policy* 54: 33-41.

Merkert, R., A. Smith, and C. Nash. 2012. "The Measurement of Transaction Costs— Evidence from European Railways." *Journal of Transport Economics and Policy* 46 (3): 349-66.

Munk-Nielsen, A. 2014. "Diesel Cars and Environmental Policy." Paper Presented at the Conference on the Future of Fuel Taxes, CTS-KTH, Stockholm, Sweden, September.

Nordhaus, W. 2015. "Climate Clubs: Overcoming Free-Riding in International Climate Policy." *American Economic Review* 105 (4): 1339-70.

Parry, I., and K. Small. 2005. "Does Britain or the United States have the Right Gasoline Tax?" *American Economic Review* 95: 1276-89.

Parry, I., and K. Small. 2009. "Should Urban Subsidies Be Reduced?" *American Economic Review* 99 (3): 700-24.

Parry, I., D. Evans, and W. E. Oates. 2014. "Are Energy Efficiency Standards Justified?" *Journal of Environmental Economics and Management* 67: 104-25.

Parry, I., D. Heine, E. Lis, and S. Li. 2014. *Getting Energy Prices Right: From Principle to Practice.* Washington, DC, US: International Monetary Fund Publication Services.

Proost, S., and K. Van Dender. 2001. "The Welfare Impacts of Alternative Policies to Address Atmospheric Pollution in Urban Road Transport." *Regional Science and Urban Economics* 31 (4): 383-411.

Proost, S., and K. Van Dender. 2012. "Energy and Environment Challenges in the Transport Sector." *Economics of Transportation* 1: 77-87.

Proost, S., F. Dunkerley, S. Van der Loo, N. Adler, J. Bröcker, and A. Korzhenevych. 2013. "Do the Selected Trans-European Transport Investments Pass the Cost Benefit Test?" *Transportation* 41 (1): 107-32.

Teulings, K., I. Ossokina, and H. De Groot. 2014. "Welfare Benefits of Agglomeration and Worker Heterogeneity" (CES-IFO Working Paper, No. 4939).

Tirachini, A., D. A. Hensher, and S. R. Jara-Díaz. 2010. "Comparing Operator and Users Costs of Light Rail, Heavy Rail and Bus Rapid Transit over a Radial Public Transport Network." *Research in Transportation Economics* 29: 231-42.

Van Dender, K. 2003. "Transport Taxes With Multiple Trip Purposes." *Scandinavian Journal of Economics* 105: 295-310.

Van der Loo, S., and S. Proost. 2014. "The European Road Pricing Game: How to Enforce Optimal Pricing in High-Transit Countries under Asymmetric Information." *Journal of Transport Economics and Policy* 47 (3): 399-418.

Van Goeverden, C., P. Rietveld, J. Koelemeijer, and P. Peeters. 2006. "Subsidies in Public Transport." *European Transport* 32: 5-25.

Van Meerkerk, J., G. Renes, and G. Ridder. 2014. "Greening the Dutch Car Fleet: The Role of Differentiated Sales Taxes" (PBL Working Paper, The Hague, Netherlands).

Vierth, I., and H. Schleusser. 2012. "Impacts of Different Environmentally Differentiated Truck Charges on Mileage, Fleet Composition and Emissions in Germany and Sweden" (CTS Working Paper 2012:22).

Vollebergh, H., and E. van der Werf. 2014. "The Role of Standards in Eco-Innovation: Lessons for Policymakers." *Review of Environmental Economics and Policy* 8 (2): 230-48.

Weismann, P. 2013. "The Genesis of the Eurovignette Directive." *European Transport* 53: Paper No. 2.

Weitzman, M. 1974. "Prices versus Quantities." *Review of Economic Studies* 41 (4): 477-91.

Wolff, H., and L. Perry. 2014. "Keep Your Clunker in the Suburb: Low Emission Zones and Adoption of Green Vehicles." *Economic Journal* 124: F481-F512.

A Comment on "Tax and Regulatory Policies for European Transport: Getting There, But in the Slow Lane"

Kurt Van Dender[1]

De Borger and Proost discuss the evolution of road transport pricing in the European Union, holding it against the yardstick of short-run marginal cost pricing, i.e., alignment of prices with marginal costs, including marginal external costs. They observe progress toward policies inspired by this principle, but note that progress is slow and that risks of tax competition or tax exporting require coordinating policies at the level of the Union. The way forward is to continue to move from vehicle and fuel taxes toward distance-based charges, with time- and place-based differentiation for congestion costs, for both cars and trucks.

The discussion touches on a great variety of important and interesting issues connected to transport pricing and transport policy more broadly. One gripe in that respect would be that better referencing would have increased the value of the work, or alternatively, that the paper should have been twice as long. Comments could be very extensive too, but I limit myself to remarks on two of the main themes, namely the role of improving transport prices in broader transport policy and the interaction between fuel taxes and external costs of air pollution and congestion.

1. The Merits and Limits of Marginal Social Cost Pricing

The paper explains what marginal social cost pricing means in the road transport sector, paying little attention to the context in which the principle is applied. Context matters, however, and largely ignoring it may lead to overstating the potential to improve welfare from price reform alone.

The argumentation for marginal social cost pricing is a direct application of the principles of welfare economics. Transport prices should foster efficiency, which means they should be in line with marginal social cost, which in turn means that marginal external costs should be charged on top of market prices.[2] Once this is accomplished, the job is done, as far as the use of available infrastructure and technologies is concerned—whatever the result in terms of traffic volumes, modal split, and levels of externalities, this result is fine because the prices are efficient and therefore the outcome is efficient too (hence the statement, for example, that modal split should not be a policy objective). In the longer run, decisions on infrastructure provision need to be guided by "unbiased assessment of needs" and support for research and development of "cleaner vehicles" is needed.

Arguing for efficient use of long-lived assets, e.g., transport infrastructure, through prices in the short and medium run makes sense as it implies getting maximal benefits out of scarce and lumpy resources and allows limiting environmental costs. However, developing the principle will only take one so far with policy preparation, and the apparent indifference as to what happens once efficient prices are implemented may not be tenable. Some additional points to consider are as follows:

- A standard relevant remark is that the distribution of benefits matters, not only the total benefits. The mantra that better policy instruments than transport pricing policies exist to pursue distributional objectives holds true in principle, but is not sufficient to justify abstracting from distributional impacts of transport policies in practice. Public debate about the implementation of distance or congestion pricing is more about who benefits and who does not than about technical design or even impacts on congestion; policy design therefore needs to address direct impacts of pricing reforms and needs to consider potential compensation mechanisms (or justify the absence thereof).
- The policy message that "there is too much emphasis on climate and energy objectives in the transport sector" is not fully justified by the analysis. The evidence presented in the paper supports the view that the impact of climate and energy policy objectives on short-run marginal cost prices is smaller than often thought, in the sense that other marginal external costs in some circumstances are higher. It does not follow, however, that they weigh too heavily in transport policy as a whole. The marginal external cost estimate of climate change used in the paper reflects current low end values of

climate damage costs of a ton of CO_2 emissions, and the estimate is the current value on rising (real) price path of CO_2 emissions. Higher values will therefore apply in the future, but since this may apply for other external costs as well, it does not immediately follow that the relative importance of climate objectives in road transport will rise even if their absolute relevance to the sector will increase. However, other ways of determining climate policy targets exist, including those that define carbon budgets (whether equivalent to those based on marginal external costs or not). Some of these emphasize the need to transform the energy basis of modern economies in order to reduce reliance on carbon-intensive fuels drastically, or even entirely by the end of the century. This, in fact, is what commonly accepted 2°C temperature increase (or less) targets require. Still a different way of stating the point is that not all currently know fossil fuel reserves should be used if the 2°C goal is to be attained.[3]

A quick glance at the history of road transport in the face of energy price changes suggests that, while fuel use clearly is lower when or where prices are higher, past price changes alone have not been sufficient to trigger transformational change in the sense of drastic reductions of fossil fuel use. This likely will hold for the near future, as current carbon values do not imply strong transport increases in many countries. Hence, a reformulation of the policy message would be that "short-run marginal cost pricing is not sufficient as a policy instrument for ambitious climate and energy policies in the transport sector." This retains important points made in the paper, including that congestion and air pollution costs are high and better policy is needed to reduce them, that pricing policies are very well suited to address some external costs of road transport, notably congestion, and that marginal abatement costs in transport presently often are higher than in other sectors.[4] It also indicates, however, that pricing is only part of the solution for some problems, including climate change.

- Getting the prices right is essential for making road transport more efficient, i.e., less wasteful. The need for other policies is partially recognized in the paper, with recommendations that long term infrastructure decisions should be guided by cost-benefit analysis,[5] that research and development for "cleaner vehicles" is required,[6] that preferential fiscal treatment of company car use should be scaled back, and that fiscal deductibility of commuting expenses is not justified under all circumstances. But policies need to be aligned more broadly, and doing so will increase the scope for adapting behavior when prices change. For example, are regulatory, governance, and institutional arrangements sufficiently conducive to innovation in the sector, technological or otherwise? Casual observation suggests they are not, and that instead there are all kinds of impediments to change. One example concerns the use of information technology to encourage car-sharing or the provision of paratransit services. Estimates of the capacity of such services to reduce costs, including external costs, while maintaining or improving quality of service (ITF 2015) may be optimistic but suggest possibilities of deep change. By contrast, the degree of experimentation and the pace of change in transport supply models are limited. This is not a matter of prices alone, even if markets are sufficiently competitive that pre-tax prices are close to marginal resource costs. The supply side should not be ignored, and this becomes all the more important when the longer run and deeper change are considered: facilitating change or steering it requires policy now and is in that sense as pressing a policy issue as is getting the prices right.

2. Fuel Taxes to Capture Marginal External Costs of Road Transport

In section 2.1, the authors reproduce Parry et al.'s (2014) formula for the second-best gasoline tax. The tax per liter equals the carbon damage per liter plus the driving-related costs per kilometer scaled down by the degree to which charging the latter provokes more fuel efficiency instead of less driving. Driving-related costs include congestion, accidents, and air pollution costs. The following points, which are all touched upon in the text but with different emphasis, may be worth noting:

• Air pollution costs are considered to be driving related, but—as is recognized and discussed at some length for gasoline and diesel—they differ between fuel types. The second-best fuel tax formula, including the air pollution component, ideally would be indexed by fuel type as driving-related costs differ between them (in contrast to what is mentioned in the paper).

   Considering air pollution costs as mainly driving related makes sense when emissions are regulated on a per kilometer basis, as is the case in the European Union for cars but not for trucks. How-

ever, when on-road performance differs from test-cycle performance and when the gaps differ systematically between fuel types
(as the paper notes is the case), then including a direct fuel tax
component (so, not scaled down) to reflect pollution costs becomes
increasingly relevant. This is all the more the case when the
driving-related component does not vary between more and less
densely populated areas.

• The driving-related component of fuel costs includes a congestion
cost, which presumably is averaged somehow over the territory
to which the fuel tax applies. The paper mentions—this deserves
to be highlighted—that this strongly limits the capability of prices
to tackle congestion, because of the strong variation of congestion
costs over time and place. Given that large shares of traffic volume
take place where there is little congestion,[7] the best uniform congestion charge (which is different from the average external congestion
cost) will be rather ineffective at curbing congestion where it is
strong.

Complementary local ("bottom-up") congestion pricing systems
can remedy this situation, and are in that sense a more straightforward option than comprehensive than nation-wide "top-down"
systems that combine distance-based charges with congestion
charges where appropriate. A concern with such reforms is that
the revenues be used productively. Standard public finance recommendations to use revenues to cut pre-existing distortionary taxes
may not be very practical when revenues are raised locally, and
earmarking the full revenues for particular purposes risks creating
inefficient spending patterns.

A uniform charge to reflect average congestion costs implies a
charge higher than marginal external costs where there is little or
no congestion. This inefficiency may be limited, however, because
raising revenue from driving may be less economically costly than
raising it via other means (including transport energy, as driving is
less elastic than energy use for driving).

Notes

1. The opinions expressed in this paper are the author's and not necessarily those of the
OECD.

2. This rule of thumb is widely used in recent literature on the subject, and it pays little
attention to the potential need for optimal deviations from Pigouvian charges (which have
been studied extensively in the public finance literature) except through acknowledgments

that revenue-raising considerations can sometimes justify taxes above marginal external costs in transport. Interactions with other tax distortions receive more attention in discussions of the use of revenues from Pigouvian charges. The rule of thumb is supported by a discussion in Fosgerau and Van Dender (2013).

3. See, for example, McGlade and Ekins (2015), who find that a third of oil reserves, half of gas reserves, and over 80 percent of coal reserves should remain unused until 2050 to meet the 2°C target.

4. A detailed analysis of taxes on energy use in 41 countries, representing around 80 percent of global energy use and of CO_2 emissions from energy use, shows that taxes on energy use in transport are on average much higher than in other sectors (OECD 2015b). Considering price signals from emissions trading systems in addition to those from specific taxes on energy use does not change the conclusion: the effective carbon rate is between €5 and €30 per ton of CO_2 for 48 percent of road transport emissions in the 41 countries and above €30 for 46 percent of transport emissions. For CO_2 emissions from other energy use, the rate is above €5 per ton for 19 percent of emissions, and it is zero for 70 percent of emissions. The indication of where to look for cheap abatement in the near terms seems rather strong, even if abstraction is made of other carbon abatement policies than taxes and trading systems (OECD 2015a; 2016).

5. But with what value of carbon or what carbon abatement objective?

6. But what are "clean vehicles," and why is there a case for directing technological change—i.e., why is pricing carbon not enough to get the direction right while the paper in general relies strongly on the power of pricing externalities alone?

7. Data for the United Kingdom show that three-quarters of traffic take place under conditions where marginal external congestion costs are less than three cents per kilometer (UK Department for Transport 2014).

References

Fosgerau, M., and K. Van Dender. 2013. "Road Pricing with Complications." *Transportation* 40 (3): 479-503.

ITF. 2015. "Urban Mobility System Upgrade." Corporate Partnership Board Report, Paris, France.

McGlade, C., and P. Ekins. 2015. "The Geographical Distribution of Fossil Fuels Unused when Limiting Global Warming to 2°C." *Nature* 517: 187-90.

OECD. 2015a. "Effective Carbon Rates on Energy in OECD & Selected Partner Economies." Paris, France.

OECD. 2015b. *Taxing Energy Use 2015: OECD and Selected Partner Economies.* Paris, France: OECD Publishing.

OECD. 2016. *Effective Carbon Rates: Pricing CO_2 Through Taxes and Emissions Trading Systems.* Paris, France: OECD Publishing.

Parry, I. W. H., D. Heine, E. Lis, and S. Li. 2014. *Getting Energy Prices Right: From Principles to Practice.* Washington DC: International Monetary Fund.

UK Department for Transport. 2014. *WebTAG Data Book.*

9 Carbon Pricing and Taxation: Overcoming Obstacles to Policy Reform in the EU

Stephen Smith[1]

Key Points for Policymakers

- Higher carbon prices or energy taxes will have a crucial role to play in achieving the major changes in energy consumption that will be needed to tackle climate change.
- Households will need to face higher energy bills, and this will provoke opposition. Part of this will focus on the impact on poorer households, for whom energy costs can constitute a particularly large part of household spending, at least in some EU countries.
- The regressive impact of higher taxes on domestic energy can be offset by a range of possible measures, so that poorer income groups are as at least as well off—or indeed better off—than before.
- Where possible, energy tax revenues should be used to cut rates of other taxes (such as income tax, payroll taxes, or VAT) to improve labor market incentives, but the benefit this gives to poor households will be small, since they pay little tax.
- Poorer households receiving social benefits will receive some compensation for higher energy prices, if rates of social benefits are automatically indexed to consumer prices. Discretionary increases in social benefits can target further help to poor households. However, such increases in public spending on benefits mean that less of the revenue from energy taxes is available for more general tax cuts.
- Even after extensive compensation, some poor households will still be worse off, because they have very high levels of energy spending. Sick and elderly people may have particularly high energy needs. Targeted assistance to improve the energy efficiency of their homes will be the most effective way of relieving these households of the burden of high energy taxes.

- Concerns that high energy taxes on business could harm industrial competitiveness have proved a major policy barrier to higher energy taxation. The best response to these concerns is to promote the fullest possible international coordination of carbon pricing and taxation measures.
- Where this cannot be achieved, businesses operating in energy-intensive, trade-exposed (EITE) sectors will face a loss of competitiveness. Less energy-intensive businesses do not face similar problems: once account is taken of exchange rate adjustments and the use of energy tax revenues to reduce other taxes, they may well benefit overall.
- Adverse effects on EITE sectors can be reduced through targeted compensation (e.g., grandfathering tradeable permits), though this has a high cost to public budgets, reducing the scope for efficiency-enhancing tax cuts.
- Exempting EITE sectors from the effects of an energy tax would mean that the largest industrial energy users do not face an incentive to cut energy use and emissions.
- Border tax adjustments would be a more efficient way of reducing the pressure on EITE sectors, facing competition from countries that have not introduced similar measures. However, they risk undermining the open international trading system, and would be difficult to define and implement.
- For practical purposes it will be desirable for carbon taxes to be increased gradually, to avoid large and abrupt effects on the competitiveness of EITE sectors. A steady and predictable escalation of carbon prices and taxes can provide effective incentives for industry to make long-term investments in carbon abatement, while giving time for gradual adjustments in sectoral output and employment.

1. Introduction

An effective policy response to the challenge of climate change will require far-reaching changes in patterns of energy production and consumption. This should include a radical change in the pattern of power generation, reducing Europe's heavy reliance on carbon-intensive fossil fuels. At the same time, significant changes in energy consumption will need to be achieved. If these are to be achieved without an excessive economic burden, it is essential that individual energy users face appropriate incentives to select the least-cost pattern of measures. Energy pricing and taxation will have a crucial role to play in guiding the individual decisions of many millions of energy users—both businesses and households. This is far better than relying on bureaucratic regulation of technologies, production processes, and products that would be less effective (some opportunities for reducing emissions, like driving less, cannot be regulated), more costly (incremental abatement costs may differ widely across programs), and pose the risk of a steady sclerosis of vital economic processes of change and innovation (the same sclerosis that, in a more dramatic form, proved the undoing of the centrally planned economies of central and eastern Europe in the 1970s and 1980s).

Many fiscal and regulatory reforms will be needed that will impact energy prices—in some cases raising prices across the board, in others removing unwarranted discrepancies in prices and taxes across different users and sectors. This paper looks at social and economic obstacles that may impede these reforms, and possible strategies to overcome these obstacles.

Some progress in energy price reform can be achieved through measures, first, to dismantle perverse incentives that already exist within the European economies, especially subsidies that encourage the production and use of carbon-intensive fuels. The aggregate value of these subsidies in the European Union has been estimated at some €39 billion in 2012 (OECD 2013).[2] This will, of course, be far from straightforward, as there are powerful economic lobbies that benefit from the status quo. However, within the European Union at least, existing commitments—in the form of the already-agreed rules on subsidy and the internal market—can strengthen the hands of reforming governments.

This is less the case when we turn to the need to ensure that carbon prices are set at an appropriate level. While the mechanism of the EU ETS is established and proven in day-to-day operation, it will need to achieve sustained, stable, and higher prices if it is to drive the required changes in energy consumption and production patterns. Through the ETS, this can be achieved only by permanently reducing the quantity of allowances so that they have a sustained scarcity value. The broad consensus of climate policy modelling suggests that within the next decade carbon prices will need to rise to €30 or more, rather than the current level of €10 or less, and to rise steadily thereafter.[3] Such a rise in EU allowance prices would be likely to provoke concerns about adverse impacts on households—especially poorer

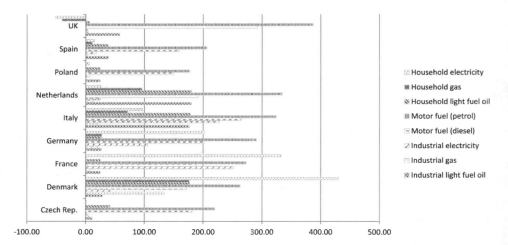

Figure 9.1
Existing taxes on energy sold to industry and households, expressed in terms of euros per ton of CO_2

Source: Author's estimates, based on data from IEA (2015) Energy Prices and Taxes, Quarterly Statistics, Fourth Quarter 2014, and IEA (2014) CO_2 Emissions from Fuel Combustion, International Energy Agency, Paris.

Notes: The estimates include all taxes on the sale of energy products, except VAT. Carbon emissions associated with electricity consumption are calculated on the basis of the average input fuel mix in the relevant country.

households—and industry—especially firms exposed to intense international competition.

In sectors not covered by the EU ETS it will be important to ensure that energy taxes provide a broadly equivalent incentive to reduce energy consumption and carbon emissions. The current situation is one in which some uses of energy are vastly more burdened by taxation than others—leading to an excessive burden of abatement in some sectors, when equivalent reductions in carbon emissions could be achieved much more cheaply in other sectors where taxes are currently too low to stimulate abatement.

This unevenness in existing taxation is illustrated in figure 9.1, which shows, for a number of EU Member States, the wide differences in existing fuel taxes both between fuels and across countries, when expressed per ton of CO_2.[4] Motor fuels are taxed much more heavily in relation to carbon content than are industrial and household purchases of fossil fuels, fuels purchased by industry tend to be taxed much less than fuels purchased by households, and there is a general tendency for gas to be taxed less than mineral oil fuels. In some countries the taxation of electricity per ton of CO_2 is very high relative to other household and industry purchases of energy, although some of the highest rates are in countries which generate most electricity from non-fossil-fuel sources, where even modest excise taxes on electricity can translate into a very high implicit tax per ton of CO_2.

Much of what needs to be done to incentivize reductions in energy use and greenhouse gas emissions has been well-understood for some considerable time. It is now more than two decades since the European Union brought forward proposals for a carbon-energy tax to tackle climate change, and a number of Member States began to introduce domestic carbon taxes. While some important progress has been made—most notably in the form of the EU ETS—other measures have stalled, including the 2011 proposals to amend the EU Energy Tax Directive, which would have taxed motor and heating fuels according to energy content and carbon dioxide emissions.

Powerful opposition to systematic environmental pricing of energy has been present throughout the policy debate, focussing on two groups of issues:

- **Distributional effects on households.** The impact of higher energy prices on household living standards, and in particular on the living standards of poorer households. Certain components of households' energy consumption, especially energy for domestic heating, have the demand characteristics of a necessity—a very low income elasticity—so that the taxation of domestic power has a strongly regressive impact on household budgets. Concerns about the adverse impact of energy taxes on the poor can be a powerful focus for political opposition to policy reform.
- **Effects on industry costs and competitiveness.** Higher energy prices to industrial users of energy have prompted widely articulated concerns about damage to the competitiveness of businesses exposed to international competition. In a number of countries where carbon pricing or other energy taxes have been proposed or introduced, industrial opposition focusing on the harm to competitiveness has forced major modifications to be made, sharply reducing the level of energy taxes paid by industry. In Sweden, for example, the substantial carbon tax introduced in 1991 taxed industrial energy users at only half the rate applying to other users; intense industrial lobbying led to a further reductions in the tax paid by industry only two years later.

This paper considers the extent to which these concerns are likely to constitute a serious obstacle to policy reform, and the scope required to overcome this opposition. It begins with an overview of the evidence relating to these two issues. To what extent are these widely articulated concerns a reflection of real, objective, obstacles to higher carbon prices? Where this is the case, what policy responses could ameliorate these adverse effects, and at what cost?

As the discussion will show, the economic substance of the distributional barriers to higher carbon prices can be overcome at relatively limited cost. Holding down energy prices is a highly inefficient way to help low-income families, as the bulk of the benefits accrue to higher-income groups. Adverse effects on industrial competitiveness, while harder to offset, will be significant only in a small number of sectors that are both energy intensive and exposed to price-sensitive international competition. If carbon tax rates are increased gradually over time, and similar policy measures are adopted in other major economies, industrial adjustment problems are likely to be limited in scale. Even where they lack real substance, however, these issues are likely to remain prominent in public debate. This paper aims to give a quantitative sense of the impacts, and some practical suggestions for overcoming these obstacles to carbon pricing reforms.

2. Distributional Effects on Households

This section provides an overview of the impact of carbon pricing on households, focusing in particular on concerns that there would be a relatively high burden on poorer households. The first section summarizes evidence on the scale of the effects. The focus here is primarily on taxes on household energy consumption (electricity and gas used for heating, lighting, etc.), but a comparison is made with the impact of taxes on motor fuels, which are already heavily taxed. The second section then discusses the extent to which measures could be identified to offset the adverse impact of carbon pricing on the living standards of the poorest households.[5]

2.1 Evidence on Distributional Effects

The energy tax changes that would be required to achieve a systematic carbon price for household consumption across different fuels will depend on the existing level of taxation of these fuels. As figure 9.1 shows, motor fuels are already subject to very heavy taxation in most

EU countries, generally well above €100 per ton of CO_2, and in some countries much higher. This may already equal or exceed the level of taxation that would be justified by the climate damage arising from motor fuel use, although there may be other reasons for high taxation of motor fuels (local air pollution and other environmental damage from fuel combustion, reducing traffic congestion, etc.). Generally, though, it is unlikely that systematic taxation of energy in relation to carbon content would require large increases in the taxation of motor fuels. Other household fuels, including heating fuels such as gas and heating oil, are much less heavily taxed[6] in many EU countries, and systematic taxation on the basis of carbon content would require substantial tax increases on some or all of these fuels. The tax increases necessary to price energy systematically in relation to its carbon content would therefore vary between fuels, and across countries, depending on their existing tax structure.

Most countries will need to increase the level of taxation on heating fuels such as gas quite significantly, to equalize carbon prices between household consumption of gas and electricity (which in some countries is subject both to an excise on electricity sold to households, and also bears an effective carbon price because carbon used to generate electricity is already priced within the EU ETS).[7] In addition, countries such as the United Kingdom, which apply a reduced rate of VAT to domestic energy, are in effect subsidizing energy consumption relative to consumer spending in general, and eliminating this subsidy by applying VAT to household energy at the standard rate would further increase the cost of household energy. These substantial increases in taxation on household purchases of energy will be the focus of most concern about the impact on households of tax reforms to implement systematic carbon pricing of energy.

The distributional impact across households of higher taxes or other policies that increase energy prices will reflect a number of elements:

- First, the impact of higher energy taxes on households will reflect the pattern of household spending on gas, electricity, and other household fuels as well as household spending on motor fuels. The effects are likely to be broadly proportional to the level of existing energy spending by households at different levels of income. While higher prices may encourage households to consume less energy—and indeed the whole point of higher taxes on household energy spending would be to provoke such behavioral

responses—these changes in consumption are likely to be relatively modest and widely spread, and will not substantially change
the pattern of household spending across households with different income levels and other characteristics.[8]

- The size of the effects on household bills will be affected by the
  extent to which taxes levied on energy production or supply
  are passed on in higher power bills and higher retail prices for
  motor fuel. Some part of the additional tax may be incident on
  suppliers and reflected in lower margins, and some part may be
  passed back to the ultimate owners of fossil fuel energy resources.
  Most estimates typically assume full pass-through to consumers,
  though there is a certain amount of evidence that the adjustment
  to this is not immediate, and that in the short term at least, less
  than 100 percent of additional energy taxes may be passed on to
  households.

- Household living standards will also be affected by indirect
  impacts arising through higher energy costs to industry, both
  directly and through the input-output structure. Where this effect
  has been investigated (e.g., by Symons et al. 2002) the distributional impact of a carbon tax passed through the input-output
  structure of industry and into the prices of all consumer goods is—
  unsurprisingly—more diffuse, and more proportional to overall
  spending, than the direct taxation of household energy purchases.
  Again, there is a question about how rapidly the increases in producers' energy costs feed through into higher product prices.

- Other fiscal instruments, such as emissions trading, would be
  likely to have similar effects to those of a tax. In the long run, the
  effects on electric power prices, for example, are likely to be very
  similar regardless of whether emissions trading allowances are
  distributed to firms for free or auctioned; in either case, the market
  price of the allowances is an opportunity cost which increases the
  marginal cost of electricity supply, and this will pass through into
  electricity prices for both household and industrial energy users.

- Many of these effects will be broadly the same, regardless of
  whether the increased tax is levied per unit of energy or per unit of
  carbon. However, a carbon tax would induce shifts in the pattern
  of energy use, including shifts away from the most heavily taxed
  fossil fuels in power generation, which would tend to dampen the
  effects of the tax on consumer energy prices to a certain extent.

The distributional effects on households can be analyzed from various different perspectives—according to household size, composition, and the age of household members, as well as by measures of household living standards. When assessing the distributional impact of taxes across households with different standards of living, two approaches can be adopted, classifying households into "rich" and "poor" either on the basis of their annual income or their total annual spending. Which of these approaches gives a better indication of household living standards is unsettled, although it is generally accepted that, where households face fluctuating incomes, and can save and borrow to smooth their consumption over periods of temporarily high or low income, household expenditure may give a better indication of long-term living standards than household income. This methodological choice makes a substantial difference to the estimated distributional incidence of energy taxes (Poterba 1989).[9]

Figures 9.2 and 9.3 summarize the overall distributional impact of taxes on each of the three main components of household energy spending in EU countries—motor fuels, electric power, and heating fuels (predominantly gas). The estimates are based on results from a recent study by Flues and Thomas (2015) of the distributional effects of existing energy taxes in OECD countries. The presentation in figures 9.2 and 9.3 aims to characterize the distributional impact of taxes on energy spending by showing how the percentage burden of the tax on each decile differs from the average burden across all households. The average percentage burden of the tax is set equal to 100, and values above 100 indicate the extent to which the burden exceeds the average for all households; these index values for each decile are then averaged across the 18 EU countries for which data are available. An index value rising with increasing income indicates a tax with a progressive distributional incidence, and a declining index value indicates a regressive distributional impact.

In figure 9.2 the relative burden of tax on rich and poor households is assessed against the yardstick of household current income. Taxes on heating fuel and electricity appear quite sharply regressive. For example, the percentage of income taken in electricity tax is on average some 80 percent higher in the poorest income decile than the average percentage, while the richest decile pays only half the average percentage of income in tax. The distributional pattern of motor fuel taxes is more complex, initially falling, then rising, then falling again with increasing income.

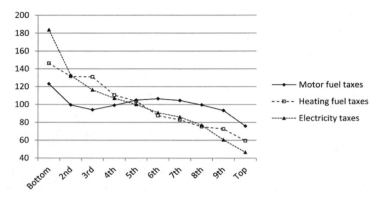

Figure 9.2
Distributional characteristics of energy taxes–income measure

Source: Author's calculations, based on data in Flues and Thomas (2015), tables 3, 5, and 8.

Notes: This shows, for each of the three energy products, the average household tax payment as a percentage of income for the relevant decile, relative to the corresponding all-decile average (set equal to 100). Households are classified into deciles on the basis of household income. The data are based on household surveys conducted in different years from 2008–2012, and are an unweighted average of 18 EU countries.

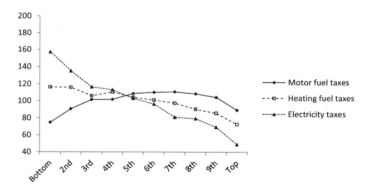

Figure 9.3
Distributional characteristics of energy taxes–expenditure measure

Source: Author's calculations, based on data in Flues and Thomas (2015), tables 4, 6, and 9.

Notes: This shows, for each of the three energy products, the average household tax payment as a percentage of household total expenditure for the relevant decile, relative to the corresponding all-decile average (set equal to 100). Households are classified into deciles on the basis of household expenditure. The data are based on household surveys conducted in different years from 2008–2012 and are an unweighted average of 18 EU countries.

Looking at the same taxes and households, but analyzing distributional impact in terms of household expenditure (figure 9.3) rather than
income shows much the same picture for taxes on electricity and household heating fuels. From this perspective, too, taxes on domestic energy
spending are, on average, clearly regressive across EU countries (though
the detailed analysis by Flues and Thomas (2015) shows some variation
between countries). The burden of tax on motor fuel, however, looks
rather different from the pattern seen in figure 9.2, especially the relative burden of tax borne by the poorest households. Across the bottom
half of the distribution, taxes on motor fuels would in fact appear progressive, with the average tax burden rising as a percentage of expenditure up to the seventh decile, and only declining at higher incomes.
Which of the two analyses gives the most accurate picture of the distributional impact of motor fuel taxes may be disputed, but it seems likely
that classifying households by income brings many more car owners
(and hence motor fuel purchasers) into the bottom decile; some of these
may be experiencing temporary fluctuations in income, and their car
ownership and consumption patterns may well be indicative of an
expectation that their longer-term income position will be higher.

Some broad conclusions may be drawn from these results and other
research literature on the distributional impact of energy taxes:[10]

- Taxes on household energy consumption (gas, electricity, coal, etc.)
  tend to be regressive, although the strength of the effect varies
  between countries, reflecting climate factors and the characteristics of the housing stock. The regressive effect seems particularly
  sharp—and to have strong political resonance—in cold, damp
  countries such as the United Kingdom, which in addition has a
  disproportionately old and poorly insulated housing stock (Smith
  1992).
- By contrast, taxes on motor fuels have a neutral or progressive
  distributional impact in many countries (Santos and Catchesides
  2005; Sterner 2012). There are significant variations across countries,
  reflecting different patterns of settlement, the availability of public
  transport, etc.
- There are also wide variations within income groups (Smith 1992;
  Healy and Clinch 2004; Ekins and Dresner 2005; Advani et al. 2013).
  The unemployed, sick, and elderly tend to have higher domestic
  energy consumption than working households with a similar level
  of income, reflecting higher needs for heating (at home during the

day, more sensitive to temperature, etc.). These variations may be as important for equity as variation across income groups.

2.2   Offsetting Policies

While the burden of taxes on carbon or energy, considered alone, may have a regressive distribution across households, the full implications for distributional equity need to take account of how the revenues from the tax will be used. Ultimately, the distributional impact that matters is that of the tax and benefit system as a whole, and if taxes on carbon or energy increase the relative burden of taxation on poorer households, this can be neutralized by using the revenues to make changes to other taxes or social benefits with a broadly offsetting pro-poor distributional impact.

Poorer households will benefit from some compensation for higher energy prices if social insurance benefits and other forms of public assistance are automatically indexed in line with increases in retail prices. Typically, however, this will only partially offset the higher costs of energy, as the price indices used to uprate benefits generally reflect the consumption "basket" of an average household, rather than poorer households, for whom energy costs would be more heavily weighted (Crawford, Smith, and Webb 1993; Callan et al. 2009). For example, in a study of a possible package of energy tax increases in the United Kingdom, Advani et al. (2013) find that even in the poorest income decile—comprising households who are heavily dependent on income from social benefits—indexation would only compensate for half the additional tax burden. How much compensation is delivered through benefit indexation will vary between countries, depending on the contribution of social benefits to household incomes.

Further compensation to poorer households could be made through discretionary increases in benefit rates, over and above the effects of indexation. To limit the amount of revenue that would be used up in providing this compensation, it could be targeted on those benefits that are predominantly received by the very poorest households, although raising the rates of "means-tested" benefits—those paid only to households whose income falls below some low-income threshold—can exacerbate problems of work incentives for households with incomes around the qualifying threshold.

The downside to paying compensation through benefit changes and other forms of lump-sum compensation is not just that it would be very expensive in terms of its impact on the public budget. It also fails to maximize the potential efficiency gains that could be achieved by using the revenue from taxes on energy or carbon to reduce the rates of existing distortionary taxes, including existing taxes on labor income, income from savings, and investment. Existing taxes impose significant distortionary costs on the economy, and these adverse effects are largely driven by the *marginal rates* at which these taxes are levied, rather than by the overall level of taxation. The efficiency benefits for the economy as a whole will typically be maximized where the revenues from energy taxes are used to cut the marginal rates at which other taxes are levied, including the marginal rate of taxes on income (income tax and payroll taxes) and on general spending (such as VAT).

However, reducing the rates of existing taxes will not, in general, give much compensation to the poor. The poorest households pay little income tax, and would therefore derive little benefit from reductions in income tax rates. As a result, there is a very sharp equity: efficiency trade-off in how the revenue is used. Lump-sum compensation through benefit changes is more effective at targeting compensation to poorer households, while using the revenue to finance tax cuts offers greater benefits in terms of economic efficiency.

- This trade-off is illustrated in figure 9.4, which shows simulated household payments of a carbon tax in the United Kingdom, across households classified by decile groups of household disposable income.
- A tax levied at the sterling equivalent of €30 per ton (without any offsetting reductions in other taxes on energy) would impose an additional tax burden per household of about £210 per annum on average (equivalent to about 1.6 percent of the existing burden of taxation on the average UK household). Using the entire carbon tax revenue to finance a lump-sum revenue return to all households would be more than enough to compensate for the additional payments of the poorest five decile groups, reflecting the fact that household spending on domestic energy and transport is lower in absolute (£ per annum) terms among poorer households than among the rich, even though it may take a higher share of their total income.
- Using the same total revenue instead to finance cuts in tax rates gives a very different pattern of revenue return, with the bulk of the benefits accruing to better-off households. The poorest households pay very little in most taxes, especially income taxes, and therefore benefit little from any reduction in tax rates, and, on average,

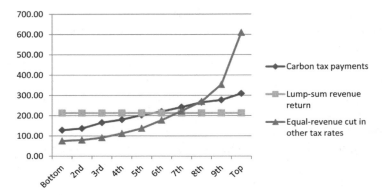

Figure 9.4
The distribution across household income groups of a carbon tax at €30 per ton, levied on household energy and transport, and two equal-cost schemes of compensation using the carbon tax revenues

Sources: Author's estimates, based on household carbon footprint data from Hargreaves et al. (2013), figure 9.3, and household tax data from ONS (2014).

Notes: The tax is assumed to apply at the sterling equivalent of €30 per ton of CO_2 to all purchases of household energy (gas, electricity, etc.) and motor fuels, and that the full burden of carbon taxation of the fuel used for public transport, including air transport, is passed on to households in higher prices. It is assumed that no offsetting reductions are made in the rates of existing taxes, such as those on motor fuels, or in the EU ETS carbon allowance costs borne by the power generation sector and aviation. The reductions in other taxes are assumed to take the form of equal proportionate reductions in the rates of all direct and indirect taxes paid by households, with an aggregate revenue cost equal to the additional revenue raised from the carbon tax.

households in the bottom two-thirds of the income distribution would pay more in carbon tax than they would receive through reductions in other taxes. Significant gains from the overall package would, however, be made by the richest two decile groups, who would benefit much more from the reduction in tax rates than they would have paid in additional energy taxes. Using the revenue from a carbon tax to finance reductions in the marginal rates of existing taxes may have important efficiency benefits, but using the entire revenue in this way would exacerbate the regressive distributional impact of the energy tax.

A further issue concerns the effectiveness of any compensation—whether changes in benefit rates or tax cuts—in compensating households who are relatively high energy users. Some disadvantaged households may be particularly high consumers of energy: for example, the sick and elderly may need warmer homes than the average, and the unemployed may be at home for much more of the day than people with jobs. The analysis up to this point has considered the net impact of energy taxes and compensation on the average position of households in the lowest income deciles. However, compensation that leaves the group as a whole no worse off may nonetheless fail to fully compensate a significant proportion of households within the group. How far this is a genuine problem, reflecting differences in households' needs for energy spending, and how far it simply reflects differences in preferences is difficult to assess.

Advani et al. (2013) simulate the impact of a possible package of energy tax increases in the United Kingdom, and show how even a very substantial and carefully targeted package of compensating adjustments in benefit rates can nonetheless leave a significant number of poorer households worse off than before the imposition of an energy tax. For example, they consider a package of additional targeted support through increases in social benefits, over and above the effects of automatic indexation, sufficient to ensure that on average households in the bottom three income deciles are fully compensated for the additional energy tax payments. Taken together with automatic indexation this absorbs nearly 60 percent of the energy tax revenues, but despite this substantial cost, almost half the households in the bottom three income deciles would still be net losers from the overall package, experiencing a net loss of at least £50 per year.

In parallel with measures to compensate disadvantaged households for higher energy costs, there would be a case for using some of the revenue to address the reasons for particularly high energy consumption by some poor households (e.g., through better home insulation) (Scott 1996; Brechling and Smith 1994). There has been persistent policy concern about the possibility of market failures in the supply or take-up of home insulation, energy efficient appliances, or other energy efficiency investments. If market failures in energy efficiency investment are particularly concentrated amongst low-income households or other vulnerable groups, this may tend to exacerbate the distributional cost of reducing energy consumption through pricing instruments. Policy measures to address the underlying market failures in energy efficiency would offer two sources of benefit. By reducing the obstacles to efficient take-up of energy efficiency improvements in poorer households, they would reduce the aggregate economic cost of achieving a given reduction in energy use, while at the same time they would act to reduce the social and distributional cost of higher energy taxation.

Table 9.1 summarizes the main options for offsetting the distributional impact of higher energy taxes, and their strengths and weaknesses. The table again highlights the trade-off between effective targeting of compensation to low-income households, and the benefits to the wider economy of using as much as possible of the revenue from carbon pricing to facilitate cuts in the rates of tax on income or consumer spending. A mix of limited but well-targeted compensation to the poorest households, coupled with measures to improve household energy efficiency, can address the distributional issues raised by carbon pricing, leaving considerable scope for energy tax revenues to finance wider tax reductions.

3.   Effects on Industry Costs and Competitiveness

3.1   The Scale of the Problem

Objections that higher energy prices would increase industry costs and harm competitiveness have been perhaps even more decisive impediments to efficient energy price and tax policies. All of the major initiatives that have proposed tax or emissions trading measures to put in place a significant price for carbon in the major industrialized economies—including the 1992 EU carbon energy tax proposal, the Clinton "Btu" tax proposal of 1993, the EU ETS, and the 2009 Waxman-Markey cap-and-trade bill (the American Clean Energy and Security Act)—included provisions to exempt or otherwise compensate industrial sectors that were likely to be adversely affected by the additional financial burden.

Concerns about the effects of climate change policies on industrial competitiveness reflect two groups of issues. One has to do with the impact on industrial activity, profits, and employment—in other words, the purely economic consequences of climate change policy. The second group of issues, considered under the heading of "carbon leakage," has to do with the effectiveness of climate policy in reducing global emissions when policy measures are taken only by a subset of countries. In this situation, global emissions may be reduced by less than the reduction in emissions from the countries taking policy action, as emissions may rise in countries outside the policy coalition. This rise in emissions elsewhere is likely to reflect two principal effects, one due to the reduction in global energy demand, and hence prices, as a result of reduced demand from the countries taking policy action, and the other operating through a competitiveness channel, a shift in carbon-intensive

Table 9.1
Offsetting the distributional impact of higher energy taxation on households

Compensate for higher energy taxes by...	Effective targeting: How well does the compensation reach the most badly affected low-income households?	Fiscal cost: What proportion of the additional energy tax revenues would be absorbed by the cost of the compensation itself, and its administration?	Impact of the compensation on incentives for reduced energy use and carbon emissions	Broader efficiency gains for the economy
cutting rate of payroll tax (e.g., UK NICs) or income tax	LIMITED. Many of the poorest households do not work, and are not affected by taxes on the labor market.	HIGH revenue cost (since the compensation is not well targeted). LOW administrative cost.	LITTLE IMPACT.	HIGH. Revenue recycling through lower tax rates on labor income increases incentives for work effort, human capital investments, etc.
raising personal income tax thresholds	LOW. Many of the poorest households pay little income tax.	MEDIUM revenue cost (the compensation is so poorly targeted). LOW administrative cost.	LITTLE IMPACT.	SMALL POSITIVE. Revenue recycling to higher-income tax thresholds reduces tax rates of some households.
cutting standard-rate VAT	MEDIUM. A higher proportion of benefits go to the poor than do with compensation through reduced labor income taxes, but most benefit still goes to better-off.	MEDIUM/HIGH revenue cost (since the compensation is poorly targeted). LOW administrative cost.	LITTLE IMPACT.	HIGH. Revenue recycling through lower sales taxes gives similar labor market benefits as income tax cuts.

(continues)

Table 9.1 (continued)

Compensate for higher energy taxes by...	Effective targeting: How well does the compensation reach the most badly affected low-income households?	Fiscal cost: What proportion of the additional energy tax revenues would be absorbed by the cost of the compensation itself, and its administration?	Impact of the compensation on incentives for reduced energy use and carbon emissions	Broader efficiency gains for the economy
indexing benefits	MEDIUM/HIGH.	LOW revenue cost. LOW administrative cost.	LITTLE IMPACT.	NEGATIVE.
targeted benefit package	HIGH.	MEDIUM.	LITTLE IMPACT.	NEGATIVE.
measures to enhance household energy efficiency	MEDIUM/HIGH. Many measures can be targeted to poor households, improving target efficiency.	HIGH.	POSITIVE. Should increase energy and carbon savings, in addition to the effect of the energy tax.	NEGATIVE.

industrial production to areas with lower carbon prices. The latter effect is the focus of policy concerns about the effects of carbon pricing on industrial competitiveness; any such relocation would reflect painful adjustments in employment and business activity in the countries taking action, without achieving any reduction in global carbon emissions.

Evidence (e.g., of direct and indirect effects, based on input-output analysis) shows that energy costs constitute a relatively small proportion of total costs for most industrial sectors, but there are a small number of "EITE" industries that are both highly energy intensive and trade exposed, in the sense that they have significant exports or face significant competition from imports, or both. Both criteria are relevant: sectors that are less energy intensive than the average would be expected in the long run to gain from the adjustment of real exchange rates that would follow introduction of a carbon tax by a limited group of countries, while sectors with largely non-tradable outputs would be insulated from pressures on competitiveness. A further consideration that in principle is relevant, though in practice may be more difficult to assess, is the nature of the market in question, as competitive pressures will be more severe in markets for price-sensitive homogeneous commodities, such as bulk steel and chemicals, than for differentiated goods where price is only one of many attributes affecting sales.

Defining criteria to identify EITE sectors is a matter of judgment. In the exercise undertaken to define sectors to receive free ETS allowance allocations under the revised EU ETS Directive 2009/29/EC three criteria were eventually defined, based on varying threshold levels of trade intensity (exports and imports as a percentage of EU sales) and cost impact (direct and indirect carbon costs at an allowance price of €30 per ton, as a percentage of gross value added):

- Trade intensity > 10% and cost impact > 5%;
- Cost impact > 30%;
- Trade intensity > 30%.

Analyzing industrial sectors at the four-digit level of the NACE classification, 146 out of a total of 258 sectors were identified as exposed to a significant risk of carbon leakage through competitiveness effects, but of these only 27 sectors qualified by virtue of the first criterion, which takes account of both cost impact and trade intensity. Similar exercises for the United States (Fischer et al. 2012) show that EITE sectors account for a relatively small part (12 percent) of total U.S. manufacturing output and less than 1 percent of total U.S. employment—though, of course, for a rather higher proportion of U.S. industry's CO_2 emissions (around half of manufacturing industry's emissions, when the indirect effects of electricity generation emissions are included).

Estimates of the likely extent of emissions leakage from unilateral carbon policy are assessed in a number of research studies.[11] Most show relatively modest overall leakage: for example, Boehringer et al. (2012) estimate that each 100 tons of abatement in countries taking policy action would result in a rise of between 5 and 20 tons in emissions elsewhere. Rather more than half of this is an effect working through the overall impact on world energy price levels, and less than half due to international displacement of industrial activity. Higher rates of leakage would, however, be experienced in some EITE sectors, especially in steel and non-ferrous metals, which are both highly energy intensive and face strong competitive pressure, leading to estimated leakage rates as high as 50 percent (Fischer and Fox 2012).

The first-best solution to these concerns about leakage and competitive disruption from unilateral carbon pricing policies is to seek international coordination. Global carbon pricing with a single worldwide carbon price—for example, implemented through a worldwide carbon emissions cap and trade scheme, or a harmonized carbon tax—would promote the most efficient pattern of abatement, and would allow the crucial issues of equitable burden-sharing to be addressed transparently through the basis on which free allowances are allocated or through the distribution of the proceeds from allowance auctions. Under a global system of carbon pricing, problems relating to industrial competitiveness would be sharply reduced, although some energy-intensive firms and industries would nonetheless face sharp competitive pressures and adjustment costs as part of the efficient adjustment of the overall pattern of industrial output to higher carbon costs.[12]

However, there is increasing recognition that a comprehensive global agreement may be unattainable for the time being, and that a coalition, mainly comprising industrialized countries, may wish to take action without equivalent policies being pursued elsewhere. In this context the question arises as to what would be the best way to respond to the problems of competitiveness and "over-adjustment" in EITE sectors. In broad terms, three options are available:

- Direct compensation of EITE sectors through revenue return or by grandfathering ETS allowances. The revenue return could take the form of reductions in other taxes such as payroll taxes, or output-based revenue redistribution.

- Sectoral exemption or part-exemption from carbon pricing for EITE sectors.
- Border tax adjustments, taxing the import of EITE goods on a basis broadly equivalent to the carbon tax that would have been incurred in their manufacture, and rebating the carbon tax on exports.

All three raise important issues, both of economic efficiency and of political economy.

To a large extent the political economy issues are common to all three approaches, and they are a crucial backdrop to the whole discussion. Compensation through revenue return, sectoral exemptions, and border tax adjustment all confer economic privileges on certain sectors. As with the free allocation of emissions trading allowances, significant resources are likely to be consumed in socially unproductive, but privately profitable, lobbying to influence the scope of these privileges. Costs will be incurred by business in trying to influence the form of the arrangements, and by government in resisting self-interested lobbying. Moreover, once sectoral exemptions or compensation measures are in place, their value to the beneficiaries is likely to make it very difficult to reverse or change the arrangements. Trade policy in general shows many examples of the extraordinary durability of sectoral trade protection measures, even those originally intended to be temporary.

From the point of view of economic and environmental efficiency, there are two key questions. The first is whether ways can be found to ameliorate the impact of high carbon prices on EITE sectors by reducing the severity of competitive pressures from their counterparts in places that do not take equivalent climate policy measures, without undermining the effectiveness of higher carbon prices in achieving reductions in carbon emissions. The second question is whether there are ways of achieving this outcome at limited budgetary cost—in other words, without dissipating too much of the revenue that could be generated from carbon taxation—since there would be significant economic gains from using this revenue to finance general tax cuts, which would reduce the burden of distortionary taxation.

3.2 Compensation Through Revenue Return

By analogy with the discussion of distributional effects on households, we might consider whether some portion of the revenue raised from higher energy taxes could be devoted to direct financial compensation to the firms most adversely affected. With energy taxes, this could take the form of a return of all or part of the revenues, as in the Swedish NO_x tax, where revenues are entirely returned to the participating firms in proportion to their output. With emissions trading, the counterpart would be free distribution of emission trading allowances to firms (e.g., grandfathering in proportion to historic emissions or allocations based on output), and this has been the general practice in most large-scale emissions trading systems, such as the U.S. Acid Rain Program, and—initially, at least—the EU ETS.

Many proposals for environmental tax measures have envisaged an explicit linkage between the revenues raised and a corresponding reduction in other taxes paid by industry, such as payroll taxes. Where this revenue return is economy-wide, much of the benefit would accrue to less carbon-intensive industries, while providing rather limited compensation to energy-intensive sectors. Tackling the problem of EITE sectors is likely to require a more targeted revenue return, concentrating the compensation on those sectors facing the highest burden of carbon tax or permit costs, and facing significant price-sensitive trade competition.

All forms of sectoral compensation raise difficult issues concerning the definition of the boundary between qualifying and non-qualifying sectors, the treatment of firms with varying levels of vertical integration, and the treatment of firms with integrated production of multiple outputs, some within and some outside the EITE sectors. However, revenue return taking the form of sector-specific reductions in other taxes such as payroll taxes raises these issues particularly acutely.

Compensation for effects on industry costs through direct return of revenues is more problematic than with households, for two reasons in particular.

First, firms differ widely in size, and there is no simple way of "scaling" the compensation to reflect such differences, without introducing potential distortions in non-energy dimensions of activity. One option would be an output-based revenue return, in which the return of revenues is keyed on current or past output of firms within the sector.[13] In effect, the tax encourages reduced emissions per unit of production, but does not encourage abatement through reductions in output. This deals with competitiveness concerns, but has the drawback that it can inhibit positive processes of economic change and innovation. Inefficient firms may be propped up by the revenue return when it would, in fact, be desirable, both on economic and environmental grounds, for them to scale back production or go out of business. Indeed, the system could create perverse incentives to maintain output at an artificially high level, simply in order to preserve entitlement to the return of revenues.

Second, while lump-sum compensation may reduce average costs of production, it may have less impact on marginal costs, and hence on output pricing. The grandfathering of emissions allowances to power companies in the EU ETS caused a massive rise in industry profits, as generators increased the price of electricity to reflect higher marginal costs, while the grandfathering largely offset the impact on average costs.

3.3 Compensation Through Sectoral Exemption

The second option is exemption or partial exemption of energy-intensive sectors. As compared with sectoral revenue return, sectoral exemption has the obvious drawback that the most important users of energy are excluded from the incentive effects of energy pricing. On the other hand, it may be possible to limit sector exemptions very precisely to EITE sectors alone, whereas most forms of revenue return based on reductions in other taxes would be liable to deliver substantial, unnecessary benefits to non-EITE sectors.

One option that has not been widely discussed in the international literature is the possibility of attaching conditions to sectoral exemption, with the aim of maintaining incentives for carbon abatement by EITE sectors, while at the same time allowing them to escape part or all of the additional fiscal burden.

A possible model might be the conditional tax reductions for energy-intensive sectors negotiated when the UK's Climate Change Levy (CCL), a tax on industrial energy use, was introduced in 2001. Certain industrial sectors were given the opportunity to reach a Climate Change Agreement (CCA) with the government, in which the firms were given an 80 percent discount on the levy in exchange for a collective agreement to undertake at least as much abatement as they would have done if subject to the full rate of the new levy. The government had considerable bargaining power in negotiating a deal of this sort, as illustrated in figure 9.5, which represents the costs and benefits of concluding a CCA from the firm's perspective. Q_0 is the level of emissions that the firm would choose in the absence of any emissions-reduction incentive, and Q_1 is the emissions level that the firm would choose if subject to

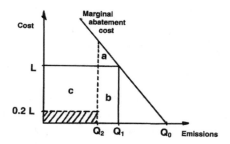

Figure 9.5
The firm's incentive to reach a Climate Change Agreement
Source: Smith and Swierzbinski (2007).

the tax at the full rate L. Taking Q_2 as the baseline in negotiation, it is clear that a sector would be willing should be willing to accept an additional abatement commitment so long as the additional abatement costs incurred (areas $a + b$) are less than the additional CCL that would otherwise be payable (areas b plus c). Area a increases with increasing emissions reductions, while area c decreases, and the net benefits of a deal are positive up to the point where area a equals area c.

How much additional abatement could in principle be demanded from firms in exchange for the 80 percent Levy discount will depend on the slope of the marginal abatement cost schedule and the level of CCL payments in the absence of any agreement. Some level of additional abatement would always be a worthwhile price for obtaining the benefit of the CCL discount, and with a linear marginal abatement cost schedule (as drawn) it would be possible to demand a substantial level of additional abatement before the gains from the CCL discount were exhausted.

Whether, in practice, the UK government sought, or could have achieved, anything like this level of additional abatement in exchange for the negotiated Climate Change Agreements is, however, a different matter. There are good reasons to doubt that it was in possession of the information needed to negotiate tough abatement targets with industry, and in any case it may not have been seeking to extract the maximum possible abatement, since the rationale for the exemption was to avoid burdening firms exposed to international competition. However, the case does illustrate that there may be scope to leverage the offer of sectoral discounts to achieve at least some of the abatement sought from carbon pricing, even in trade-exposed sectors.

3.4 Border Tax Adjustments

The third option addresses more directly the reason for concerns about competitiveness—the exposure of firms to competitors elsewhere that do not face similar increases in carbon costs. Border tax adjustments would neutralize this disadvantage by charging taxes on competing imports and rebating taxes on exports. Imports would need to be charged a tax equal to the direct and indirect carbon costs that would incurred if they had been produced within the domestic tax regime, while imports would be refunded tax equal to the carbon costs incurred in the course of their manufacture.

There are significant legal impediments to introducing arrangements for border tax adjustments (Zhang 2012), especially where—as in this case—the adjustments aim to take account of the actual or assumed production processes involved in the manufacture of a product, rather than the characteristics of the product itself.

Border tax adjustments will need to be based on assumptions about the carbon content of imported and exported products. These assumptions will be contentious, and cannot be straightforwardly derived from objective evidence. Schedules of adjustment rates will need to be drawn up with sufficient detail that they differentiate appropriately between goods with very different carbon requirements in manufacture, while not making excessive adjustments that exceed the carbon costs that would have been incurred, or in the case of exports, actually were incurred, in the course of manufacture. Although the tax adjustments on traded goods made in the context of the operation of VAT systems are often suggested as a precedent for carbon tax adjustments, there is a crucial and highly significant distinction: with VAT, an exact tax adjustment can be made, since the tax content (including the VAT paid on intermediate goods used in the course of production) can be precisely calculated as a percentage of the value of the traded commodity, whereas the direct and indirect carbon tax paid in the course of the manufacture of a good would require a detailed knowledge of the entire life-history of the product, and of the intermediate goods used in the course of its manufacture. The carbon tax content of a traded good cannot be judged from the characteristics or price of the traded good, and exact rebating of carbon taxes will be impossible, especially where there is a range of different production techniques involving different levels of pollution. If the border tax adjustments are calculated on the basis of average carbon content, then they will over-compensate some firms and provide inadequate compensation for others.

This is not necessarily an undesirable property of border tax adjustments. It means that firms still face strong incentives to reduce carbon content, since they incur the full carbon price for any carbon used, while at the same time they benefit from a refund on any exported goods based on average, rather than actual, carbon content.

Much more than either of the other offsetting policies, border tax adjustments for carbon taxes raise difficult questions about the assessment of climate change policies in other countries. The logic of border tax adjustments implies that they should be applied to trade with countries that do not pursue climate change policies of equivalent stringency. There will be many difficulties in making systematic judgments about what level and forms of environmental protection would count as "equivalent." Where a trading partner has no climate change policy at all, the matter is straightforward, but should a foreign carbon tax at half the domestic level trigger the border tax adjustment, and if so, at what level? What account should be taken of excise taxes on energy that may impose much the same financial burden as a carbon price? More difficult still, how should border tax adjustments be applied to trade with foreign countries that operate equally stringent (or more stringent) policies, but not using the same instruments? It will be particularly difficult to assess equivalence where countries pursue climate change policies using conventional "command-and-control" regulation, since this does not reveal a single clear carbon price that can be used to assess equivalence.

The main obstacles to border tax adjustments are these difficulties of practical application, and the more general—and undoubtedly worrying—risk that using trade taxes in this context could open the door to a more general erosion of the open international trading system through retaliatory measures. These issues aside, border tax adjustments have clear merits, compared with the available alternatives. In contrast to sectoral exemption, they would ensure that even energy-intensive, trade-exposed firms face strong incentives for carbon abatement. In contrast to compensation through revenue return or grandfathering, border tax adjustments do not forego the scope to use the revenues from carbon taxation to finance tax cuts and reduce the distortionary burden of taxation.

Table 9.2 summarizes the strengths and weaknesses of the various options for offsetting the adverse impact of higher energy taxation on the international competitiveness of energy-intensive, trade-exposed (EITE) industrial sectors. This again shows that international coordination

Table 9.2
Offsetting the adverse impact of higher energy taxation on the international competitiveness of energy-intensive, trade-exposed (EITE) industrial sectors

	Effective targeting: How well does the measure reduce excessive competitive impact on EITE sectors?	Cost: What would be the revenue foregone?	Impact on incentives for reduced energy use and carbon emissions	Impact of the compensation on revenue-raising efficiency
Use carbon tax revenues to cut rate of payroll tax to industry in general	POOR. Firms in EITE sectors are likely to benefit less from a general reduction in payroll tax than the additional energy costs they would face.	HIGH. Even if most or all of the additional tax revenue was used to cut payroll tax, the benefit to EITE sectors would be modest.	GOOD. Using the revenues in this way does not undermine incentives to reduce carbon emissions.	POSITIVE. Revenue recycling through lower tax rates on payroll income avoids adverse effects on revenue-raising efficiency.
Pursue international coordination	GOOD. If all competitors face the same high energy costs, any effect on the competitive position of individual firms is part of efficient adjustment.	NO BUDGETARY COST.	GOOD.	NO EFFECT.

(continues)

Table 9.2 (continued)

	Effective targeting: How well does the measure reduce excessive competitive impact on EITE sectors?	Cost: What would be the revenue foregone?	Impact on incentives for reduced energy use and carbon emissions	Impact of the compensation on revenue-raising efficiency
Exempt EITE firms from energy tax	EXCESSIVE. EITE sectors would benefit from any exchange rate adjustment and general revenue return. Partial exemption may be more justified.	MEDIUM. Revenue foregone can be limited if EITE sectors benefit from reduced tax rate, rather than full exemption.	BAD. Full exemption means the most energy-intensive firms face no incentive to cut emissions.	UNCLEAR. Sectoral exemption implies various conflicting effects on tax-raising efficiency.
Sectoral compensation (e.g., free ETS allowances, sectorally targeted reductions in non-energy taxes)	UNCLEAR. Depends on impact on EITE firms' pricing behavior in international markets. Danger that compensation is hard to remove, and outlives its initial rationale.	MEDIUM.	GOOD. EITE firms face full energy taxes, and thus have strong incentives to reduce energy and carbon use.	MODERATE. Reduces the revenue available for general reductions in tax rates.
Border tax adjustments	HIGH.	LOW/possibly POSITIVE. Some energy taxes would be refunded to exporters, but border tax would be collected on imports.	GOOD. Does not undermine incentives for EITE firms to cut emissions (except on exports).	NO EFFECT.

is the best approach, and assesses the relative merits of the alternatives in terms of how well they can be targeted to EITE sectors (rather than wasting resources on compensation to firms that do not need it), the overall budgetary impact, the impact on incentives for carbon abatement, and the impact on revenue-raising efficiency. General tax cuts score well in relation to abatement incentives and revenue-raising efficiency, but are less effective at targeting the EITE sectors where the main competitiveness issues would arise. Exemption, sectoral compensation, and border tax adjustments can be better targeted, and, of these three, border tax adjustments perform better than exemptions and compensation in terms of the criteria covered by the table.

4. Conclusions

Reforms to the pricing and taxation of energy to ensure that energy users face the full social costs of their consumption could substantially increase the cost of fossil fuels. While assessments of the social cost of carbon vary widely, the evidence points toward pricing carbon at €30 or more. For many energy uses this is significantly higher than current levels, with the exception of motor fuels which are already taxed more heavily than this in most European countries.

Higher taxes that increase household energy bills will be liable to provoke significant opposition. Part of this will focus on the impact on poorer households, for whom household energy costs can constitute a particularly large part of household spending, in some EU countries at least. The extent to which this is true varies between Member States, though this is a matter that would merit further research. Taxes on motor fuels are probably much less regressively distributed in the European Union than in the United States, especially in densely populated urban areas with good public transport infrastructure, but these are already high, and so are unlikely to be increased much by efficient carbon pricing. The largest impact on household spending will be on household heating fuels—gas and coal, in particular—which bear little tax in many Member States, and to a certain extent on electricity, where a higher EU ETS allowance price for the carbon used by power generators would feed through into higher prices to consumers.

The regressive impact of higher prices for domestic energy can, on average, be largely offset, at modest budgetary cost, by targeted assistance to poorer households, and the problem of poorer households with higher-than-average energy needs may be eased by measures targeted at the underlying sources of these high needs, especially measures directed at improving household energy efficiency. Significant additional revenues would remain, even after incurring the cost of these offsetting measures, and could facilitate reductions in other distortionary taxes, especially income tax, although the scale of income tax reductions is unlikely to be dramatic.

Concerns about adverse impacts on industrial competitiveness have proved a major barrier to higher energy taxation, though adverse effects are likely to be limited to a small number of sectors which are *both* energy intensive *and* exposed to significant price competition from international competitors. As with households, the revenues generated from taxing industrial energy use could facilitate tax reductions—for example, in payroll taxes—that would ensure that on average industrial energy users face no increase in overall tax burden. Energy-intensive sectors would, of course, be incompletely compensated, while sectors with low energy needs would benefit more from the reductions in other taxes than they would pay in higher energy prices. However there is a growing burden of evidence that international displacement of industry by environmental regulation—in this case, so-called carbon leakage—is modest. Obviously, these risks to competitiveness would be reduced by international coordination of carbon pricing measures. However, even without international coordination, the need for measures to offset the impact of higher energy taxes on energy-intensive firms is—viewed objectively—very limited indeed.

Further, it should be noted that many of the effects of energy taxation on the international competitive position of energy-intensive firms would also arise with other forms of regulation that do not impose any additional direct fiscal burden on the firms. A significant part of the energy cost of firms arises from their use of electricity, and electricity prices will be liable to be increased by any measures that increase the marginal cost of power supply, regardless of whether they increase the financial burden on firm in the power sector. Free distribution of ETS allowances did not prevent a sharp increase in electricity prices in line with the impact of carbon allowance prices on marginal costs, and a similar effect would be expected even from conventional regulation, if it increases the marginal cost of carbon-intensive production.

Even if there is little real substance to loudly voiced concerns about competitiveness, it may be difficult to avoid some form of response. Even though they appear the best-targeted approach, political economy concerns about the risk to the open world trading system may rule out the use of border tax adjustments—countervailing taxes on import of energy-intensive goods from countries that do not impose similar energy taxes. If these cannot be employed, the alternatives may be sectoral exemptions or some form of lump-sum financial compensation (or, equivalently in the case of emissions trading, the grandfathering of allowances). Lump-sum compensation to firms is wasteful of revenues and inefficient, though it would have the merit of preserving the marginal incentive for carbon abatement at the efficient level. Unconditional sectoral exemptions would mean that some of the most energy-intensive sectors faced little pressure to reduce their energy intensity and carbon emissions. Conditional sectoral exemptions offer an alternative option, allowing energy-intensive firms to benefit from exemption (which may be partial, time-bound, and conditional on policy developments in competitor countries) in exchange for legally binding commitments for abatement at least as great as the tax would have induced. Such an approach can offer substantial generosity, in terms of fiscal burden, while at the same time strengthening abatement incentives.

Notes

1. This is a revised version of a paper presented at the CESIfo/EC/IMF/PBL conference *Energy Tax and Regulatory Policy in Europe: Reform Priorities and Research Needs,* November 13-14, 2014, Ifo Institute, Munich, Germany.

2. Within this total direct budgetary support to energy users is probably no more than €1 billion, and direct support to producers is of the order of €5 billion. The largest part of the total estimated subsidy is comprised of tax expenditures—subsidies delivered through the tax system in the form of preferential tax treatment for production and use of fossil fuels (Oosterhuis et al. 2014).

3. The long-run carbon price required will depend on the climate stabilization goal that policy aims to achieve. While there is considerable uncertainty and a wide range of estimates in the research literature, Bosetti et al. (2012) conclude that limiting mean projected warming to about 3.6°C would require a global carbon price starting at roughly \$20 (€18) in 2020 and rising at 3 to 5 percent per year, while a tax at roughly twice this level would be needed to keep mean projected warming below 3°C. It will be noted that these stabilization objectives are modest by comparison with the focus of current international policy discussions on restricting mean projected warming to only 2°C, which would imply substantially more aggressive policy. Looking at this matter from another perspective, research has developed estimates of the "social cost of carbon," the value of the world-wide damage caused by emitting one additional ton of carbon dioxide. These are also subject to substantial uncertainty, but a recent review by a U.S. Interagency Working Group proposed a central estimate for use in policy assessments of \$43 (€39) for emissions in 2020 (valued in 2007 prices) (Greenstone et al. 2013).

4. The taxes included in figure 9.1 are, in the main, excise taxes. VAT is excluded from this analysis; for fuel used by industry, VAT is not relevant, as the VAT mechanism

refunds VAT on industry purchases, while for household purchases, the taxation of household spending through VAT should be regarded as part of the general revenue-raising system, rather than a mechanism for pricing energy-related environmental effects.

5. The focus of the discussion here is on distributional effects of carbon pricing in European countries. Recent contributions to a similar debate in the United States include Dinan (2012) and Mathur and Morris (2014).

6. In most EU Member States, household purchases of domestic energy are subject to a reduced rate of VAT, and therefore benefit from a substantial subsidy, compared with taxation of all household consumption at a uniform rate. In addition to taxing these fuels on the basis of their carbon content, eliminating this subsidy would require domestic energy to be taxed at the standard VAT rate.

7. Power generation is within the scope of the EU ETS, and household electricity bills therefore already reflect the cost of ETS allowances to cover the carbon dioxide emissions associated with electricity production. While EU ETS prices remain low, the impact on domestic electricity bills is small, but if ETS allowance prices were to rise in the longer term this would be expected to feed through into household bills in the same way as a tax rise.

8. These responses are simulated using micro-data-based estimated demand systems for Spain in Labandeira and Labeaga (1999) and for Sweden in Brännlund and Nordström (2004). Wier (2005) incorporates the effect of actual consumption changes in assessing the effect of a carbon tax introduced a decade earlier in Denmark.

9. Poterba (1991) shows that a carbon tax in the United States would be dramatically more regressive when analyzed on the basis of household income than household expenditure. A \$100/ton carbon tax would take 10 percent of the total income of households in the lowest income decile, but only 4 percent of the total spending of households in the bottom decile assessed on the basis of household spending. Smith (1992) presents similar calculations for the United Kingdom, showing less difference between the two bases, and suggests that this may reflect less income volatility in the UK labor market than in the United States.

10. For a thorough assessment of relevant literature, see Kosonen (2012).

11. See, for example, Böhringer et al. (2012) and the survey by Zhang (2012).

12. Controlling climate change will require a range of adjustments, one of which will be lower consumption of energy-intensive products. Some plants that produce these products will need to close down as part of the efficient pattern of abatement, and where climate change policy is implemented on a global basis, national policy measures should not inhibit this process of plant closures and rationalizations, except where there are grounds to believe that it is happening too rapidly for the economy to adjust.

13. An example in practice is the NO_x tax in Sweden, where revenues are returned to the firms in proportion to their output. The effect is equivalent to an emissions trading system, in which free permits are allocated to firms in proportion to their output.

References

Advani, Arun, Paul Johnson, Andrew Leicester, and George Stoye. 2013. "Household Energy Use in Britain: A Distributional Analysis." IFS Report R85. Institute for Fiscal Studies, London, UK.

Böhringer, Christoph, Jared Carbone, and Thomas Rutherford. 2012. "Unilateral Climate Policy Design: Efficiency and Equity Implications of Alternative Instruments to Reduce Carbon Leakage." *Energy Economics* 34 (Supplement 2): S208-17.

Bosetti, Valentina, Sergey Paltsev, John Reilly, and Carlo Carraro. 2012. "Emissions Pricing to Stabilize Global Climate." In *Fiscal Policy to Mitigate Climate Change: A Guide for Policymakers*, eds. Ruud de Mooij, Michael Keen, and Ian W. H. Parry. Washington, DC: International Monetary Fund.

Brännlund, Runar, and Jonas Nordström. 2004. "Carbon Tax Simulations Using a Household Demand Model." *European Economic Review* 48: 211-33.

Brechling, Vanessa, and Stephen Smith. 1994. "Household Energy Efficiency in the UK." *Fiscal Studies* 15: 44-56.

Callan, Tim, Sean Lyons, Susan Scott, Richard S. J. Tol, and Stefano Verde. 2009. "The Distributional Implications of a Carbon Tax in Ireland." *Energy Policy* 37: 407-12.

Crawford, Ian, Stephen Smith, and Steven Webb. 1993. *VAT on Domestic Energy*. IFS Commentary No. 39, Institute for Fiscal Studies, London, UK.

Dinan, Terry. 2012. "Offsetting a Carbon Tax's Costs on Low-Income Households." Working Paper 2012-16, Congressional Budget Office, Washington, DC, US.

Ekins, Paul, and Simon Dresner. 2005. "Economic Instruments to Improve UK Home Energy Efficiency without Negative Social Impacts." *Fiscal Studies* 27: 47-74.

Fischer, Carolyn, and Alan Fox. 2012. "Comparing Policies to Combat Emissions Leakage: Border Tax Adjustments versus Rebates." *Journal of Environmental Economics and Management* 64 (2): 199-216.

Fischer, Carolyn, Richard Morgenstern, and Nathan Richardson. 2012. "Carbon Taxes and Energy Intensive Trade Exposed Industries: Impacts and Options." Paper Presented at Resources for the Future "Roundtable Discussion on the Economics of Future US Fiscal and Carbon Policy," October 23, 2013.

Flues, Florens, and Alastair Thomas. 2015. "The Distributional Effects of Energy Taxes." OECD Taxation Working Paper No. 23, OECD, Paris.

Greenstone, Michael, Elizabeth Kopits, and Ann Wolverton. 2013. "Developing a Social Cost of Carbon for US Regulatory Analysis: A Methodology and Interpretation." *Review of Environmental Economics and Policy* 7 (1): 23-46.

Hargreaves, Katy, Ian Preston, Vicki White, and Joshua Thumim. 2013. "The Distribution of Household CO_2 Emissions in Great Britain." Supplementary Project Paper No 1. Updated Version, March 2013. JRF Programme Paper, "Climate Change and Social Justice." Joseph Rowntree Foundation, York, UK.

Healy, John D., and J. Peter Clinch. 2004. "Quantifying the Severity of Fuel Poverty, its Relationship With Poor Housing and Reasons for Non-Investment in Energy-Saving Measures in Ireland." *Energy Policy* 32: 207-20.

Kosonen, Katri. 2012. "Regressivity of Environmental Taxation: Myth or Reality?" In *Handbook of Research on Environmental Taxation*, eds. Janet Milne and Mikael Skou Andersen. Cheltenham, UK: Edward Elgar Publishing.

Labandeira, Xavier, and Jose-Maria Labeaga. 1999. "Combining Input–Output Analysis and Micro-Simulation to Assess the Effects of Carbon Taxation on Spanish Households." *Fiscal Studies* 30: 305-20.

Mathur, Aparna, and Adele C. Morris. 2014. "Distributional Effects of a Carbon Tax in Broader US Fiscal Reform." *Energy Policy* 66: 326-34.

OECD. 2013. "Inventory of Estimated Budgetary Support and Tax Expenditures for Fossil Fuels 2013." Organisation for Economic Co-operation and Development, Paris, France.

ONS. 2014. "The Effect of Taxes and Benefits on Household Income, 2012/13." UK Office for National Statistics.

Oosterhuis, Frans, Helen Ding, Laurent Franckx, Paolo Razzini, and Country Experts. 2014. "Enhancing Comparability of Data in Estimated Budgetary Support and Tax Expenditures for Fossil Fuels: Final Report for DG Environment." European Commission, August.

Poterba, J. M. 1989. "Lifetime Incidence and the Distributional Burden of Excise Taxes." *American Economic Review: Papers and Proceedings* 79: 325-30.

Poterba, J. M. 1991. "Tax Policy to Combat Global Warming: On Designing a Carbon Tax." In *Global Warming: Economic Policy Responses*, eds. R. Dornbusch and J. M. Poterba. Cambridge, MA, US: MIT Press.

Santos, Georgina, and T. Catchesides. 2005. "Distributional Consequences of Gasoline Taxation in the United Kingdom." *Transportation Research Record* 1924: 103-11.

Scott, Sue. 1996. "Social Welfare Fuel Allowances—To Heat the Sky?" (ESRI Working Paper No. 74. ESRI Dublin).

Smith, Stephen. 1992. "The Distributional Consequences of Taxes on Energy and the Carbon Content of Fuels." *European Economy*, Special Edition No. 1: 241-68.

Smith, Stephen. 1994. "Who Pays for Climate Change Policies? Distributional Side Effects and Policy Responses." In *The Economics of Climate Change*, ed. OECD. Proceedings of an OECD/IEA Conference: 277-99. OECD, Paris, France.

Smith, Stephen, and Joseph Swierzbinski. 2007. "Assessing the Performance of the UK Emissions Trading Scheme." *Environmental and Resource Economics* 37: 131-58.

Sterner, Thomas. 2012. "Distributional Effects of Taxing Transport Fuels." *Energy Policy* 41: 75-83.

Symons, Elizabeth, Stefan Speck, and John Proops. 2002. "The Distributional Effects of Carbon and Energy Taxes: The Cases of France, Spain, Italy, Germany and UK." *European Environment* 12: 203-12.

Wier, Mette, Katja Birr-Pedersen, Henrik Klinge Jacobsen, and Jacob Klok. 2005. "Are CO_2 Taxes Regressive? Evidence from the Danish Experience." *Ecological Economics* 52: 239-51.

Zhang, ZhongXiang. 2012. "Competitiveness and Leakage Concerns and Border Carbon Adjustments." FEEM Nota di Lavoro 2012.080, Fondazione Eni Enrico Mattei, Milan, Italy.

A Comment on "Carbon Pricing and Taxation: Overcoming Obstacles to Policy Reform in the EU"

Felix Chr. Matthes

Carbon pricing is without any doubt a crucial if not a central element of climate and energy policies designed to achieve greenhouse gas emissions reductions. A broad variety of carbon pricing approaches have been implemented in the past and an even broader variety of carbon pricing mechanisms are discussed in the context of the future climate policy regime (OECD and WBG 2015; PMR and ICAP 2016; WBG 2016). Three issues are, however, of outstanding importance for the debate and, probably more importantly, for the practical implementation of carbon pricing schemes:

1. The role of carbon pricing in the climate and energy policy mix;
2. The fundamental design choice between price and quantity control;
3. The concerns that often lead to a reluctance to make use or broaden the use of carbon pricing approaches: the distributional impacts for households on the one hand and competitiveness as well as carbon leakage concerns of energy-intensive industries in a world of unequal carbon pricing.

An appropriate assessment on the role of carbon pricing in the broader climate and energy policy mix requires careful reflections on the four mechanisms that can deliver greenhouse gas emission reductions (IEA 2016a, 47):

- Changing the operation and the dispatch of existing production assets and/or;
- Changing the patterns of new investments and/or;
- Changing the patterns of disinvestments and/or;
- Changing the patterns of downstream production and consumption decisions via the pass-through of carbon costs to commodity and product prices.

There is a broad consensus that undistorted carbon prices have already and will have significant impacts on operation and dispatch decisions as well disinvestment decisions at least in economies with liberalized markets. Theoretical reflections and empirical analysis on the impact of real-world carbon pricing approaches on investment decisions (IEA 2011; IEA 2016b; Matthes 2010) indicate that complementary policies will be needed in many cases to trigger sufficient and far-sighted investments in low- or zero-carbon technologies. The pass-through of carbon prices along the value chain will depend on market structures as well as the exposure to competition in production from jurisdictions with no or different carbon price levels.

The choice of carbon pricing mechanism and its positioning in the broader climate and energy policy mix (reaching from carbon pricing to standards, incentive programs, and capacity remuneration mechanisms) depends, on the one hand, on the specific circumstances of the jurisdiction, sectors or markets. In matured market economies with liberalized (energy) markets, the efficiency gains from using carbon pricing mechanisms will be typically more significant than in jurisdictions with regulated or state-controlled markets, as can be found in many emerging economies. On the other hand, and probably more importantly for OECD countries, the ambition level of greenhouse gas emission reductions is an important dimension for the choice, the design, and the integration of carbon pricing mechanisms. Deep decarbonization trajectories over a period of a few decades will require a broader range of complementary policies to carbon pricing mechanisms. Carbon pricing mechanisms can in many cases play a fundamental role in the policy mix but can also be of a complementary nature in some cases, depending on sectors, structures of markets and capital stocks, or other specific factors (PMR and ICAP 2016).

The choice of price or quantity-based carbon pricing mechanisms depends on economic core beliefs as well as on political, regulatory, and at least cultural traditions or the respective windows of opportunities. Over the course of the last decade, another perspective on the choice between price-based and quantity-based carbon pricing mechanisms became more and more important. The significant volatilities and disruptions in global and regional energy and commodity markets and the related abatement costs make it increasingly difficult to fix appropriate carbon taxes or levies. The highly volatile costs of fuel switches in the Continental European electricity markets, between 5 and 50 euros per metric ton of carbon dioxide between 2005 and 2015, mark the importance of responsive carbon pricing in market environments, which are characterized by the "new normal" of extremely volatile commodity prices. In this context, emissions trading systems seem to be raising increasing attention. The empirical evidence shows, however, that most carbon pricing instruments include hybrid elements. Advanced emission trading systems (e.g., in California, the United Kingdom, the European Union, or South Korea) integrate price elements like price floors, price collars, or market stability reserves, on the one hand. On the other hand, typical carbon tax systems (as implemented or discussed in Chile or South Africa) integrate quantity mechanisms, e.g., the use of emission reduction credits for tax compliance. The choice for a certain carbon pricing mechanism should also reflect two additional dimensions:

In the emerging global climate policy regime, based on a pledge-and-review approach, the integration or the linking of carbon pricing mechanisms will be of increasing importance. The respective potentials of quantity-based mechanisms or elements will emerge as a significant criterion for design decisions.

Although carbon pricing mechanisms are primarily economic instruments, design elements that deliver complementary functionalities could increase the effectiveness and the dynamic efficiency of the instrument: the clear visibility of long-term consistency requirements that are delivered by long-term caps could classify emissions trading systems as economic instruments with a complementary function of informational instruments.

Even if there is a certain trend of convergence between quantity and price-based carbon pricing mechanisms and the role of carbon pricing mechanisms could go beyond economic effects in a narrow sense, the different nature of challenges and solutions with regard to political and public acceptance deserves some reflection. Among the many factors that influence political and public acceptance, distributional effects are of key importance, and specifically the impacts of carbon pricing mechanisms on low-income households and on industrial competitiveness and/or carbon leakage.

With respect to the impacts of carbon pricing on low-income households, there is a remarkable difference between different jurisdictions, essentially depending on the broader political and regulatory framework. For jurisdictions with traditionally strong social security systems (in parts of Europe) the distributional impacts on households have never played a key role for the political and public acceptance of carbon pricing, whereas in other jurisdictions (the United Kingdom, the United

States, Australia, and South Africa) specific provisions to deal with these types of distributional impacts were essential elements of the political and public debate. Complementary policies with no or limited links to carbon pricing mechanisms can also play a significant role for political and public acceptance with regard to low-income households but this depends on the broader political and regulatory framework.

Although the evidence on the impacts of carbon pricing on industrial competitiveness or the respective carbon leakage from ex post evaluations is significantly less than from ex ante modelling (PMR 2015) the respective debates are a key element for the acceptance on any carbon pricing mechanism. Although addressing competitiveness and carbon leakage by complementary instruments with no or limited links to carbon pricing mechanisms, e.g., by border adjustment mechanisms, has been broadly discussed among analysts, they have been rarely implemented, essentially by legal or political concerns on trade policies and politics. These concerns reflect again the broader political and regulatory framework which can build major barriers to deal with distributional and acceptance issues by mechanisms that are not directly linked to carbon pricing mechanisms.

If concerns on distributional effects and their implications on political and public acceptance can only partly be addressed by more or less fully separated (compensation) mechanisms, the integration of such mechanisms into the carbon pricing instruments will emerge as a significant issue.

The textbook-style compensation mechanism is the use of revenues from carbon pricing instruments to lower distorting taxes, e.g., on labor costs, raising the "double dividend." Although the macroeconomic efficiency gains should be most significant for this compensation approach, it has been rarely used for carbon or energy taxes and almost never for emissions trading systems.

In contrast to this, targeted compensation has received major attention in a variety of carbon pricing mechanisms, ranging from free allocation or dynamic allocation in emission trading systems, to direct compensation payments, to private households or industries in a variety of carbon tax and emissions trading systems. Considering the visibility of compensation mechanisms or payments, they seem to be much more attractive in overcoming barriers to the implementation of carbon pricing mechanisms, at least from a political economy perspective.

There is, however, a third group of compensation mechanisms that have received a certain level of attraction for several carbon pricing mechanisms. Using revenues from carbon taxes or from auctions in emission trading systems for innovation has proved to be a powerful complement to carbon pricing mechanisms from the perspective of political and public acceptance (e.g., the use of auctioning revenues from the EU emissions trading scheme for technology innovation or using the revenues from the carbon tax in Chile for the reform of the education system).

The systematic combination of much more narrow, more specific, and more tailor-made direct compensation mechanisms (to raise public acceptance and to avoid carbon leakage) and the conscious creation of revenues from carbon pricing mechanisms and their use in lowering distortive taxes and for innovation (to increase the macroeconomic efficiency and to raise public acceptance) is probably the type of hybrid mechanism that seems to be necessary to make carbon pricing mechanisms an effective and efficient element of future-proof climate and energy policies. Balancing the effectiveness, (macroeconomic) efficiency, and visibility of compensation mechanisms (as a key determinant of political and public acceptance) is an essential element for designing successful real-world implementations of carbon pricing mechanisms.

References

IEA (International Energy Agency). 2011. "Summing Up the Parts: Combining Policy Instruments for Least-Cost Climate Mitigation Strategies." IEA, Paris, France.

IEA. 2016a. "Energy, Climate Change & Environment 2016 Insights." IEA, Paris, France.

IEA. 2016b. "Re-Powering Markets: Market Design and Regulation during the Transition to Low-Carbon Power Systems." IEA, Paris, France.

Matthes, Felix Chr. 2010. "Greenhouse Gas Emissions Trading and Complementary Policies. Developing a Smart Mix for Ambitious Climate Policies." Report Commissioned by the German Federal Ministry for the Environment, Nature Conservation and Nuclear Safety. Öko-Institut, Berlin, Germany.

Organisation for Economic Co-operation and Development (OECD) and World Bank Group (WBG). 2015. "The FASTER Principles for Successful Carbon Pricing: An Approach Based on Initial Experience." World Bank Group, Washington, DC, US.

Partnership for Market Readiness (PMR). 2015. "Carbon Leakage: Theory, Evidence and Policy Design." World Bank, Washington, DC, US.

Partnership for Market Readiness (PMR) and International Carbon Action Partnership (ICAP). 2016. "Emissions Trading in Practice: A Handbook on Design and Implementation." World Bank, Washington, DC, US. License: Creative Commons Attribution CC BY 3.0 IGO Partner.

World Bank Group (WBG). 2016. "State and Trends of Carbon Pricing 2016." World Bank Group, Washington, DC, US.

Contributors

Mikael Skou Andersen, Aarhus University

Niels Anger, European Commission

Bruno De Borger, University of Antwerp

Antoine Dechezleprêtre, London School of Economics

Jos Delbeke, European Commission

Ottmar Edenhofer, Potsdam Institute for Climate Impact Research, Technical University of Berlin, and Mercator Research Institute of Global Commons and Climate Change

Christian Flachsland, Hertie School of Governance and Mercator Research Institute of Global Commons and Climate Change

Beatriz Gaitan, Potsdam Institute for Climate Impact Research

Polona Gregorin, European Commission

Cameron Hepburn, University of Oxford and London School of Economics

Alan Krupnick, Resources for the Future

Andreas Löschel, University of Münster

Claudio Marcantonini, European University Institute

Felix Christian Matthes, Öko-Institut

Paul Nahmmacher, Potsdam Institute for Climate Impact Research and Technical University of Berlin

Ian Parry, International Monetary Fund

Karen Pittel, Ifo Institute and University of Munich

David Popp, Syracuse University

Stef Proost, KU Leuven

Christina Roolfs, Potsdam Institute for Climate Impact Research and Technical University of Berlin

Bert Saveyn, JRC, European Commission

Oliver Schenker, Frankfurt School of Finance & Management

Stephen Smith, University College London

Alexander Teytelboym, University of Oxford

Kurt Van Dender, OECD

Herman Vollebergh, PBL Netherlands Environmental Assessment
    Agency and Tilburg University

Nils-Henrik M. von der Fehr, University of Oslo

Zhongmin Wang, Resources for the Future

Georg Zachmann, Breugel

Index

Acemoglu, D., 193, 194
ACER (Agency for the Cooperation of Energy Regulators), 83
Adgate, J. L., 241–42
Advani, Arun, 317
Aghion, P., 178, 189
AIDS treatment, 187
Airbus, 16
Air pollution. *See also* Greenhouse gas (GHG) emission reduction targets
  motor vehicles and, 272–75, 279, 289, 300–301
  shale gas development and, 238
Alternative fuels, 189, 265, 275–76, 288. *See also* Biofuels
Ambec, S., 177
American Clean Energy and Security Act (2009), 318
Andersen, Mikael Skou, 129
Anger, Niels, 163
Attaran, A., 187
Auctioning
  emission allowances by individual countries, 9
  fiscal properties and use of auction revenues, 7
  full auctioning as recommended model, 20–21
  renewables and, 141
  reserve price on auctions, 23n9
  revenues from, 13, 218–19

Australia
  Carbon Pricing Mechanism (repealed), 11, 12, 24n19
  shale gas resources in, 224, 230
Austria
  electricity market in, 87n16
  optimal per capita transfers and, 42
  toll roads in, 291n8
  truck charging system in, 284–85
Automobiles. *See* Electric vehicles; Motor vehicles; Road transport
Aviation
  Carbon Offsetting and Reduction Scheme for International Aviation (CORSIA), 16
  controversy over coverage of, 16
  within-EEA aviation emissions, 9, 10, 16

Back-loading, 13, 21, 29, 32–33, 35, 55n2
Baker Hughes (fracking service company), 233, 249n4
Banking and borrowing rules, 4, 23n10
Barbose, G. L., 150
Barnett play (Texas), 226, 227–28, 229
Barroso Commission, 129
Basso, L. J., 291–92n15
Belgium
  carbon tax in, 129
  distance-based charges on transport in, 284